Black Tigers

A Grammar of Chinese Rubbings

Black Tigers

A Grammar of Chinese Rubbings

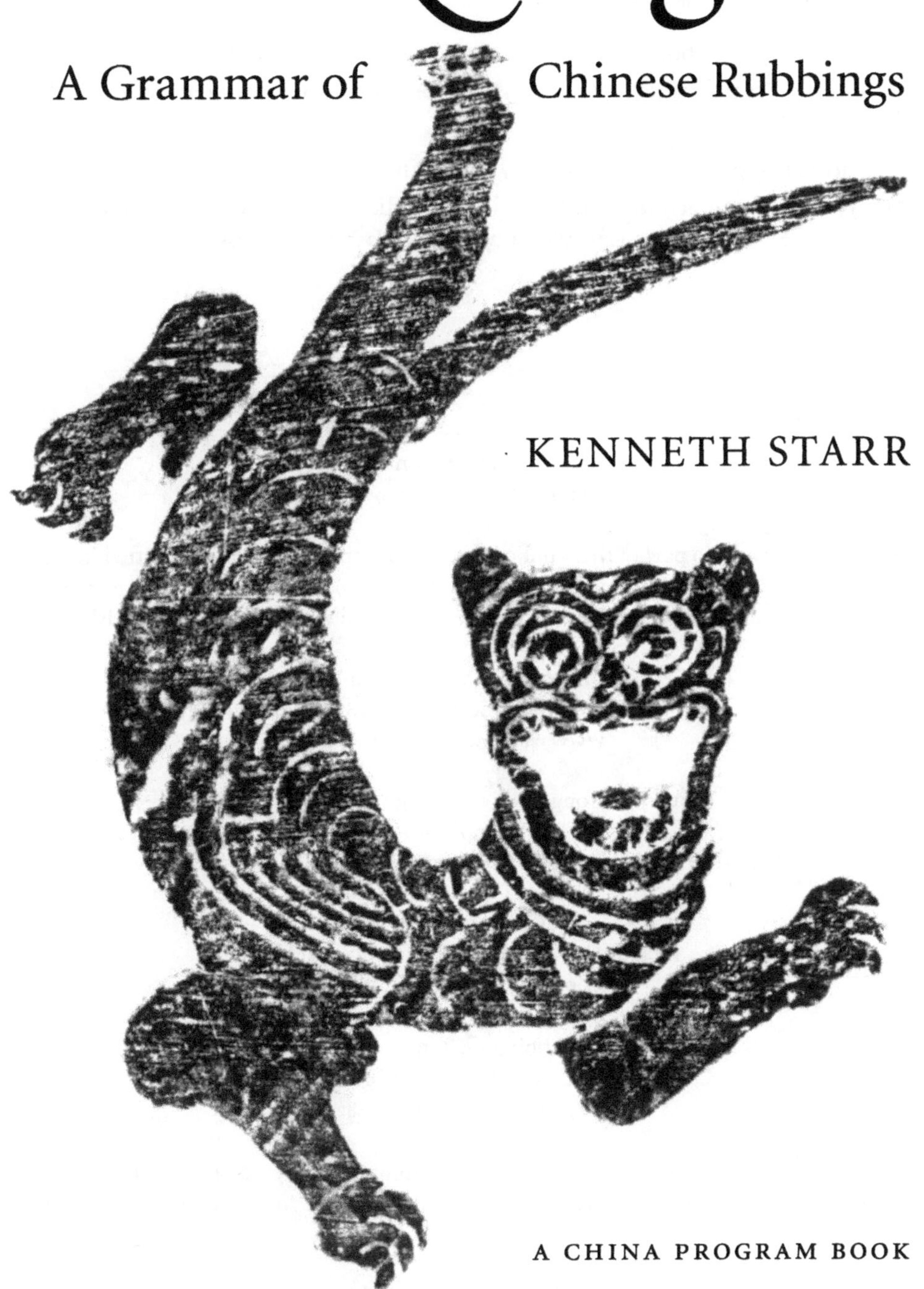

KENNETH STARR

A CHINA PROGRAM BOOK

UNIVERSITY OF WASHINGTON PRESS • *Seattle and London*

Black Tigers: A Grammar of Chinese Rubbings
is published with the assistance of the Getty Foundation.

Additional support was provided by the China Studies Program, a division of the Henry M. Jackson School of International Studies at the University of Washington.

Designed by Veronica Seyd
12 11 10 09 08 5 4 3 2 1

University of Washington Press
P.O. Box 50096, Seattle, WA 98145 U.S.A.
www.washington.edu/uwpress

Library of Congress Cataloging-in-Publication Data
Starr, Kenneth.
Black tigers : a grammar of Chinese rubbings / Kenneth Starr. —1st.
p. cm.
A China program book
Includes bibliographical references and index.
ISBN 978-0-98826-6 (cl. : alk. paper)
ISBN 978-0-295-98811-5 (pbk. : alk. paper)
1. Rubbing—China. I. Title.
NC915.R8S73 2008
760—dc22 2007040825

The paper used in this publication meets the minimum requirements of American National Standard for Information Sciences—Permanence of Paper for Printed Library Materials, ANSI Z39.48–1984.

Cover image: Pictorial relief from the cave tombs of Shih-tzu-wan, Le-shan; a leaping tiger. Courtesy of the C. V. Starr East Asian Library, University of California

For BJ and Leslie, and for Winfield, who left us too soon

Contents

Preface

DESPITE the centrality of rubbings in Chinese culture over a millennium and a half, Westerners have given them but passing attention. My interest in rubbings began in 1953, when I became curator of East Asian Archeology and Ethnology at the Field Museum of Natural History, a major holder of Chinese rubbings. I found that Western descriptions of their history and materials and methods rarely ran more than a few pages, and those on connoisseurship not even that.

Moving more deeply into the subject, I discovered a wealth of Chinese sources on rubbings and became increasingly intrigued by them. In 1960 I spent nine months in Taiwan, immersing myself in the lore of rubbings at the National Central Library, the Institute of History and Philology, the Academia Sinica, and other public and private collections. I had long and fruitful conversations with colleagues and collectors, took voluminous notes and hundreds of photographs, and learned how to make rubbings. Subsequent trips to Taiwan and all across China, including Xinjiang and Tibet, and to museums, libraries, and historic sites, broadened and deepened my interest and experience.

It was the growing fascination with this singularly Chinese cultural phenomenon that led me to undertake a synoptic, discipline-neutral treatment of rubbings: their history, materials and techniques, and connoisseurship. The present book treats the first two aspects, with cost considerations requiring elimination of connoisseurship and many illustrations.

In writing on rubbings, I think of the proverb *Ban men nong fu,* "wielding the ax at the door of [Lu] Ban [god of carpenters]." As excuse, I can but plead fascination with Chinese rubbings for half a century. Rubbings represent one small, but brilliant, facet of the jewel of Chinese culture. They provide clear insights into the rich and infinitely varied intellectual and aesthetic history of China, the rigorous discipline of classical scholarship, the way in which traditional scholars viewed their world, and the exquisite subtleties of Chinese high culture and connoisseurship.

KENNETH STARR
Shanggu Zhai
(Study for Cherishing Antiquity)

Acknowledgments

IN EXPRESSING appreciation for the counsel and assistance of colleagues over the years, I again turn to a Chinese saw, *yin shui, si yuan*, "when drinking the water, think of the spring." In the United States, I especially am beholden to Tsuen-hsuin Tsien, with his unsurpassed knowledge of writing in early China; to Hoshien Tchen, friend and colleague at the Field Museum; and to Robert E. Harrist Jr., who read the manuscript and was singularly encouraging and helpful. Staffs at the Library of Congress and the Freer Gallery of Art and Sackler Gallery of Art Library were endlessly accommodating. I also fondly and gratefully remember Paul H. Clyde and Cornelius Osgood, my professors, respectively at Duke and at Yale.

Taiwan colleagues gave me strong support during my several research trips. I owe my greatest debt to Su Yinghui, who had a broad and deep familiarity with rubbings and their literature, and who arranged full access to the rubbings collections in the National Central Library. He also generously introduced me to his wide circle of scholarly and collector colleagues, who freely shared their knowledge and collections. Professor Su was ever at hand in personal matters, and I shall never forget his kindness. Over the years of my visits, half a hundred other Taiwan scholars, collectors, and artisans provided invaluable information on rubbings. I am deeply grateful to them all, as I am to the Field Museum, the American Council of Learned Societies, and the Social Science Research Council for supporting my Taiwan fieldwork.

In China, assistance was generous during my visits to the Xi'an Beilin, the Palace Museum, and other museums. In my six visits to the Beilin, Ma Ji, assistant to the director, gave greatly of his time and extensive knowledge of "old stones" and rubbings. He was extraordinarily kind, patient, and helpful, as was Yao Jinxu, an experienced rubbing artisan. Li Yingji, at the Palace Museum in Beijing, was equally accommodating during my visits and by mail following. At the Dai Temple (Dai Miao) in Taian in 1993, Liu Hui gave me full access to the museum and took me by car to the remote Later Han mortuary site at Xiaotang Shan. In Japan in 1960, Sueji Umehara demonstrated rubbing jades and bronze mirrors at his home in Kyoto, and Fujii Zenzaburo at the Yurinkan was very gracious.

At home, David Howell, known to his colleagues as Golden Fingers for his computer adroitness, ever was on call when my feeble skills faltered, as was Leslie Starr. Lorri

Hagman, Patron Saint of Stone Inscriptions at the University of Washington Press, was forbearing and supportive throughout, and Marilyn Trueblood and Xavier Callahan facilitated the editing.

Above all, I owe BJ a debt that I never can repay. For sixty-five years she truly has been the light of my life, never complaining about the endless hours, over many years, that I spent pursuing "old stones" and "black tigers." How can one ever fully express one's gratitude for such devotion and understanding?

Black Tigers

A Grammar of Chinese Rubbings

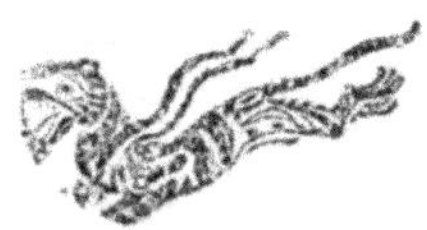

1 / The History and Functions of Rubbings

Rubbings are ink-on-paper copies of engraved or cast inscriptions and designs on what are mostly cultural objects of metal, stone, and other firm substances. The rubbing technique originated in China, but the exact date and circumstances of the technique's origin are less certain, mainly because of the paucity of extant documented early rubbings. Dating is also difficult because of the differing interpretations of early terms for copying, especially of stone inscriptions (stone was the first and thereafter most common material on which the Chinese used the technique). Finally, there is no precise knowledge of when paper and ink attained a quality suitable for making rubbings.

Views on the inception of the rubbing technique range from the Han to the Tang, as follows.

Han Dynasty (206 B.C.E.–220 C.E.)

Orthodox Chinese sources assign the initial application of the technique to the Han dynasty, including the Former (Western) Han (206 B.C.E.–8 C.E.) and the Later (Eastern) Han (25–220 C.E.). Conservative scholars have drawn primarily on three traditional sources: the second-century dictionary *Explanation of Words and Elucidation of Characters* (Shuowen jiezi); *The History of the Later Han Dynasty* (Hou Han shu); and *Extension of the String of Pearls on the Spring and Autumn Annals* (Yanfan lu).

The first of these sources, *Shuowen jiezi,* a dictionary by Xu Shen (d.120 C.E.?), makes no specific mention of rubbings, but some scholars single out one passage as evidence that the technique was known in the Han. Rong Geng observes that "in the preface of the *Shuowen jiezi,* Xu Shen states that 'people throughout the country often found ritual vessels [*dingyi*] in mountain streams whose inscriptions surely were the ancient script [*guwen*] of early times;' [and so] those ritual-vessel inscriptions already were collected by people in the Han."[1] Traditionalists may be correct in inferring that Han scholars had an active interest in pre-Han inscriptions, but they are on less firm ground in judging that they collected them as rubbings.

The second source is Fan Ye's *The History of the Later Han Dynasty.* In the biographical section, under the entry for the eminent scholar-official and calligrapher Cai

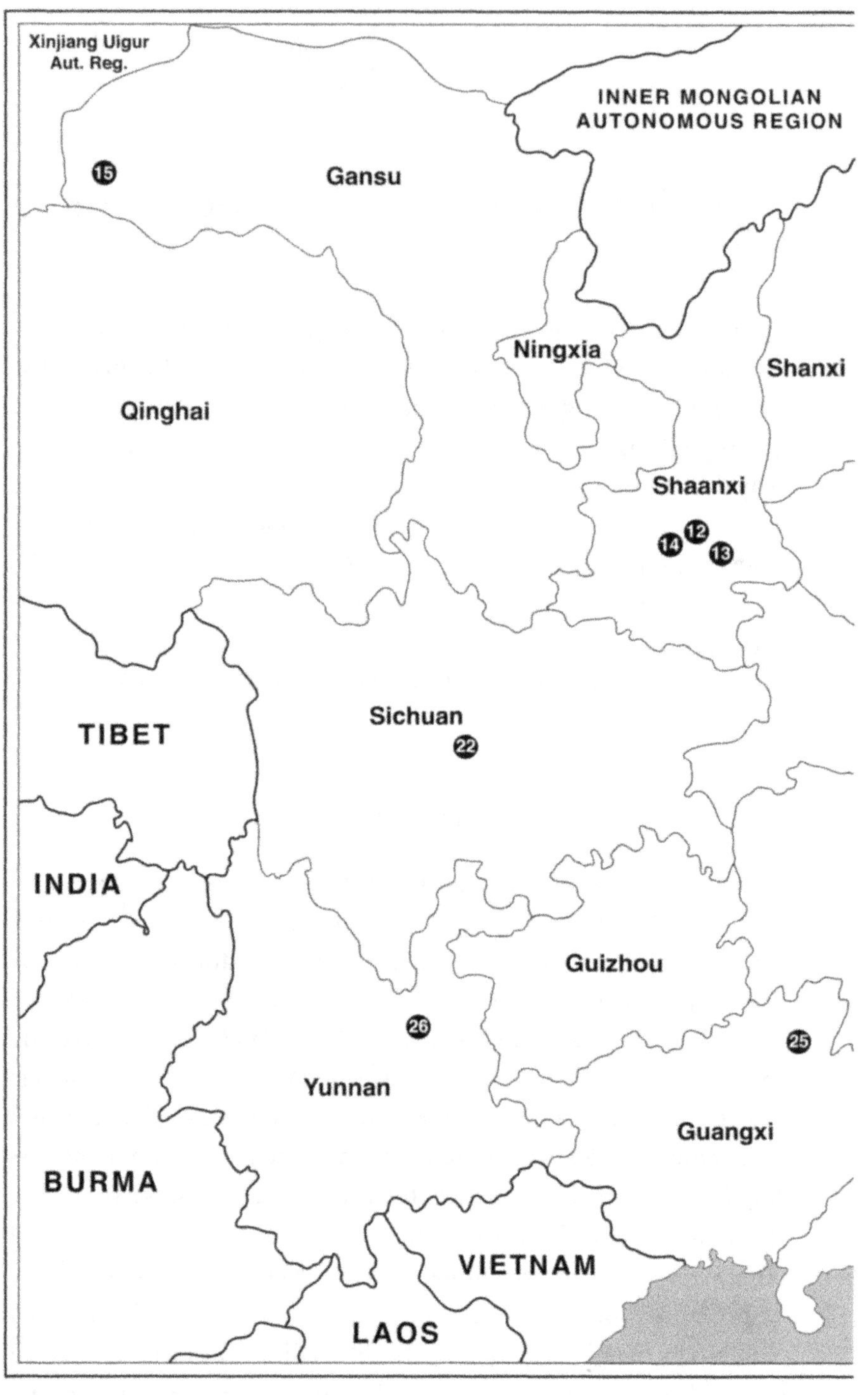
Xinjiang Uigur
Aut. Reg.
INNER MONGOLIAN
AUTONOMOUS REGION
15
Gansu
Ningxia
Shanxi
Qinghai
Shaanxi
12
14
13
Sichuan
22
TIBET
INDIA
Guizhou
26
25
Yunnan
Guangxi
BURMA
VIETNAM
LAOS

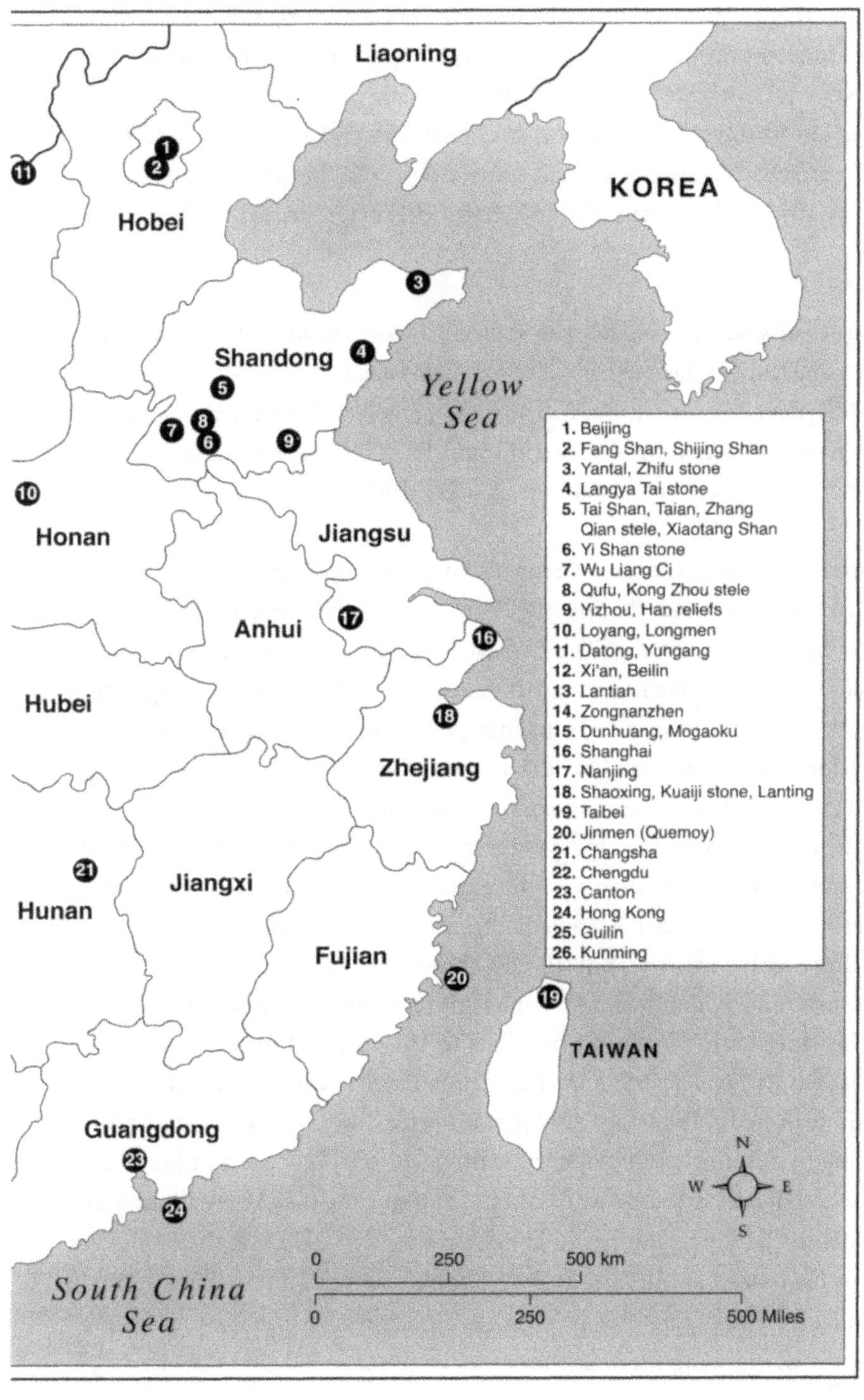
Liaoning
KOREA
Hobei
Shandong
Yellow Sea
Honan
Jiangsu
Anhui
Hubei
Zhejiang
Jiangxi
Hunan
Fujian
TAIWAN
Guangdong
South China Sea
1. Beijing
2. Fang Shan, Shijing Shan
3. Yantal, Zhifu stone
4. Langya Tai stone
5. Tai Shan, Taian, Zhang Qian stele, Xiaotang Shan
6. Yi Shan stone
7. Wu Liang Ci
8. Qufu, Kong Zhou stele
9. Yizhou, Han reliefs
10. Loyang, Longmen
11. Datong, Yungang
12. Xi'an, Beilin
13. Lantian
14. Zongnanzhen
15. Dunhuang, Mogaoku
16. Shanghai
17. Nanjing
18. Shaoxing, Kuaiji stone, Lanting
19. Taibei
20. Jinmen (Quemoy)
21. Changsha
22. Chengdu
23. Canton
24. Hong Kong
25. Guilin
26. Kunming
N
W
E
S
0 250 500 km
0 250 500 Miles

Yong (133–92 C.E.), there is an account of the great furor that accompanied the completion of the first stone engraving of the then known corpus of six Confucian classics. That historic event was initiated in the fourth year (175 C.E.) of Emperor Lingdi's Xiping-reign period to provide an official, standard text and was completed in 183 C.E. (fig. 1.1). *The History of the Later Han Dynasty* credits Cai, but others contributed. Parts of the *bafen* script, a late form of Han clerical (*li*) script, are said to be in Cai's hand:[2]

> Lingdi gave permission for it, and [Cai] Yong then in his own hand wrote the texts for the stone tablets and had workmen engrave and erect them outside the gate of the National Academy [in Luoyang]. Thereafter, Confucianists and scholars all accepted [them] as standard. When the tablets first were erected, the vehicles of those who came to see and copy [*mo*[b]*xie*]* them numbered more than a thousand a day.[3]

Conservative interpretation is that *mo*[c]*xie* means "making rubbings."[4]

The third source is *Extension of the String of Pearls on the Spring and Autumn Annals*, published in 1175 by Cheng Dachang. The *Extension* attributes to Qin-Han times the initial use of a copying technique known as "moisten with ink" (*lamo*).[5] Cheng judges "moisten with ink" to be rubbing, but its meaning is unclear. Of incidental interest is the possible relationship of "wax ink" to "dry rubbing," described in chapter 5.

Modern writers reject a Han date for the origin of rubbing. First, there are no extant rubbings from the Han or the following several centuries, despite more than a century of intensive archaeology and the discovery of a great volume and variety of highly perishable materials, including paper and silk. Tomorrow's archaeology may provide rubbings from these early centuries, but till now there are none.

Second, circumstantial evidence for a Han date is unconvincing, especially as regards terminology. The chief basis for dating rubbings to the Han is the reference to the Xiping Stone Classics in *The History of the Later Han*. Critical opinion holds that traditionalists misinterpreted this passage, and that it means "copying by writing" rather than "reproducing by rubbing": "Copying by writing [*mo*[b]*xie*] is wasteful of time and energy, besides which it is easy to make mistakes. If at that time they knew about making rubbings [*chuanta*[b]], they certainly would not have used *mo*[b]*xie*, and the onlookers surely would not have been so numerous."[6] Li Shuhua suggests that perhaps one is unjustified even in translating *mo*[b]*xie* as "make exact copies," while Carter observes that we have no way of knowing whether the copies were exact: "At that time they still

*Superscript letters distinguish homophones that are written with different Chinese characters; see Appendixes 2 and 3.

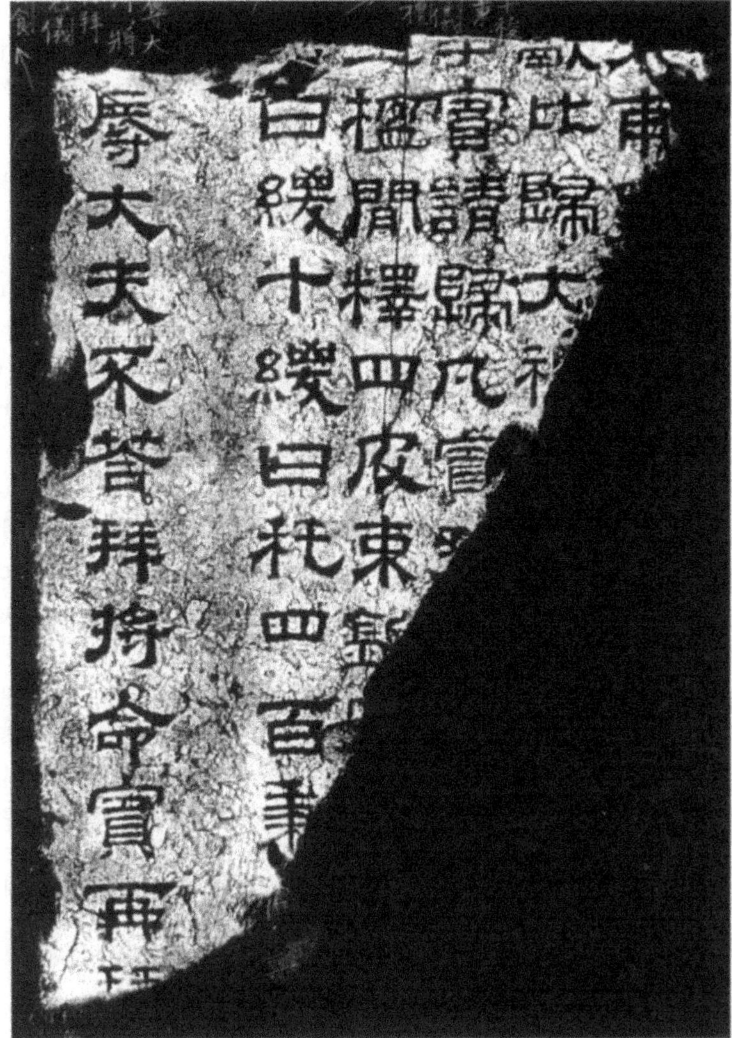

FIG. 1.1. Fragment, *Book of Etiquette and Ceremonial* (Yi li), Xiping Stone Classics (183 C.E.). Author's collection. Photograph by the author.

did not know about making rubbings [*mo*[a]*ta*[a]], and . . . therefore the term *mo*[b]*xie* had the meaning of imitatively to transcribe, not to make a rubbing [*mo*[b]*ta*[a]]."[7] Tsien concurs that *moxie* [*mo*[b]*xie*] "seems to mean 'handwriting from a copy' rather than 'make exact copies' by squeezing [rubbing]," concluding that "the origin of taking impressions from inscriptions cannot be definitely traced."[8]

Terms clearly relatable to rubbing do not occur until several centuries after the Han. Wei Zheng's *History of the Sui Dynasty* (Sui shu) uses *chuanta*,[a] still used for the process, to refer to rubbings from the Liang period.[9] "The regular word for rubbing, *t'a* [*ta*ᵇ], . . . did not come into use until the T'ang dynasty. The view is sometimes held that the word *mo*[b] . . . as used in the Han dynasty was the equivalent of *t'a* [*ta*ᵇ] . . . but it is by no means certain."[10] Wang Chi-chen cites a Tang date for *ta*ᵃ (or *tuo*) used synonymously with *yin,* a general term for printing.[11] The terms *ta*ᵇ and *ta*ᶜ, referring to rubbings makers (*tashu shou*), were common in the Tang and the Song, as were *da* (strike) or *dade* (strike-obtain) for "rubbing" and *daben,* "a rubbing."[12]

A third reason for caution in assigning a Han date to the initial use of the technique involves the origin and currency of paper. Although paper was known when the Xiping Stone Classics were cut in 175 C.E., its use seems not to have been common, and "squeezing from stone or other hard surfaces was made possible only when paper was perfected. The earlier specimens of paper of the second and third centuries, discovered in northwestern China and Chinese Turkestan, are thick and rough and do not seem suitable for taking impressions for inscriptions."[13] Reflecting the uncertainty, the same authority observes that "apparently the quality of paper during the later part of the second century C.E. must have been greatly improved, with variety of selection . . . [and] the cost . . . considerably reduced, so that . . . paper became a popular material for writing."[14]

There is no knowledge of when paper was of a quality to make rubbings, but there is an intimate relationship between the qualities of the paper (thickness, elasticity, texture, finish) and the character of the inscription or motif being copied (size, width, depth, state of preservation). One can make an adequate copy of a large-character inscription in good state with relatively coarse paper. Rubbing fine inscriptions on oracle bones and jades demands good, thin paper, as does making a quality rubbing (*jing taben*).

NORTHERN AND SOUTHERN DYNASTIES (420–589 C.E.)

Modern writers assign the inception of the rubbing technique to the Northern and Southern dynasties. Wang Guowei states that "the rubbing technique [*ta*ᵃ*mo*ᵃ] originated in rubbing [*ta*ᵃ] the Stone Classics in the Northern and Southern dynasties, and then in time was used to rub the stones cut by Qin [Shihuang]."[15] Some writers place the event in the Northern (Later) Wei; others, in the Liang.

NORTHERN WEI DYNASTY (386–534 C.E.)

On the basis of literary references to an event in 450, Li Shuhua states that "in the fifth century (or even earlier) China already knew the method of rubbing [*mo*ᵇ*ta*ᵇ] stone tablets."[16] He draws on the vicissitudes of the Mount Yi stone (*Yi Shan keshi*), one of seven stones cut by Qin Shihuang following his unification of China in 221 B.C.E., as

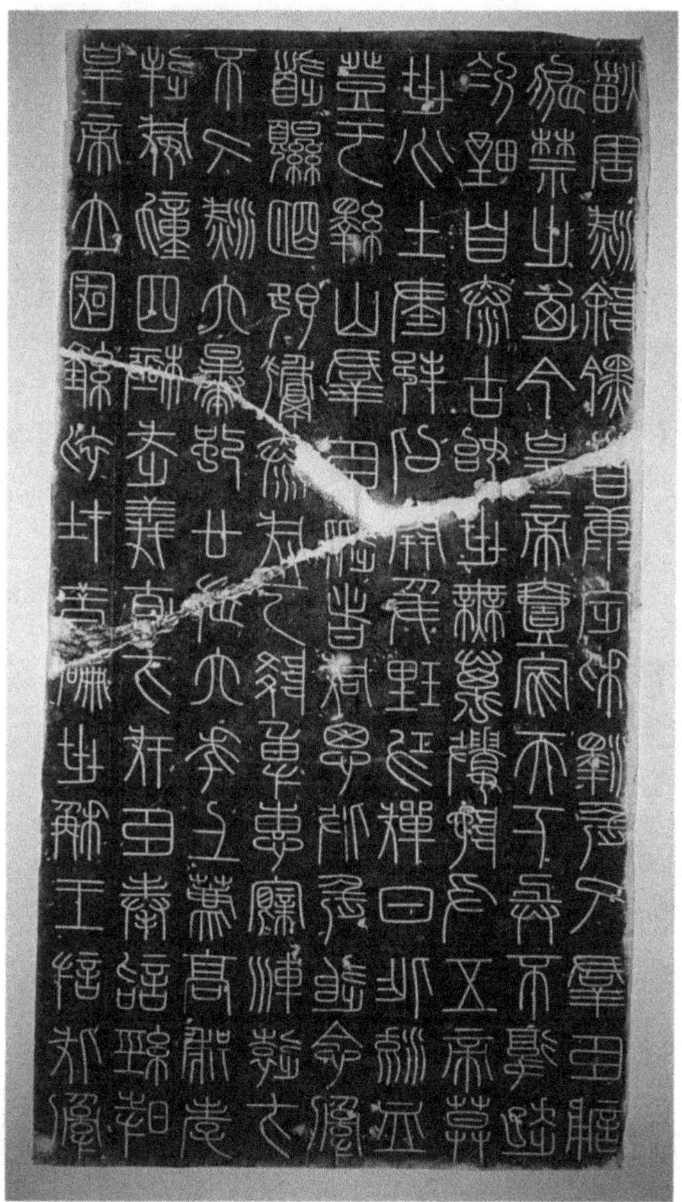

Fig. 1.2. Recut (993) of the Yi Shan stone, front face (221 B.C.E.). Courtesy Xi'an Beilin Museum.

sacrifice to the gods and ancient emperors, and as validation of his conquests.[17] All are recorded in Sima Qian's *Records of the Grand Historiographer* (Shiji) except the Mount Yi stone, which was listed in *The History of the Later Han Dynasty.*[18] Save for the Langya Tai stone, these "handed down" inscriptions most likely are later recuts (plate 1; figs. 1.2–1.3).

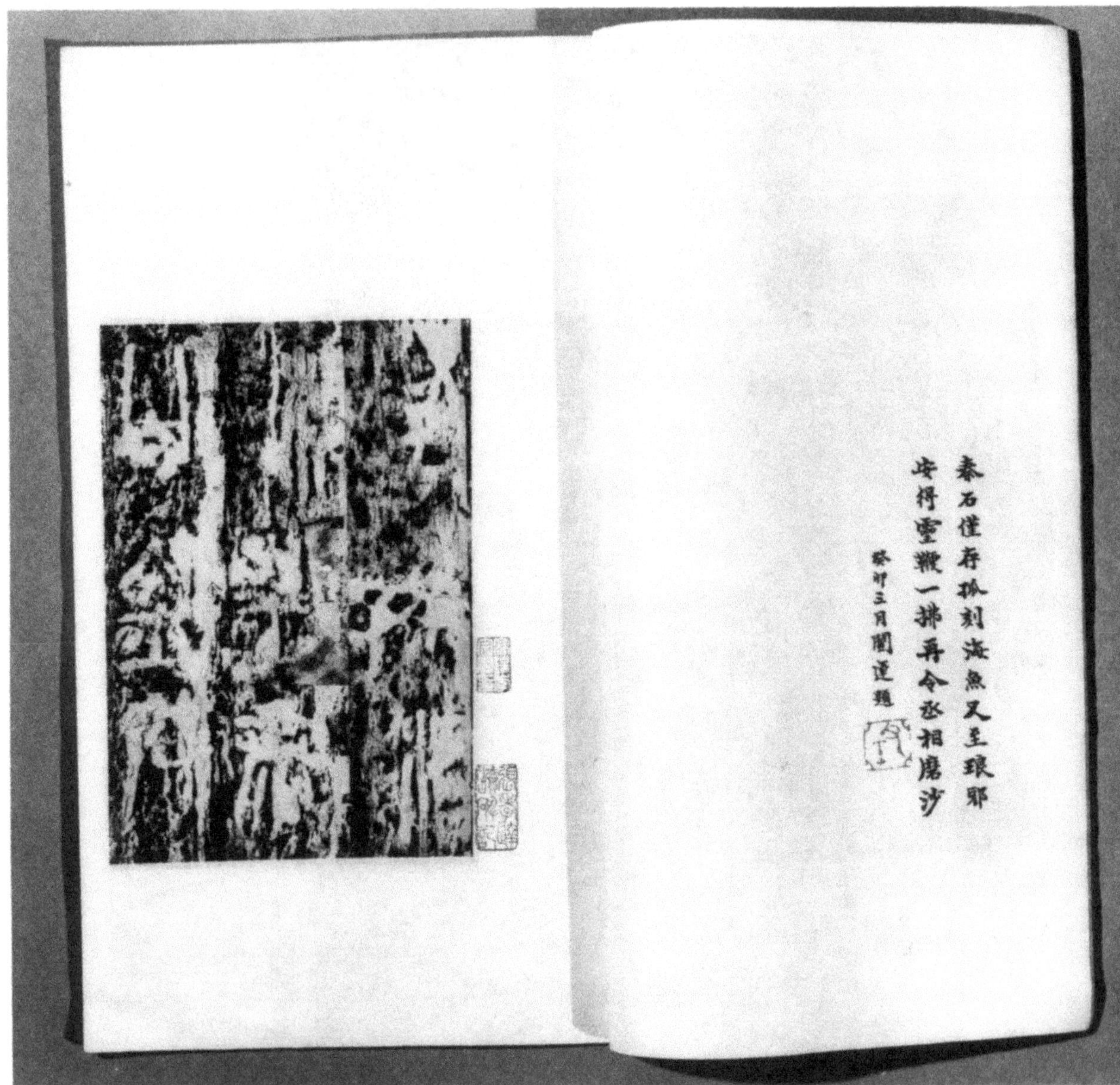

Fig. 1.3. Book-mounted "old" rubbing of the Langya Tai stone (218 B.C.E.). Early Qing dynasty, modern annotations. The Field Museum of Natural History, 233919.

The history of the Mount Yi stone is pertinent for rubbings. Praising the virtues and accomplishments of Qin, the front text described the chaos of earlier times and the way that the August Thearch "unified all under heaven under one lineage" and "enabled the black-haired people to live in peace and tranquillity."[19] The rear face held a shorter inscription by Er Shi, the First Emperor's son. Both inscriptions were in the newly created small-seal (*xiaozhuan*) script of Li Si, Shihuang's chief minister.

The original stone disappeared early. In the Southern Tang (937–975 C.E.), Xu Xuan obtained a hand copy (*mo^c ben*), and in the fourth year (993 C.E.) of Chunhua in the Northern Song, Zheng Wenbao, a Xi'an classicist and seal-script specialist, penned the inscription for a stone copy (*mo^c ke*) that is still in the Forest of Stone Tablets (Beilin) in Xi'an.[20]

Record of What Mr. Feng Has Seen and Heard (Feng shi wenjian ji), a Tang antiquarian work by Feng Yan, states that it stood from 219 B.C.E. until 450 C.E., when the Northern Wei emperor Taiwu Di overturned it.[21] Taiwu Di is said to have acted out of malice against the First Emperor, execrated by the Confucians for his excesses against traditional institutions, including the destruction of their books. The Song historian Sima Guang confirms the event and date in *Comprehensive Mirror for Aiding Government* (Zizhi tongjian).[22] Feng adds that "thereafter, people in succeeding ages made rubbings [*mo^b ta^a*] considering it to be a [calligraphic] model."[23] Sometime prior to the Tang Kaiyuan reign (713–741 C.E.), disgruntled by so many outsiders coming to copy the inscription, local people set a fire that largely destroyed the stone, ending the rubbing of Li Si's even then highly regarded calligraphy.[24]

Subsequent centuries saw many recuttings of Li's calligraphy in stone and wood, such as the 993 C.E. recut.[25] Feng's statement that "people in succeeding ages made rubbings" likely refers to the period from the Northern Wei to the Tang, when the burning of the stone reportedly occurred, and by which point there were recuttings.[26] This conclusion is based in part on two sources: a poem by Du Fu (712–770 C.E.), who notes that the recuts were done in jujube wood (*zaomu*), but that the characters were "fat," not true to the original; and *Discussing Stones* (Yushi), Ye Changchi's classic nineteenth-century study on stone inscriptions.[27]

Li Shuhua inclines toward the earlier part of the span, concluding that "making rubbings [*mo^b ta^b*] probably began in the Northern and Southern dynasties."[28] Because of events relating to the Yi Shan stone, he concludes that "in the fifth century (or even earlier) China already knew the method of rubbing [*mo^b ta^b*] stone tablets."[29] That period corresponds to the Northern Wei.

LIANG DYNASTY (502–556 C.E.)

The registry of classics (*jingji zhi*) in *The History of the Sui Dynasty* is the chief source of inferences that rubbings were known in the Liang.[30] Modern writers note that the history includes titles of the Kuaiji inscription and the Later Han and Wei Stone Classics.[31] Annotations indicate that the Liang imperial library formerly also held copies, recorded as paper rolls (*juan*), but that by the Sui they were lost or incomplete.

Listing the Han and post-Han stone cuts of Confucian, Buddhist, and Daoist classics, Qu and Chang conclude:

> Despite the fact that there were many stone cuts of the classical texts [in the Later Han and the early post-Han], before Xiao Liang they still did not understand about rubbing [*chuanta*[b]]. . . . Although we do not know about the beginnings of rubbing, we can determine that it originated approximately in the Xiao Liang. The minor studies (*xiaoxue*) division of the bibliographical section of *The History of the Sui Dynasty* records stone classics cut in a single style of script [*yi zi shi jing*] and those cut in three styles [*san zi shi jing*], and the original notations under each classic all speak of such-and-such a number of rolls of Liang [titles], which are rubbings [*chui*[b]*ta*[b] *zhi mo*[a]*ben*] from the Liang.[32]

The annals section of *The History of the Sui Dynasty* traces the troubled history of the Xiping Stone Classics, describing the natural and human attrition over centuries. Noting that early Tang efforts to recover these stone texts produced fewer than one-tenth of the original number, the Sui annals conclude that "rubbings [*chuanta*[a] *zhi ben*] of them still are in the Imperial Archives [Bifu]."[33] Modern scholars conclude that "these are the rubbed [*chuanta*[a]] Stone Classics of the Northern dynasties."[34]

There is no consensus on origins during the Liang. Some believe that rubbing was common then.[35] Others are guarded, noting that "although evidence concerning ink squeezing is found no earlier than the first part of the sixth century C.E., the . . . method might have been inherited from previous dynasties."[36] Still others suggest that the Liang saw the initial use of the technique, but they conclude that, "as for the term 'transmitted rubbings' [*chuanta*[a] *zhi ben*] in . . . the Sui [history], whether it actually meant going to the stone tablet and laying on ink still is difficult to determine."[37] Luo Zhenyu believed that the technique was initiated only in the Tang, in part because of the very small number of proven extant Tang rubbings, in part because of similarities between the bamboo paper and heavy ink of some of the rubbings attributed to the Tang and those known to date from the Ming.[38]

In summary, there is general agreement on assigning the inception of the rubbing technique to the Northern and Southern dynasties, with majority opinion inclined toward the Liang.

SUI DYNASTY (581–618 C.E.)

There is no need to linger on dating the innovation to the Sui. On the basis of Sui history, even cautious students allow that it took place at least a full century before the earliest known rubbing from the first years of the Tang.

TANG DYNASTY (618–907 C.E.)

With the advent of the Tang, there are both extant rubbings and sure literary evidence. A small number of rubbings derive from or are attributed to the Tang, with five as examples.

The earliest known, and only dated, Tang rubbing is a fragment of a rhymed composition known as *The Eulogy on the Hot Springs* (Wenquan ming). It is one of a small group of rubbings found at Mogaoku, the Caves of the Thousand Buddhas (*Qianfo dong*), near Dunhuang, in westernmost Gansu. Paul Pelliot discovered it in 1908 and took it to the Bibliothèque Nationale.[39] The rubbing, of relatively thin, heavily inked, badly worn, but still surprisingly resilient paper, consists of forty-eight lines from the lower part of the inscription and so carries no heading. The text lauds the qualities of a hot spring, and thus its name. There are no records of the inscription, and it contains neither the author's name nor the date. Fortunately, both are known, the one through scholarship and the other through happy circumstance. Luo Zhenyu deduced that both text and calligraphy in standard script (*zhengshu*) were by the second Tang emperor, Taizong (r. 627–649), a devotee of calligraphy, especially that of Wang Xizhi. Luo inferred that three tabooed characters in the inscription were written in the full form permitted only to the emperor.[40] The fragment luckily carried part of a single line of an anonymous note, dated the fourth year (654), eighth month of the Yonghui, the initial reign period of Emperor Gaozong, who succeeded Taizong (fig. 1.4).[41]

Other extant rubbings judged to be from the Tang era are undated, among them two that are also from Dunhuang. One is a rubbing of the Huadu Temple Stele (*Huadu Si bei*); in full title, "Inscription on a reliquary pagoda for Master Yongzhan, former monk at Huadu Temple" (*Huadu Si gu seng Yongzhan shi sheli taming*). The inscription records that the pagoda was built in 631 at Huadu Si, a Buddhist temple at Qimingdui, at the foot of the Zhongnan Shan, south of the Wei River, southern Shaanxi.[42] Li Baiyao composed the text, and Ouyang Xun (557–641) wrote it in a greatly admired style said to resemble straight trees and curving iron. The inscription had disappeared by the end of the thirteenth century.

Xie Jin (1369–1415) cites Fan Wo, writing in the Longxing-reign period (1163–1164), early in the Southern Song, and recording the turbulent history of the tablet, including its destruction.[43] Rubbings of the stone already were extremely rare by the Southern Song. Weng Fanggang (1733–1818) owned a genuine edition (*zhenben*), believed by him to be Tang, but which more likely was a Tang hand copy (*linben*), rare enough. Several editions of the inscription may be Song, but probably not Tang.

The rubbing consists of six initial leaves (twelve faces) cut-mounted as a small booklet. Aurel Stein found five leaves, with 197 characters, at Dunhuang, in March 1907.[44] Paul Pelliot found one leaf, carrying the initial text, in December of that year.[45] The

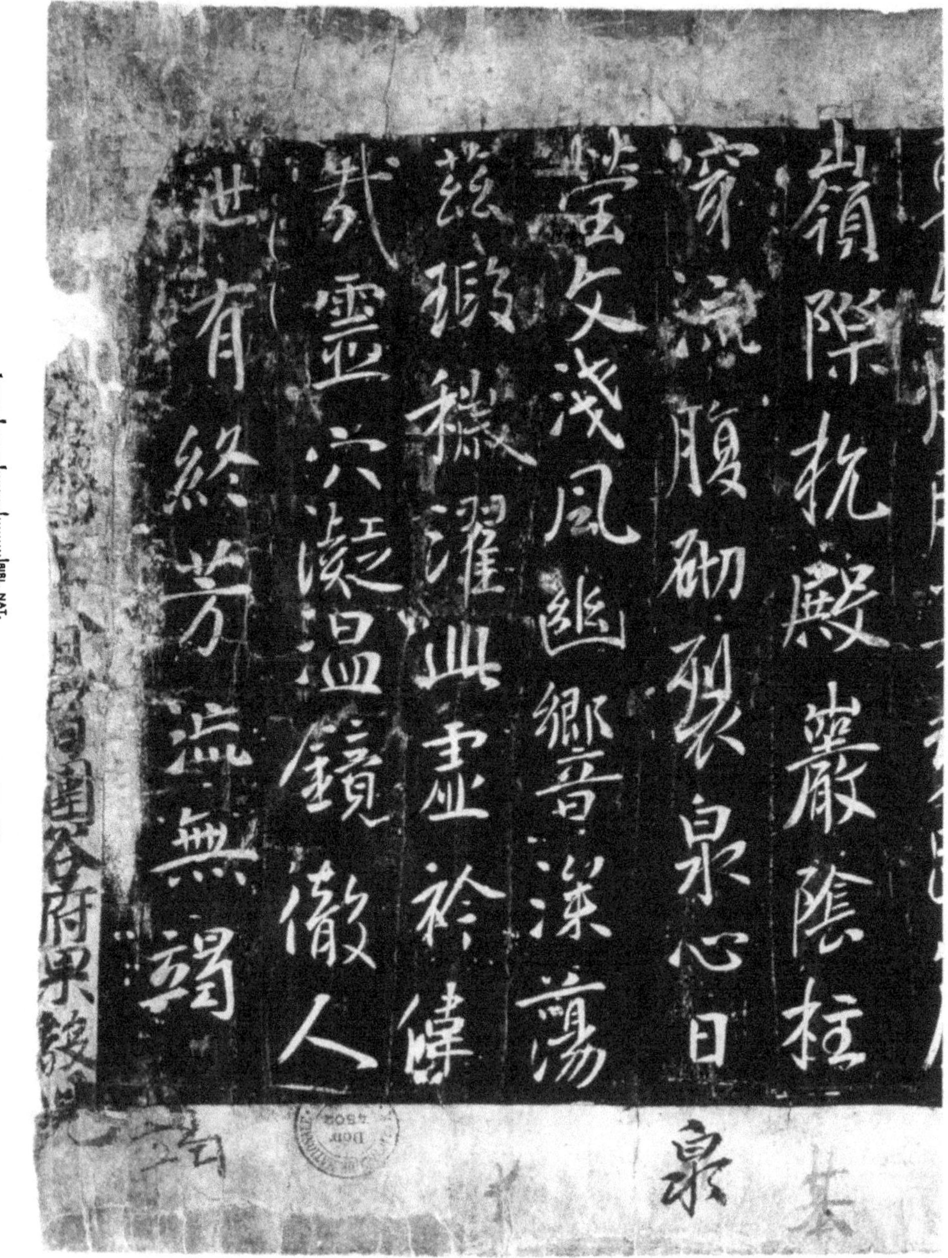

FIG. 1.4. Final, dated page of Ouyang Xun's *Hot Springs Inscription* (Wenquan ming), 654. Courtesy Bibliothèque Nationale de France.

rubbing is undated, with no commentary, seals, or other datable features, but most scholars, judging from its characteristics and its finding at Dunhuang, believe it to be Tang.[46]

The paper is light buff, markedly fibrous, but surprisingly thin, and in excellent condition.[47] The rubbing work was crude, with poor tamping and careless inking. The format and manner of mounting show up clearly in the Stein specimen, with the Tang artisan following the same principles as do his modern counterparts, producing a raincoat mount (*suoyi biao*), described in chapter 6. The after-inking of the support paper to harmonize it with the rubbing text was uneven, a sign of poor workmanship.[48] The artisan "bound" the booklet simply by gluing the edges of the pages, and it had no seals or inscriptions.[49]

The other Dunhuang rubbing, also found by Pelliot and generally considered to be Tang, is of a stone inscription of Liu Gongquan's standard-script *Diamond Sutra* (Liu Gongquan kaishu Jingang jing, fig. 1.5). Liu wrote it in 824 as a horizontal scroll. The paper is thin but tough; the ink, black but not glossy; the rubbing work, standard. The rubbing is judged to be from the ninth century, toward the end of the Tang, for three reasons. First, the Dunhuang manuscripts, especially those in the secret walled chamber, ranged from the early fifth to the late tenth centuries, with none later than 996. Of the eighteen pieces listed in *Serindia*, thirteen were dated or datable, and of these, eight were specifically or generally Tang, with only one, dated 991, closely post-Tang.[50] Second, Tangut military pressures, thought to have occasioned the secreting of the manuscripts, greatly lessened religious activities at the caves by the early Song. And, third, the chamber seems to have been sealed about 1035.[51]

Luo Zhenyu represents the prevailing view that the rubbing is Tang: "From all the writings, we know that at the time the stele had a great name, and because the transmitted rubbings were very numerous, and because the stone subsequently was destroyed, it was therefore recut again and again, and by Song times people no longer could see the original cutting."[52]

Two other rubbings are attributed to the Tang.[53] One is a rubbing of the *Duke Fang Liang Stele* (Fang Liang Gong bei) erected in honor of Fang Xuanling (578–648), ennobled duke by Tang Taizong. In the standard script of Chu Suiliang, the inscription is more than a thousand characters long.[54] The other rubbing is of the *Confucius Temple Stele* (Kongzi miaotang [zhi] bei) with both text and calligraphy by Yu Shinan (558–638), still actively imitated.[55] The inscription is dated 21 January 627, in the reign of Gaozu, first Tang emperor. The date of the rubbing is uncertain, leading Luo Zhenyu to observe that there is no way of knowing if the piece actually is Tang, this in the context of an analysis of another moot Tang rubbing of the *Sacred Scripture Pillar erected by Na Luoyan* (Na Luoyan jian zunsheng jingchuang), cut by a female Buddhist disciple.[56]

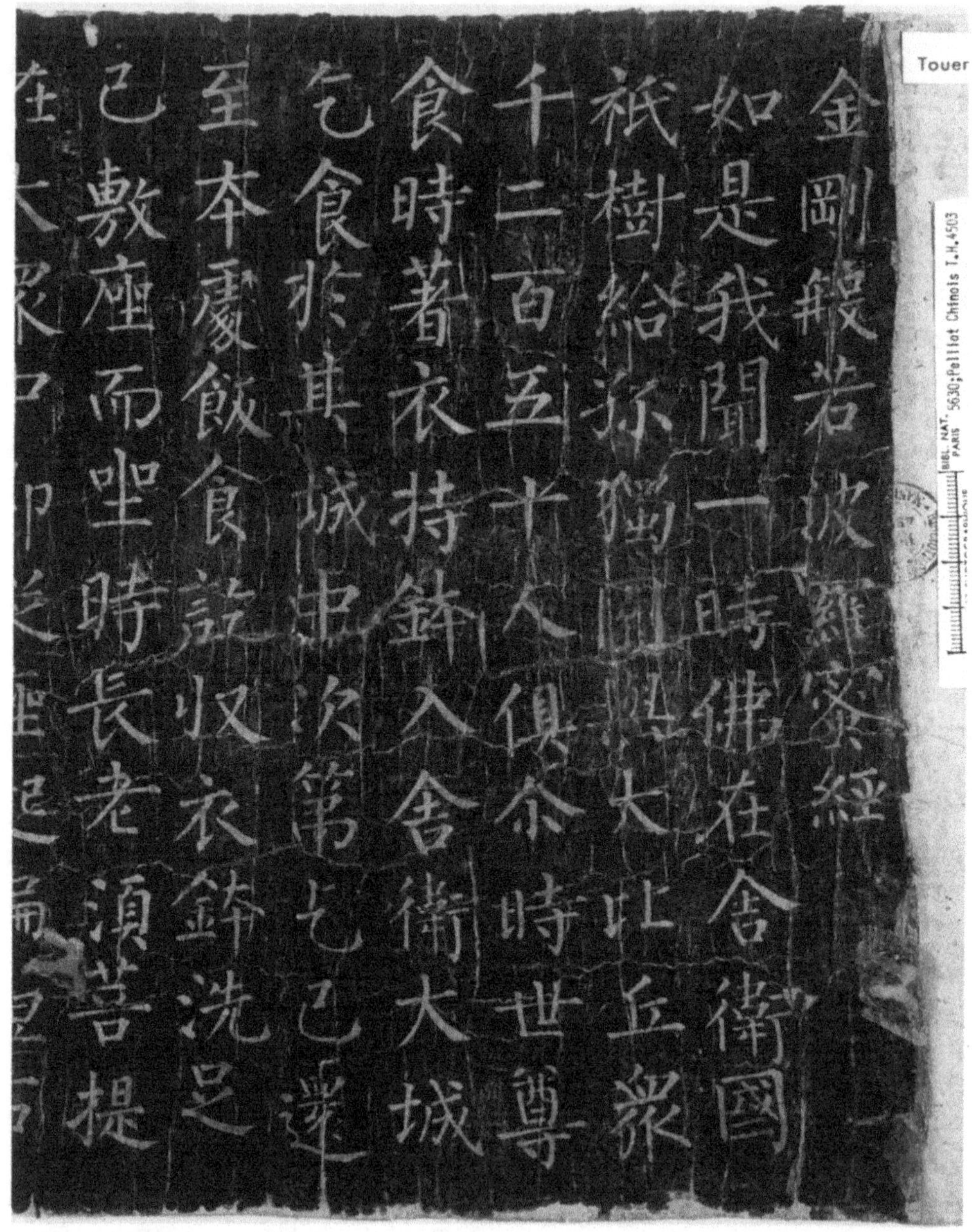

金剛般若波羅蜜經
如是我聞一時佛在舍衛國
祇樹給孤獨園與大比丘衆
千二百五十人俱尒時世尊
食時著衣持鉢入舍衛大城
乞食於其城中次第乞已還
至本處飯食訖收衣鉢洗足
已敷座而坐時長老須菩提
在大衆中即從座起偏袒右

Fig. 1.5. First page of Liu Gongquan's *Diamond Sutra* (Jingang jing), 824. Courtesy Bibliothèque Nationale de France.

Close students attribute only a small number of rubbings to the Tang, for, as Luo understatedly observes, "Song rubbings are not easy to come by, and Tang rubbings thus are very few."[57] Luo was cautious, pointing out that these early rubbings "used mulberry paper and heavy ink . . . no different from Ming rubbings, and the rubbing technique [*zhanla zhi fa*] became refined only in the Song . . . [although] it certainly did not attain that marking post–Song times."[58]

Tang literary references to rubbings are abundant and clear, bulwarking evidence that the technique was well established. *Codes and Regulations of the Six Boards of the Tang Dynasty* (Tang liudian), written in the early eighth century by or in the name of Emperor Xuanzong (713–755), contains a series of references to rubbings. The Institute for the Advancement of Literature (Hongwenguan) of the Chancellery (Menxiasheng) maintained three rubbings makers (*ta*[c]*shu shou*): "[The section was] established in the twenty-third year [649] of Zhenguan, and by the third year [663] of Longshuo there were 949 rolls of calligraphic models [*fashu*] in the section. [They were] mounted, and the section's rubbing work stopped. The section was reestablished in the first year [705] of Shenlong."[59]

The Academy of Scholarly Worthies (Jixiandian shuyuan) also had six rubbings makers (*ta*[b]*shu shou*). *Codes and Regulations* states that "the Academy of Heaven (Qianyuandian) first established two people [to make rubbings]. In the fourteenth year [of Kaiyuan, 726, the office] petitioned to increase the number to six, and they selected the people and had an official the same [rank] as an auxiliary (*zhiyuan*)."[60] The threefold increase in personnel strongly suggests a much greater interest in rubbings in the early eighth century. The Institute for the Veneration of Literature (Chongwenguan) also maintained two rubbings makers (*ta*[c]*shu shou*).[61] That office was directly under the Crown Prince, with a scholarly staff that supervised the collections of classical and other texts and taught the scholar-officials and the emperors themselves.

The "Record of Officialdom" (Baiguan zhi) of *The Old History of the Tang Dynasty* (Jiu Tang shu) and *The New History of the Tang Dynasty* (Xin Tang shu) includes similar references to rubbings personnel (*ta*[b]*shu shou*).[62] These rosters often lump rubbings artisans with other minor personnel, suggesting that rubbings were systematically collected, but that those who made them had the status of clerks, as is still true today.

Other Tang references to rubbings are Sima Zhen's *Commentary on the Records of the Grand Historian* (Shiji suoyin) of Sima Qian and Dou Ji's "Prose Poem on Explaining Calligraphy" (Shushu fu).[63] Both use *daben* ("strike" and "book") for a rubbing, the same term that occurs in a dated colophon (813) to *The Sacred Scripture Pillar Erected by Na Luoyan* and in other Tang inscriptions.[64]

Of high interest is a reference to a rubbing by Ennin (793–864), the Japanese Buddhist monk who made a pilgrimage to Tang China in 838–847. Ennin, touring temples in the Wutai Shan region of Shanxi, visited the Golden Pavilion Temple (Jin'ge Si), where "he also saw a picture of an impression of the Buddha's foot. . . . Ennin recorded in his diary the label under this painting, telling how it had been copied from a rubbing [Japanese, *datoku*; Chinese, *dade*] of the original footprint in India and brought back to Ch'ang-an [Xi'an] by a Chinese envoy in 649."[65] This account speaks of a date five years earlier than the Hot Springs rubbing, reinforcing the point that the technique was common by the early Tang.

Because of extant Tang rubbings and frequent Tang literary references to rubbings and personnel, modern writers, whether or not they agree that making rubbings began only in the Tang, concur that the technique was solidly established by then.[66] "Since the persons assigned to making rubbings were so numerous, there must have been many rubbings. It can be seen that, by the beginning of the Tang, making rubbings [*mo*[b]*ta*[b]] was extremely common."[67]

Many writers consider that cutting texts in stone and, subsequently, in wood at this period was done specifically to make rubbings: "At the outset they rubbed [*ta*[b]] only stonecuts; later they substituted woodcuts for stonecuts and used [the rubbing technique] to rub [*ta*[b]] those woodcuts."[68]

In summary, there is but a minuscule possibility that the rubbing technique originated in the Han. There is a strong likelihood that it was invented in the Northern and Southern dynasties, in the Northern Wei or, more narrowly, in the Liang, in the late fifth or early sixth century. There is virtual certainty that the practice was known in the Sui, in the late sixth or early seventh centuries, and it is solid fact that rubbings were common by the beginning of the Tang, early in the seventh century.

FUNCTIONS OF RUBBINGS

Inextricably bound to the history of rubbings are their functions in Chinese culture. Broadly, their principal function has been to reproduce intellectually or aesthetically valued matter that was incised, cast, or molded on clay, metal, stone, wood, and other firm substances. Rubbing was the only means the Chinese had of mechanically reproducing such materials until the invention of woodblock printing three and a half centuries later. The need for faithful copies has sustained the technique for a millennium and a half, despite the subsequent invention of more sophisticated forms of reproduction.

The Early Centuries

Throughout its history, the rubbing technique has served mainly to copy inscriptions, as against pictures. Further, the Chinese initially used the technique to copy inscriptions on stone, rather than those on metal, and it is important to distinguish between two chronological sequences. The first relates to substances and objects on which the

Chinese cut, cast, or molded inscriptive or pictorial matter.[69] From late prehistoric and early dynastic times to the Tang, when wood blocks became the primary printing medium, the Chinese recorded a broad range of subject matter susceptible to rubbing, with stone and iron of growing importance in the Han, especially the Later Han, and after that for recordation, civil and religious.[70]

The second chronological sequence is that in which the Chinese applied the rubbing technique. Despite the much earlier inscriptions on pottery, shell and bone, and metal, the cultural focus of the Chinese when they devised the technique, and for seven centuries after, was on stone inscriptions. There has been no correlation between the two sequences: through the centuries, the Chinese applied the technique to those substances, objects, or subjects of current intellectual or aesthetic interest, regardless of age.

The focus of the Chinese when they devised the rubbing technique was on stone inscriptions, initially the classics, but continuing, as in the Kaicheng edition of 837 (fig. 1.6), because through the Qing dynasty, knowledge of the classics was a requisite for an official position as well as the mark of a proper education. Stone also served commemorative and edictal functions, proliferating in the Later Han and continuing to the present day. Stone texts provided a guarantee of textual integrity, but as surrogates, rubbings also served a guaranteeing as well as a duplicating function. Religion, especially Buddhism, was a second major spur. Apart from Buddhism's role in developing woodblock printing, in which rubbings played a central part, the faith was in its time of greatest vitality, with exchanges with India of people and ideas, translations of Buddhist canons, and Buddhist art, breathtakingly exemplified at Dunhuang from the fourth century on, in sculptures at Yungang, largely from the fifth century, and at Longmen from the fifth and sixth centuries.[71] Of particular note was the monumental engraving of the complete Buddhist canon on walls of and stone tablets in nine grottoes on Stone Sutra Mountain (Shijing Shan), high above Cloud Dwelling Monastery (Yunju Si), an Early Tang temple in Fang Shan County, southwest of Beijing (plate 2). "The Fang Shan Stone Sutras are . . . Beijing's Dunhuang, a national treasure . . . [and] the largest [collection of] engraved Buddhist texts in the world. . . . [The work] began in . . . the Sui and ended in the late Ming, . . . continuing a thousand years. The immensity of the labor and the magnitude of the engravings warrant the designation 'the greatest in the world.'"[72]

This custom of cutting the Buddhist stone sutras flourished in the Northern Qi (550–577), before the formulation of the doctrine of *mofa,* the predicted decline and end of Buddhist Law.[73] Proselytization and fear of suppression occasioned cuttings on cliffs, grotto walls, and tablets, with devotees making rubbings. The Yunju Si engravings are an example, as are the 824 edition of the *Diamond Sutra* and the Na Luoyan and other scripture pillars (fig. 1.7). A colophon to the Na Luoyan pillar states that the Buddhist disciple erected it and made rubbings, and so "to some extent the purpose of erecting

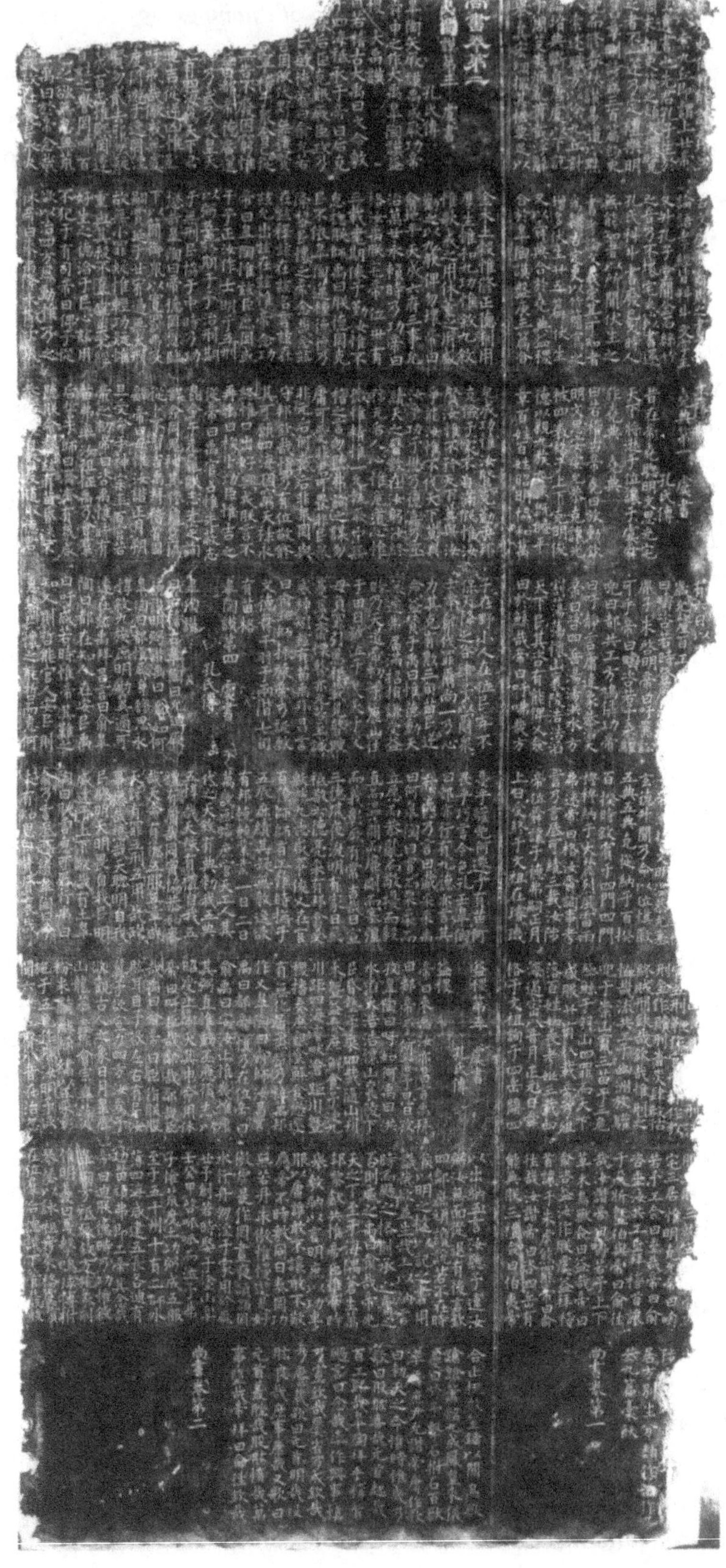

(*opposite*) FIG. 1.6. *Book of Documents* (Shang shu), *juan* 2, Kaicheng Stone Classics (837). Courtesy Xi'an Beilin Museum.

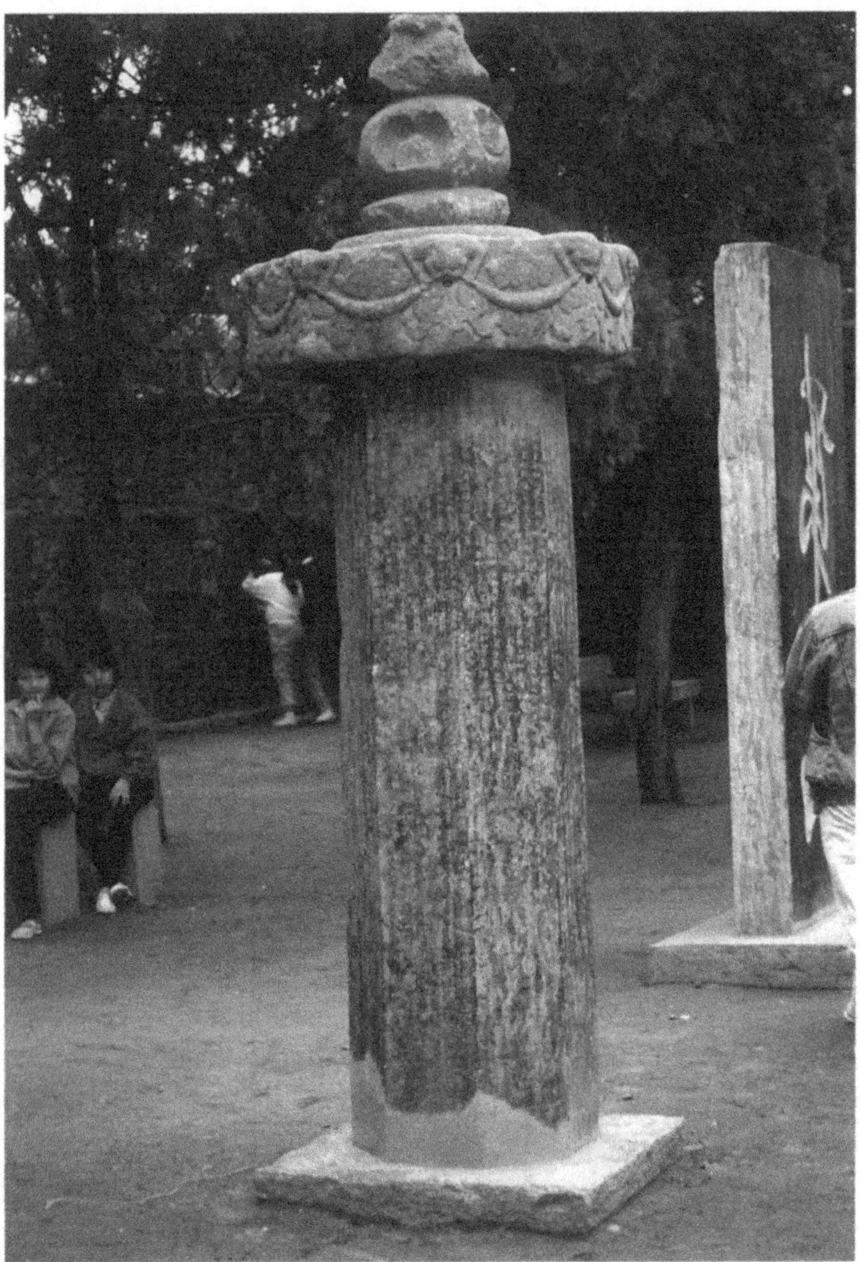

FIG. 1.7. Buddhist scripture pillar (*jingchuang*). Five Dynasties, Jin, 940 C.E. Taian, Dai Temple, 1993. Photograph by the author.

the stone was just to make rubbings [*daben*] for distribution."[74] In lesser measure, the Daoists also cut and rubbed their canons on stone, especially *The Classic on the Way and Its Power* (Daode jing) and the *Classic on the Central Court* (Huangting jing), said to have been written by Wang Xizhi, and prized for its calligraphic importance.[75]

The remaining major stimulus for rubbings in the early period was what was even then a strong interest in calligraphy, with extant examples of rubbings whose primary raison d'être was aesthetic as well as references to rubbings, the inspiration for which sprang from an appreciation of fine calligraphy and poetry, commonly combined. The rubbings of the calligraphies of Ouyang Xun's *Huadu Temple Stele* and Liu Gongquan's *Diamond Sutra* from Dunhuang generally are accepted as Tang, and their making and preservation almost certainly were inspired as much by aesthetics as by faith. References in *The History of the Sui Dynasty* to rubbings of Li Si's calligraphy include one to Shihuang's Kuaiji inscription, said to have been composed in his small-seal script.[76] The concise listing says nothing of its calligraphic value, but, given the Confucian establishment's implacable hatred of the First Emperor, one can posit that the copying was motivated in significant measure by appreciation of Li's hand rather than by its imperial content. One comes to the same conclusion with respect to rubbings of the Yi Shan and Tai Shan stones. In *Record of What Mr. Feng Has Seen and Heard,* Feng Yan describes the overturning of the Yi Shan stone and adds that succeeding generations made rubbings of it, considering Li's small-seal script a calligraphic model.[77]

Further documentation of early interest in calligraphy comes from the Tang references to Du Fu and Dou Ji in "Prose Poem on Explaining Calligraphy," both referring to local people cutting the text of the destroyed Yi Shan stone in wood as a substitute.[78] The clear implication is that the woodcut copy was a calligraphic model, and that rubbings, rather than prints, were made from the block: "Specimens of writing by famous calligraphers cut on stone were later transferred to wooden blocks, which were engraved with positive inscriptions, but in intaglio form similar to those on stone, and squeezes [rubbings] were made from them . . . as models of calligraphy."[79] This practice continued strongly into modern times.

Extant rubbings and literary references to rubbings as calligraphic models confirm that the Chinese of the period rubbed inscriptions primarily for their calligraphy. Figure 1.8 shows a rubbing of *Stele of the Sacred Teachings of San Zang* [Xuan Zang] *of the Great Tang* [dynasty] (Da Tang San Zang shengjiao bei), also known as *Stele of the Compiled* [-characters] *Preface to Wang Xizhi's Sacred Teachings* (Ji Wang Xizhi shengjiao xu bei), or simply *Compiled* [-characters] *Wang Stele* (Ji Wang bei). The inscription was neither composed nor written by Wang Xizhi. In 648, Tang Taizong composed the text

(opposite) FIG. 1.8. *Preface to the Sacred Teachings of San Zang* (Xuan Zang) *Tablet* (*Da Tang San Zang shengjiao bei xu bei*), 672. Courtesy Xi'an Beilin Museum.

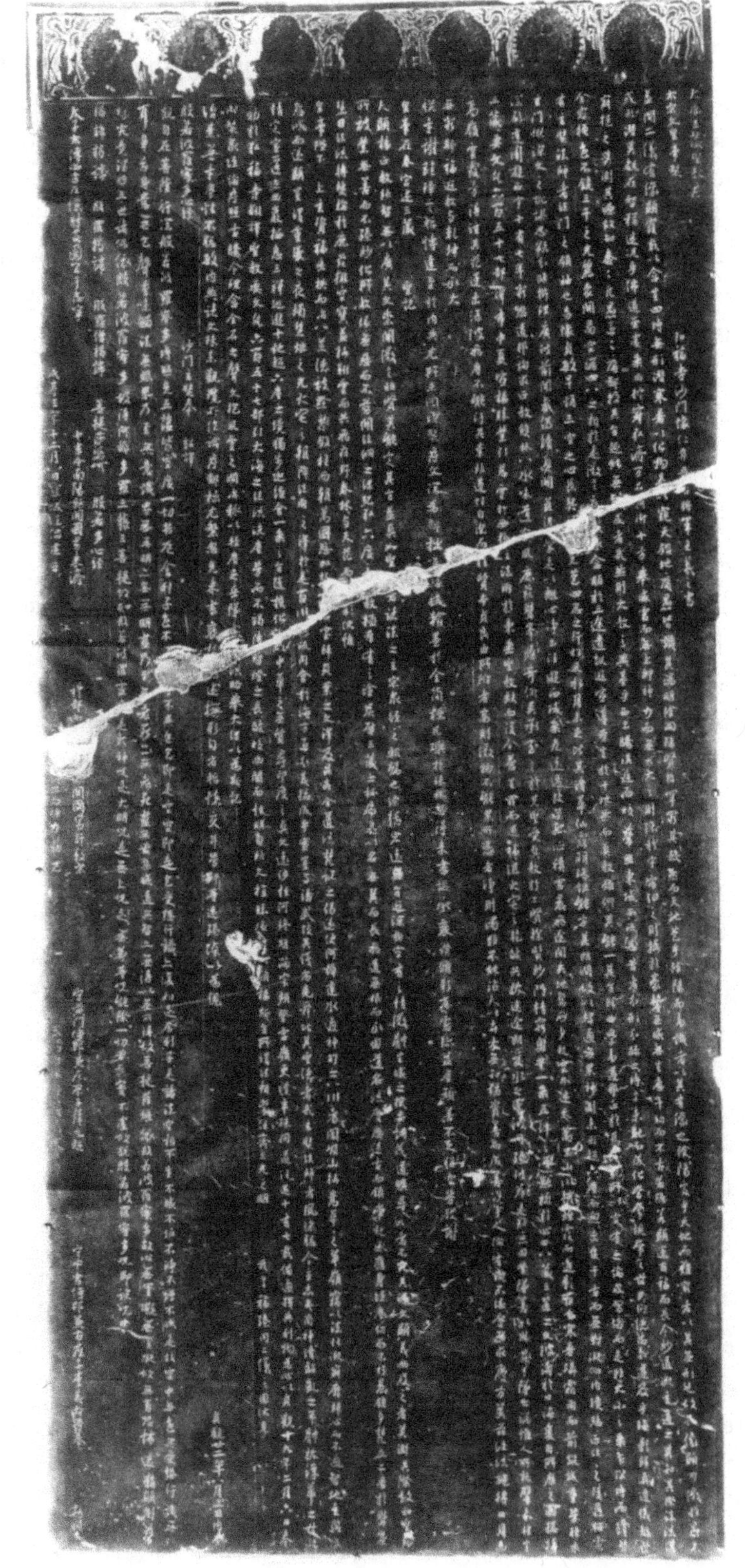

in honor of the Buddhist pilgrim Xuan Zang. Tang Gaozong (r. 649–683) ordered Huairen, a monk, calligrapher, and descendant of Wang, to copy individual characters from various specimens of Wang's calligraphy in the imperial collection, forming a composite duplicate of the famous piece: "It was one of the first *t'ieh* [*tie*] to be cut in stone . . . [and] could be easily and widely distributed . . . in the form of rubbings, an advantage . . . so far . . . enjoyed only by *pei* [*bei*]."[80] The deep and abiding Chinese affinity for calligraphic art has been a major factor in the continuing vitality of the rubbing technique.

Song Dynasty (960–1280)

By the Song, rubbings were well-established features of Chinese culture, but with changes in function, some products of the invention of woodblock printing in Tang, for the new technique fulfilled the duplicative function more efficiently. The changes were of degree rather than order, and rubbings continued to serve intellectual and aesthetic functions.

The classics continued as a stimulus, with conservatism binding Confucians to stone and rubbings as "the one official and orthodox method for the reduplication of standard texts, . . . [and so] the use of rubbings . . . continued a parallel existence."[81] In addition to those cut in the Han, the Wei, and the Tang, Confucians engraved the classics in the Shu (Five Dynasties), the Northern Song, the Southern Song, and the Qing, with "each important dynasty considering it a duty thus to conserve the results of the best textual criticism of the day."[82] Chen Yuanlong (1652–1736) described a series of genuine and spurious Song stone texts, on the basis of character forms and physical attributes.[83] Rubbings also served to copy commemorative inscriptions, such as the *Stele of the Benevolent Sage Equal to Heaven of the Eastern Mountain Peak* (Dongyue Tianqi Rensheng Di bei), marking the expansion in 1013 of the Dai Temple (Dai Miao) in Taian, Shandong (fig. 1.9).

Religion continued to stimulate the production of rubbings. Buddhists relied on stone and rubbings, as represented by the Fang Shan cuttings, and Daoists also followed the traditional propensity for stone texts.

Aesthetics also spurred production, centering on the stone-cut brushmanship of famous calligraphers, with calligraphy a major art by the Eastern Jin (317–420 C.E.) and increasing in the Song and after.[84] Such calligraphies in stone and wood were copied as *fatie*—models with intaglio characters cut in normal orientation, rather than in reverse, as in woodblock printing—and then rubbed. That practice seems to have begun no later than the Tang and most likely earlier, given the literary references to Li Si's calligraphy on the Yi Shan and Kuaiji stones.

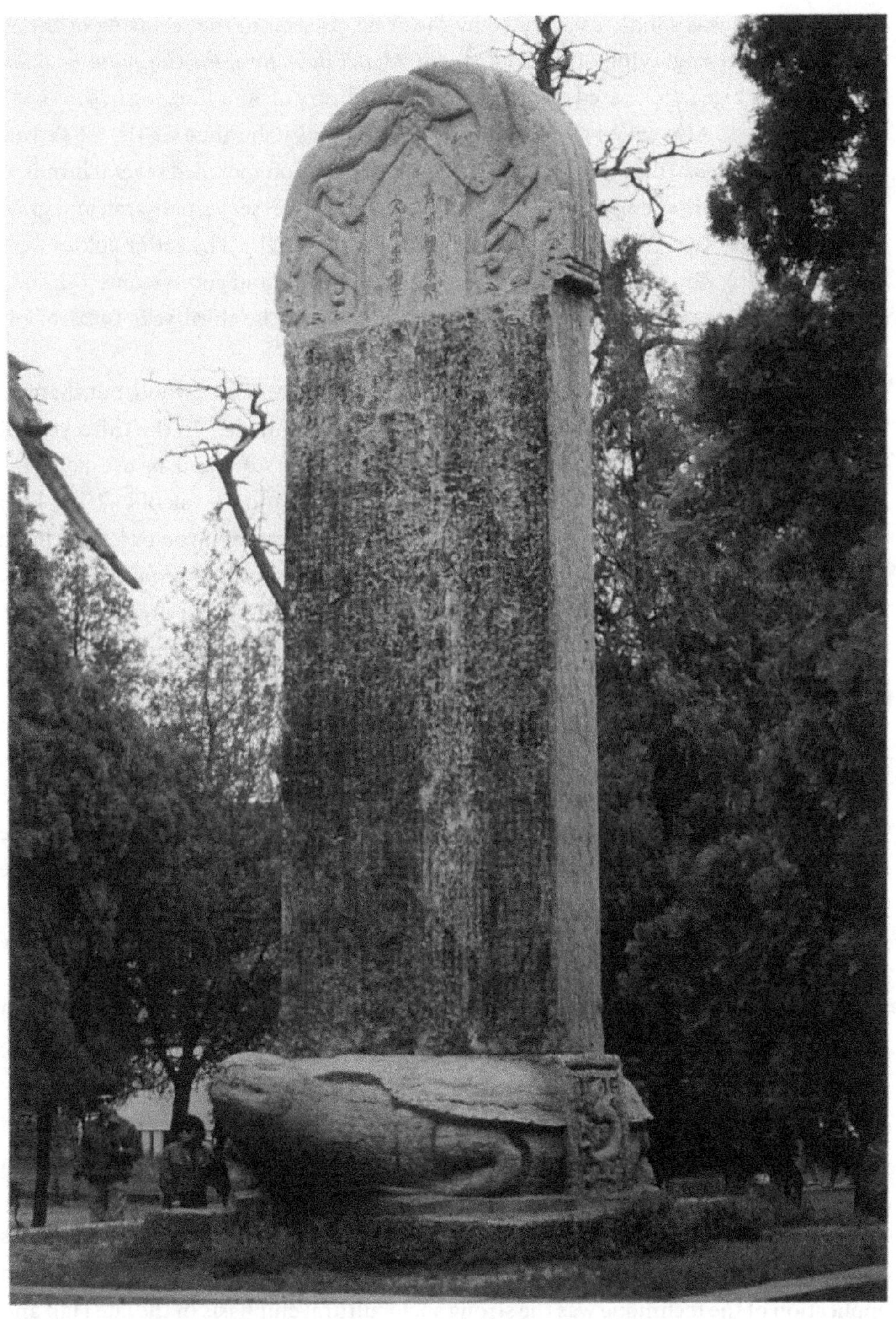

FIG. 1.9. *Stele Commemorating the Expansion of the Dai Temple* (*Dongyue Tianqi Rensheng Di bei*), 1013. Taian, Dai Temple, 1993. Photograph by the author.

The process was solidly established by the Song, as seen in the recutting of the Yi Shan Stone. The engraving of the *Calligraphy Model Book from the Chunhua Pavilion* (Chunhua Ge bige fatie), based on models from the library of Song Taizong (r. 976–998), was a landmark. Also called the *Chunhua Ge Model Book* (Chunhua Ge tie), or *Private Cabinet Model Book* (Bige tie), the comprehensive collection included several hundred calligraphies of earlier emperors, officials, inventors of large-seal, small-seal, and grass scripts, and the "two Wangs," Wang Xizhi and Wang Xianzhi. The calligraphies were copied by Wang Zhu, a renowned calligrapher of the time, and cut in stone. Tai Zong ordered rubbings, which were put up in ten volumes in the third year (992) of his Chunhua reign and presented to high ministers.[85]

Opinion differs about whether the set was cut in both stone and wood, but that it is certain that it was done in stone, and that rubbings were made: "In the third year of Shunhua (992), an edict was issued to cut these facsimiles in stone and, by use of Ch'ên-hsin-t'ang [Chengxin Tang, Hall of the Pure Heart] paper and the ink of Li T'ing-kuei [Li Tinggui, fl. 937–975], to make rubbings . . . in such a way that if you pass your hand over them the ink will not soil your hand."[86] Commenting on the *Chunhua Ge fatie,* Carter states that "lithography was thus the recognized method of preserving exact copies of beautiful calligraphy. When the stone blocks became broken through constant use, they were mended with silver wire, the impression of which could often be detected in the rubbing. During the later years of the Sung period these lithograph books of 992 were treasured as great rarities."[87] When stone sets were lost, rubbings served as models for new copies and for stone or wood recuts, from which fresh rubbings or woodblock prints were made down the centuries.[88] As a result of this copying, "there are many doubts about the authenticity of even these [calligraphic examples in the *Calligraphy Model Book from the Chunhua Pavilion*]."[89] Bai Qianshen adds that, "unfortunately, none of the original works of calligraphy reproduced in the *Chunhuage tie* have survived. Although it includes some fakes, the original *Chunhuage tie* has preserved many ancient works of calligraphy and tells us exactly what was in the imperial calligraphy collection during the early Song period."[90] Despite its uncertainties, the *tie* "has been deemed the *ketie zhi zu* ('the ancestor of calligraphy model-book engraving')."[91] Stone rubbing continued along with woodblock printing, for rubbings provided accuracy that no other method then known could ensure, and accuracy was vital with calligraphy, where subtleties of line and proportion are essential.

There are no extant rubbings or sure literary references to evidence use of rubbings to capture bronze inscriptions much before the Song. The main reason for the delayed application of the technique was the strong sociocultural emphasis in the late Han and the early post-Han on official stone editions of the classics. Another reason "for the neglect of bronze inscriptions was probably their inaccessibility, since they were usually kept in private or imperial collections."[92]

In the Northern Song, "collecting and cataloging rubbings of ancient bronzes and stelae . . . became popular among the Chinese literati. . . . Collecting rubbings of inscriptions on ancient objects was intended to forward studies of the classics and historiography rather than calligraphic learning. *Jinshi xue*, or the study of ancient metal and stone objects, also matured as a scholarly discipline."[93]

Among the earliest books to record inscriptions on metal were *Record of Ding Vessels* (Ding lu), by Yu Li (502–561 C.E.), and *Record of Ancient and Modern Swords* (Gujin daojian lu), by Tao Hongjing (502–556 C.E.). *Record of Ding Vessels* is an annotated list of sixty-three tripod and tetrapod *ding* cauldrons, ranging from the mythological Nine Tripods of Emperor Yu to historical vessels, the latest of which, now lost, was associated with Wang Xizhi (303–361 C.E.). *Record of Ancient and Modern Swords* includes swords from the time of the legendary emperor Yu to the Three Kingdoms (220–265 C.E.):

> Their . . . work, at the latest, could not have been later than the time of Liang [emperor] Yuandi (552). Therefore, at that time, this [type of] study was not yet flourishing, and at best one only can regard it as the developmental period of metal-and-stone [epigraphical] research [*jinshi xue*]. The phenomenon of "families having their [collections of ancient] objects, and [of] people being familiar with their inscriptions," causing epigraphical studies to grow and become popular, actually appeared in the Song and flowered in the Qing.[94]

There is no agreement on when rubbings of bronze inscriptions first were made, with the consensus being that "the technique of squeezing inscriptions from bronze and other objects was probably later than that from stone."[95] Su Yinghui refers to early studies of bronze inscriptions:

> Rubbing [*chuanta*[a]] inscriptions and designs on metal (at the latest, it could not have been later than the Sui or the Tang) and stone, although we still cannot determine their beginnings, both were flourishing by the Song. In the Song, from the time of Emperor Zhenzong [998–1022], Confucians organized the ancient *ding* tripods of Qianzhou [Shaanxi] and so initiated the beginning of research into ancient objects.[96]

Although Su suggests that the rubbing of metals began no later than the Sui or the Tang, he cites Wang Guowei's view that "with respect to rubbing [*ta*[a]] inscriptions on sacrificial vessels, there is no information prior to the Zhao Song [960–1279]."[97]

That the application of the rubbing technique to bronze inscriptions did occur then is documented in *Treatise on the Zhou Script* (Zhou shi), by Zhai Qinian: "In the third year [1051] of [the reign of] Huangyou, an imperial order was issued to take out the ceremonial vessels from Xia, Shang, and Zhou that had been preserved by the Imperial

Archives (Bige) and the Chamberlain for Ceremonies (Taichang), and to hand them over to the Musician in Chief (Taiyue) [section of the Taichang] for statistical comparison. The order was also issued to rub their inscriptions [*mo*ᵃ*kuan*] for presentation to high officials."[98] It seems that "this is the only recorded reference to Song-era rubbing [*mo*ᵃ*ta*ᵃ] of ceremonial vessels. . . . From that time on, the various specialists increased, and the records daily became more abundant; and then metal-and-stone studies proliferated and became the great profession of the time!"[99]

Rong Geng also cites *Treatise on the Zhou Script,* noting that "this was the beginning of making rubbings [*ta*ᵃ *mo*ᵃ] of ceremonial vessels." He continues:

> Unfortunately, *Illustrations of Antiquities* (Kaogu tu) [by Lü Dalin, late eleventh century] and *Inscriptions on Ritual Vessels* (Zhongding kuanshi) [by Wang Houzhi, late twelfth century], and such books could not rely on rubbings (*mo*ᵃ*ben*) at all [but used woodblock illustrations].[100]

The conclusion is that using rubbings for illustrating the bronzes had not yet become common in the Southern Song. That there was greatly increased interest in bronze inscriptions in the Song, and with it an added emphasis on rubbings to copy them, gains support from the strong Song renaissance of interest in the classical period, notably in Confucian philosophy and in art. In the latter area, the revival was marked by close attention to pre-Han bronzes and other objects because of their historical and epigraphical content.

Post-Song Dynasty

Following the spur of interest during the Song, there was no renewal of interest in metal-and-stone studies until the early Qing, when rubbings of ancient steles again became popular.[101] Over the intervening centuries, rubbings and the rubbing technique seem to have continued with little major change. In the Qing, there were significant changes in and additions to what was cut in stone and rubbed, a trend that was especially marked in the late eighteenth century, crested in the nineteenth, and continues to the present. There was diminished reliance on rubbings for copying stone-cut Confucian classics, and although an edition was cut during the Qing, in the last decade of the eighteenth century, the original guaranteeing and duplicating functions had long since ended, and the cutting was largely a bow to tradition. The cutting of commemorative, edictal, and other inscriptions continued, carrying on the tradition (fig. 1.10). Similarly, Buddhism and Daoism no longer depended significantly on stone but did continue to cut and rub stone inscriptions (fig. 1.11).[102] Figure 1.12 shows a rubbing of the heading of a handwritten Qing copy of *Classic on the Way and Its Power in the Hand of Songxue* [*daoren,* Zhao Mengfu's literary name] (Songxue shu Daode jing).

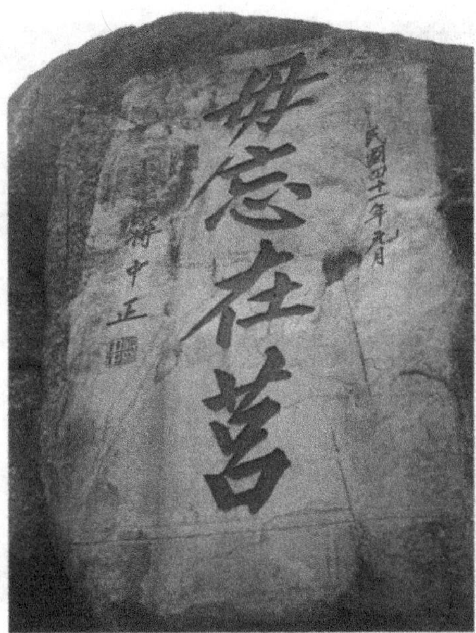

FIG. 1.10. *Don't forget Ju* (Wu wang zai Ju). Calligraphy of Chiang Kaishek (1952), Quemoy Island, 1960. Photograph by the author.

The aesthetic stimulus for rubbings continued undiminished, with rubbings of exemplary calligraphy made, prized, and preserved in stone, and commonly inscribed on smoothed boulders and cliff faces (*moyai*, plate 3). The last edition of the *Chunhua Ge fatie*, on display at the Beilin, was cut in Shaanxi in the third year (1646) of the Qing Shunzhi reign, with woodblock used for all subsequent editions (fig. 1.13). The continuing cultural preoccupation with calligraphic art has strongly sustained the rubbing technique, as witness the ready availability of calligraphic models in China and other Asian countries, and in Western countries touched by Chinese culture over the centuries, not to mention contemporary private and public collections, both Asian and, increasingly, Western.[103] This reverence for fine brushwork continues to manifest itself in the new China, as seen in the appreciation of traditional as well as modern calligraphers, including Mao Zedong, whose brushwork during his tenure was omnipresent, and Zhou Enlai, whose hand is considered better.

Finally, in the Qing era and the modern period there was an expanding use for copying other substances, objects, and subjects not known earlier. The late Qing also saw a significant advance in the technique itself, described in chapter 5.

Rubbing inscriptions on the ancient bronzes seems to have become popular by the Song. Whether the technique was also used then to copy their decor is not known, but majority opinion inclines against such application. That interest greatly increased in

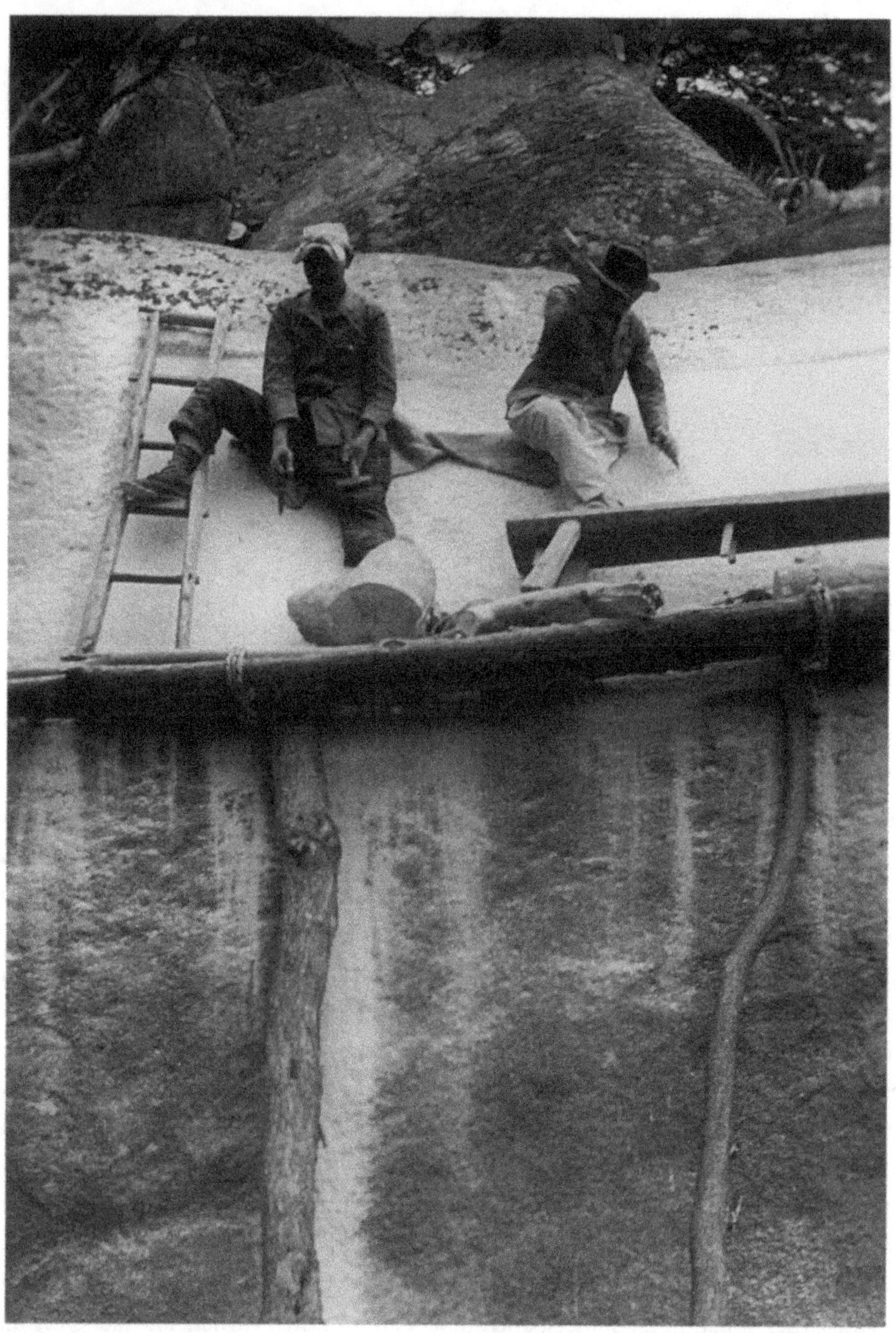

FIG. 1.11. Daoist "smoothed cliff." White Cloud Grotto, Lao Shan, Shandong, 1948. Photograph by the author.

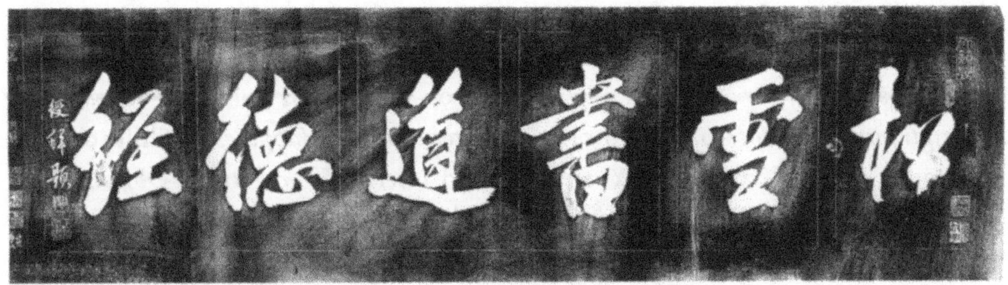

FIG. 1.12. Heading of a handwritten recut (1858) of *The Classic of the Way and Its Power* (Daode jing), calligraphy of Zhao Mengfu (1254–1322). The Field Museum of Natural History, 233334.

FIG. 1.13. Calligraphic models of historic emperors, recut (1646) of the *Chunhua Ge tie* (992). Freer Gallery of Art, Smithsonian Institution, gift of Peking University, F1980.70.1.

the late Qing, as witness the innovation of three-dimensional composite rubbings (*quanxing taben*), also described in chapter 5. Rubbings then began to find favor in book illustration, for "after Jiaqing [1796–1820], Qian Dian published *Research on Inscriptions on Ancient Objects in the Hall of Sixteen Eternal Happinesses* [Shiliu changle tang guqi kuanshi], and Ruan Yuan published *Inscriptions on Ritual Objects in the Studio of Accumulated Antiquities* [Jigu Zhai zhongding kuanshi], and thus rubbings [*ta*ᵃ*ben*] first were accorded respect by people."[104] This tendency, which accelerated in the nineteenth century, continued to do so in the twentieth and into the twenty-first, despite the availability of photography, and rubbings are standard in publications and museum exhibits. Continuity of traditional patterns clearly continues, despite China's violent political, social, and cultural disruptions.

The greatest change in the rubbing technique in recent centuries has been its extended use. The initial use of the technique, from its inception through the Tang, focused on stone, with the Song extending it to metal. Those two materials have constituted its most significant applications, as attested by the traditional name, "metal-and-stone studies," *jinshi xue*, applied since the Song to epigraphical studies. The usage continues in the bibliographical classification of rubbings, "metal-and-stone section" (*jinshi bu*), that is used in Chinese libraries and museums.

In the Qing, during or soon after the Qianlong (1736–1795) and Jiaqing (1796–1820) periods, scholars and collectors extended the technique. While maintaining their primary interest in inscriptions on the favored bronze and stone, they broadened their focus to include inscriptions and pictorials on new materials, as in the shell-and-bone and bronze inscriptions at Anyang, capital of the Shang dynasty, and the subsequent proliferation of finds representing the lives of commoners at a host of other prehistoric and historic sites. This broadened interest, and the concomitant use of rubbings, were fruits of the heightened interest in historiography during the Qing, and in paleography and other modern and contemporary language studies. The application of the technique through the centuries followed whatever were the current scholarly and connoisseurship interests, and in modern and contemporary times these have encompassed a full range of substances, objects, and subjects, providing a comprehensive view of Chinese history, society, and culture over the millennia.[105]

Rubbings, ubiquitous in China, are still a source of high interest a millennium and a half after their invention. One has only to pay a holiday visit to the Xi'an Beilin or other local imitative "forests of steles" all across China to appreciate the continuing reverence for inscriptions and designs on ancient cultural objects, and the interest in rubbings made of them.[106]

Along with other changes that marked rubbings, the Qing, especially from the eighteenth century on, also saw innovations in the technique. It is to this subject that we turn in the following chapters.

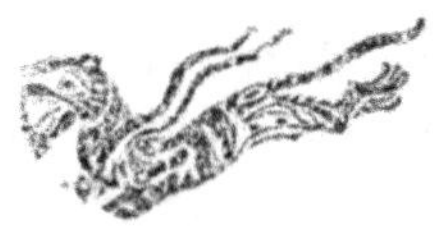

2 / Orchid Root and Rhinoceros-Tail Hair

In describing the materials and methods used to make Chinese rubbings, one needs to clarify the meanings of and relationships between two pairs of terms and the phenomena to which they apply. The terms are "simple rubbing" and "composite rubbing," and "wet technique" and "dry technique."

SIMPLE AND COMPOSITE RUBBINGS

Ordinary Chinese rubbings are ink-on-paper representations of intaglio and relief inscriptions or designs on metal, stone, and other firm substances. Such representations are two-dimensional and can be called "simple rubbings" (figs. 2.1, 3.1, 4.6). Simple rubbings commonly represent intaglio or relief texts or pictures on surfaces that are flat—such as, most commonly, a stele—or slightly curved. The resulting effect is strictly two-dimensional. As the depth of the relief or the degree of surface curvature increases, the simple rubbing becomes a progressively less successful means of representation.

Rubbings also occur as composite rubbings (*quanxing taben*, "full-form rubbings"), representations of objects in the round, particularly the ancient ritual bronzes. Other names include *liti ta* ("three-dimensional rubbing"), *qixing ta* ("vessel-form rubbing"), and *tuxing ta* ("pictorial rubbing").[1] Although still two-dimensional, such rubbings have a strong three-dimensional quality and differ markedly in effect from simple rubbings (see figs. 5.2–5.3).

The terms *simple* and *composite* carry double meanings. First, they refer to the differences in the appearances of the images. Second, they connote differences between the techniques used to make them. Both are Chinese in origin and go under the name *taben*, "rubbing," in one of its three variant character forms (see Appendix 2).

WET AND DRY TECHNIQUES

Traditionally, the Chinese have used two different techniques to make simple or composite rubbings. Marked by distinctive materials and methods, these are "wet technique" and "dry technique," or "wet rubbing" and "dry rubbing." The differences between the two center in the way in which the paper is laid, wet or dry; how it is manipulated; and the state in which the ink is applied, moist or solid. The wet technique is more standard, more widely applicable, and historically and culturally more significant than the dry technique. In the wet technique, used for simple as well as composite rubbings, one wets the paper in applying it to the host, tamps it into tight apposition, and, when it is appropriately dry, applies moist ink. In the dry technique, one applies the paper dry, does not tamp or manipulate the paper, and lays on dry coloring. Figure 2.1 illustrates the two types.

One further clarification will be helpful, that having to do with the schizophrenic relationship between the rubbing and the host object. There is a tendency on the part of those who find fascination in rubbings to accord them lives of their own, forgetting that they are surrogates for original objects, often still extant, but, in many cases, not. In the latter situation, rubbings assume some of the qualities of the originals, especially if the rubbing is a *guben,* "unique edition," a sole existing copy of a lost original object. The focus in these pages is on the rubbings, but one always needs to remember that they are but very convenient, useful, and often very attractive reflections of original objects.

The following account focuses largely on making simple rubbings by the wet technique, because of their greater historical significance and abundance. Chapters 2 through 4 treat materials and methods for making simple and wet rubbings; chapter 5 deals with those for composite and dry rubbings.

The materials and methods used to make a simple rubbing by the wet technique basically are the same regardless of the substance, object, or subject. The account emphasizes those used to copy inscriptions and pictures on stone, especially steles, the first and thenceforth most common cultural object on which the Chinese have practiced the technique across fifteen centuries, and on metal, particularly the ancient ritual bronzes. Through the centuries, especially in recent times, the Chinese used the technique on a wide variety of other substances, objects, and subjects, each posing special challenges. Massive steles with large, deeply cut inscriptions require very different materials and methods from those appropriate for the finely incised, often fragile Shang divination shells and bones, or carved ivory and bone hairpins. Highly polished surfaces, such as surfaces of jade or glass, demand very different treatment from the rough surfaces of eroded steles, or the porous surfaces of pottery and wood. Within similar categories of objects, specific types often require special consideration. Among the ancient bronzes, certain types require special attention because of their size or shape, the nature of their relief, the location of their inscriptions or design elements, and their condition. Images of revered figures often receive special attention. Finally, materials and techniques differ for making rubbings indoors and out, in different seasons of the year, or even at different times of day.

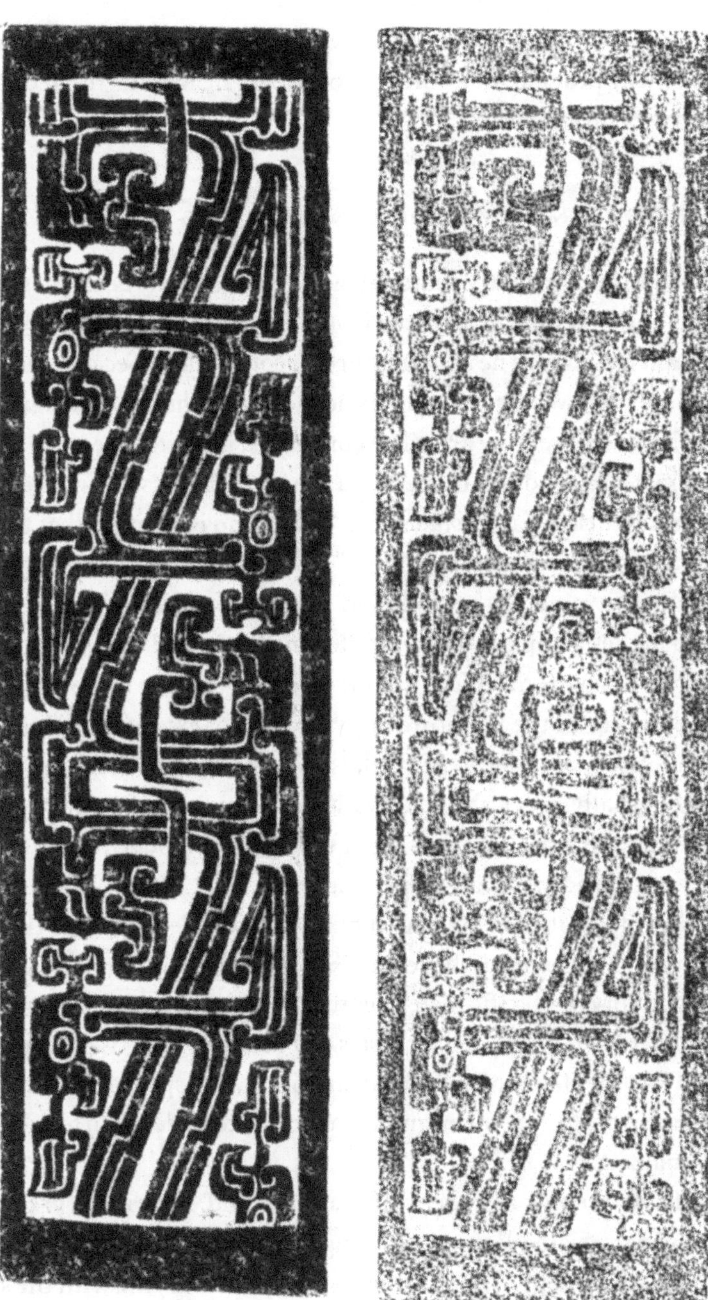

Fig. 2.1. Simple wet (left) and dry (right) rubbings of an Eastern Zhou bronze architectural element. The Field Museum of Natural History, 127363. Rubbings and photographs by the author.

Materials and techniques are personal, varying with the artisan. Mention of but a few variations will provide an awareness of the intricacies of the technique and an appreciation of its mystique.

HISTORICAL INFORMATION ON MATERIALS AND TECHNIQUES

There is little information on the materials and methods that the Chinese used to make rubbings in the early centuries after the invention of the technique, largely because of the lack of extant rubbings. The matter is further complicated because making rubbings in China traditionally was a craft and was not accorded the same recognition as painting, calligraphy, and other fine arts. The consensus, given their essential simplicity, is that the basic materials and techniques used in ancient times were similar to those used in more recent centuries. Carter states that "there is no indication that the method has materially changed from the earliest times," while Tsien observes that "we assume that it was generally the same as that followed in modern practice."[2] The materials and methods used in the early period were limited in variety and quality as compared with those used in the Song, from which time onward they became more refined.[3] Although difficult to document in the literature or by analysis of extant rubbings, this progress is reflected in references to the expanded use of the technique and the greater variety of materials, especially paper and ink, available in the Song and after. A small corpus of data on rubbing materials derives from the later premodern centuries but largely centers in the two basic materials, paper and ink.

Much of the information about the rubbing process derives from the period since about 1800. From then forward, the record is more active and detailed, including views about the desirability of specific materials and techniques, with differences of opinion traceable to preferences of the time or tastes of a collector or artisan. Chinese connoisseurs believed that the choice of materials was critical, and specialists during this period devoted great care to selecting them, giving particular consideration to subtle differences in type and quality.[4]

In order of use, the five categories of materials and equipment used to make wet rubbings are papers, sizing liquids, tamping tools, inks, and ink dabbers. The work also involves an assortment of miscellaneous materials, varying with the situation and artisan predilections.

Papers

Of the four components in the Chinese writing complex—paper, ink, inkstone, and brush, the *si bao,* "four precious" (stationery articles)—paper is the most prized, and one of the most amply described.[5] Seventeenth- and eighteenth-century European

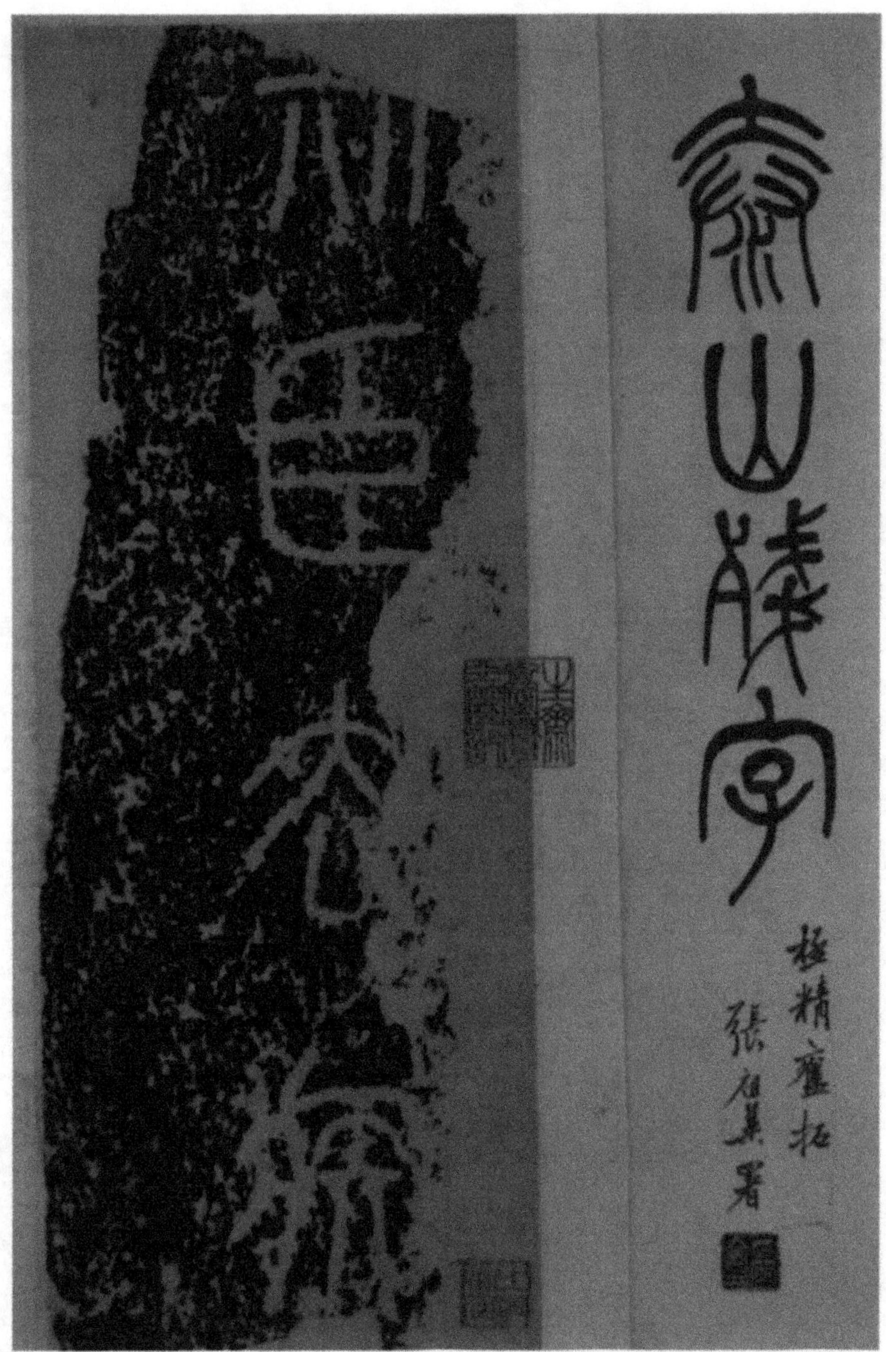

PLATE 1. Book-mounted "quality" old rubbing, fragment of the Tai Shan stone (219 B.C.E.). Early Qing dynasty. Colophon by Zhang Zuyi, late Qing. The Field Museum of Natural History, 233917.

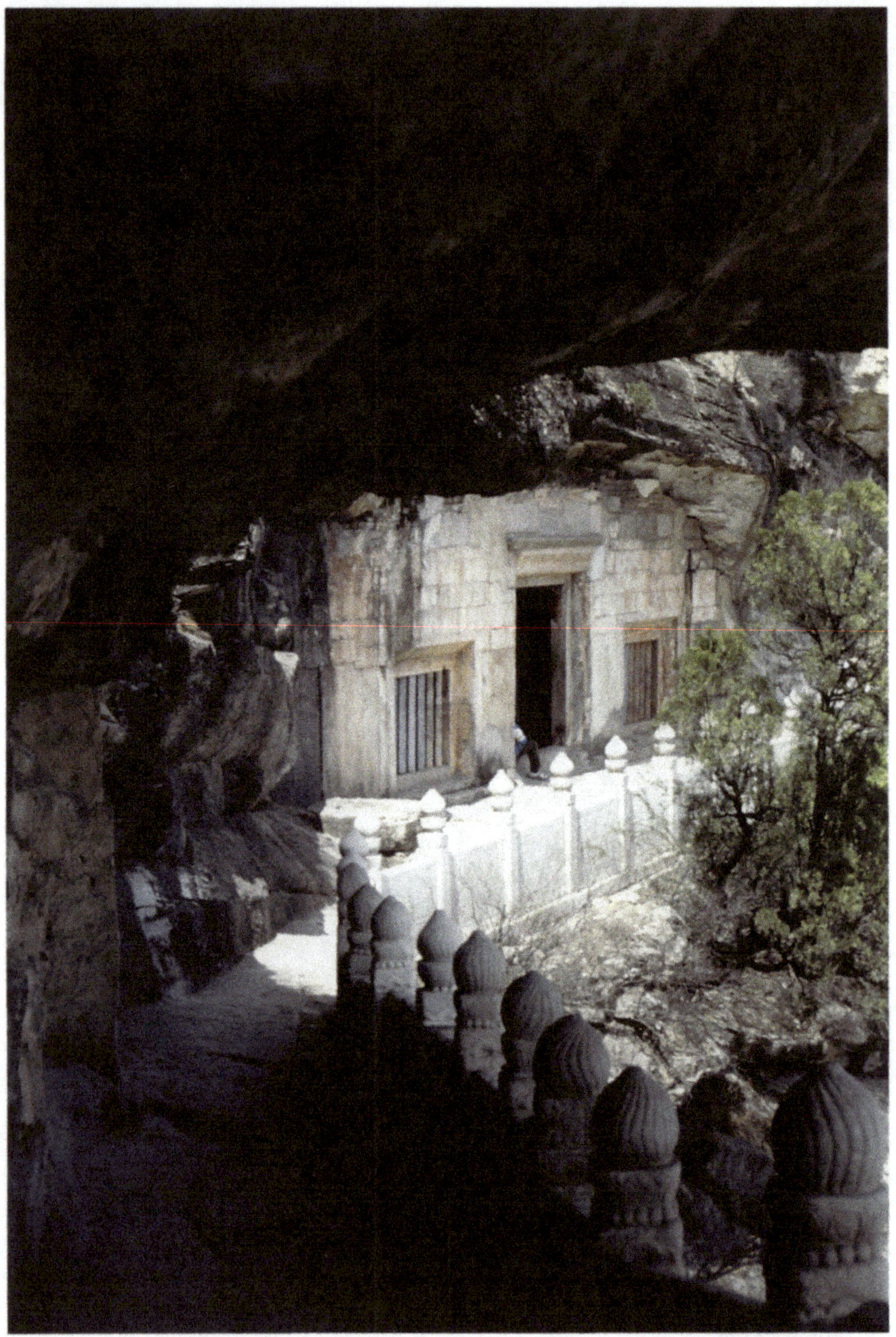

PLATE 2. Cave at Stone Sutra Mountain. Hebei, Fang Shan, 1993. Photograph by the author.

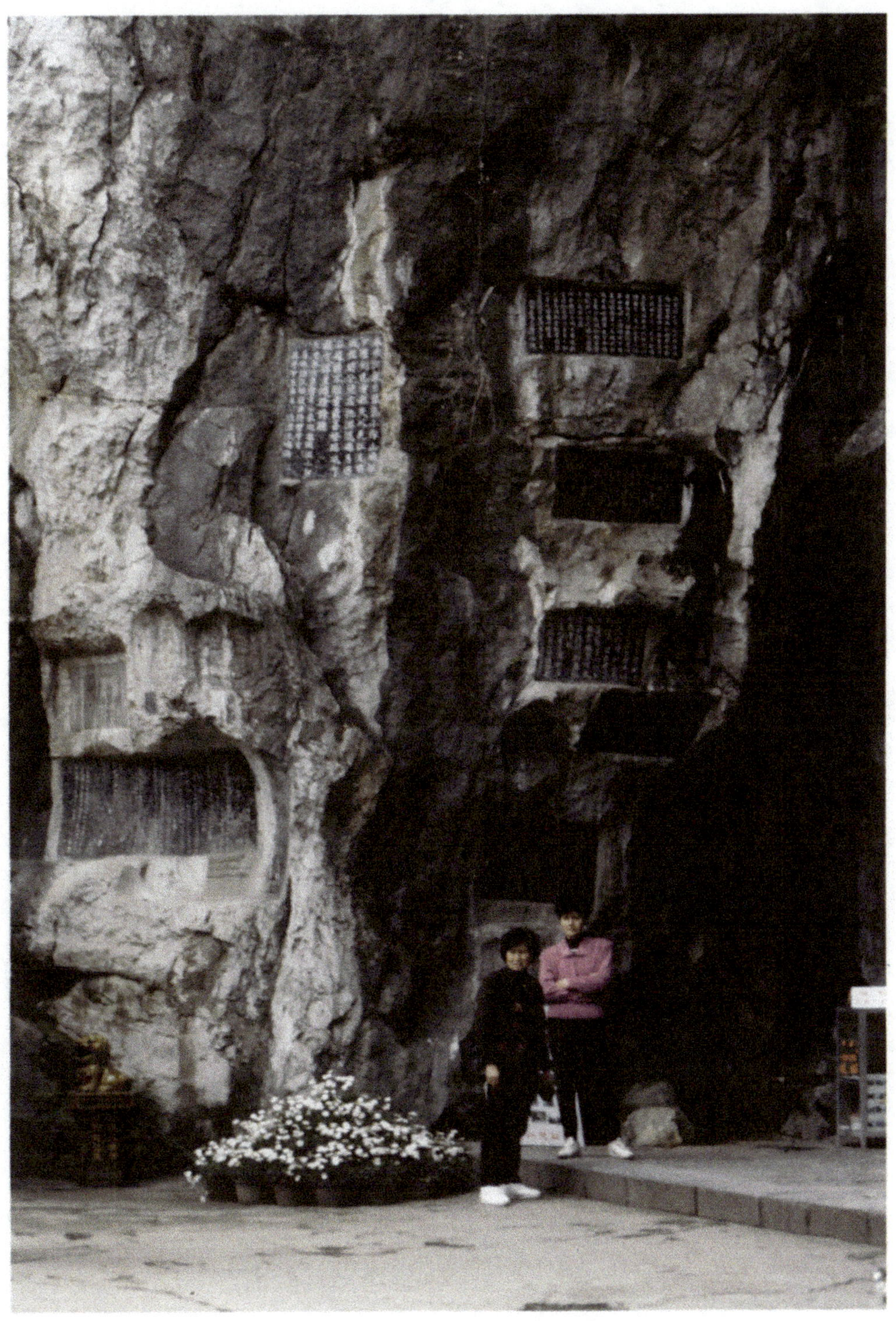

PLATE 3. "Smoothed cliff" calligraphy. Guilin, Diecai Shan, 1993. Photograph by the author.

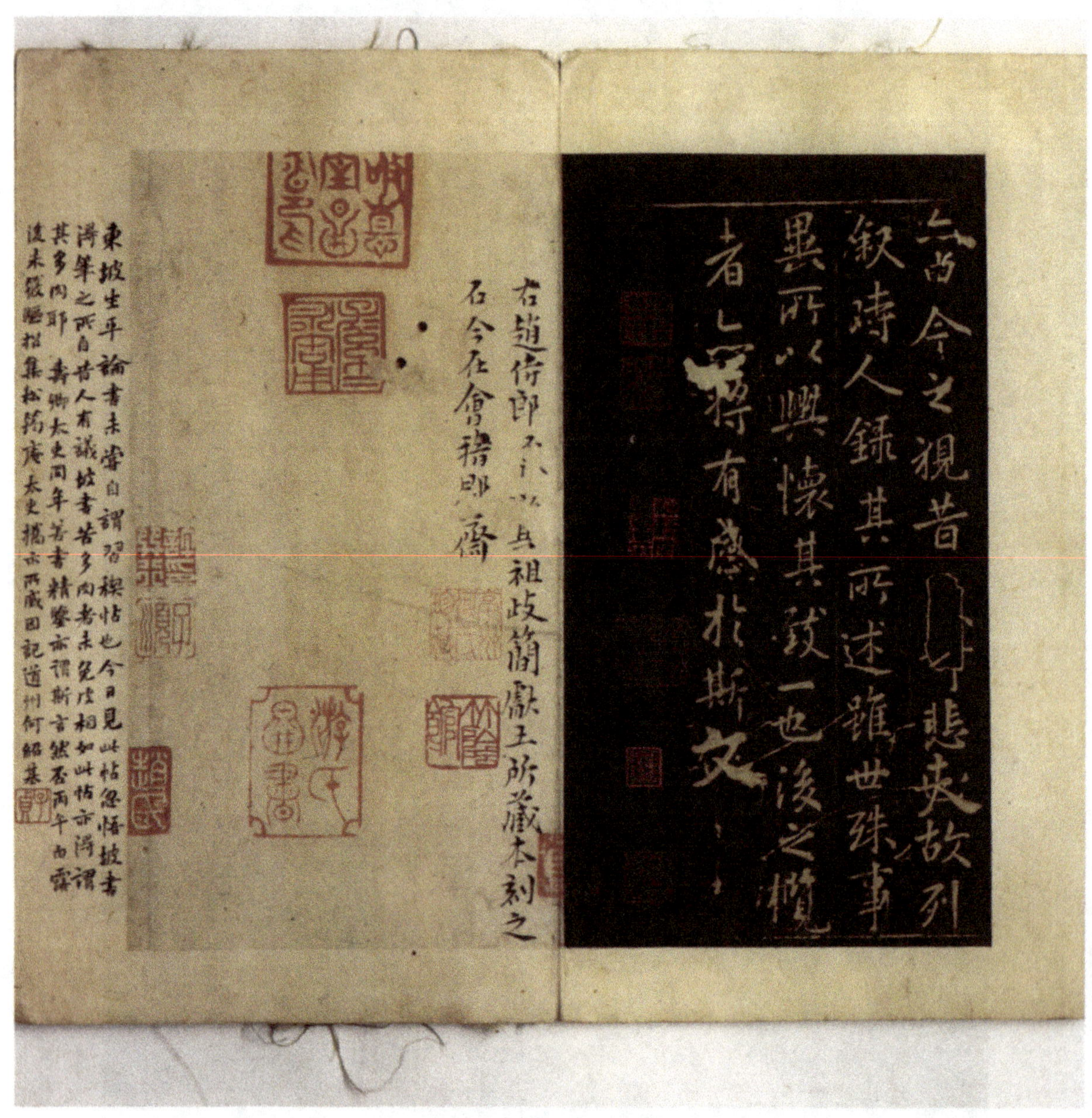

PLATE 4. "Continuous" album-mounted "layered ink" rubbing of *True Lanting* (Lanting zhenben): calligraphy of Wang Xizhi (303–361 C.E.), colophons, seals, vermiculations, and *goudiao* deletion. Song rubbing, ca. 1140–1278. The Field Museum of Natural History, 233914.

Plate 5. *True Lanting* (Lanting zhenben), silk-faced pasteboard covers and redwood box with carved label. Song. The Field Museum of Natural History, 233914.

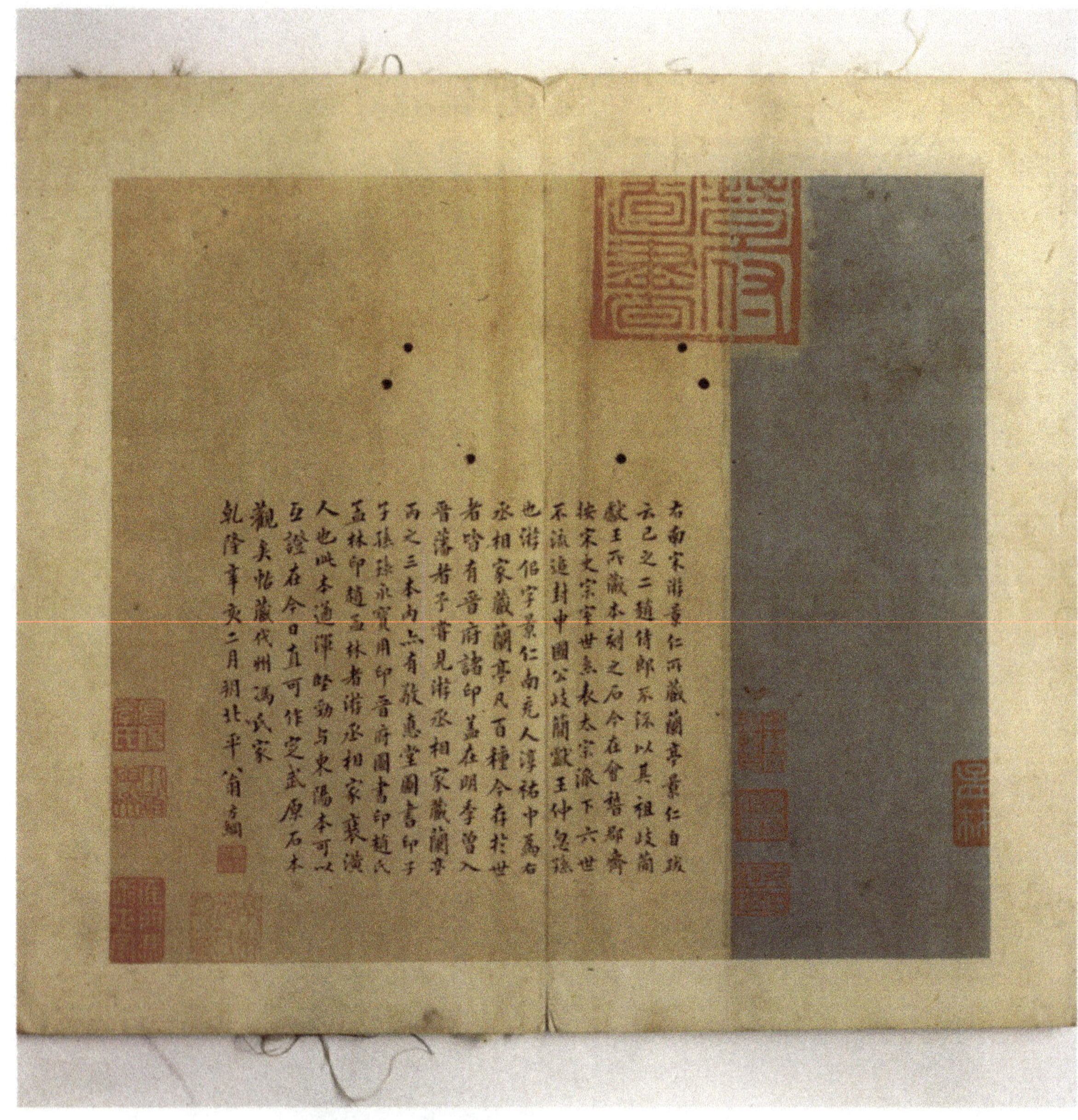

PLATE 6. "Quality" rubbing (ca. 1140–1278) of the *Lanting Calligraph* (Lanting tie). Buff and blue papers, typical mounting style of You Si (Southern Song). Colophon by Weng Fanggang (1733–1818). The Field Museum of Natural History, 233914.

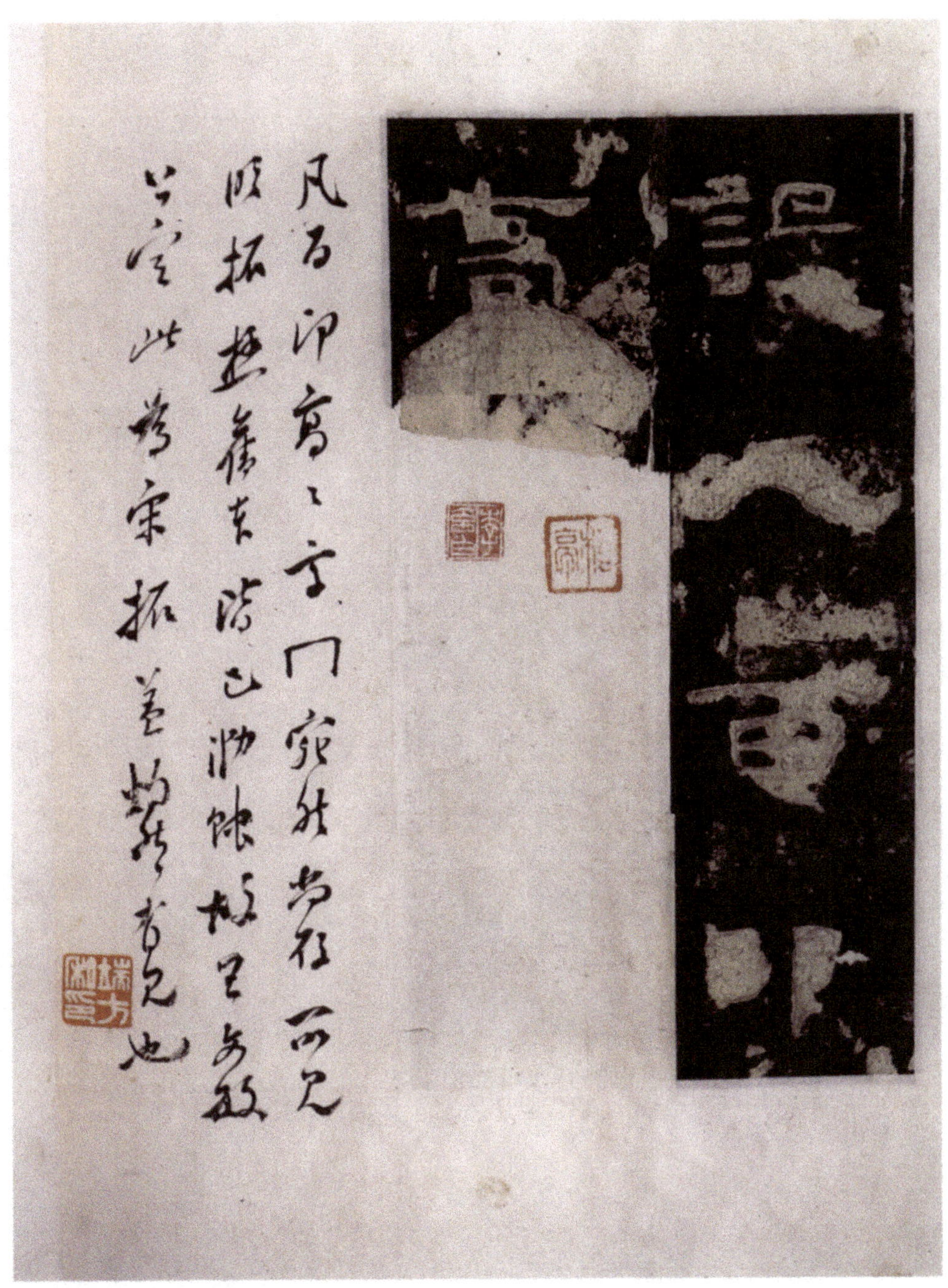

PLATE 7. Book-mounted "quality" rubbing of the *Kong Zhou Stele* (Kong Zhou bei, 163 C.E.): eroded *gao* character dating the rubbing to the Song dynasty, with affirmative colophon by Duan Fang (1861–1911). The Field Museum of Natural History, 233915.

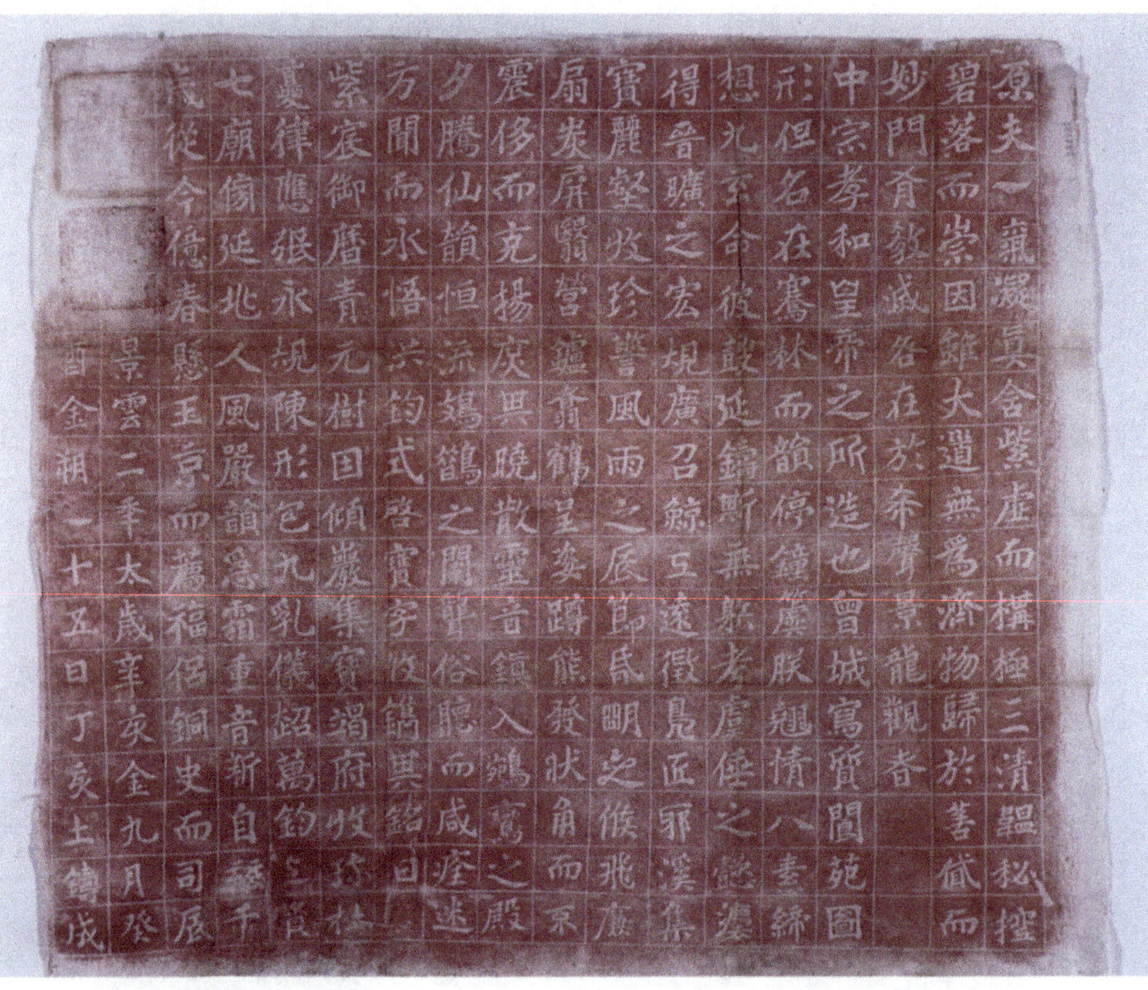

PLATE 8. Vermilion rubbing of a Daoist bronze-bell inscription by Tang Ruizong (711). Xi'an, Jinglong Temple. Standard script, with residual seal and clerical styles. The Field Museum of Natural History, 244795.

travelers to China were keenly interested in the papers, praising them for their fineness, softness, whiteness, and uniformity. They also commented on their length, with leaves 10 to 12 feet long.[6] Du Halde especially remarked on the papers' "extraordinary length," important for rubbings.[7]

Papers used for rubbing divide into rubbing papers proper and working papers. The rubbing paper should be of good quality, thin, fine, and even-textured yet strong and tough so as not to tear under the considerable stresses of the work. The better to take the ink, the paper also should be soft and pliable with a slight tooth, rather than hard and brittle with a glaze. Finally, the paper should be clear white, without gray or yellow cast, and should be free of blemishes, including visible fibers. These characteristics are especially important in rubbing bronzes, finely incised objects, and quality rubbings (*jingta*).

The type and quality of the paper will vary, with the character of the host object and the nature of the relief being paramount considerations. Thus the quality of the paper used to rub ancient bronzes must be superior to that used for steles.[8] Finely incised Shang divination inscriptions demand fine, thin paper, such as *mianlian*. Grosser inscriptions or designs on stone, where the relief or intaglio often is pronounced, require a heavier, tougher paper, such as *pi* or double-weight Xuan (*shuang Xuan*), to bear the strain of tamping it onto irregular, rough surfaces, into large or deep intaglio, or around relief:

> If the ordinary thin and soft paper were used [for rubbing large and deeply cut inscriptions], it would have a tendency to break when . . . dabbed with a stiff brush [in tamping], as the depth of the line would be too much for the stretch of the soft and brittle paper used. . . . In this contingency, it is necessary to use heavier paper, further buffered with a still heavier mulberry-bark paper with a much greater stretch. . . . In the case of extremely fine incised lines, it will be necessary to use a thinner paper than usual.[9]

Song sources attest to the attention that even then was paid to high-quality rubbing papers, with particular mention of Chengxin Tang paper in rubbing the *Chunhua Ge Model Book* (Chunhua Ge tie).[10] One can cite the preferences of two nineteenth-century metal-and-stone specialists (*jinshijia*), Wu Shifen (1796–1856) and Chen Jieqi (1813–1884).[11] Wu suggests that "in cases of steles with large characters, one should use good-quality, pure *pi* paper, while in cases of small steles with small characters, one should use fine, thin *mianlian* paper."[12]

Especially exalted in the world of rubbings was Chen Jieqi (1813–84), from Wei County, Shandong. Chen is remembered for his scholarly writing, fame as a collector, and reputation as a rubbings aficionado: "With respect to [the rubbings of] the stone cuts collected by the Chen family, they used the [more demanding] technique of rubbing ritual [bronze] vessels to rub all of them, and the Xuan paper that was used was incomparably strong and thin."[13]

Chen Jieqi himself also makes specific comment about rubbing papers:

> Formerly they used [Wang] Liuji's *mianlian* fan-material paper, with the popular name of "seventeen knives" (*shiqi dao*), but nowadays they do not have it. At present, the thinnest one is called *jingpi*, but compared with the older [paper] it certainly is not as thin and, further, not as soft. The paper is coarse and has a grayish cast because the workmanship is not good. Zhang Shuwei [Zhang Tingqi] has excellent rubbings on [blank sheets of] flyleaf paper taken from Song books. Using Ming *luowen* paper to make them, moreover, is less excellent. The yellow color of Governor Su's rubbing paper also is elegant. Nowadays, the paper is thick and coarse, and although one still can rub stone [inscriptions with it], if one makes rubbings of bronzes, one cannot achieve the finest [effects].[14]

Writing some six or seven decades later, Rong Geng amplified Chen's comments: "Wang Liuji's thin *mianlian* paper is very good, and one can use it. Before the Marco Polo Bridge incident [with Japan, 1937], each quire of 95 sheets cost about five *yuan*. In other provinces it is not easy to obtain. The *liansi* paper of Hangzhou is brittle in nature and is not very usable."[15] A few years earlier, in the late thirties, Jiang Xuanyi had provided more information about the types and qualities of modern papers best suited for rubbing stone cuts:

> For large areas, use [Wang] Liuji Xuan paper; for small areas, heavy *lianshi* paper. For small articles [with fine inscriptions], use Liuji *mianlian* fan-[material] paper [or] *jingpi lian*; and for high-relief carving, *pi* paper. To sum up, for large areas one can use slightly heavier paper (if it is too thick, it does not dry easily, and so those who make rubbings avoid using [it]); using long-fiber [paper, the better] to soak up water without tearing, is preferable. In rubbing small objects, using a little thinner [paper] is desirable. One certainly should not use papers that are coarse, brittle, and of a limy nature, and one absolutely should not use those with an aluminous nature. If one makes a rubbing of sculpture with low, flat relief, one still can use *lianshi* or Xuan paper, but unless one uses tough [but] soft and smooth *pi* paper for rounded relief, then one cannot achieve fine work. (*Lianqi* [paper] is a product of Jing County [Anhui], *liansi* [paper] is a product of Jiangxi, and *cangjing jian* [paper], imitative of Song [paper], is a product of Xin'an [County, Jiangxi].) One can use all these, but paper made from the roots and bark of the paper mulberry are not satisfactory to use.[16]

Jiang also commented on modern papers used in various parts of China for making stone rubbings, and he specified the papers commonly seen in rubbings from the respective provinces and localities, marking their salient characteristics.[17] In Shaanxi, in the north, better rubbings usually are made on good *lianshi* paper, the best of which is white and fine of grain, although a little thin. Poorer types are thick, coarse, uneven in texture, yellowish or reddish in tone, and low in absorbency. The province also produces *pi* paper, some of it fine, some coarse. Shanxi paper is coarse and muddy in color, tending to reddish-yellow. As seen in rubbings from Hebei, especially Beijing, the common paper for rubbings is *maotou* paper, which otherwise is used to paper windows. Beijing craftsmen also use two varieties of *pi* paper, one called *gaofei pi* paper, marked by a reddish cast, and the other described as being coarse and resembling mulberry paper, but a little purer. The paper from Henan is cited as coarse, of poor color, and not very receptive of ink. In Shandong the rubbings are made on *lianshi* or *pi* paper, the latter a bit thinner than that of Beijing. Rubbings from Jiangsu and Zhejiang are on *liaoban lianshi* paper, and those from Fujian and Guangdong are on the well-known Xuan paper. Rubbings from Korea and Manchuria generally are on Korean *pi* paper, which Jiang characterized as coarse, muddy, yellowish-red, and low in absorbency. Museum artisans in Taibei (1960) preferred thin, even, lustrous *lianshi* paper for rubbing stones, but with that paper hard to obtain in Taiwan, they used *mian zhi*, which was said to have irregularities and poor absorbency. Makers of commercial rubbings customarily use the cheapest available local paper.

On the whole, papers made in south China, particularly the papermaking areas of the southeast, are said to be superior and are preferable to those from north China. Southern papers are characterized as strong, thin, and good for making quality rubbings (*jingta*[a]); northern papers are described as being thick, coarse, and not very receptive of ink.[18] Tangentially, the south always has produced fine papers but poor stone for making steles, whereas the north generally has produced paper of lesser quality but an abundance of fine, hard stele stone.[19]

Over the centuries, artisans have valued certain papers.[20] Chinese connoisseurs judge older papers to be superior to more recent ones, but older types now are very rare. Even when obtainable, papers such as blank flyleaves from Song woodblock editions nowadays are deemed too valuable for making rubbings. Some of the standard papers traditionally used to make rubbings are still produced in China and can be purchased in Chinese stationery shops in China and the West, especially in larger cities.[21] The quality of these papers varies appreciably, and one needs to emphasize that, apart from type, weight, and other pertinent considerations, papers judged superior for rubbings are white, even-textured, fine and soft, with a slight tooth, long-fibered, strong, ductile, and properly absorbent. Xuan paper, which comes in a number of types and weights for different kinds of line, manifests these qualities and so is widely used for making good rubbings. Conversely, inferior papers are muddy in color, gray or yellowish, coarse, hard, uneven in texture, and low in absorbency. In selecting papers for rubbing, one also should avoid those made with alum or other deleterious chemicals.[22] For average work, any of a large number of available papers will be satisfactory: "It does no harm if one samples many kinds of papers and experimentally rubs things, for one very likely will find the best ones."[23] This experimental approach is typical in making rubbings.

All that has been said relates to the rubbing paper proper. The artisan also often employs working papers to absorb water from the wet rubbing paper and protect it from maceration in tamping. Generally one paper serves, but sometimes two are named. The generic names of the two are "absorb-water paper" (*xishui zhi*) and "assisting paper" or "liner paper" (*chen zhi*).[24]

The absorb-water paper draws excess moisture from the freshly laid wet rubbing paper. When used separately from the liner paper, the absorb-water paper is used first, following the application of the water or size to the rubbing paper. In the copying of stone inscriptions, Jiang advises that, preparatory to rubbing, "one can ready several tens of sheets, with fineness and absorbency desirable. Exemplary types are *yuanshu* paper and *cabai* paper."[25]

The liner paper protects the moist rubbing paper from abrasion by the brushes and other tamping tools. For smaller objects, such as bronzes, Jiang Xuanyi names "strike-stele paper" (*qiaobei zhi*), which is strong, thin, fine, and relatively nonabsorbent.[26] He further notes that in rubbing bronzes he often has used the very fine paper (*xiangyan xi zhi*) that backed the foil in cigarette packages, again nicely illustrating the experimental approach to materials and methods.

One paper frequently serves both functions, and the absorb-water paper generally is cited. The quality and weight of the working papers, as with those of the actual rubbing papers, varies with the type of relief and the quality of line. If the subject is a hairbreadth shell-and-bone inscription, one can employ scraps of the same fine paper that one uses for the rubbing. In copying a grosser inscription, one would use one or more sheets of heavier weight.

Water and Sizing Liquids

All references to making wet rubbings speak of some sort of liquid with which the artisan wets the rubbing paper to relax it in applying it to the surface being copied. References differ, however, with respect to its type and function. Different substances and objects require variant approaches. The simplest formula prescribes clear water, with descriptions often referring merely to moistening the rubbing paper.[27] Detailed descriptions may specify using clear water, as does Chen Jieqi, who observes that "formerly, they used clear water on the paper."[28] Another writer states, "As far as I know, the paper is not prepared with any sizing."[29]

Other accounts suggest an aqueous solution containing some glutinous substance. The simplest solution, traditional, was the excess water in which rice has been boiled. Chen states that "later they used rice-water on the paper, which [being glutinous] is better than clear water."[30] Jiang Xuanyi also suggests using the diluted broth in which rice has been cooked.[31] The disadvantage of rice water is that it attracts vermin. The material used by the Chinese in recent times for sizing the rubbing paper is *baiji,* the corm of *Bletilla striata,* a species of the orchid family native to various parts of eastern Asia.[32]

In the mid-nineteenth century, Chen Jieqi noted that "at present they use Zhang Shuwei's method of making a strong decoction of *baiji* glue and putting it on the [rubbing] paper, but it is only a descriptive note in a letter, and I have not seen a rubbing made by such method."[33] This statement may evidence an early use of *baiji* for sizing. Whether or not such is the case, using *baiji* became common in subsequent decades, especially for rubbing bronzes and other smaller objects, and those with irregular or glossy surfaces. In 1941, Rong Geng stated that "nowadays they steep *baiji* in boiling water to produce glue. One spreads the paper on the object [to be copied], uses a brush to dip into the *baiji* solution, and spreads it on the paper."[34] Others also cite *baiji* as the standard adhesive.[35] Alternatively, "a slightly adhesive stiffening [may be] obtained from a sea water alga, somewhat resembling agar-agar, by dissolving a few fragments of the seaweed in boiling water in a bowl."[36]

Chinese pharmacies and pharmaceutical sections of many groceries, East and West, stock *baiji* for their traditional customers as a palliative for the lungs, liver, and stomach. *Baiji* is a small, irregularly shaped corm that, when dried and thinly sliced, is translucent, yellowish, with a slightly sweetish smell. It comes in three forms: natural corms, small chunks, or, most convenient in making rubbings, thin, shredded slices (fig. 2.2). One should not confuse *baiji* with *baizhi,* the root of the fragrant iris (*Angelica anomala, Pall.*) that the Chinese use for nasal inhalation and general bodily health.

There is little mention of the strength of these glutinous solutions, but the concentration varies with the nature of the surface being rubbed, type of rubbing paper, and working conditions, especially the level of wind and degrees of heat and humidity. In general, the solutions should be weak, glutinous, but not glue, or else there is the danger of pasting the rubbing paper to the surface. If one uses rice water, one should remember that the Chinese regularly use cooked rice for paste, and so the solution should be quite dilute. For rubbing small objects in the studio, one can start with a moderate-sized pinch of *baiji* flakes in a cup of boiling water and modify the strength

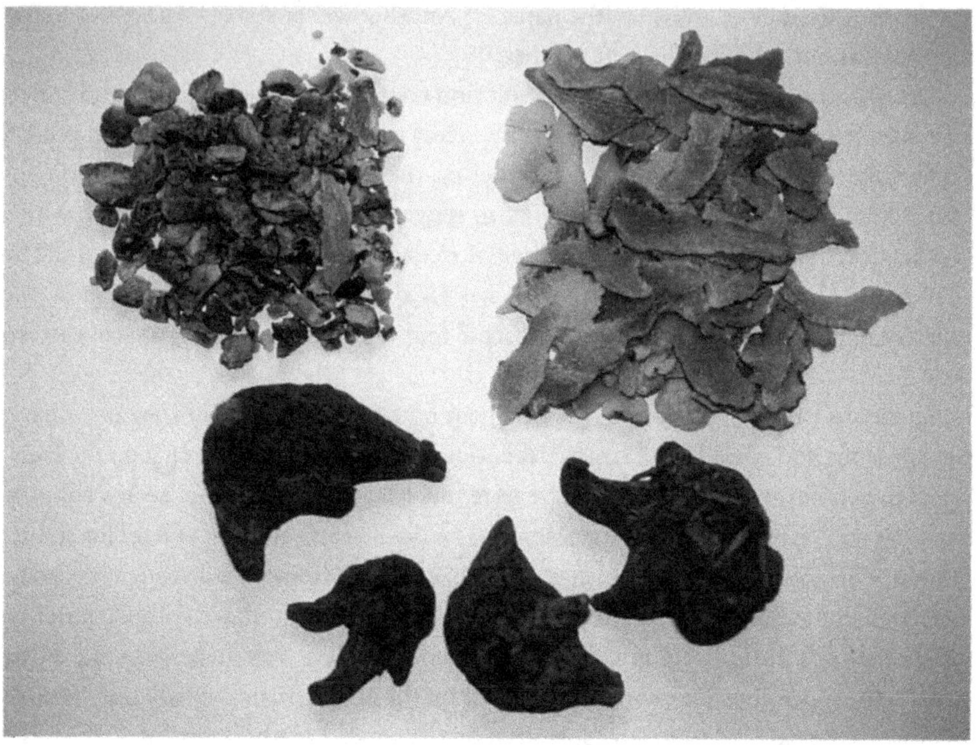

FIG. 2.2. *Baiji* corms, chunks, and slices. Photograph by the author.

up or down as the situation demands.[37] For rubbing steles, one should prepare larger amounts, and for rubbing bronzes or other objects that require tight adhesion of the rubbing paper, as on glossy surfaces, one should make a stronger solution. One either can pour boiling water on the thin slices and steep them or place the *baiji* in a little water and boil the mixture for five or ten minutes, with the latter method extracting the most from the *baiji*.[38] Macerating the flakes also helps to extract more from them. One can cook the flakes until the solution is of the desired strength, longer for greater stickiness, and test it by rubbing it between one's fingers. If one wants a very strong concoction, one can cook it until it is thicker and dilute it as needed. One should strain the sizing solutions, whether of *baiji*, rice water, or agar-agar, or else tiny bits of the material will adhere to the rubbing paper, catch the ink in the inking stage, and flaw the rubbing.

In summary, more recent opinion inclines toward adding a glutinous size to the water for wetting the rubbing paper. One should not use commercial adhesives that contain deleterious chemicals: "As for bad things to put on the paper, nothing is worse than glue containing alum, for alum damages the stone and makes the paper brittle [as well]."[39]

Views differ slightly with respect to the functions of the liquids, especially those containing a glutinous additive. Some describe the seaweed solution as "a slightly adhesive stiffening . . . for moistening the thin paper to make it workable and, after drying, to retain the molded form."[40] Clear water alone serves the first of these two functions, and Chinese sources do not speak of the second. In making wet rubbings, there is no effort to retain the molded form of completed rubbings, and, as described below, they normally are flattened when the finished rubbing is pulled. Glutinous additives also act as a stiffening size. Chinese writers sometimes emphasize the importance of using a glutinous additive to hold the rubbing paper to the surface being copied, especially with smooth, glossy objects such as jade, or in adverse working situations, as with drying and lifting wind or sun.

It is pertinent to note that the use of glutinous additives has differed over time and from place to place in China. Artisans in Beijing and in Taibei, to cite two examples, used *baiji* to size the rubbing paper, as did Chen Jieqi earlier in Shandong. Those at the Beilin preferred plain water in rubbing steles, achieving the adhesion with a specially prepared commercial ink containing glue.[41]

Rubbing Equipment

The rubbing process involves a wide variety of tools, depending on the object and its inscription or pictorial. All are simple, often made by the artisans themselves (figs. 2.3–2.8).

SMOOTHING AND TAMPING TOOLS. One of the most important steps in making a rubbing is putting the paper into tight apposition with the surface being copied. This can be achieved with brushes, pads, mallets, felt, and even needles, to lay the paper and tamp or press it into or around the relief.

Brushes. Several types of brushes are used for cleaning, wetting, smoothing, and tamping. Stone cuts in outdoor settings usually require initial cleaning. For this, one uses a medium stiff brush, with bristles that are strong enough for the work, but not so stiff as to abrade the inscription or design, or spall loose pieces. Natural-fiber brushes are preferable.

Wetting and smoothing brushes with longer, softer bristles help to lay the rubbing paper. It is "a soft brush that is used to smooth the paper and push to the edges air pockets that might have formed."[42] Depending on the situation, artisans employ several types of smoothing brushes. Most common is a short-haired, soft-bristled coir brush (*zongshua*) or paste brush (*husao*) used by scroll mounters (fig. 2.3).[43] One can have them made to order or purchase them in the market, where they differ slightly from

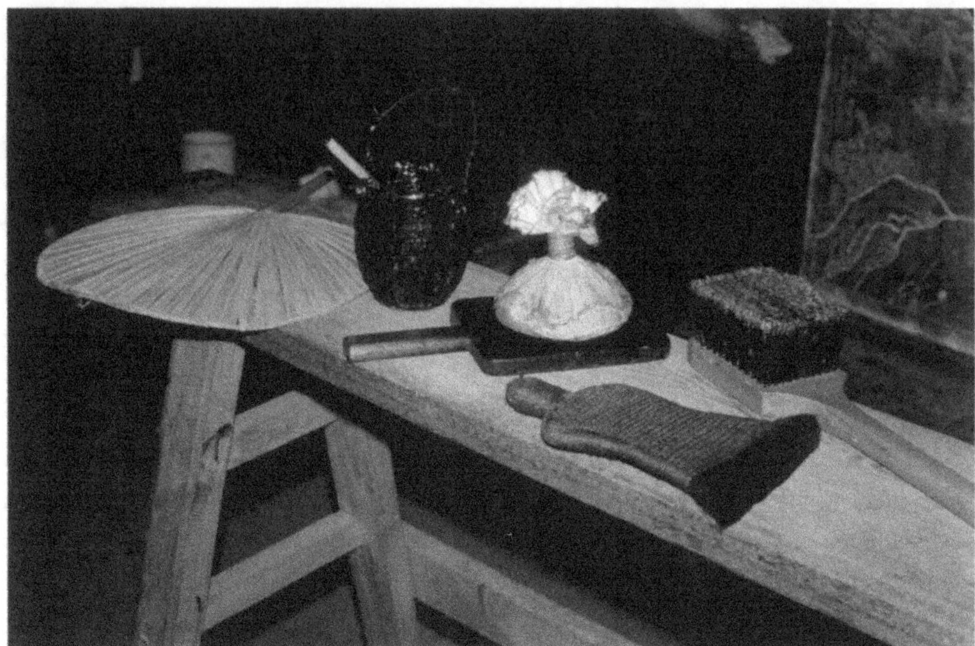

Fig. 2.3. Stele-rubbing equipment. Xi'an Beilin Museum, 1980. Photograph by the author.

north to south, being thicker in the north and thinner in the south.[44] One softens the fiber ends by soaking and rubbing them back and forth in a solution of water and sand, scissoring the ends even and slightly rounded, and washing the brush clean. Another type of smoothing brush, for smaller objects, and again speaking of the inventive quality that marks the rubbing technique, includes toothbrushes.[45] They again should be of soft natural fibers and are especially useful for rubbing fine inscriptions and those inside bronze vessels. For smoothing fine paper laid on very small, fragile objects, such as oracle bones, one can use a traditional Chinese goat-hair writing brush whose point has been cut evenly blunt.[46]

Brushes of a very different type are used to tamp the rubbing paper down into or around the relief. "Formerly [for bronzes and smaller objects, instead of a brush] they used a felt roll (fine white blankets, into which they did not let anything dirty; they rolled it tightly [in columnar form], used a tape to bind it tight completely [for its full length], cut the two ends even [and slightly rounded], and [used vertically] it served the purpose). . . . [For support] they used a bronze crossbow bolt wrapped in thin fine felt."[47] Pressing down firmly with such a felt roll poses far less danger to a delicate object than does tamping with a brush or pounding with a mallet.[48]

Chen Jieqi noted that, by his time, brushes of similar shape were used instead of a felt roll: "Nowadays, they use a brush made of hair (those of rhinoceros tail are superior

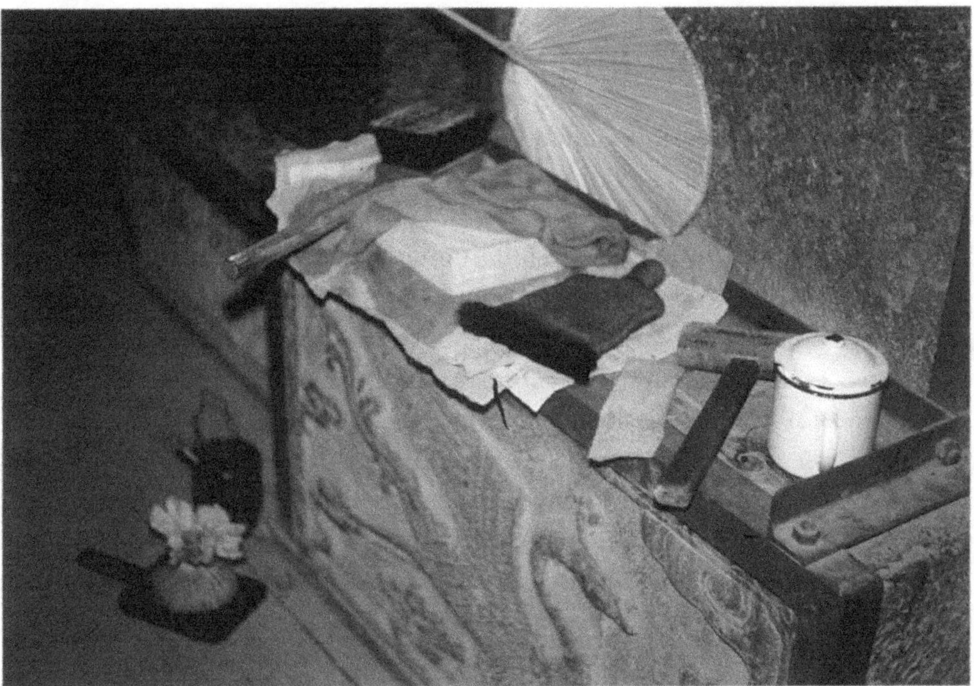

Fig. 2.4. Stele-rubbing equipment. Xi'an Beilin Museum, 1981. Photograph by the author.

to ones of goat hair)."[49] Rong Geng supplements Chen's exotic recommendation with a description of a common material to make these brushes:

> Nowadays they use a cylindrical coir-palm [*zonglü*] brush. The length is 3 *cun* [about 10 centimeters], the diameter, about 7 or 8 *fen* [about 2.5 centimeters], and one can make two or three sizes. One should leave the two ends unbound but bind it tightly with a cord in the middle. When one uses it the first time, [one] soak[s] it in boiling water and then strike[s] it [the ends] on a stone to soften it, after which one can use it [fig. 2.5].[50]

Jiang Xuanyi confirms this description of what he calls the "coir tiger" (*zong laohu*).[51] The length should be 3 or 4 *cun,* and the edges should be trimmed carefully to make the two ends even and eliminate stray hairs that might stick out and tear the rubbing paper or damage the object. He suggests the sort of brush used by antiquarians to polish jade, with a worn one preferable. One should prepare several different sizes for work on ancient bronzes, jades, potsherds, and other small objects.

These brushes can be of various materials and of many shapes and sizes, depending on the character, size, and condition of the object being copied and on the artisan's preference. For rubbing steles, they have fairly stiff and closely set bristles of animal hair or vegetable fiber. Other materials also may be used, especially other types of hair. Horsehair closely resembles coir and seems to be the material next preferred for tamping brushes: "A stiff, long, narrow, finely made two-ended brush [may be] produced by binding a bundle of horsehair around the middle. The ends are cut square, and one end is bigger than the other."[52] Jun Yu also recommends a horsetail-hair brush.[53] Such brushes can be set in bamboo handles and are inexpensive in the Chinese market. Both hairs and handle should be rounded a little, the one by cutting and the other by sanding, to produce a more effective tamping brush. Having described making columnar palm-fiber brushes, Rong notes that "using human hair to produce [such a brush] is even better."[54] This especially holds for fine work, as on shell-and-bone inscriptions (figs. 2.5 and 4.1). The brushes are 10 to 15 centimeters long and about 1.5 to 2 centimeters in diameter, with the ends clipped off flat and even. They are tightly wrapped with string to within 3 or 4 millimeters from one end, for shallow line, and about 1 centimeter from the other end, for ordinary depths.

One of the salient qualities required of the materials used to make these brushes is that they be stiff. Caution is necessary, however, for if the bristles are too stiff, or if the worker has too heavy a hand, the bristles will abrade the paper and, over time, damage the object as well, gradually but relentlessly dulling the sharp edges of the characters or designs: "One greatly should fear round-bristled, hard brushes and should consider not using them as the best [course]."[55] The longer a brush is used, the softer and less abrasive it becomes, and so is a better tool. This process can be accelerated by soaking the brush in boiling water and pounding it on a stone, softening the bristles and wearing off their sharp edges. For very fine work, one can use a brush with equally stiff, though finer, bristles.[56] For tamping very fragile pieces, one also can use a softer brush made of slightly longer hair, such as a worn-down Chinese pen.[57]

Tamping brushes vary in type, size, and shape, depending on the nature of the object and the artisan's preference. The original object—faint divination inscription, delicate jade design, massive stele—determines the material and form of brush. In copying bronze inscriptions, "one uses those with handles where the characters are on a flat surface; while one uses those that are round and without handles, inserting them into a bamboo tube where the characters are deep inside the belly."[58]

Pads. In some situations, artisans use pads to press the wet rubbing paper onto the surface, especially for relief. One type is a loose cotton pad that one uses to press the rubbing paper into or around the relief. A reference to the technique used in the Chen household for rubbing bronze vessels notes that in addition to using good quality Xuan paper, they also were careful of the manner in which they pressed the paper down: they "did not use a tamper to make the rubbing, but instead used a cotton pad lightly to press" the paper down.[59] One also can use a damp towel or a moistened pad to bring

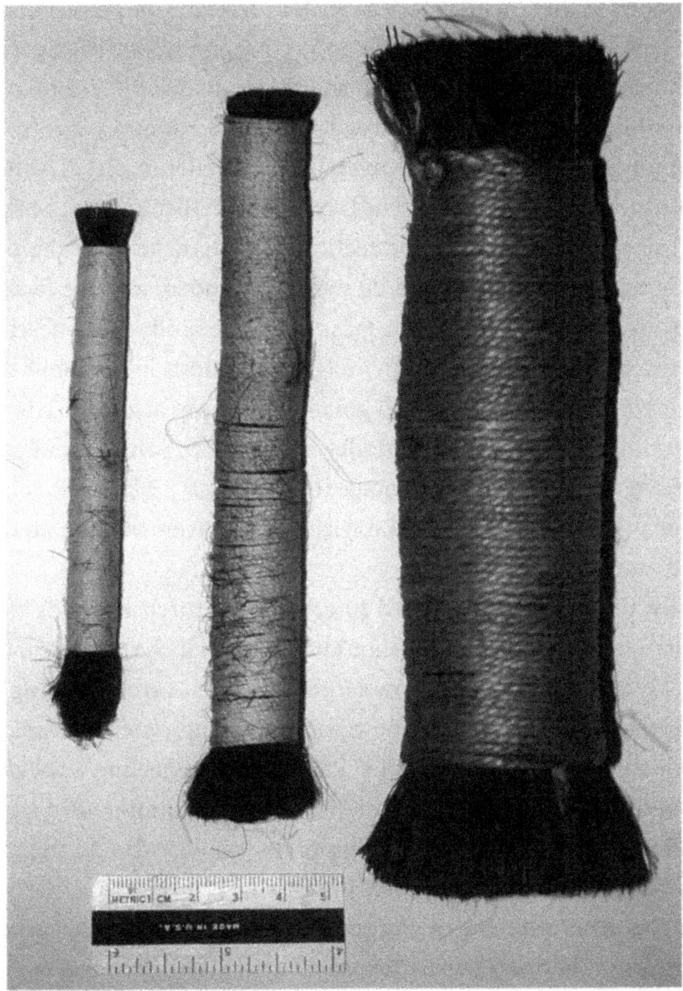

Fig. 2.5. Columnar coir tamping brushes. Author's collection. Photograph by the author.

out some types of line.[60] A small pad sometimes is helpful in pressing down the rubbing paper around the edges of small objects or into fine intaglio line preliminary to tamping, but one must be careful not to leave stray fibers on the paper.[61] Clean white toweling also absorbs excess water from the paper and presses it gently into wide, deep intaglio or around relievo. A second type of pad, useful for pressing the damp paper on sculptures, is made of cotton waste wrapped in thin *chou* silk.[62]

Mallets and Felt, and Needles. In copying stele inscriptions, artisans also use wooden mallets (*muchui*) to tamp the paper, the mallet blows cushioned by a pad of fine felt or woolen cloth (figs. 2.4 and 4.3). Wu Shifen refers to using "a *ding*-character [T-shaped] flat-headed wooden mallet," while modern writers describe the preferred material, size, and shape of these mallets in detail, noting that one can have them specially made in a carpentry shop.[63] For strength, the head should be made of heavier wood, while the handle can be of lighter material. The head should be about 3.5 *cun* (12 centimeters) long, and its diameter, 1.5 *cun* (5 centimeters) for a smaller mallet. The handle should be about 6.5 *cun* (21 centimeters) long. The faces of the mallet must be perfectly smooth, without grain or tool marks, for imperfections can damage both the paper and the object. The edges of the mallet should be slightly rounded, and the faces themselves, slightly convex, achieved by shaping the faces with fine sandpaper oneself, rather than entrusting the work to a carpenter. If there is the slightest doubt about the convexity, it is better to leave the faces flat, for too great a curvature also can damage the paper and the object. Gulik refers to using "a mallet covered with soft leather," a modification designed to lessen the possibility of damage to the object.[64] Matteo Ricci also spoke of employing a small mallet, in conjunction with several layers of cloth, to tamp the rubbing paper into apposition.[65]

Traditionally, the Chinese have used fine, loose-textured felt pads to cushion the mallet blows (see fig. 4.3). The texture should not be too loose, for the felt will soak up water too quickly and also will push down into the intaglio areas, placing undue strain on the rubbing paper. Pure hair felt is best, for it soaks up water less rapidly than does the cheaper felt adulterated with cotton.[66] Pads of flannel or fine wool cloth (*rongbu*), fashioned from old overcoats, hats, and blankets, were recommended for drawing out excess moisture and spreading the tamping pressure. One should prepare several of these pads and exchange them when they become wet.

Finally, for fine inscriptions and designs on very delicate objects, especially oracle bones, one can use a blunted needle to press the paper into the line. This is called "walking the needle" (*zouzhen*).

FANS. Fans also help to dry the rubbing paper. The time-honored variety is a palm-leaf fan (fig. 2.3), but where electricity is available, workers speed the process with electric fans (fig. 2.6) or heaters.[67]

INKS. The most common coloring agent used to make rubbings is the remarkable substance known as Chinese ink. This compound is so familiar to Chinese writers on rubbings that they often fail to describe it at all, or they make only passing mention of it, assuming that the reader will be familiar with the traditional literature on ink and its ingredients, manufacture, variant forms, special qualities, and cultural roles. Chen Jieqi and Rong Geng, who at times describe in detail the preferred types of other materials used to make rubbings, and who carefully prescribe inking techniques and define desired effects, say very little about types of inks. Some authors do provide information,

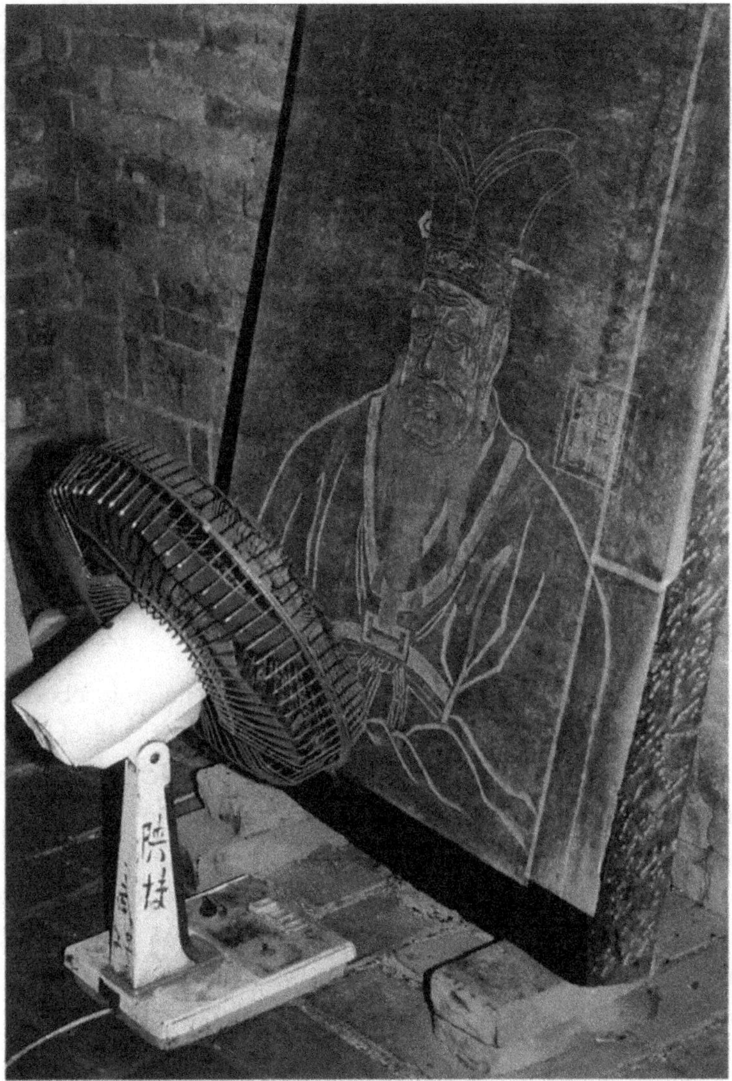

FIG. 2.6. Felted paper, drying with an electric fan. Xi'an Beilin Museum, 1993. Photograph by the author.

but their comments generally are brief, as are those of Wu Shifen, who merely advises using fragrant ink (*xiangmo*), a good quality of ink, not coarse smoke (*cuyan*), made from heavier soot lower in the chimney; while Wang Chi-chen merely recommends "regular Chinese ink."[68] Other writers also dismiss the subject, speaking only of "ordinary Chinese ink."[69] There are occasional references to inks used to make rubbings, as when Cao Zhao (Ming) notes that artisans used Chengxin Tang paper and Li Tinggui ink to rub the *Chunhua Ge Model Book* in the late tenth century.[70]

The advantages of Chinese ink are several. First and foremost, the ink is unfading over centuries and millennia, as attested by neolithic finds. Second, it is waterproof. Third, it is convenient, for one can make ink any time, any place, in any needed amount, and mix it in any desired consistency or intensity by varying the amount of water, important for painters and calligraphers as well as for rubbing artisans.

Finally, there is an aspect of Chinese ink that relates to rubbings and their nicknames, "black tigers" (*hei laohu*) and "ink tigers" (*mo*ª *laohu*). Most informants have agreed that *hei laohu* is an alternative name for rubbings, with *hei,* "black," carrying two connotations: the first, that of black as a color; the second, "black-hearted" (*heixin*), which is derived and refers to dealers who traffic in fake rubbings. One informant stated that the term *mo*ª *laohu* refers to calligraphy rather than to rubbings; another observed that some people use the two names interchangeably, with yet others noting that the usage differed from person to person and place to place, but that *mo*ª *laohu* was not normally used for rubbings. The more common nickname for rubbings is *hei laohu,* "black tigers."[71]

INKS FOR MAKING RUBBINGS

Many Chinese writers say little about preferred inks for making rubbings, save that modern artisans prefer oil-smoke ink (*youyan mo*) because of its blackness and sheen. As with paper and other materials, traditionalists favor older inks over present-day inks, which often have a coarser nature and a greater amount of glue.[72] This preference is not entirely a matter of scholarly purism, for older inks, and papers as well, were made of natural ingredients, and the product was marked by fine texture, ready solubility, uniformity, and good color and covering power. Older inks also show a glossy effect not marking many newer inks.

Inks used to make rubbings occur in four forms: water-based, or liquid; powdered; oil-based; and solid, or wax-based (fig. 2.7).

Liquid Ink

There is specific guidance on liquid-ink rubbing (*mozhi ta*).[73] One can buy liquid ink (*mozhi, moshui*) or make one's own, preparing a little or a lot, depending on the situation. For rubbing a small object, one either can grind an ink stick in a little water on an inkstone, as for calligraphy, or grind a small piece of ink stick into powder, mix it with a bit of glue (*jiaoshui*), and boil it in a little water to produce ink of a consistency such that an experimental drop slowly will penetrate a scrap of rubbing paper.

In rubbing a stele, one must have a larger supply. One approach is to make a quantity of ink from solid inks, but freshly prepared ink often is not well dissolved, and so the ink will be lumpy and uneven in tone. One remedy, seen at the Beilin and other

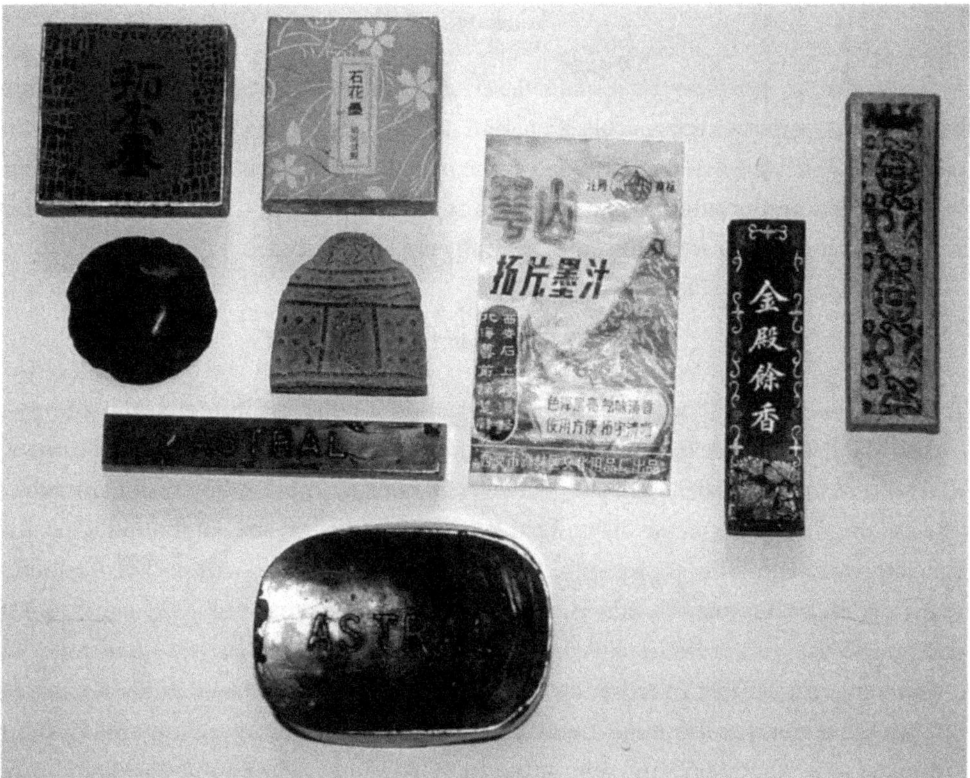

Fig. 2.7. Inks. Author's collection. Photograph by the author.

sites where artisans produce large quantities of rubbings, is to soak ink sticks in small buckets for extended periods, adding new sticks and fresh water as necessary to produce a viscous ink. Thus, even though one works for ten years, the "everlasting inkpot" is never empty (fig. 2.3), and the artisan always has well-dissolved ink. Ink thus prepared also gradually loses its gluey nature, a change that purists consider to be an advantage. As an alternative to soaking ink sticks, one can powder them or buy the powder already ground and mix it with a little glue and hot water. One also can purchase commercial inks, but they often have chemical additives, with deleterious effects on the rubbing paper and the host. Most such inks are used for brush writing and so are more dilute than ink for rubbings.

Some specialty inks are compounded specifically for making rubbings, such as that with the brand name *Hua Shan,* made in Xi'an and used at the Beilin. It contains glue, negating the need for a glutinous additive in wetting the rubbing paper.[74] The label claims that the ink is glossy black, pleasant to smell, and easy to use, and that it produces clear characters (fig. 2.7). Whether homemade or commercial, the ink should be of good quality.

Powdered Ink

Artisans also use powdered ink (*mofen*), self-ground or bought, to make powder rubbings (*fenta*), with two approaches. One is to sprinkle the powdered ink on a wet stamp pad, from which the artisan carries it to the paper. The other is to dab the powdered ink directly onto the rubbing paper when it is 50 to 60 percent dry.[75] Both approaches are crude, produce poor results, and generally are to be avoided.

Oil-Based Ink

Youmo ta, "oil ink rubbings," are made with *youmo,* similar to Chinese seal ink (*yinse*), except that it is black instead of red. One prepares it by macerating and boiling leaves of the moxa plant (*ai*), a species of the genus *Artemesia,* and mixing them with lampblack and castor or other vegetable oils to form a sticky, slightly mushy compound. One also can add colors and other ingredients.[76] Sueji Umehara carried a little packet of rubbing materials, including oil ink (*abura zumi*), when visiting museums. One can find the compound, as part of rubbing kits, in shops specializing in Japanese art supplies.

Youmo is convenient in traveling. It is intensely black and provides good contrast but has the major disadvantage that it leaves oily, ever-expanding yellow rings around the inked areas that bleed into adjoining stored rubbings. The compound therefore is useful only for temporary study purposes.

Wax-Based Ink

The inking agents described so far all have liquids, water, or oil, as their vehicles. As mentioned above, the Chinese at an early stage may have used stone ink (*shimo*), graphite, for rubbing, but that is speculation. For dry rubbings, they now use a compound akin to "heelball," used to dry-rub Western mortuary brasses and tombstones. Chinese *lamo,* here "wax ink," is an ink cake made of a hard variety of wax (*baila*) and lampblack. Such cakes are utilitarian, but one can find them in a variety of colors and culturally meaningful forms, such as ancient musical instruments and bronze bells, hence the Japanese name "bell inks" (*tsurigane zumi,* fig. 2.7). These wax inks generally are made of softer wax and not favored by the Chinese.

One makes such ink cakes by melting either hard carnauba or softer candilla wax, stirring in finely powdered ink sticks or carbon black, and molding the mixture in a Chinese wine cup or a small bowl or mortar. The resulting cake is a low cone, rounded on its lower, working side, flat on its upper side, about 5 or 6 centimeters in diameter and 2 or so centimeters high. Figure 2.7 illustrates a selection of inks and other materials used in the wet and dry techniques.

Colored Inks

The Chinese also use red, blue, green, and orange colors to make decorative rubbings or those prized for intellectual or aesthetic reasons.[77] The most common color is red, a preference that extends back in China to Upper Paleolithic times, when red ocher (hematite) was used in a mortuary context (plate 8).[78] The Chinese also used vermilion, as well as lampblack ink, for designs and symbols in the neolithic and for writing from Shang times.[79] The common source of red for inks through the centuries has been cinnabar.[80] As adaptable as lampblack, vermilion can be mixed with glue and used in stick form in the study, prepared in aqueous solution, or as *yinse,* the mushy seal ink.[81]

Largely quoting the *Yu shi,* Jiang Xuanyi provides a bit of lore on making vermilion rubbings:

> Artisans certainly will use [the cheaper] red ocher [*tuzhu*] for vermilion rubbings, but better ones are [made with genuine] vermilion [*yinzhu*]. If one does not include chicken-egg albumen [*jizibai*] in the color compound, the vermilion will come loose. Generally speaking, [however], ones rubbed with chicken-egg albumen will develop weevils in time, and if one puts them together with good rubbings, the insects surely will increase, and there will be no end to it. When mounting vermilion-rubbed "unique rubbings" [*zhuta guben*], one can apply a weak solution of borax, camphor, and alcohol, adding water.[82]

Egg white is said to add sheen to the vermilion, and some hold that it is only the cheap vermilion made from ocher that attracts insects, for true vermilion is poisonous and discourages insects and vermin.[83] The problems in dealing with blue and green rubbings are similar to those marking vermilion rubbings.[84]

DABBERS

When the rubbing paper is tamped into tight contact with the surface being copied, and the paper is suitably dry, one applies the ink. This usually is done with a dabber (*tabao* or *tapu,* the most common terms; *paibao*; *pubao*; or just *pu*) of a form and size appropriate for the host, the nature of the inscription or design, and the preference of the artisan. The most common form is of an inverted mushroom, with the rounded head as the dabbing surface and the "stem" as the handle (figs. 2.3, 2.8–2.9). A standard dabber consists of a piece of fine-textured material wrapped around a small bunch of resilient material. The recommended cloth for rubbing fine line is unfigured thin *chou* silk, which holds less ink, for the outer wrapping, and wool, cotton, or silk waste for the inner wadding.[85] Fine cotton cloth, which holds more liquid, is a second choice for

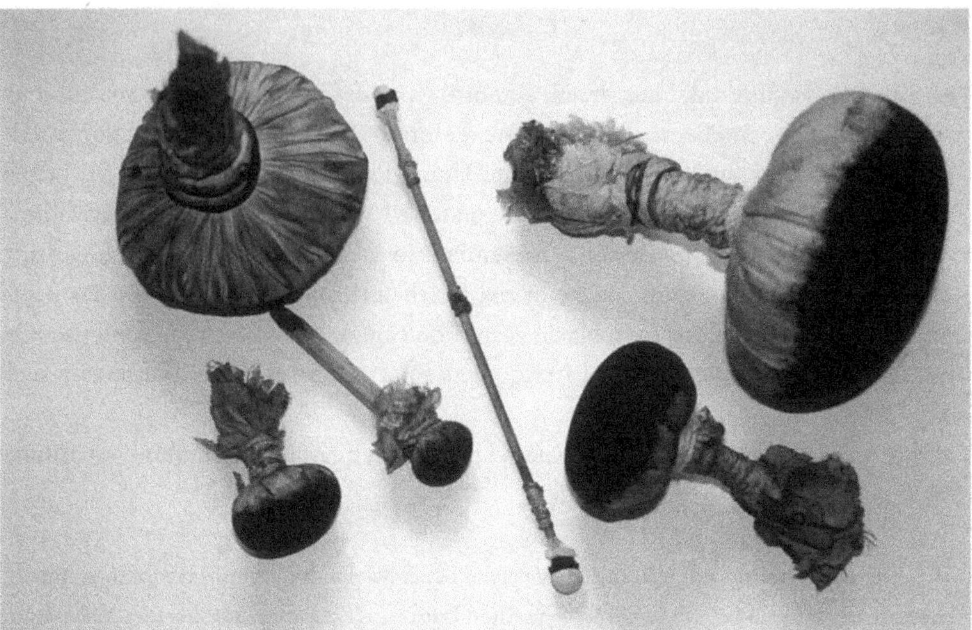

FIG. 2.8. Ink dabbers. Author's collection. Photograph by the author.

the outer wrapping. The essential qualities of the outer wrapping are that it be of fine weave and have no nap.

Referring especially to rubbing bronzes, Chen Jieqi described the traditional preference for a dabber: "For the outside . . . one uses a layer of *bai* silk, while for the inside one packs new cotton [as wadding], binding it tight. Old *bai* silk is economical, but is not as good as *yuansi* silk."[86] Rong Geng amplifies:

> For the dabber, one can use either two layers of plain thin *chou* silk or one layer of plain [heavier] *duan* satin, with the plain satin being excellent. Buying a thirty-year-old *tianqing jinyin* satin outer jacket, cutting it up and using it, moreover, is utilizing waste material. The dabber size differs with the size of the vessel, with the diameter about 2 to 4 *fen* [0.5 centimeter to 1.3 centimeter]. When tied, it is like a round ball, and one must press it and flatten it a little.[87]

Contemporary descriptions expand and vary. One recommends that the dabber have five layers rather than two or three.[88] For fine line, the outermost layer, amply large, should be either thin *chou* silk, with that made in Puyuanzhen, Jiaxing County, Zhejiang, specifically recommended, or thin *ling* silk. Fine cotton cloth suffices for heavier line. The second, third, and fourth layers should be of commensurate size. The second layer should be fine felt; the third, an interlay of oiled paper or cloth to impede

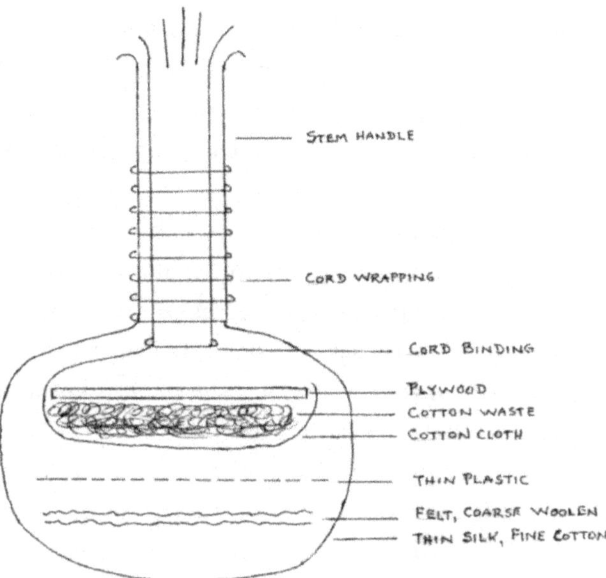

FIG. 2.9. Construction of a dabber. Sketch by the author.

the liquid ink from soaking into the core; the fourth, compared with Chen Jieqi's scraps of *yuansi* silk, fine felt; and the fifth, innermost layer, waste cotton. Some accounts speak of the liquid-resistant interlayer, while others do not. The dabber stem should be stiff and lined with cotton or silk for extra strength; otherwise, it will be thin and weak, like a rat's tail. The binding cord should be cotton rather than synthetic fiber, which slips. The outer layer of silk can be doubled back over the stem for security and tied again.

The head of the dabber should be compact, not spongy, so that it does not deposit ink in the incised line. The working surface should be flat, with the edges rounded, or else they will accumulate ink and deposit ugly ink blotches, "ink pigs" (*moshi*), on the rubbing. One should make a graduated series of dabbers, large ones, 15 centimeters or so in diameter, for rubbing broad steles, and small ones, finger-tip size or less, for capturing the spirit of the ancient bronzes.[89] For hairline oracle-bone inscriptions, one should use a dabber of 1 *cun* (about 3 centimeters in diameter) for larger, flatter pieces, and of 3 or 4 *fen* (1.0 to 1.3 centimeters) for small fragments, very fine line, or irregular areas such as joints. Extremely fine detail may require a tiny dabber, just a few millimeters, and of especially fine materials and make. It should be of a size relative to that of the subject matter so that the ink tone will be even.[90] Other specialists supplement these descriptions of the *tabao,* some in great detail.[91]

There are many variations on the basic materials and construction. Instead of cotton waste for the core, one can use sheep or camel wool, with the latter particularly recommended for its elasticity and for washability when stained with ink. Although initially more expensive, camel hair is more economical in the long run. Where camel hair is not as easily had as it is in north China, raw cotton serves. Heavy woolen cloth (*ni*), such as that used for winter coats, also is good, for it absorbs and holds ink and releases it evenly.

The ink-resistant interlayer between the outer silk cloth and the cotton or wool core impedes the ink from soaking into the core and making it soggy. Earlier artisans used oiled paper or cloth, but thin plastic or rubber is common today, with greater impermeability, flexibility, and durability. The raw cotton or wool core is wrapped in the interlay and the outer silk or cotton covering, the whole is kneaded to work out lumps, and the stem is wrapped tightly with string.

Dabbers vary with the situation. For inking extensive flat areas, such as steles or mortuary tiles, artisans use large round or rectangular dabbers fashioned of a thin plywood support to one face of which one are fastened the core, interlay, and cover materials (see fig. 4.6). For places difficult of access, one can modify the dabber form endlessly. One can fasten it to the end of a length of bamboo or wood to reach inscriptions in deep-bellied vessels, and for pinpoint work, one can use a small dowel, half the diameter of a pencil. For inscriptions in hard-to-reach places, long-nosed pincers will hold the dabber, and for those in awkward spots, as under pitcher-type handles on bronze *jue* wine cups, one can use a narrow splint of bamboo or wood, akin to a tongue depressor, around which one wraps the silk, interlay, and cotton combination.[92] Finally, inscriptions and designs on pottery often are so uneven, deep, and narrow as to preclude the use of even a tiny dabber. In such situations one can apply very dry ink with a cut-off Chinese writing brush.[93]

One can find ready-made dabbers in Asian, especially Japanese, art-supply shops as part of rubbing kits. Such dabbers commonly have a cotton rather than silk outer cover and, being of coarser weave, are not suitable for inking very fine line. Westerners can find dabber components in fabric stores and upholstery shops.

OUTDOOR WORK

Many objects are in a location or of a size and character that require copying on the spot, such as the tens of thousands of steles, ubiquitous through the length and breadth of China for two millennia. Other inscribed or decorated objects also are omnipresent: pillars of stone, bronze and iron, including Buddhist scripture pillars; bases and backs of images, and sometimes their fronts and sides as well, such as those in rock-cut niches; cliff-smoothed inscriptions; wellheads; *biane* panels over gates; bells and ceremonial vessels; stone and tile pictorial reliefs; and pottery bricks and tiles, to name some of the most common.[94] Each type and situation will require its own response and imaginative solution.

Many of these cultural objects long since have been abandoned and must be sought out, as appealingly noted by Lu Shihua (1714–1779): "Whenever I travel about in leisurely manner, I pay close attention to traces left by the ancients in the form of time-worn stone engravings in the mountains and along the water margins, even risking danger. Moreover, I have to examine [them] carefully."[95]

The search is particularly keen in the case of steles, in which antiquarian interest in China always has run high. Wu Shifen observes that "throughout the countryside, famous scenic places, ancient tombs, and old [Buddhist and Daoist] monasteries generally abound in stele inscriptions, and one with great care must minutely search them all out."[96] Wu emphasizes that old abandoned steles often were broken up and used as stepping-stones, pillar plinths, rice mortars, and even as foundation stones for new structures.[97] One also must pay particular attention because old inscriptions sometimes were ground down in later periods.[98] Often, however, either vestiges of the inscription still remain and may be copied or only the front face has been ground down, while the heading, back face, and side faces remain untouched.

Writing in 1939, Jiang Xuanyi echoes Wu's comments of seven or eight decades earlier:

> [The Song poet Su] Dongpo thought that traveling 10,000 *li* [Chinese miles] and reading 10,000 *juan* of books was the painter's credo, and I feel that scholars of antiquity also can observe [this precept] as a jade law. In China, engraved stones mostly are scattered about, abandoned in old monasteries deep in the mountains, and except for [the assemblage in] the Beilin, our country as a rule has not collected and stored them in museums. Newly excavated [antiquities] all are bought and sold by villagers, and nowadays there sometimes is news of the plundering of tombs and the [clandestine] opening of grave mounds. Moreover, all [these randomly collected antiquities] are scattered in the four directions. Therefore, the road to searching for old relics primarily is in traveling, but aimless traveling cannot result in success. Thus, investigating metal-and-stone records, gazetteers, maps, stele catalogues, and travel accounts beforehand is very important.[99]

Jiang ends his account with an eloquent statement that affords revealing insight into the mystique of Chinese antiquarians and, for that matter, antiquarians everywhere:

> All who enjoy metal-and-stone studies find pleasure in traveling, in high mountains and along great rivers, in gray mists and rosy clouds, in venerable Buddhist monasteries and neglected cave shrines, and in fragmentary remains and crumbling cliffs. Travel [of this kind] certainly is an appropriate way of expressing one's feelings. A love of metal-

> and-stone [inscriptions] is like turning [one's face] toward the ancients, like going back into the [cultural] memory.[100]

For Jiang, "traveling" means an on-foot search for old inscribed monuments, known as *fangbei* (visiting steles) or, more broadly, *fanggu* (visiting relics), and in this respect, as did Lu Shihua and Wu Shifen, he shows an attitude often assumed not to exist among traditionally conservative Chinese scholars. He describes the needs of the search in some detail, including simple dress, a stout staff, and tools for rough work and constructing scaffolds and uprighting steles.[101]

One also needs materials for recording data. These include a camera, to photograph the stele and its setting; a compass or, today, global-positioning equipment, to determine the location and orientation of the stone; a metric rule for precise measuring; and, finally, a notebook and a pencil, to record field notes on the stone and its inscription in order to compensate for insufficiencies in the rubbings and photographs. It is of particular importance that the searcher take along a small corpus of reference books to help locate and identify inscriptions. As Jiang piously counsels, "While resting, one should not avoid books."[102]

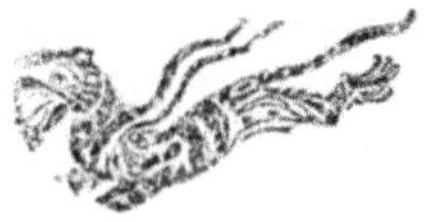

3 / The Gentle Art

THERE is little information on rubbing materials and techniques used in the early and middle centuries. There is more information about both in recent centuries, especially in the middle and late Qing, when metal-and-stone studies (*jinshi xue*) reached their height. As normally practiced, the process divides into five stages: preliminary considerations; selecting, fitting, wetting, and laying the paper; tamping; inking; and removing the rubbing, documentation, and preservation.

PRELIMINARY CONSIDERATIONS

The first consideration is selecting the host object, with the primary criterion being cultural: the intellectual or aesthetic value of the inscription or pictorial.[1] A second criterion involves technical aspects, for although the rubbing technique has wide application, it has limitations. Ideally, it is for copying intaglio or relief on firm, flat, or slightly curved surfaces. The relief should be low or, at most, medium, for as it increases, the rubbing technique becomes ever less suitable, and the result, ever more tortured. One can use the technique on high relief, even the full round, as described in chapters 5 and 6, but only by dint of effort not always commensurate with the results.

The physical condition of the host object is a third important criterion. The manipulations involved in the rubbing process frequently result in great stress on the object. One always should proceed with circumspection, but special care often is imperative. Ancient pottery or archaic jades, the latter often thin and fragile, may have faint cracks or hidden faults that will open in the tamping stages. The ritual bronzes, although often massive and heavy, can be quite thin or badly corroded, with their flaws not always observable macroscopically: "Corroded pieces easily are damaged, and although they are whole and still make a sound [when tapped], their basic composition already has changed to verdigris [*qinglu*]. They will not bear being struck or abraded, and being regretful after [the damage is done] is not like guarding against [it] beforehand."[2] Ancient bronze weapons and coins also frequently are thin, bent, and badly corroded and so also must be handled with great care.[3] Evidencing the caution characteristic of Chinese connoisseurs, Chen Jieqi warns that massive or corroded bronze vessels should not be entrusted to unsophisticated people for study or rubbing, while fragile old coins and other small objects should not be given over to rough hands, children, or strangers.[4]

If there are doubts about the condition of an object, there are alternative methods of handling fragile specimens.[5] The traditional approach is to trace the inscription (*mo^c wen*).[6] This age-old method, which is the only recourse for inlaid or extremely fine and shallow inscriptions, is widely practiced because of its simplicity and safety. A second method, the surface of the object permitting, is to rub a light coat of oil-based ink on the intaglio with one's finger, lay on a very thin piece of paper, and obtain a print by lightly wiping or brushing the paper. The resulting print will be negative, but one can obtain a positive by reversing the paper and tracing the inscription or design against a light source. This method has the great disadvantage of staining both the object—especially if its surface is absorbent, as with pottery or wood—and the rubbing paper. A third method is to make a mold of the original and, from that, a cast. The cast then can be rubbed as though it were the original, although the resulting rubbing will not be as faithful as one from the original. As this method is troublesome and not without its dangers to the object, one should use it as a last resort. Within the bounds of these three criteria—cultural, technical, and physical condition—virtually any object is fair game for rubbing.

The selective process still must consider a fourth criterion, the completeness of the subject matter being copied. One must check the inscription or design closely, for a particular inscription or design may be complete or fragmentary, or it may be complete in itself but incomplete in that it is but part of a series. It also may have distinctive features, such as a cancellation (*goudiao*), as in Wang Xizhi's *Lanting Preface* (Lanting xu, plate 4). One must have a close familiarity with the history of the object and a keen knowledge of pertinent reference works.

It is important to rub not only the main front face of a stele but also other inscribed or decorated faces, such as the heading (*bei'e*), back, and sides. This is especially important where for political or religious reasons the front face is effaced.[7] Similarly, one must pay attention to all the faces of a fallen stone, such as the Han reliefs at Nanyang, near Yizhou, southeastern Shandong. Stone doors and pillars at the site lie scattered about with one or more faces down, and with great effort they must be turned over to capture the reliefs.[8] Many elegant stone cuts have been used as building foundations, and one should make every effort to capture the reliefs by any means possible, for to miss even one is like "leaving a pearl in the depths of the ocean."[9] If one cannot gain access to all the faces, scholarly integrity requires that one report the fact. Capturing all the elements of a stele or relief at the time also may save returning several hundred *li* to rub something vital that one overlooked on the original visit. One also should give equal attention to rubbing all the faces of inscribed or decorated tiles.[10] Thorough workers rub not only the inscribed or decorated but also their plain surfaces, for record-keeping purposes. Referring to steles, Wu Shifen advises that one "also carefully rub areas where there are no characters."[11] In a note he adds that "in recent times [commercial] rubbers generally are sparing of paper and ink, often rubbing a large stele of more than one *zhang* [3.3 meters] with but a [single] sheet of paper [but skipping blank or spalled areas]," and he opines that such a situation is a matter for great regret.[12] Copying of plain surfaces is characteristic mainly of rubbings made by or for scholars and collectors. Ordinary commercial rubbings usually include only the primary surfaces, and sometimes, to save paper and ink, not even all of those (see fig. 7.3).

Attention to blank or missing parts also is requisite for mortuary bricks and tiles as well as for the endless variety of smaller objects that have composed the awesome range of Chinese material culture through time and space. Chen Jieqi advises that, in addition to rubbing the dramatic side panels of bronze *zhong* bells, one also should rub their top surfaces for the dimensions of the bell to be clear. Similarly, in rubbing the décor of a *zun* wine jar, one should capture the entire circling band.[13] In rubbing jade plaques, one must rub not only the inscribed or decorated faces and the plain faces but also the edges, to show the thickness and surface texture, and in rubbing a tubular object, such as a jade flute, one should rub the end of the tube as well as of its length, to show the diameter and thickness.[14] Other examples include the circumferences and tops of jade bracelets; the edges of jade *bi* discs, inkstones (fig. 3.1), and bronze mirrors (fig. 3.2); architectural components (fig. 3.3); and the smallest bits of decorated objects.[15] One must rub the edges of inscribed shell-and-bone fragments with particular care, to enable scholar-detectives to rejoin separated fragments.[16]

Working Conditions

Working outdoors requires initial preparations for good results, often extensive and demanding, and differing with the nature of the object and the working conditions. This especially is so with steles, which often have eroded, spalled, uneven surfaces, and with cliff-smoothed inscriptions. First considerations, even before preparations begin, are the season and the weather.[17] Spring and fall are the best times for making rubbings. Summer heat dries the rubbing paper too quickly, vegetation requires clearing, and insects are annoying. Dead of winter also is a bad time, for winter winds make it difficult to control the paper, the wetted paper dries slowly, and one's fingers stiffen. As for weather, rain wets the delicate rubbing paper, wind makes it difficult to control, and a strong, drying sun lifts it off the relief prematurely.

One often must devise special means of rubbing monumental outdoor objects.[18] For tall steles, many of which stand 5 meters or more, one must construct a scaffold, and a partly fallen stone may necessitate lying on one's back. For cliff-smoothed and cave

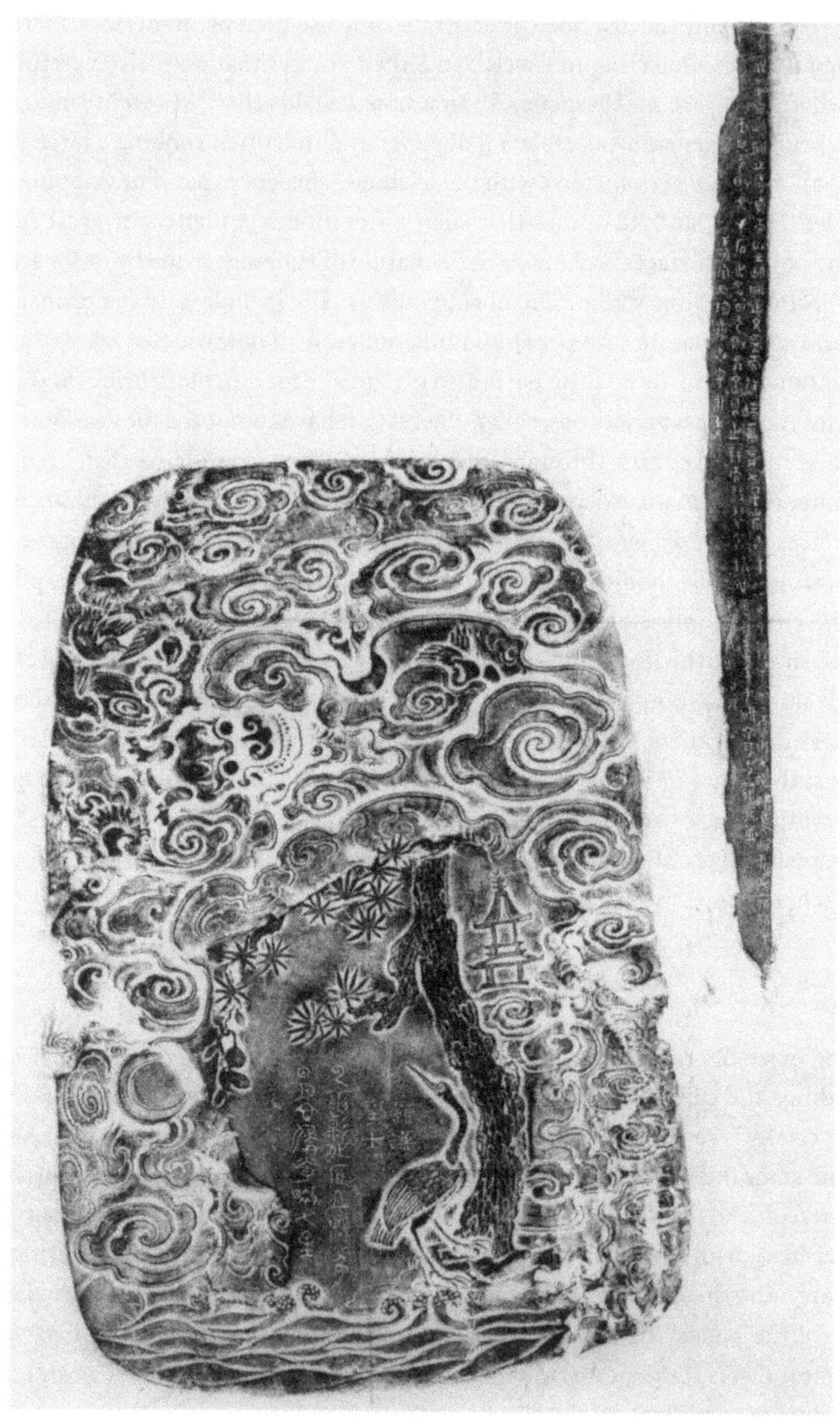

FIG. 3.1. Inkstone with edge inscription. Undated. Freer Gallery of Art, Smithsonian Institution, gift of Peking University, F1980.39.

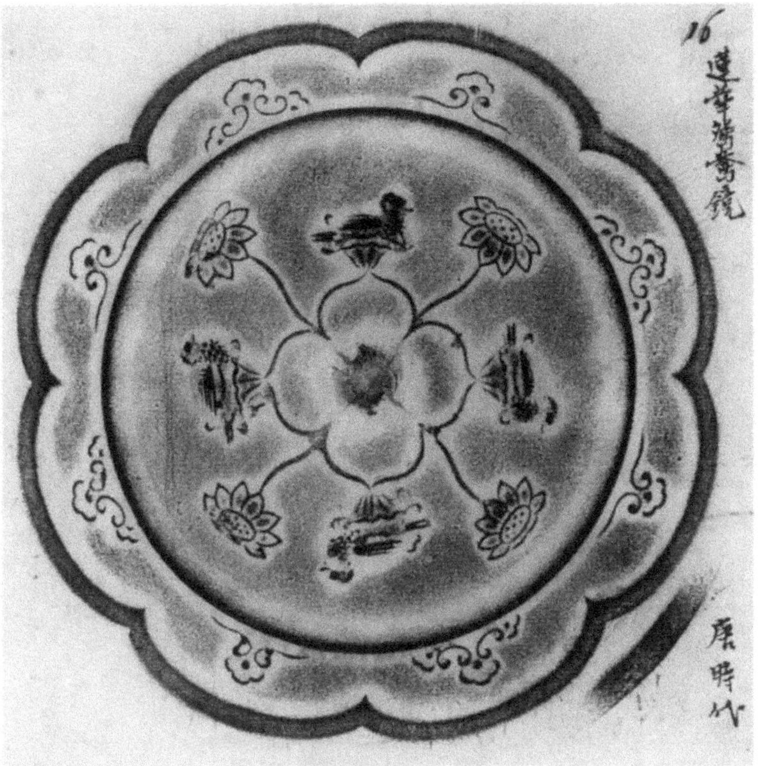

Fig. 3.2. Slitting the rubbing paper over the bail and rubbing the edge of a Tang bronze mirror. Freer Gallery of Art, Smithsonian Institution, gift of Peking University, F1980.36.

inscriptions, one must construct a scaffold or drop a platform from above. Exemplary is a group of Sui and Tang rock-cut Buddhist sculptures at Wanfo Tang, in Tuoli township, southwest of Beijing, where the figures are in a pitch-black cavern, across a 10-foot chasm, 15 feet above an underground stream. In such situations, one must devise whatever means one can.

One must clear away undergrowth and dirt from around a stone, especially its base, and clean it of dust, cobwebs, dirt, and moss or lichen, using water and a fiber brush to bring out detail.[19] The fibers of the brush should be natural and not so stiff as to damage the edges of the characters or the lines of clay mortuary tiles. As bits of ancient objects often are spalling and loose, one should examine the surface minutely for faults.

Finally, it is essential to record basic measurements of objects, with each type requiring special consideration. Stone inscriptions commonly require figures for at least the height and width of the inscribed faces, traditionally in *zhang* and *chi*, and the dimensions of characters in *cun* and *fen* (nowadays, in metric measures). The idiosyncrasies

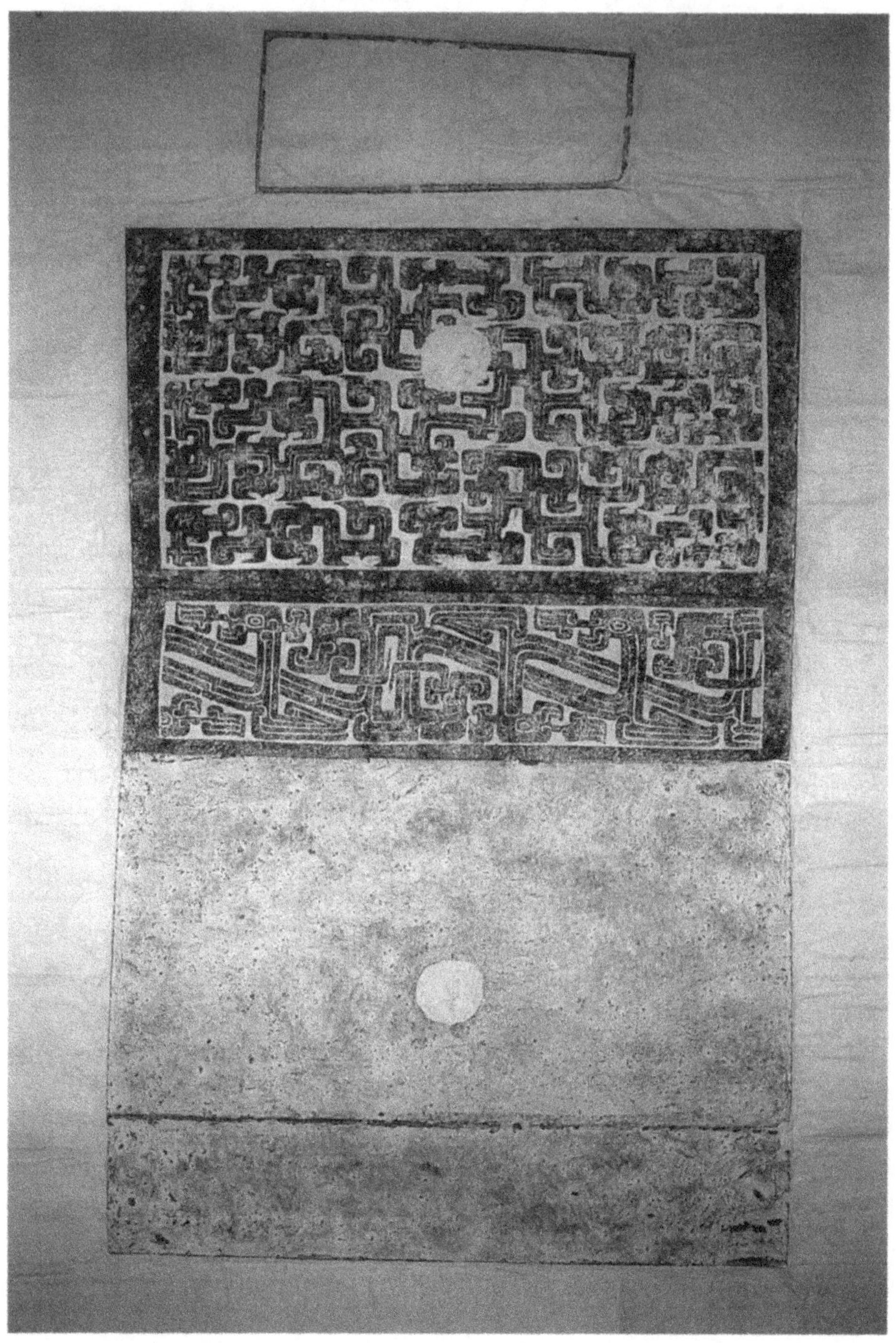

Fig. 3.3. Simple rubbing showing all faces of an Eastern Zhou bronze architectural element. The Field Museum of Natural History, 127363. Rubbing and photograph by the author.

or cultural importance of the object may suggest additional measurements. Bi Yuan and Ruan Yuan record the Qin Langya Tai *keshi* at Langya Tai, Zhucheng County, southeastern Shandong, as being 1 *zhang* and 5 *chi* high, 6 *chi* wide in its lower part, 5 *chi* wide in its midpart, 3 *chi* in its upper part, 2 *chi* and 3 *cun* at its top, and 2 *chi* and 3 *cun* thick in its north-south axis.[20] One also should photograph or sketch the object. Illustrations and notes are important, especially with pictorial reliefs, such as at Wu Liang Ci, the Later Han Wu family shrine in Shandong, where there are multiple levels and scenes, and about which many uncertainties remain.[21]

Cleaning smaller objects in the studio requires equal care, with each type requiring slightly different treatment. First, one must be painstakingly careful not to damage the piece, for inexpert cleaning can damage a rare specimen to the point where its intellectual, aesthetic, or monetary value is lessened or lost. Second, the finer the line of an inscription or design, the more important sharp definition becomes. In order to obtain the clearest possible reproduction, one should clean the object as thoroughly as its nature and condition permit, for one can capture in a rubbing only such relief as actually exists. One also must remember that every tiny speck of foreign matter on the surface of the object will appear in the subsequent inking, when it is impossible to rectify the situation.

Removing Earth and Corrosion

The most common unwanted substance is plain old earth, there naturally or by the hand of one who hopes to heighten the aura of antiquity or cover faults and repairs. The removal of earth encrustation and lichen seldom lessens the scientific or aesthetic value of a piece, but the work must be done by a specialist, especially if the piece is fragile. The dirt encrustation on hoary steles, although generally easier to deal with than that on small, delicate objects, or verdigris on bronzes, still requires close attention, for in removing encrusted earth one inadvertently may open up an underlying hidden crack or speed a spall.[22]

Careful removal of earth encrustation is essential in the case of delicate objects and very fine inscriptions, such as those on oracle shells and bones, and on ancient jades, so that there is no damage to either object or inscription.[23] With the piece solidly supported as described below, one carefully brushes the dirt away with a small columnar, human-hair brush, lightly moistened with water. If the earth fill in the characters is too resistant, one can use a dull needle or, preferably, a bamboo splint, to pick off the earth. One must not probe the incisions roughly or hastily but work with exquisite care, moving from the center line outward toward the edges of the characters, carefully, carefully picking and lifting the earth with an upward motion, small bit by small bit.

One must be particularly attentive to not marring the edges of the characters, adversely affecting their aesthetic qualities.

Of markedly different nature is the corrosion on ancient bronze and iron objects. Because of their intense interest in ancient bronze inscriptions, the Chinese through the centuries have been particularly concerned about verdigris and have devoted close attention to the problem, especially as it bears on the sanctity of the inscriptions and the fidelity of the resulting rubbings. Traditionally, the Chinese have looked with great suspicion on heavy-handed mechanical and radical chemical methods in dealing with verdigris, for such approaches can result in irreparable damage to the object and its inscription. As with preserving other antiquities, the Chinese have preferred gentle, natural approaches.

Chen Jieqi (1813–1884) clearly reflects this view. He first emphasizes that scraping verdigris with a sharp knife is the most reprehensible of all methods, for in doing so lies the great danger of scratching the surface of the object and altering the spirit of the original inscription. Chinese scholars and connoisseurs are so sophisticated in calligraphic art that they are sensitive to the slightest alteration in the form of an ancient character. They are fearful about making a scratch that might be mistaken for a brush-stroke or marring the edge of a stroke so that it would alter the original form or change its spirit: "Scraping with a knife is the worst [method of removing verdigris], for when there are knife scars, one loses the overall ancient quality. Its [i.e., knife scraping's] damaging the original edges [of the characters] is especially [bad], for it [results in] totally losing the authentic quality of the ancients and changes the characters into those in the hearts of modern people, to characters in the hand of people today."[24]

Scraping the verdigris with a wire brush "also harms the edges of the characters and damages the patina. Seeing the [underlying] body [and] removing the [original] bronze is like wronging the ancient writing."[25]

One also can use a needle to pick the verdigris away:

> Picking with a needle also is a possibility. One should use a large blunt needle, and from the exact center line of the stroke [of the character] repeatedly go back and forth, allowing the verdigris to lift by itself. Moreover, as always, one should not touch the edges of the characters, use the needle to scrape, or permit the needle to go outside the stroke and make a scratch. Further, regarding a point [in a character or stroke] where it is not proper to go farther, if one continues, then one especially should not use a sharp needle or employ excessive force. Not knowing about the bed of the character, and whether the bronze is thin, or whether the old bronze is rotten, will result in piercing the bronze and making a hole or, even if [the needle] is blunt, surely will result in breakage.[26]

Jiang Xuanyi amplifies many of Chen's points about mechanically removing verdigris with a sharp knife, wire brush, or sharp needle.[27] He also notes common problems and preferred approaches:

> Where earth encrustation and verdigris have accumulated over a long period, basically one can remove it by scraping it away. Using a bamboo needle is best, and in keeping with the natural depth [of the characters], one from the exact center of the brushstroke must scrape away the verdigris down inside the stroke. One certainly should not touch the edges of the characters, for the edges are the original bronze, and scraping them away damages the forms [of the characters]. Although the edges of the characters still may have a few spots of verdigris, one can leave them. Further, there are situations where the characters float on top of the blue-green verdigris, which develops from inside the bronze. . . . If one scrapes away the verdigris, the characters also will come off along with the verdigris and end up becoming a hole.[28]

Chemical methods of removing verdigris also are not without their dangers. After warning the reader that one should not use vinegar in such situations, Chen Jieqi adds the following bit of esoterica:

> Acids can remove blue-green spots but cannot take away red spots; acids only change them to purple. Zhang Shuwei . . . of Jiaxing [Zhejiang] has a method of removing verdigris from inside characters [of bronze inscriptions]. I do not know the details [of the process], but only have seen that the characters [cleaned by this technique] are genuine [*zhen*] but "fat" [*fei*, disproportionately wide from overcleaning]. The characters are clear, but if one compares them with those in old rubbings [of the inscriptions] that did not have the verdigris removed, then the exactness of the essential [aesthetic] quality is far removed. I do not accept [Zhang's method] and so do not wish to hear about it![29]

This quotation illustrates Chen's cautious approach to removing verdigris and affords nice insight into the conservative purism of traditional Chinese scholars and the importance that they attached to such matters. The passage further suggests that he was not of one mind with Zhang in many areas, for one will recall that Chen was reserved in his judgment about Zhang's use of *baiji* for sizing the paper.

Jiang Xuanyi exemplifies the care with which traditionalists approached such matters. He differentiates seven types of liquids for soaking and loosening unwanted encrustations, ranging from plain well water to dilute hydrochloric acid:

> Well water is not as good as river water, river water is not as good as rainwater, and rainwater is not as good as water in which rice has been rinsed. Further, one can use water [in which one has] steeped ash from burning young bamboo shoots (when the shoot

> becomes bamboo, the alkaline quality is a little stronger) and apply it [to the encrustation]. [This solution] then is stronger than water in which rice has been rinsed, [and in turn again] an alkali solution [made from the burning of mature bamboo] is stronger than [the solution made from] ashes of young bamboo shoots. . . . [Beyond these], it is best not to use the stronger dilute hydrochloric acid![30]

Although Jiang cautions about using hydrochloric acid, manifesting the traditional strong suspicion of manmade chemicals, he allows that under certain circumstances one can use it if it is sufficiently dilute. Even so, one must watch the results of the chemical action constantly so that no harm is done to the object.

Chen Jieqi describes the preferred traditional manner of removing verdigris by combining chemical and mechanical methods:

> Where corrosion on an ancient [bronze] object is heavy, first soak it for several days in water in which rice has been rinsed, and then remove it. Then take the large red fruit of the hill haw [*shanzha(zi)*, *Crataegus cuneata*, the wild hawthorn], remove the skin and seeds, use a mortar and pestle to pound [the meat to a consistency] like mud, and apply [the paste] on the corrosion. One must spread [it] evenly and liberally, approximately 1 *fen* thick, wait until it is nine-tenths dry, and then remove it. One cannot allow it to become too dry, and so cannot not let it go beyond the point of being nine-tenths dry. After removing it, take advantage of its [residual] moistness, and, using a bamboo knife or a dull steel knife (keeping in mind not damaging the ancient object), firmly pare away the earth and corrosion. If you cannot remove [all the accretion], then use the hill-haw paste again, applying it as before. If one proceeds several times in this manner, there will be no situations in which it is impossible to remove the corrosion. (Certainly one should not use force to a point of damaging the ancient object.)
>
> Where the corrosion on ancient objects is thin, if there is an inscription that one can see but cannot rub, or that one can rub but that is indecipherable and not clear, apply hill-haw paste as described above. Wait until it is nine-tenths dry, then clear it away, and immediately use a sharp point of bamboo or a steel embroidery needle (blunt its point, so as not to damage the object). For the sake of the appearance of the character, scrape it without using great force, and the corrosion automatically will split open as its meets the knife. If one scraping does not remove the corrosion, then apply [the hill-haw paste] a second time, with scraping [the object] clean as the goal, but one cannot be impatient. This is a method that proves effective every time it is used.[31]

In proceeding, on the one hand, one must be thoughtful of the object, especially if it is heavy, unwieldy, oddly shaped, or in poor condition. Examples include *jue* wine cups, *ding* cauldrons, *zun* wine jars, *you* wine jars, and *zhong* bells with their projecting bosses. All are easily abraded and so must be moved with great care, especially when their mouths, sides, or bases carry inscriptions.[32] Thin areas, corroded places, and convexities or protrusions require special handling.[33]

On the other hand, one must be equally considerate of inscriptions or designs, for, apart from the danger of abrading them in moving, there is the even greater danger of marring the edges of the strokes in the cleaning process. Of a different nature, but no less needful of caution, are situations in which the verdigris has erupted from beneath the surface of the bronze in such a manner that the inscription or design "floats" on its surface.[34] Such eruptions, especially characteristic of bronze mirrors, should not be scraped off, lest the inscription or design also be carried away. For removing corrosion on seals, Chen Jieqi recommends soaking the seals in oil, the kind unspecified, for several months. After such treatment, the corrosion readily can be removed.[35]

The primary consideration in the mind of the old-school Chinese scholar-connoisseur was the safety of the object and, of equal if not greater importance, the integrity of the inscription. No action ever should be taken that will endanger the latter, for even the slightest damage is irreversible, and the inscription once marred never can be returned to its original physical or aesthetic condition but, to the extent of the damage, is forever lost. If there is the slightest doubt about the safety of either the object or its inscription, one is obliged to eschew cleaning it and either rub it as is or, if the rubbing process also threatens the object, turn to one of the safer methods of copying.

Chen Jieqi provides clear and valuable insight into the caution that characterized the traditional Chinese attitude toward the sanctity of the ancient bronzes and their inscriptions:

> Being regretful afterward [about damaging a corroded bronze piece] is not like being watchful beforehand. Because I love them [the ancient bronzes], I cannot but take care of them. To force those who do not love [the bronzes] and make them love [them], to force those who cannot be trusted [with them], moreover, is both foolish and vexing. Liansheng [courtesy name of Wang Yirong, 1845–1900] says that the striae on metal [the ancient bronzes] and the veins of stones [steles] are to be loved as if they were one's own muscle and flesh! How can one not make rubbings, and yet how can one minutely oversee it [the work]? The only recourse is to seek out a careful, trustworthy person to oversee it, and there will be no loss![36]

Chen several times emphasizes the dangers involved in trusting one's precious objects to strangers or to thoughtless and unsophisticated people, and he similarly stresses the need for careful workers.[37] Even skilled workmanship and painstaking attention are not enough. The ideal situation is one in which the person doing the cleaning of the characters is intimately familiar with the calligraphic style of the inscription: "The characters of the ancients have strength, they have style, and therefore they have [an essential] spirit. If the person who does the scraping is familiar with how they [the ancients] used strength, [and] what the style was, and [with this knowledge] scrapes them, then one will not lose their spirit!"[38]

Chen continues in this vein, emphasizing that "skillful work and great carefulness perhaps also can bring it off, but [skill and care] are not equal to a scholar understanding the approach to cutting the ancient *zhuan* [seal script]."[39] Cleaning and rubbing ancient objects and their inscriptions thus will require not only technical knowledge and careful work but also a keen aesthetic sense and a close familiarity with the history and aesthetics of calligraphic art. One also must be in the proper frame of mind: "When scraping characters, one needs a quiet mind and a concentrated eye, doing the work when the heart is relaxed and the hand is steady. . . . If the spirit is weary, then one should not scrape, and if there is someone at hand with an upsetting matter, then one should not scrape."[40]

By way of final sober statement on cleaning bronzes, Chen warns that "if there is a single mistake, one cannot rectify it, and so one cannot not be cautious about it."[41] After thus impressing upon his reader the possible dangers involved in cleaning and rubbing ancient bronzes, however, Chen philosophizes, opining that "being cautious to the point of not daring to scrape [an object], and of not being willing to rub it, also does not result in good, for if one cannot transmit antiquity, how is it any different from not having the object [at all]?"[42]

Special Treatments

Some types of objects may require other initial treatment. Handling bronze vessels may result in scratching, especially if they are massive and heavy, or if they are of unusual shape, with bulging bellies or protruding rims, handles, bosses, or feet. Chen Jieqi advises protecting the inscriptions by wrapping the pieces with soft cloth or by temporarily pasting paper on them with harmless rice paste so that they can be safely manipulated in rubbing.[43] Bronze vessels that require particular care include *zun* wine jars, *you* wine jars, *gu* beakers, *zhi* tankards, *fu* trays, *gui* tureens, *pan* basins, *yi* ewers, and *dou* stem dishes.

Different in function is the preparatory treatment that highly porous materials receive. These include low-fired-ceramic ancient bricks and tiles, clay sealings, and earthenware molds as well as wooden objects and plaster casts. Such soft, loose-textured, and absorbent materials take the wetted rubbing paper much more readily if they first are coated lightly with white wax (*baila*).[44] In some of these situations, one also may use alum water, which, however, some authorities discourage because of its deleterious effect on the rubbing paper.[45] Ceramic pieces marked by loose bits of glaze also do well with such a thin coating of wax, if indeed one dares rub them at all.

Once properly cleaned and prepared for rubbing, the object must be solidly positioned. Generally, there is no problem with large, massive objects of stone, metal, or tile that one finds on mountainsides, in old temples, or in ancient tombs and shrines, for these stand sturdily, set in the earth or supported on a base. If the object being copied is smaller or is broken or fragile, one must position it securely. This is done primarily to protect the object but also to ensure that it is solidly set, for any movement in the process can result in a ruined rubbing. Larger mobile pieces, such as bronze vessels, especially those with irregular shapes or projections, must be laid on their sides or turned upside down to capture their inscriptions or motifs. Awkward, heavy pieces, such as *zhong* bells with their projecting nipples, can be set on an old chair cushion and thus protected from abrasion, a solution that also allows for easy shifting.[46] Smaller objects also may require a cushion or, for very small pieces, such as jades, curving potsherds, or bent old coins, a similar support.[47]

Evidencing the subtleties that characterize the rubbing technique, Chen Jieqi notes that for supporting and protecting small objects, "in the winter, the table should have felt padding [to hold the piece], and in the summer, one should use a soft pad made of paper from an old [Chinese] book to hold it."[48] Elsewhere Chen again refers to using an old book, specifically for supporting ancient coins, and he adds that if one moistens the paper, the object will not shift on the working surface:[49]

> Summing up, using a soft pad of appropriate size that does not readily shift is safe. If one wishes to keep [the object] on the table without its moving, one can moisten it [on the underside], and then it will not move. If the object is hard and slippery, one can use flour to dust it, and then one can manage it.[50]

For extremely fragile objects, such as very thin and delicate old jades, worn or corroded coins, or fragments of inscribed shell or bone, one must prepare a special support. In rubbing fragile oracle bones, specialists shape a foundation of softened beeswax (fig. 3.4).[51] It should conform precisely to the shape of the bone, and once the piece is set, one should cut the sides of the foundation straight down from the edge of the bone. This last is important, for when the thin rubbing paper is laid on the bone, it must be pressed down crisply over the edge all around, permitting a trim line in inking.

Two points of caution may be made on using such a beeswax base. First, one must be certain that the piece of bone is well set, with no part, however small, unsupported. Aside from their normally fragile condition, fragments often are glued together and will come apart if not handled with care. The solidness of the piece can be tested by

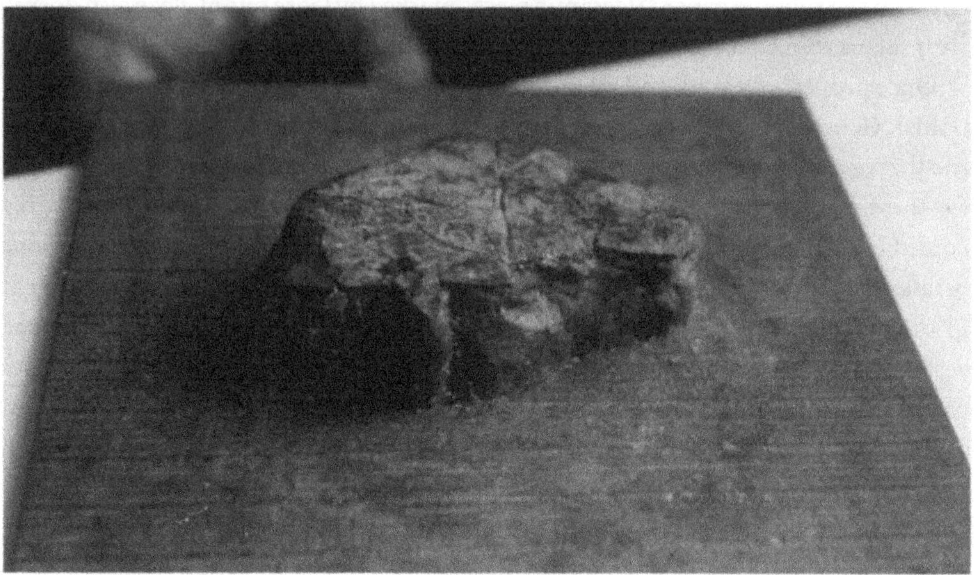

FIG. 3.4. Beeswax support for an oracle bone. Institute of History and Philology, Academia Sinica, Taiwan, Republic of China, 1960. Photograph by the author.

tapping it after it is in position. Should there be a hollow sound anywhere, one must reset the bone, for otherwise it may break in the process, especially in tamping. Second, as the beeswax is tacky, one must take care that the fragile object being supported does not stick. One can prevent this by laying thin strips of scrap rubbing paper or waxed paper between the object and the foundation. The preferred approach is to lay narrow strips of the paper around the edges of the foundation, about 1 centimeter wide, depending on the size of the bone. There should be just enough points of contact with the wax to hold the object in position. In that way, the bone will not stick too tightly to the wax and can be released by carefully inserting a knife or spatula along the edges. Materials other than beeswax also may be used, so long as they contain no harmful substances.[52]

The specific methods of guaranteeing that the object is safely and securely supported are quite varied and depend upon the nature, size, shape, and condition of the piece.

Record Keeping

When the object is clean and its inscriptive and pictorial elements are clear, one should record its identifying features. These include especially its name, which often derives from its inscription, such as that on the *Mao Gong ding* tripod or on *Ju dao*, knife-money (*daobu*), from the small Zhou state of Ju, in modern southeastern Shandong.

One also must set down important measurements of objects, depending on their forms and special features and their importance. Among ceremonial bronze vessels, *ding* cauldrons require figures on their height, depth, mouth diameter, belly circumference, the height and width of their ears, and their weight.[53] Vessels with auxiliary or idiosyncratic features, such as lugs, handles, and nipples, require additional measurements. Bronze *ge* dagger axes require measures for the length and width of the neck (*hu*) and the lengths of the butt (*nei*) and blade (*yuan*).[54] The familiar round coin with the square central hole, used from the Han on, requires only a record of its diameter and weight, but odd-shaped ancient coins require a wider range of measures.[55] Zhou spade coins (*bu*) require figures on the total length, the length of the socket (head), the width of the shoulder, the width of the feet, sometimes the length and width of the space between the feet, and the weight. "Knife money," especially unique specimens, requires measures of the overall length, the length and width of the handle and the body, the diameter of the terminal ring and its opening, and the weight.[56] Jade *bi* discs, whose central hole (*hao*) is smaller than the solid portion (*rou*), and *huan* discs, of which the opposite is true, require that one record the overall diameter, the width of the *rou*, the diameter of the *hao*, and the thickness.[57] For models in recording such measurements, which are as diverse as the kinds of objects, one can refer to catalogues of bronze and stone, jades, weapons, mirrors, coins, seals, and other objects.

One should photograph the objects, for rubbings and photographs supplement each other. Chinese and Japanese works on antiquarian subjects continue to use both techniques to illustrate objects as well as their inscriptions or motifs.

If one is to make a faithful rubbing, one must study the host closely, carefully analyzing its relief and noting its significant physical and aesthetic features, for once the rubbing paper covers the surface, those features disappear. One should try to predict where problems might occur and visualize how the finished rubbing will turn out. With an eye to absolute fidelity, artisans make experimental rubbings of important objects to determine where the difficulties lie and how best to deal with them.

Readying the rubbing paraphernalia, particularly the paper and ink, is the last consideration before one begins rubbing. Time is an important factor in the process, and one must be able to lay hands quickly on materials and equipment.

SELECTING, FITTING, WETTING, AND LAYING THE PAPER

The first step in the rubbing process is laying the paper on the surface to be copied, as smoothly as possible. First, one must determine what type of rubbing paper will best suit one's purpose. The standard paper for making rubbings is Xuan paper of several weights, but the selection depends on the physical qualities of the host and the type of rubbing that one is making. Steles, because of their outdoor situation, their size, their generally larger and more deeply cut inscriptions, and, with older stones, their roughness of surface, require heavier paper than do small objects with fine inscriptions that one rubs in the studio. Chen Jieqi had this in mind when he observed that the papers of his day were thick and coarse and adequate for rubbing stones, but not of such quality as to allow for the finest effects in rubbing bronzes.[58] For large areas, one should use *Liuji* Xuan paper of slightly heavier weight.[59] The paper, however, should not be too thick, for it will not dry readily, and the fibers should be long so that the paper will soak up water and yet not tear. For smaller areas, one can use heavier *lianshi* paper, and for small articles, thinner *Liuji mianlian* fan paper.[60]

The nature of the relief is also a guide. Stone reliefs range from very fine intaglio inscriptions and pictures through low relief, high relief, and sculpture in the round.[61] For the first two categories, one should choose fine thin paper, such as *mianlian*. *Lianshi* or Xuan papers are satisfactory for low relief, but heavier, good-quality *pi* paper is the preference for the last three categories. Fineness of the characters is also a cardinal factor. Wu Shifen emphasizes this when he suggests that for large steles and large characters one should use fine, good-quality *pi* paper and for small stones and small characters, fine thin *mianlian*.[62] Specifying a local variety, he adds in a note that the fine, white *Shaanxi maotou* paper is good.[63] *Mianlian* almost always is the preferred paper for copying fine line, such as (*Liuji*) *mianlian*, which is for rubbing the extremely fine oracle inscriptions.[64] Specialists at the Historical Museum in Taibei preferred *liansi* (*lianshi*) paper for its thinness, evenness, and luster. It was said to be of two types, one sized with alum (*fan*, *mingfan*) and the other, the preferred type, without. *Liansi* paper, made in Fujian and Jiangxi, was difficult to find in Taiwan at the time, and so they used *mianlian* despite its shortcomings, including irregularities and poorer absorption, requiring *baiji* solution over the entire surface, not just at the edges.

One must select the paper with an eye to the kind of rubbing that one wishes to make. With standard rubbings, the matter is of no great importance, but if one wishes to make special rubbings, such as cicada-wing rubbings (*chanyi ta*[a]), described below, one should use thin, fine *mianlian*.[65] In all cases, one should select paper that is free of blemishes. I shall speak further of paper selection in referring to kinds of objects susceptible to rubbing and several special types of rubbings that one can make.

RELATED CONSIDERATIONS

Despite the expense, one should not be miserly with rubbing paper. It must be large enough to accommodate the main text and headings as well as commentaries, seals, and other trappings of connoisseurship.[66] This especially is so for steles.[67] Bronze vessels also require plenty of paper, with certain classes particularly needful, such as *zun* goblets, *you* wine jars, *jue* wine cups, *jue* wine goblets, *guang* jars, *jia* wine cups, *gu* beakers, and *zhi* tankards.[68] Also demanding larger sheets are *zhong* bells and irregularly shaped *ge* dagger axes, *mao* lance heads (see fig. 6.2), and *qu* halberds.[69] Finally, for the endless variety of small articles, one can prepare a large number of standard sheets, two or three times the size of the object, to allow for colophons, seals, and memorabilia.[70] A second consideration in laying the rubbing paper is orientation of its grain: "It is better for the vein of the paper to run vertically, not horizontally."[71] One also should use the smoother top surface (*zhengmian*).

In rubbing steles, one must cut or shape the rubbing paper to fit the full stone, including blank borders plus a little extra. Larger steles, many of which are several meters high, with widths proportionate, require multiple sheets. The artisan usually starts at the top and proceeds down the stone, laying the lower sheets atop those above, but sometimes the reverse is true. There is similar variation in positioning the papers from right to left or left to right. The preferred method of adding these sheets is to overlap them slightly, about 4 or 5 *fen*, about 1 centimeter, to save paper.[72] One must plan the overlaps carefully so as not to fall on the inscription, especially if the characters are small, and then felt the sheets in the tamping process.[73] The glutinous quality of the ink and the sizing liquid, if one is used, ensure the bond. The felted sheets almost become one, and even if they separate, matching them is easy because of the clear line between the inked and uninked paper.

Some commercial rubbings, especially of large steles, show that the upper sheet was rubbed first, then the lower sheets rubbed separately, with the artisan repeating 5 to 7 centimeters of the higher part of the inscription just rubbed. With the entire inscription copied, the rubber may paste the sheets together in an approximate match. Although easier, and necessary if working conditions are poor, this latter method is less accurate and wastes paper. When one is working outside, especially in rough terrain, precutting the rubbing paper to size saves time at the site and lessens the risk of damaging the paper if there is a wind. Artisans at the Beilin precut their paper.

There often is mention of some types of bronze vessels that present particular challenges in fitting the paper. Among those most often singled out because of their strong curvature or irregular shape are *ding* cauldrons, *pan* basins, *jue* wine goblets, *zhong* bells, and mirrors.

Rubbing *ding* cauldrons and *pan* basins is difficult, especially if they are large and cumbersome. The *Mao Gong ding* and *San shi pan* are named as being especially challenging if one is to avoid creases in laying the paper, and if one cannot do so, one must arrange the paper so that the creases do not fall on the inscriptions (figs. 3.5–3.6).[74] Shallow, and commonly with a low ring foot, *pan* have an interior bottom that slopes gently up and outward to its periphery, at which point it curves sharply upward to form the low sides. Although the exterior is decorated, the interior bottom and sides usually carry the main inscription or decoration and are the primary rubbing focus. The slope

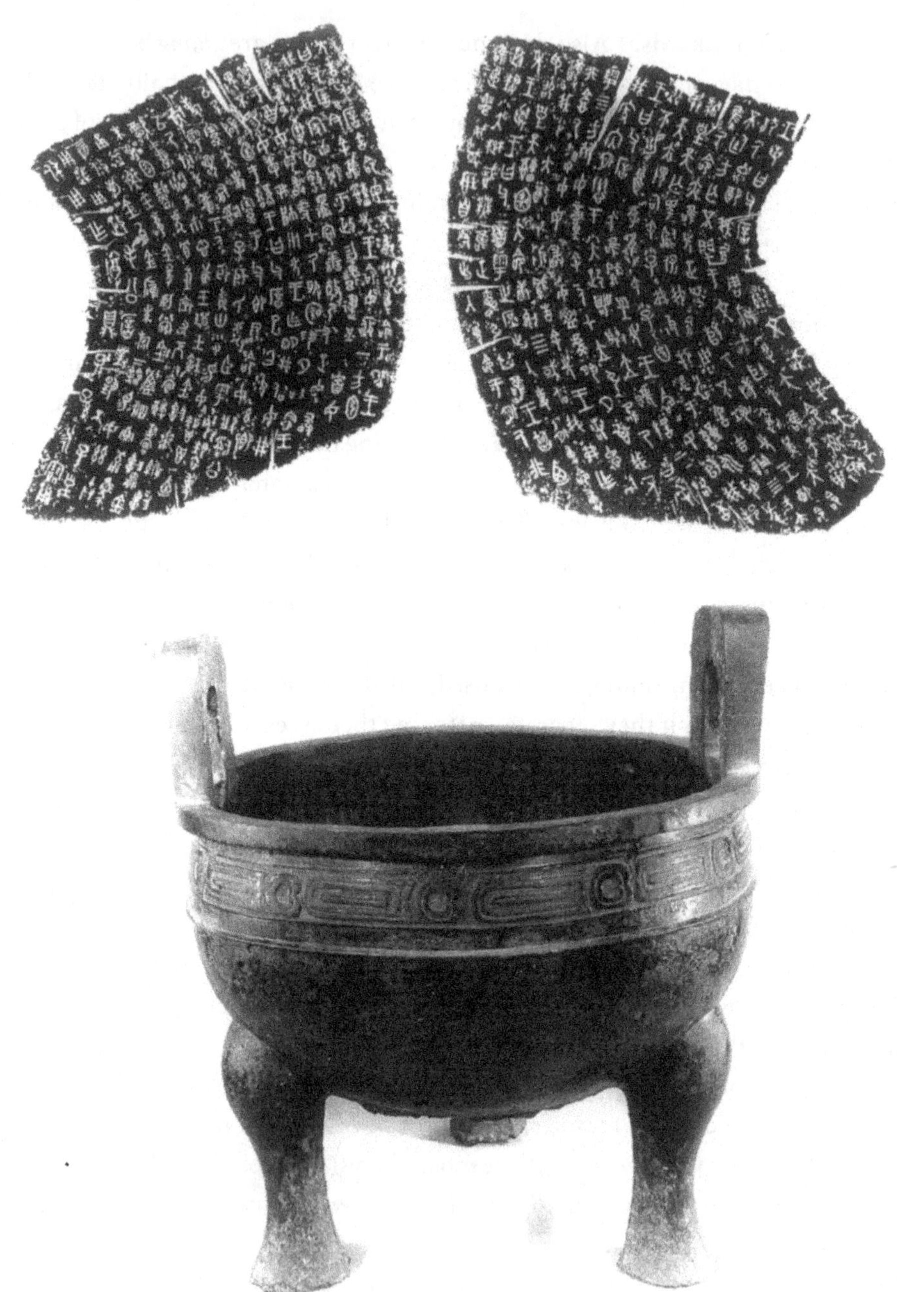

FIG. 3.5. *Mao Gong ding* cauldron (827–782 B.C.E.). Courtesy National Palace Museum, Taibei, Taiwan, Republic of China.

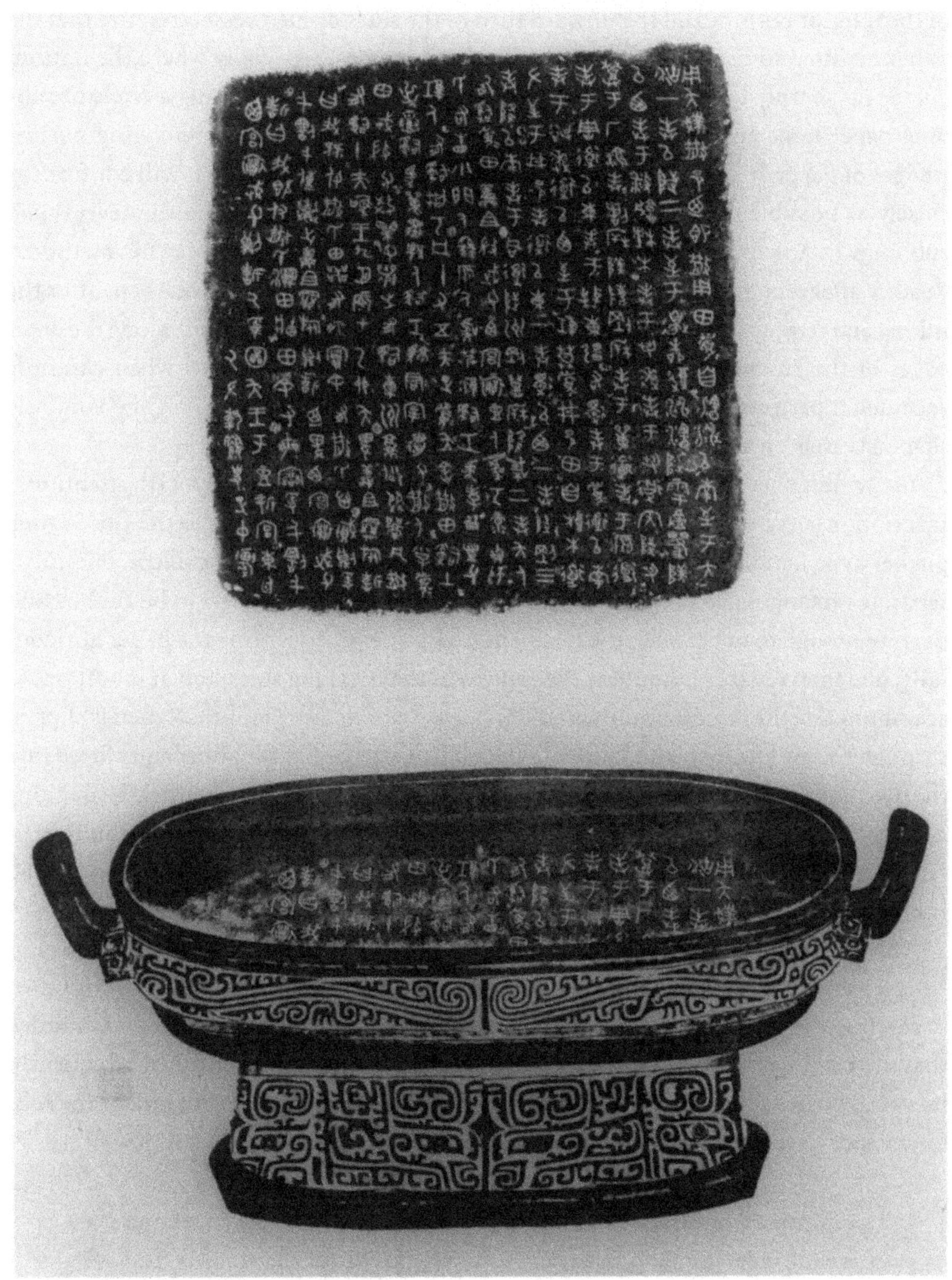

FIG. 3.6. *San shi pan* basin, Western Zhou. Courtesy National Palace Museum, Taibei, Taiwan, Republic of China.

of the interior bottom and the upward turn of the sides of such vessels require that the paper be fitted to lie as flat as possible, without creases, especially where the bottom curves up sharply to form the sides. One accomplishes this by cutting a circle of rubbing paper large enough to fit the interior of the basin and then removing narrow wedges of paper at appropriate points around the perimeter so that it will conform as closely as possible to the interior bottom and sides (fig. 3.5). Among the several *pan* rubbings in *Shang Zhou yiqi tongkao*, one example clearly evidences this method.[75] Readily apparent also are places where the paper creased in laying and then, after the inking and removal, opened out again, showing white "lines" that occur along the outer edges of the rubbing. Although the technique is imperfect at best, when carefully executed it permits copying the relief on the curving interior of the *pan* and similarly shaped vessels on a single sheet.[76]

Jue wine goblets also frequently are mentioned as requiring special attention.[77] Inscriptions occur most often on the exterior, within or contiguous to the close-lying, pitcher-type handle. To capture such an inscription and its flanking decor, one cuts a separate rectangular piece of paper long enough to span the section to be rubbed and narrow enough to fit between the two handle abutments. Orienting the paper horizontally, one then scissors cutouts at the centers of the two long sides, top and bottom, to accommodate the handle abutments. This strip, with its two "mouths," then is slipped through the handle loop and laid onto the body, with the handle abutments fitted into the two mouths. In many cases, the location and shape of the inscription and its flanking decor require that the paper be cut in some other form, such as, commonly an L, ⊦, or H.[78] With the paper cut and fitted, one can proceed with the wetting, tamping, and inking.

The need for cutting and fitting the rubbing paper is not limited to vessels. *Zhong* bells also require prior cutting and fitting, especially with their top handles and rows of side bosses (fig. 3.7).[79] In some cases, these bosses are sufficiently stubby and rounded that the rubbing paper can be laid lightly over them and their tops inked. Frequently, however, bosses project so far or so pointedly that it is necessary to cut and fit the rubbing paper to accommodate them:

> In rubbing *zhong* bells, one first must use [a separate piece of] paper and make [a pattern with] holes [for the bosses], and then slip [this pattern down] over the bosses on the side panels [of the bell]. If the holes are too big, then one must paste paper [around them] and make them smaller. . . . Using this paper pattern, one spreads it on the [more costly] *mianlian* paper, and with a [moistened Chinese] writing brush pokes [corresponding] holes in it. . . . [Finally,] one should record on the paper pattern that it is of such-and-such a *zhong* bell and preserve it.[80] An alternative method, apparently common in Chen's time, was to represent bosses in three-quarter view.[81]

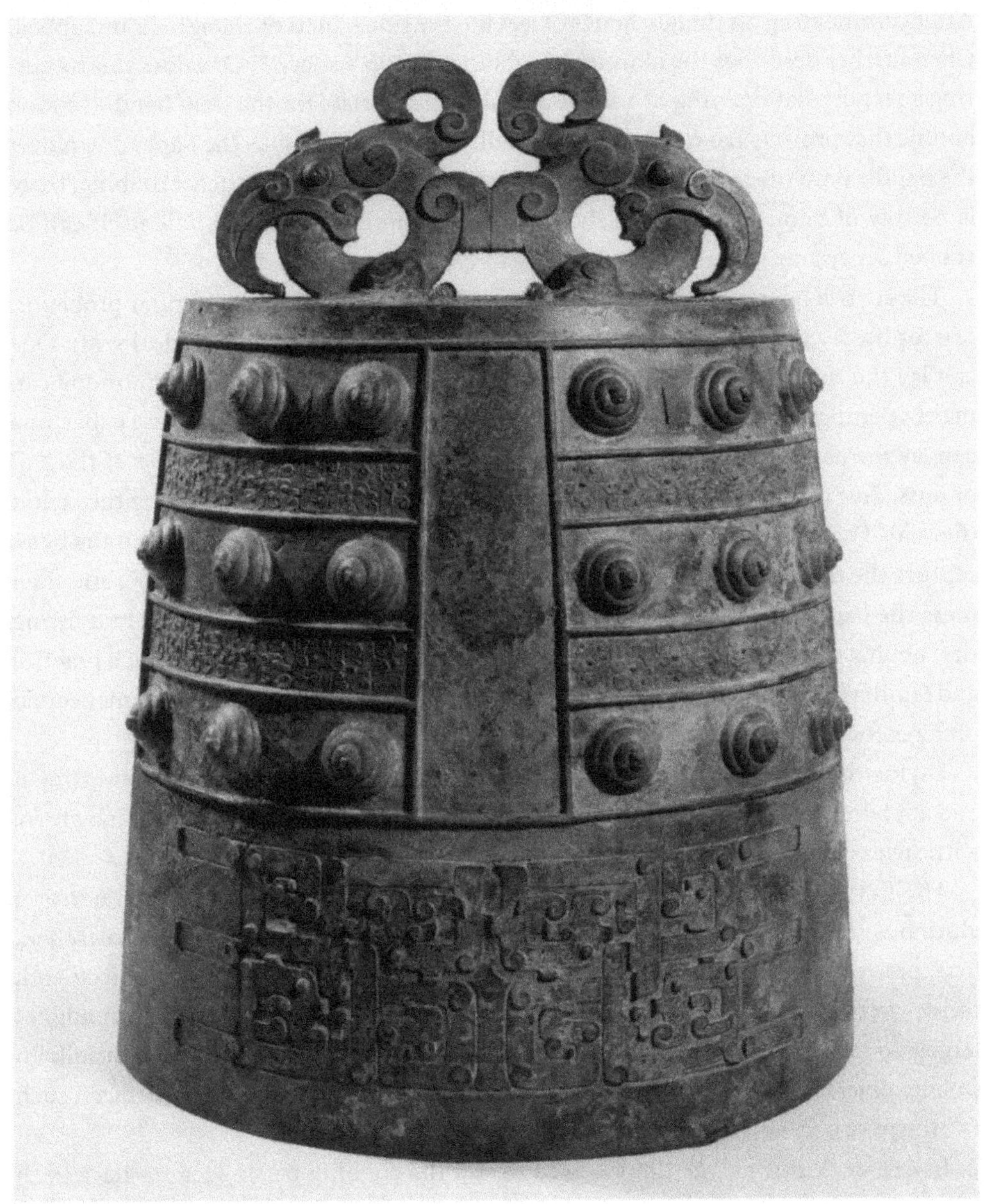

FIG. 3.7. Eastern Zhou *zhong* bell. Freer Gallery of Art, Smithsonian Institution, purchase, F1941.9.

After commenting on the aesthetics of leaving the side panels of *zhong* bells unrubbed, Chen further describes the manner of rubbing the top surface.[82] One does this by cutting a rectangular opening of a shape and size appropriate for the stem handle or loop handle that projects from the top of the bell, and one then drops the paper down over the handle onto the bell and rubs the entire top surface. Without such a rubbing, there is no way of knowing the bell's shape. The sides and top of the handle itself can be rubbed separately.

The central bosses and bails on the backs of bronze mirrors pose similar problems. Mirror bosses generally are low and rounded and are much easier to deal with. One can lay the rubbing paper lightly over the boss or bail and ink the paper, or one can make openings for them.[83] As an alternative to poking a hole in the rubbing paper, one can lay the dry rubbing paper on the mirror, mark the paper at the center of the bail or boss, and make cruciform slits, with their intersection points matching the center (fig. 3.2). The slits allow the artisan to press the rubbing paper down around the boss, capture the relief right up to its base, peel the paper when the inking is done, and then press the paper flat, closing the hole. In all situations that require cutting and fitting the rubbing paper, ingenuity must be partner to skill, and one must have much practice and familiarity with precedent to obtain superior results. Personal taste and intellectual preferences also are factors.

Laying the rubbing paper smoothly on the surface of the object involves wetting it and applying it. Some artisans combine the two steps, while others take them by turn, with steles differing from bronzes and they, from oracle bones.

The first step consists of wetting the rubbing paper with either plain water or a glutinous size, with three different approaches. In order of commonness, these are, first, prewetting the paper; second, wetting as it hangs or lies on the dry object; and, third, wetting the object and laying the dry paper on it. The first approach applies largely to steles and other large flat objects, the second and third, more especially to smaller objects, such as oracle bones, and those with irregular shapes or surfaces, such as bronze vessels and rough stones.

In earlier centuries, the liquids used to wet the rubbing paper seem to have been either clear water or, when a size was required, rice water, both still used today.[84] The past century or so has seen the increasing use of *baiji* as a glutinous additive. Today, *baiji* commonly is used in rubbing smaller objects, such as small bronze sculptures, objects with smooth or glossy surfaces, and those with fine, shallow inscriptions, such as oracle bones. A glutinous size sometimes is used supplementally with larger objects, such as steles.[85]

The strength of the solution depends on the substance of the host, its type, the subject matter, the kind of rubbing desired, and the working conditions. Objects with hard, smooth, glossy surfaces, such as jade, glass, and porcelain, require heavier applications of *baiji*.[86] One also must adjust the strength to compensate for adverse atmospheric conditions. Outside, the sun, the wind, and low humidity require stronger size or covering the paper to prevent premature drying and lifting. Inside work may call for lower heat, higher humidity, or covering. One also has to consider the type of rubbing that one is making. Quality rubbings (*jingta*), with their superior workmanship, require longer to make and demand a heavier *baiji* size so that the paper does not pull away from the relief too soon.[87] Similarly, black-gold rubbings (*wujin ta*), characterized by thickly laid, glossy ink, also require heavier gluten.[88] If one needs to make additional applications, one should add size gradually rather than in one strong and possibly adhesive application.

Once decided on the type and amount of the wetting liquid, one further must determine how to apply the rubbing paper, with three approaches common. First, the worker can premeasure, precut, prefold, and prewet the dry paper and apply it, unfolding it onto the surface, as in hanging wallpaper (fig. 3.8).[89] This approach is most suitable for large flat surfaces, such as steles. It has the advantages that, when properly done, it facilitates managing the paper, distributes the liquid evenly, and prevents it from drying too quickly. The method is particularly useful in controlling the paper while working on large surfaces, or in unfavorable working conditions. Second, the rubber can apply the paper in the form of a dry, open sheet and then wet it as it lies on the surface. This method, usable both for steles and for smaller objects, such as bronze mirrors, jades, and oracle bones (fig. 3.9), is easier to use and lessens the danger of tearing the paper. Third, one can wet the object and then apply the dry open sheet, wetting it further as necessary (fig. 3.10). This last approach is usable both for steles and for other objects.

Chen Jieqi comments on the first two approaches:

> Formerly they used clear water on the [rubbing] paper, folded it, wet it thoroughly, blew it open, laid it on [the surface being copied], and the rubbing could be done quickly, and the paper, easily lifted off. Rubbing paper with water put on [after the paper is laid] is not easy to lift off, and moreover, there is water in the [intaglio] characters, and the [degree] of dryness and wetness of each is uneven.[90]

Stanley and Wang Chi-chen also specify prewetting the paper, the former recommending seaweed solution, and the latter, "previously moistened" paper, wet with clear water only, "not . . . with any sizing to make it adhere to the stone."[91] Beilin artisans use this method to rub steles, readying small stacks of precut, prefolded, and prewetted paper beforehand (fig. 2.4).

As with every trade, there are tricks to folding and wetting the rubbing paper, which when dry is quite strong but when wet is easily torn. In the first step, the artisan cuts

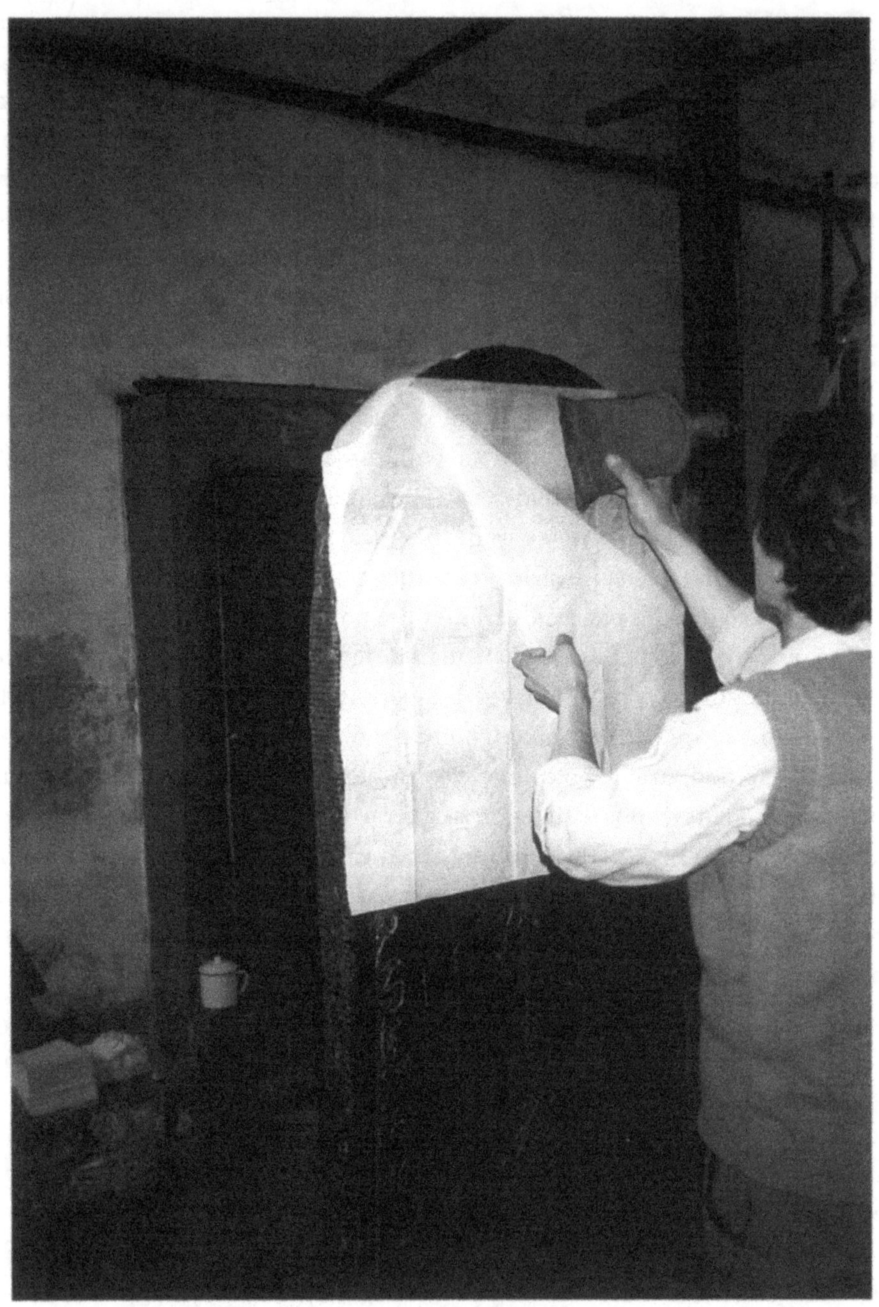

Fig. 3.8. Unfolding and smoothing prewetted paper. Xi'an Beilin Museum, 1987. Photograph by the author.

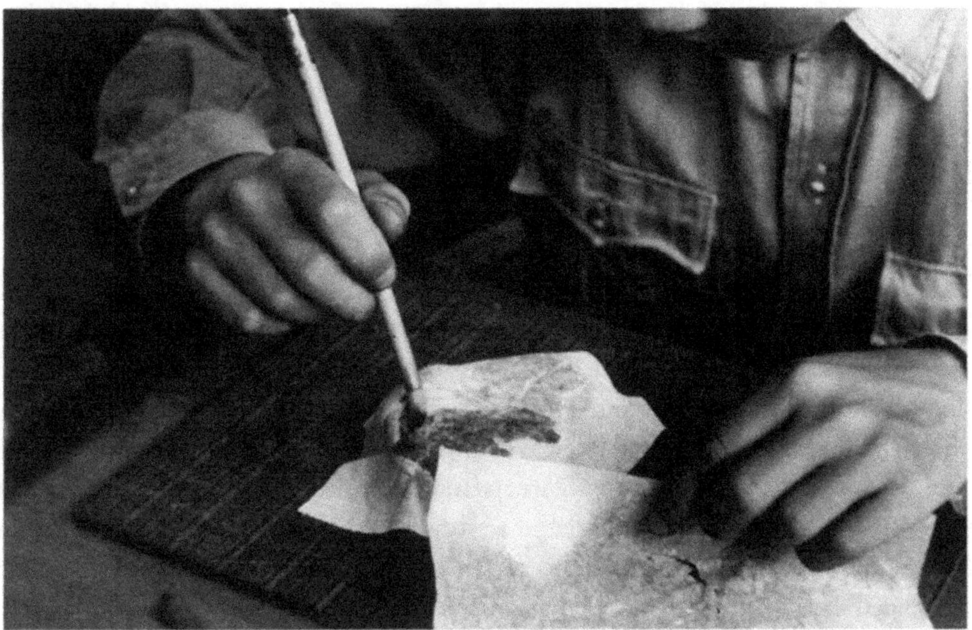

Fig. 3.9. Applying dry rubbing paper to an oracle bone, then wetting it. Institute of History and Philology, Academia Sincia, Taiwan, 1960. Photograph by the author.

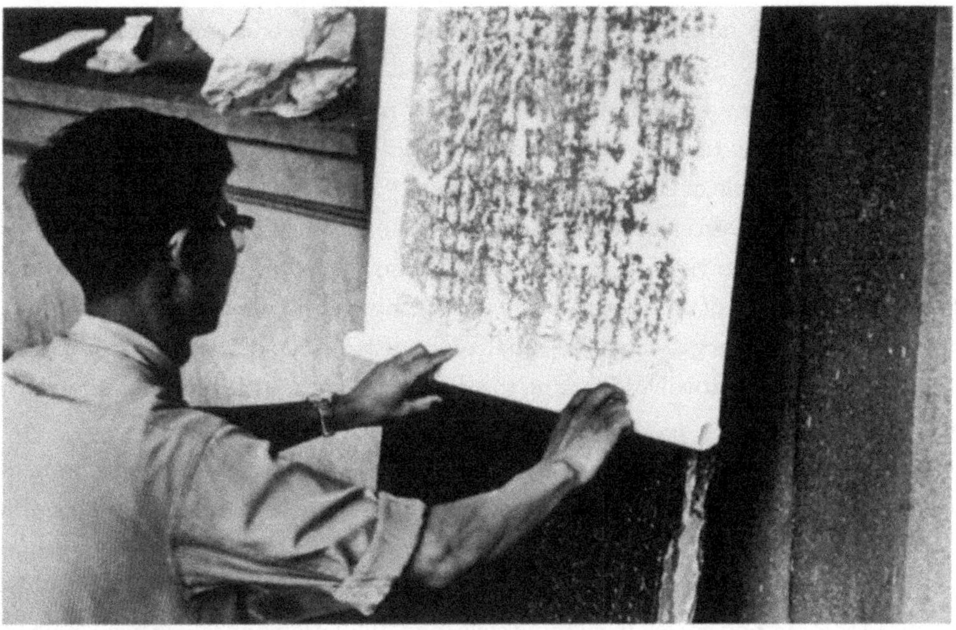

Fig. 3.10. Wetting a stele before laying the paper. National Historical Museum, Taibei, Taiwan, 1960. Photograph by the author.

the requisite number of sheets of dry rubbing paper to fit the stone and folds each in a prescribed pattern. Fold one carries the bottom of the long sheet up to about 1.5 centimeters from the top, and the fold is lightly creased. Fold two again carries the bottom of the once-folded sheet up to 1.5 centimeters of the previous edge, and the second fold is creased. Fold three repeats the process, so that the thrice-folded sheet now is wide and narrow. Fold four then carries the left end of this folded sheet to within 1.5 centimeters of the right edge. The product of this process is a packet of square folded sheets.

In the second step, the artisan wets the folded papers with plain water, by turns dipping the four edges of the folded sheets in a container of warm water, wetting them about 1–2 centimeters all around, allowing the moisture to diffuse slowly and evenly through the sheets. In rubbing steles, Wu Shifen varies the method by dampening the folded paper with a wet hand towel, as also does Jiang Xuanyi, while Chen Jieqi and Rong Geng merely refer to folding and wetting the rubbing paper.[92] These methods allow a moderate amount of water to seep by osmosis gradually and evenly through the folded sheets. The paper should be damp, but not wet, for then it is very difficult to open it without tearing it.

The artisan then stacks these prewetted sheets for use, bundling them in a damp cloth or plastic sheet to prevent premature, uneven drying. Apart from providing even distribution of moisture, the method requires less water and enables the rubber to spend less time tamping. One felts on additional sheets of prewetted paper as needed.

There are many personal variations on this basic method. Orient Lee (Lee Tung-fang) described a variation that as a boy he saw employed in rubbing stone-cut poems of Su Dongpo at the Temple of Confucius in Yangzhou.[93] The artisan first washed the stone and dried it with a clean cloth. He then laid down a dampened clean white cotton cloth slightly larger than the rubbing paper, laid the rubbing paper on it, and in turn covered it with another piece of dampened cloth, sandwiching it. Finally, he gently patted the top cloth to remove excess water and equalize the distribution of that which remained. Yet another variation involves hanging the dry paper on the stele and then pressing a wet cloth against it.

Rong Geng recommends the second method of wetting the paper in rubbing bronzes, common in his time. Having described making *baiji* gluten, he states that one "lays the paper on the object, one dips a brush into the *baiji* solution, spreads it on the paper, and uses a damp towel to press it down."[94] Artisans at Academia Sinica, in Taiwan, practiced this method as well in rubbing steles and divination bones, as Sueji Umehara did in rubbing a jade *bi* disc and a Tang mirror at his home in Kyoto (February 1960), cutting the paper to fit the objects, so as not to waste the fine, thirty-year-old paper that he had bought years earlier in Shanghai, laying it dry, and then brushing on water.

Jun Yu similarly recommends first laying and then wetting the paper, emphasizing that in laying the rubbing paper on smooth, glossy jade objects one must use a stronger *baiji* solution to prevent the paper from lifting.[95] Zhang Xuan also followed this approach.[96] One must be careful not to use so much *baiji* that the rubbing paper sticks to the object, and so it sometimes is better to use plain water if one needs to rewet the paper. If one wets the paper after it is in position, one should use a brush with soft bristles and work from the center of the object toward the edges to release air bubbles and prevent wrinkling.

Other artisans use the third approach, prewetting the surface of the stele, dousing it and cleaning it at the same time. Some artisans additionally wet the cleaned stone with *baiji* solution.[97] With the stone wet, they apply the dry rubbing paper to the top of the stone, unroll it down the stone, brush it smooth as it unrolls to release air bubbles, and then wet the paper further with a wet towel or a brush as needed. One specialist at Academia Sinica also used the method in rubbing interior inscriptions on the ceremonial bronzes—wetting the bronze with *baiji*, laying the rubbing paper, tamping it with a human-hair brush and intermediate sheet, and then inking the inscription.[98]

The size and shape of the object and the nature of the working situation also determine whether to prewet or postwet the paper. In rubbing a small, flat object in the studio, it is simpler to lay on the dry sheet and wet it lightly, taking care not to flood the inscription or design, while for a large stele done outside when there is a breeze, one may find it more convenient to prefold and prewet the sheet, unfolding it as one works.

Judging from majority opinion, with practice at the Beilin as an example, the best tradition favors prewetting over postwetting, especially for steles, and frowns on dousing the stone. Such a procedure, however, is not without its appreciable difficulties, for Asian papers are fragile when wet. This particularly obtains with very thin papers and papers of lesser quality, and so great care is requisite in opening out the folded, wetted large sheets.[99] Keeping in mind the old saw "better safe than sorry," the beginner is well advised to lay the dry rubbing paper smoothly on the dry object and judiciously wet it with a soft brush. That method is preferable to first wetting the object, for it is easier to adjust the rubbing paper on the dry object, and there is less likelihood of flooding the inscription or design.

The second step in laying, often combined with wetting, is actually applying the rubbing paper. Allowing for the real difficulties that stem from their monumental size and outdoor locations, the papering of standard steles is straightforward. The ease and speed with which professional artisans work is deceptive, however. With a medium-size stele as the first example, and assuming that one uses one of the two preferred methods, the procedure is as follows.

In executing the first approach, the artisan blows open the first fold of the premeasured, precut, prefolded, and prewetted rubbing paper, positioning it straight along the top edge of the stone, laying it against the stele so that the corner of the folded paper (the center of the sheet in its unfolded state) is at the center of the stone, and tacking it down by tamping. He then unfolds the paper down the stone, brushing it from the center out, smoothing it onto the surface with a soft, long-haired brush in a motion used in writing the Chinese character *ren*, "human." If wrinkles or bubbles persist, one must gently lift the sheet, float it like a bedsheet, and reposition it. When certain that the paper hangs straight, free of wrinkles and bubbles, the artisan tamps the moist rubbing paper with a handled coir brush (fig. 4.2), periodically using the smoothing brush. When the size of the stele requires, one felts on additional prewetted sheets. When the need to conserve paper dictates, the artisan felts on smaller pieces of paper, using a wooden mallet and felt pad.

If the paper begins to lift, one can remoisten it with a damp towel or a soft brush while not breaking the flow of the process.[100] One also can drape a lightly dampened cloth or a thin sheet of plastic over a portion of the surface to prevent premature drying.

In the second approach, the artisan measures the rubbing paper and cuts it to size, with extra space for colophons and seals, preparing additional sheets if the size of the stone dictates. One puts the full sheet of rubbing paper to the dry stone, tacking it down along the top edge with rice water, rice paste, or *baiji*. It is important to hang it straight, for if one starts just a tad crooked at the top, the paper is very off at the bottom, and adjusting the wet paper can be challenging. Then, using a soft brush or a lightly wetted hand towel, the rubber moistens the paper with clear water or a glutinous additive.[101] The procedure then follows that used in the first approach. Applying the paper dry, and then wetting it, works better in rubbing stones whose surfaces are irregular, as from spalling. One must use whatever works to capture the inscription or design, with adaptability a key to success.

For the third approach, one prewets the stone and then lays on the dry paper, wetting it further, as necessary, with toweling or a sponge. Artisans may douse a stele with a bucket of water, a procedure that is not recommended, for the water fills the intaglio or cracked areas of the stone, causing the subsequent inking to bleed. The same situation will occur if one washes the stele beforehand but does not dry it carefully, and this is said to be a problem particularly with Xuan paper.[102] Excess water also adds to the weight of the rubbing paper, increasing the likelihood of tearing. It is helpful, especially if one is working outside in low humidity or wind, to tack down the edges, especially the top edge, of the rubbing paper with rice water, rice paste, or *baiji*.[103] All are pure, with no chemicals, and so protect both the stone and the paper. One also can use a dab of ink, which contains glue, but such a practice can result in a fuzzy rubbing, especially if the characters are fine.[104] Ink also penetrates the paper and blackens the stone, but as the most frequently rubbed stones are black anyway from centuries of rubbing, the additional dabs are of little consequence.

Along with hanging the paper straight, one also should attend to irregularities in the paper, such as larger fibers, and adjust the paper so that they do not lie atop important inscriptions or designs. Subsequent inking highlights such irregularities and mars the rubbing.

Next, one lightly brushes out the wetted paper on the surface of the stele, using a soft coir or hair brush made of presoftened natural bristles that will not abrade or tear the delicate wet rubbing paper.[105] Some artisans use a bunched towel for initially pressing the paper against the stone and working out the air bubbles. This aspect of the process is particularly important and must be carried out with great care so that the paper lies smooth and free of wrinkles. Generally, one brushing will do to place the paper in contact with the stone and its inscription, at least an inscription with large characters.[106] The recommended pattern is to start brushing from the top center of the stone, with the right hand wielding the brush and the left hand holding the lower part of the paper slightly away from the surface of the stele to prevent its prematurely being drawn to the stone. One then proceeds down the stele, moving from side to side, and from the center outward to the right and left sides as one goes, working air bubbles outward to the edges of the stone.[107] If not released, the bubbles will be pressed flat in the tamping, forming wrinkles that the inking will highlight. If the stone is especially broad, two people can brush at the same time, coordinating their movements.[108] In brushing and smoothing, one must strike a balance, brushing firmly enough, even holding the brush with both hands for greater strength, but not brushing so vigorously as to tear the wet rubbing paper, especially where the stone is uneven.[109] One also must work quickly, brushing on the paper thoroughly before it dries and lifts.

In some situations, especially with relief, a wad of absorbent toweling substitutes for a brush. Used with a gentle rolling motion, toweling molds the paper around the relief, works the bubbles outward to the edges of the stone, and absorbs excess moisture. One also may eliminate bubbles and wrinkles by carefully lifting and adjusting the paper.[110]

When the rubbing paper is brushed smooth on the surface, one can secure it to the edges of the stone by wetting it with glutinous size and tamping it with a small mallet used with an intermediate piece of clean white felt or similar soft, absorbent material (figs. 2.4, 4.3).[111] Next, one should use "one brush" of rice water or *baiji* solution over the smoothed rubbing paper to help hold it to the stone.[112] The preference for clear water or rice water in rubbing steles stems both from tradition and from the greater expense of *baiji*. In laying paper on high-relief or rough stone sculptures, clear water can be insufficient to hold the paper, and one should use *baiji*. Finally, in the brushing process, especially for large, deeply cut characters, one can protect the delicate wet rubbing paper by interposing between it and the brush or toweling a dry sheet of less expensive strike-stele paper, such as *maotai*.[113]

This account applies to laying the open, dry sheet of paper on the stone, but essentially the same method is used if one elects to prefold and prewet the rubbing paper, unfolding it down the stele.[114] The description of laying the paper applies especially to steles that are in good condition, regular in form, even of surface, with inscriptions of medium or large line.

The challenge of laying the paper is difficult enough on a flat stele. As noted above, it becomes much more so with the strongly curved surfaces that characterize many ancient bronzes, such as round-bellied *ding* cauldrons and *lei* and *hu* jars.[115] The difficulty in adjusting the flat sheet of rubbing paper to the curved surface of bronzes shows clearly in the inked creases that mark many rubbings of these types of vessels.

Chen Jieqi notes that the deep, rounded interior of *ding* cauldrons is particularly troublesome in laying the paper so that wrinkles and creases do not fall on the inscription.[116] The classic example is the *Mao Gong ding* cauldron (fig. 3.5), the rubbing of which is particularly demanding because of its strong curvature and its lengthy interior inscription of 497 characters. Rong Geng expands on Chen:

> The *Mao Gong ding* cauldron is large, the characters [on the curved inside] are numerous, and so laying the paper is very difficult. Mr. Chen [with great skill,] used [only] two sheets of paper to make a rubbing, and with some adjustment [of the paper he] was able to cause the creases not [to fall] on the characters. . . . [Viceroy] Duanfang's rubbing [of the same vessel] using four sheets [instead of two] is [a case of] the difficult and the easy being widely separated, [for using two sheets of paper and dividing the inscription in half vertically requires much more skill than does using four sheets and dividing it in quarters].[117]

Liu Yuanjian, at the Institute of History and Philology in Taiwan, made rubbings of the famous inscription. His method was to wet the vessel interior with *baiji* solution and then lay the paper dry, using both two and four sheets.

The *Mao Gong ding* is not the only vessel specifically named as being particularly challenging, for "of vessels that are difficult to rub, none exceeds the two *Qi Hou lei* jars."[118] Inscriptions on *lei* jars commonly are on the inside of the mouth, which curves strongly in both horizontal and vertical planes and so can be very troublesome in both the laying and inking stages. Chen advises dealing with the curving surfaces of the jars by not rubbing the middle lines of the inscription, by adjusting the paper to make as good a rubbing as possible, and then by going back and additionally rubbing the individual lines one by one to copy the inscription, the essential consideration.[119] The goal is to capture the inscriptions with the fewest sheets. The *San pan* or *San shi pan*, the San clan *pan* vessel, whose inscription documents a Shang-dynasty border dispute, is a further example of an inscription that is difficult to rub on a single sheet, with its curving interior and its long inscription, nineteen lines and 348 characters (fig. 3.6).

Such difficult cases aside, the method of laying the rubbing paper on the surfaces of bronze vessels is the same as that used in putting paper to steles. Being curved and marked by finer detail, however, bronzes require thinner and better paper, such as *mianlian*, and more skill and care, especially in cutting and fitting. Despite their odd shapes and great weight, however, bronzes can be rubbed indoors. There also is not a need for such large sheets of paper, or for prefolding and prewetting the paper. It is common to lay the paper on the bronze dry, wet it with a brush dipped in *baiji* solution, and press it down with a damp towel or, for fine detail, a cotton pad. As the area covered generally is small compared with steles, there seldom is need for lapping or rewetting the rubbing paper, but if there is need to do so, one can use a fine brush or an atomizer. To reach the working surface down inside deep-bodied vessels such as *hu* vases, one attaches a handle to the smoothing brush.[120]

Steles and bronze vessels represent the main challenges in laying the rubbing paper, but other situations also can be demanding, such as "cliff smoothings," with their religious texts and poetic and calligraphic compositions (plate 3, fig. 1.11). The sites commonly are in exposed and wild places difficult of access, and the rock faces are characterized by expansive, uneven, and often deteriorated surfaces, and so artisans spread the open sheets of paper on the rock surface, with others to help with large inscriptions. Dabbing with a damp towel often is preferable to using a brush for wetting and pressing the paper onto the irregular surface. With the paper laid, one brushes it lightly to ensure contact and quickly applies the ink to avoid the challenges of wind and sun. The inking technique, described in chapter 4, can differ from that used in rubbing steles and bronzes.

Other types of objects sometimes present novel challenges but generally are less troublesome to rub. Small articles, such as inscribed and decorated jades, coins, pottery, shell, and ivory and bone, generally manifest finer line and smaller detail and so require finer and thinner paper, such as *mianlian* or *liansi* (*lianshi*). Very small objects, such as tiny fragments of pottery or bone, may require wrapping the rubbing paper around the piece or supporting it on a foundation. Artisans at the Institute of History and Philology cut and fitted the paper and then wet it as it lay on the bone or shell. *Baiji* commonly is used to size the paper in rubbing small objects, and one applies the solution and smooths the paper with a small, fine, soft-brush Chinese brush pen, its pointed tip cut blunt (fig. 3.9).[121] A bit of cotton also can be used initially to press the paper down and release air bubbles, although one must be watchful not to leave fibers on the paper. In smoothing the paper on fragile surfaces, such as old jade and oracle bones, one must be very careful not to use undue pressure, lest one break the piece.

Smooth, glossy surfaces, such as those that mark jade, glass, and porcelain, require a heavier concentration of *baiji*. For soft, friable surfaces, such as plaster, that tend to disintegrate when wet, one must be particularly careful in wetting, laying, and manipulating the paper. Smaller inscribed or decorated objects also may have curving or irregular surfaces. Oracle inscriptions often occur on uneven, curving joints of bones, and if the thin paper cannot be laid without creases, it must be adjusted so that the wrinkles fall on uninscribed areas.[122] Whatever the object being rubbed, the goal in laying the paper remains the same: to apply it over the surface smoothly and tightly, with an even an amount of moisture.

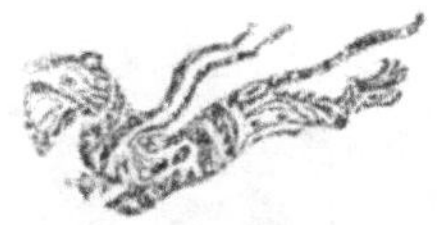

4 / Gentler Still

WHEN the wet rubbing paper is smooth and wrinkle-free on the surface of the object, one presses gently with a clean cotton cloth to achieve further contact between paper and object. One also can use intermediate absorbent paper (*xishui zhi*) to tighten contact and draw out excess moisture.[1] One then is ready for the tamping.

The primary function of tamping, arguably the most important phase of the rubbing process, is to place the rubbing paper into tight apposition with the surface of the object so that the inked impression will be fully faithful. Fidelity is important, not only for faithful transmission of the intellectual and aesthetic content but also for connoisseurship, especially dating. Secondary to this appositive function is the drying effect. Ink cannot be laid on until the rubbing paper is sufficiently dry to prevent bleeding, a state that varies with the fineness of the line and moistness of the ink.

Summarizing these two related functions in rubbing bronzes, Rong Geng advises that "next, spread [a sheet of] dry [liner] paper on the [wet rubbing] paper, [and], using a palm-fiber brush or a brush of human hair, strike it lightly, on one hand, pressing the paper into the [intaglio] characters and, on the other, causing it to dry quickly."[2] One tamps with a variety of materials and tools, including intermediate papers, towels, felt rolls, brushes, mallets and pads, and needles.

When the wet rubbing paper is smooth and in light contact with the object, the rubber may interpose a second sheet between the tamping brush and the rubbing paper. This sheet goes by the generic names of "liner paper" (*chen zhi*) and "strike-stele paper" (*qiaobei zhi*). For steles and larger objects, it generally is of a heavier and coarser grade than that used to make the rubbing. For smaller objects and fine line, it may be scraps of thin self paper (fig. 4.1).

This intermediate sheet serves several purposes. First, it absorbs excess moisture from the wet rubbing paper.[3] Second, it helps to press the rubbing paper into fine intaglio line. Third, where the relief is greater than average, the extra layer cushions the tamping, diffuses pressure, and eases strain on the rubbing paper. Fourth, it catches hairs that fall from the tamping brush and would mar the inking. The need for the absorptive function varies, depending on the levels of temperature and humidity and on the method the rubber uses to wet the rubbing paper. Generally, there will be less

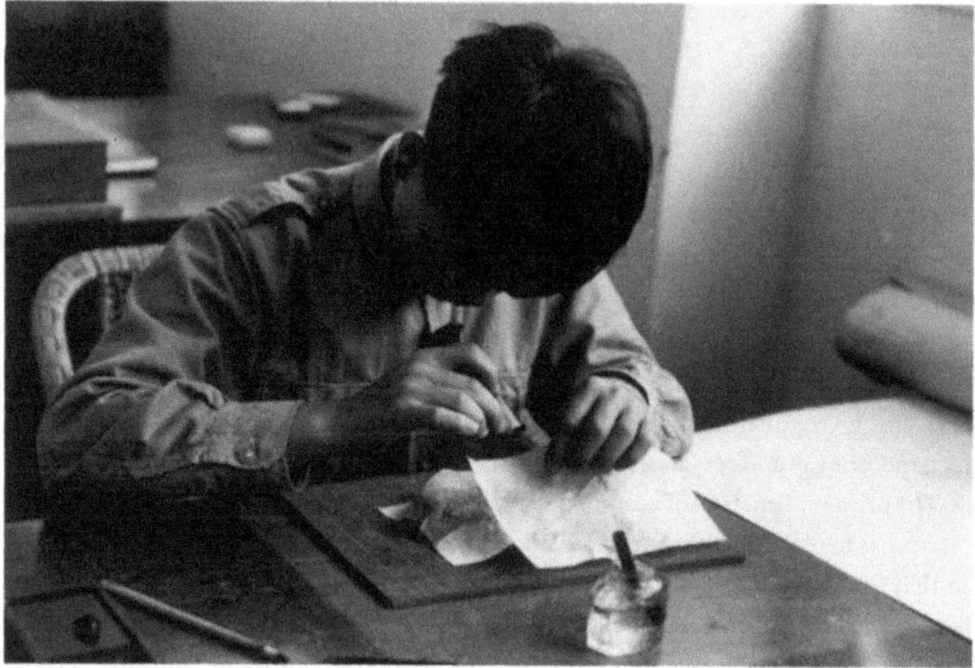

FIG. 4.1. Using intermediate paper in tamping paper on an oracle bone. Institute of History and Philology, Academia Sinica, Taiwan, 1960. Photograph by the author.

need for absorptive paper if one prewets the paper rather than wetting the object beforehand or wetting the rubbing paper after it is on the object.

The intermediate paper is useful for rubbing pictorial reliefs as well as smaller objects, with two layers for greater absorption and cushioning.[4] If the paper becomes wet, one must replace it. If it sticks to the sized rubbing paper, one can tamp less firmly and jiggle it as one tamps, holding the paper with one's left hand and tamping with the right. One should use ever finer cushioning paper as the rubbing paper dries, to deal more effectively with fine detail.

Initial smoothing with the soft coir brush is insufficient to press the paper into tight contact with the relief, and one must use other tools. In former times, rubbers used columnar rolls of fine white felt, stiffened with bronze crossbow bolts, to tamp the paper, especially in rubbing the ancient bronzes. In more recent times they have used a coir tiger (*zong laohu*), similar in form but made of palm fiber bound with cord or wire (see fig. 2.5). The brushes vary with the substance of the host, its type and size, the nature of relief, and its condition, and they are used especially in studio work.

For small, delicate cultural objects, artisans make smaller versions from human hair wrapped with cord (figs. 2.5 and 4.1). These smaller versions are more effective for tamping the paper into fine line, such as that on Shang oracle bones and hairpins, early

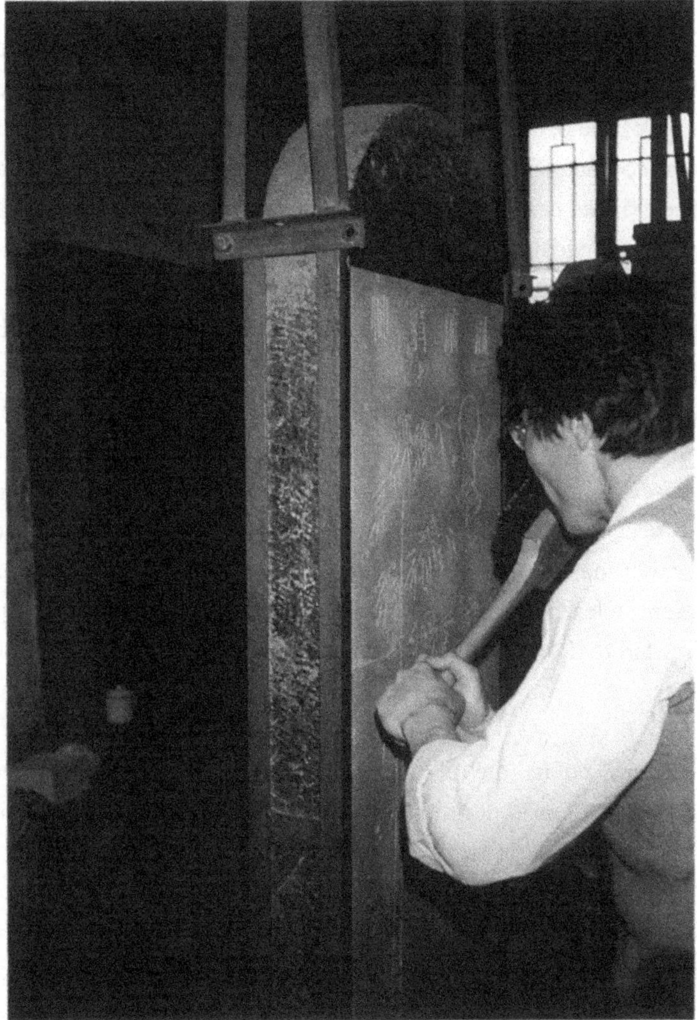

FIG. 4.2. Tamping with a handled brush. Xi'an Beilin Museum, 1987. Photograph by the author.

jades, and on later inkstones and mirrors. The human-hair versions also are safer to use on fragile objects. For massive steles, artisans commonly employ a handled coir-fiber brush, which they wield with surprising vigor, often using both hands for greater force (fig. 4.2). The choice of brush also depends on the type and weight of the rubbing paper. Coir tigers are not recommended for deep intaglio line or relief, given the greater risk of tearing the paper.[5]

The role of the cushioning paper is important in using a tamping brush, for without it, three harmful results can occur. First, the rubbing paper can wear through, exposing the object, risking damage to the inscription or design, and necessitating a patch. Second, the tamping can abrade the rubbing paper, creating a fuzzy surface that precludes achieving a crisp line in the inking—a particular concern with fine, shallow line. Third, too much tamping may paste the paper to the object if one uses a glutinous size.

The function of the brushes, as with all the tamping tools, is to place the rubbing paper into tight contact with the relief. One uses the brush, properly made and with the ends of the bristles carefully softened, to tamp the paper into intaglio line. The tamping should be vertical, to lessen the abrading effect, and one may need to provide extra tamping where fineness or complexity of the line requires.

Mallets used with felt or wool pads are common tamping tools, especially in rubbing steles, with both mallets and pads varying in size, depending on the bulk of the object and the nature and size of the line (fig. 4.3). Mallet and pad are effective in capturing fine, shallow line.[6] Pads also are helpful in spreading the impact of the mallet in rubbing deeper inscriptions, lessening the risk of stretching the wet paper beyond its limits. Care is necessary, for if the pad is too thin and the pounding too heavy, the rubbing paper will mash or tear. One also has to be watchful not to damage the host, especially ancient steles, many of which, millennia old, are cracked or spalling, in which cases one is limited to lightly brushing on the paper.[7] The proper use of the mallet and felt is as follows:

> Taking advantage of its [the rubbing paper's] still being moist, use the left hand to hold the fine felt [pad], place it on the rubbing paper, and with the right hand use the mallet and evenly tamp it. First, tamp the [blank] upper part [of the stone, and] then extend to [the parts with] the inscription or design. One certainly should not tamp [randomly] once in this place, [then] once on that edge, then move from the inscription to the [uninscribed] border. Rather, [one should] tamp everywhere in sequence. Regardless of whether the various areas have inscriptions or not, one must tamp them all equally. In cases where the inscription or design is fine, one can do a little extra light tamping, but if one tamps only the fine parts, then the four edges and the corners of the paper prematurely will dry and lift off the stone.[8]

One can use a loose pad to press the paper into intaglio line or around the relief, especially for small, delicate objects, fine detail on larger objects, friable surfaces, or relief.

Despite the comment by Chen Jieqi that using a felt roll no longer was in vogue, Jiang recommends one, minus the bronze crossbow bolt, for tamping small, extremely thin, or fragile objects:[9] "If the lines are fine and in high relief, and the depressed spaces are correspondingly large, it may be necessary to use a pad moistened with water to dab the lines, to bring them out instead of using a stiff brush to force the paper to follow the depressed surface."[10] Such pads should be loose rather than compact, fashioned of

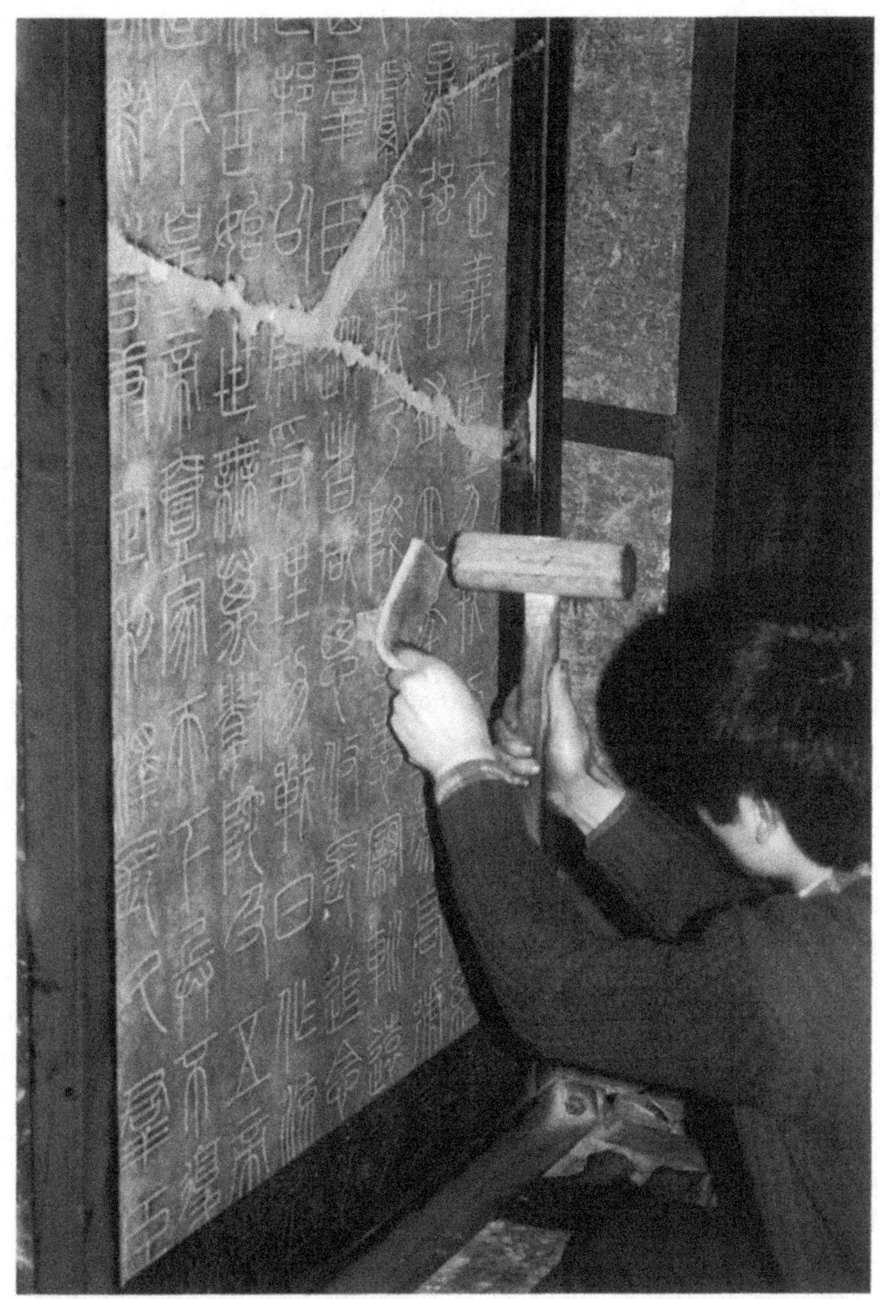

FIG. 4.3. Tamping with mallet and pad. Xi'an, Beilin, 1993. Photograph by the author.

a piece of *ling* or *chou* silk of appropriate size and shape within which one wraps cotton waste; one also can use a clean dry mushroom dabber of the kind used for inking.[11] Jiang specifies the types of relief for which such wads are most useful, including various forms of low and high relief, and sculpture in the round. One should use a light touch, gently pressing the rubbing paper against the relief so that the paper does not break in conforming to concavities and convexities. Used with a gentle but firm hand and a dabbing or slightly rolling motion, toweling serves to press the paper down around the relief and absorb excess moisture. For fine work, one can use a small wad of clean cheesecloth or cotton. Such a technique neither suffices for very fine work nor guarantees the sharpness of line achieved by patient tamping with brush and protective paper but is useful for certain types of relief.

In places difficult of access, one can modify the brushes and pads. In tamping the rubbing paper into inscriptions cast on the interior bottoms of deep-bellied *you* wine jars, one must use a long, straight coir-fiber tamping brush or a shorter one inserted into a bamboo tube; in pressing the paper into inscriptions or designs under pitcher-type handles of *jue* wine cups, one can hold a small cotton ball with long-nosed pliers and work at right angles.[12] As in every aspect of rubbing, ingenuity is a prime requisite.

In some situations, these tamping methods may be insufficient to press the paper down into very fine line, such as incised shell-and-bone inscriptions. When the lines of such inscriptions are not fully clear after tamping by usual methods, one further can "walk the needle," described earlier.[13]

Several general comments on tamping are in order. First, one should give equal consideration to all parts of the relief, tamping evenly across the entire surface, regardless of whether it carries an inscription or design. Those new to rubbing often concentrate on the inscribed or decorated areas, paying less attention to plain areas, with two dismaying results: the rubbing paper may pull away prematurely from the insufficiently tamped areas; and the liner paper will draw more moisture from the heavily tamped areas, which then will be dry enough for inking before the less heavily tamped areas are. The rubber may try to save time and materials by rewetting and retamping the unruly parts of the paper, but even if one is successful, one destroys the unity of the work.[14] Second, one should tamp from the center outward, working unwanted wrinkles and air bubbles to the edges. Third, one should shift the liner paper as one tamps, to prevent its sticking to the rubbing paper, especially if one has used a glutinous size. Shifting the liner paper has the additional benefit of allowing one to check the effectiveness of the tamping and the gradual whitening of the rubbing paper as it dries. Fourth, despite the delicate nature of the wet rubbing paper, one must tamp with a firm hand or else the paper will pull away from the surface prematurely. Even if the paper stays tight to the end of the work, it may not conform closely to the finer parts of the inscription or design, and the subsequent inking will not sharply reflect the original line. Fifth, in addition to firmness, a clean, rhythmic movement is essential: "A good tamping technique is clean and exact, [executed] without hesitation, like a hawk striking a small bird, rising and falling, all with a rhythm."[15]

The primary tamping function is to ensure tight contact between the rubbing paper and the relief. The secondary function is to dry the paper, for only after the excess moisture is drawn out can one can lay on the ink. The paper must be evenly dry in inking, for if there is differential moisture, the ink in moister areas will bleed, causing a fuzzy image. Finally, because the moisture in the damp rubbing paper drains downward, the paper on the upper part of a standing stele dries more quickly.

In wind and sun, the rubbing paper dries too quickly and lifts before the tamping is done. A puckish breeze may float the paper off the stone and onto one's head and shoulders, as happened to me in front of a group of joking soldiers on Quemoy Island. The drying tendency can be slowed by laying a lightly dampened cotton cloth or a thin sheet of plastic over the tamped areas, or by using an atomizer to mist areas that are drying too rapidly. If the paper lifts too much one may have to begin anew.[16] Another option, recommended only if the format of the inscription or design allows, is to wet, tamp, and ink one section of the object at a time. Such an approach risks achieving an uneven ink tone but sometimes is the only option when the surface area is large, or when sun and wind result in premature drying and lifting.

A similar difficulty arises in dry interiors, especially in winter. One can ease the situation by lowering the temperature and raising the humidity, slowing the drying of the rubbing paper. One also can brush on additional sizing and retamp the paper, perhaps doing so several times, despite the inherent challenges. The number of applications relates to the humidity level and the strength of the solution as well as to the features of the object, its glossiness, the degree of relief, and the fineness of detail. The goal is to hold the rubbing paper to the surface to the end of the process while not gluing it down.

Well-made rubbings clearly manifest careful tamping, for the quality of the tamping directly affects the sharpness of the inked reproduction. If the characters or design elements of the original are fresh and sharp, and if the tamping is careful, the lines of the inked copy will appear as if drawn with a razor. Even when the original is imperfect, as is common, the rubbing must be absolutely faithful or else its intellectual as well as its aesthetic qualities will suffer. Fidelity is particularly important in dating rubbings, as described in chapter 7. Preliminary photographs and sketches are aids in tamping, for with the rubbing paper covering the object, they help in seeing where one must be particularly attentive in tamping.

Speaking of the need for sharp definition in inking, but implicitly referring to that in tamping, Chen Jieqi emphasizes that "most important in it [the inking], is that the lines of the characters must be exact, and even more that the characters must be full-bodied. . . . If the edges of the characters are exact and [the characters] are full-bodied, then one can capture the spirit of the original."[17]

The need for patient, careful tamping exists in rubbing any object, but its importance is vital in copying exceedingly fine and shallow inscriptions, such as those on divinatory shells and bones, whose lines often are but a fraction of a millimeter wide and deep. Rong Geng describes the difficulty involved in rubbing extremely fine line and emphasizes the need for practice in copying such material:

> [When] beginning to make rubbings, one first can experiment with large-character inscriptions and gradually extend [one's efforts] to smaller ones. Some workers are quite self-confident in rubbing [inscriptions on] bronze vessels, but if they rub [fine inscriptions on] shells and bones, at first [the results are] poor and blurred. After a few days, [they] gradually become clearer. Although [the inscriptions] may be extremely shallow and small, a good worker will nevertheless be able to rub them and bring them out.[18]

If one hopes to achieve good results, one must use the proper tamping technique: "Falling short of it by even a hair results in a difference [in the finished rubbing] of a thousand *li*."[19]

Among the fine points of tamping, one must watch that hairs from the tamping brush do not fall on the rubbing paper and become embedded, for they will show up in the ensuing inking. One should tamp evenly and methodically over the whole surface, line by line, character by character, tamping selectively where fineness or faintness of detail demands. One can verify the thoroughness of the tamping by watching to see that the inscription or design comes evenly through the damp rubbing paper, or by throwing a raking light across the paper to check its apposition. A small flashlight or mirror is helpful in ferreting out places, sometimes very small, that one may have tamped inadequately or missed entirely, the result being a less faithful reproduction.

One must be very careful not to pierce or abrade the rubbing paper with the tamping brush.[20] Further, apart from selecting the correct weight of paper for the situation, one also must pay attention to the amount of strain that the wet paper will tolerate:

> A stiff but closely set brush then is used to dab evenly all over the covered surface until the paper is forced into every incised line. This should be done lightly and tentatively at first, until one has found out just how much pressure and stretching the paper will stand (according to the breadth and depth of the incised line) without breaking. . . . It is evident that if ordinary thin and soft paper were used [for rubbing large and deeply cut line], it would have a tendency to break when dabbed with a stiff brush, as the depth of the line would be too much for the stretch of the soft and brittle [rubbing] paper. . . . In case of extremely fine incised lines, it will be necessary to use . . . greater diligence in forcing the

> paper well into the lines. . . . In the case of unusually thick and deep lines, it is not necessary to force the paper down until it reaches the bottom of the incision. . . . The same caution should be taken in the case of raised characters or designs with depressed spaces between them.[21]

Equal care is necessary in tamping the paper on relief, especially high relief.[22] To lessen the abrading effects of the tamping, the strokes should be even and regular and as nearly vertical as possible: "Tamping straight down is particularly important."[23] Finally, and of no small significance in achieving a good result, one must tamp with a contented heart.[24]

If one tears the rubbing paper in tamping, one can felt on a patch of self paper.[25] The paper type and grain of the patch should match those of the parent sheet, and the felting should be done promptly while the rubbing paper still is moist. Such repairs are common, especially with rubbings of large objects. Patches show in the subsequent inking, and so one should try to avoid the need for such repairs. Artisans also felt papers when large steles require multiple, overlapping sheets of rubbing paper or, to save paper, piece remnants (see fig. 2.6).

Aside from damaging the rubbing paper, there is the greater danger of damaging the lines of the original inscription or motif with the tamping brushes.[26] The possibility of such damage is obvious in the case of soft clay objects, and that of harm to metal and stone objects is less likely, but the matter is relative. Given the hardness of the bristles of some tamping brushes, the number of tamping strokes necessary to make a single rubbing, and the countless rubbings that rubbers have made of famous steles and bronzes—over centuries, in many cases—tamping gradually but relentlessly wears away the edges of the inscriptions or designs. Referring to the famous "Forest of Stones," Ye Changchi reported that his "friends coming from Guanzhong [Shaanxi] to Xi'an tell of the rubbing of the Beilin steles and of the *dangdang* sounds [of the tamping] day and night without end, and so how can the tablets not be destroyed? Although stone for making steles is hard, how can it be otherwise in cases of tablets rubbed like this?"[27] One hears the same sound at the Beilin today, where artisans make rubbings for sale. Ye spells out what happens:

> [In cases of] steles that have been assaulted and damaged [by continuous rubbing over long periods], none of the empty ground surrounding the characters is damaged, but each of the characters has become but a hole and is blurred beyond recognition. As one looks at them, they are like columns of white egrets or groups of white butterflies. . . . Although one fixedly studies [the effaced inscription], one cannot see a single brushstroke, one cannot make out a single character. Although there is a stele, it is as if there is no stele [inscription] at all![28]

In order to prevent or at least slow damage to rare inscriptions, extreme care is mandatory in the rubbing process.

Not to be overlooked, either, is the danger of tamping a thin or fragile specimen so firmly that it breaks. A cardinal rule is to tamp only as firmly as the nature (material, thickness, and strength) and condition (sound, or broken or cracked) of the object allows. One must watch for breaks or spalling areas on stones or clay objects, or for thin or corroded areas on metal ones. One can become so deeply absorbed in tamping, especially in making a quality rubbing (*jingta*), that one forgets the object beneath, sometimes with unfortunate consequences.[29]

INKING

The tamping done, one ascertains the degree of moistness of the paper to determine if it is appropriately dry to proceed with inking. The color of the rubbing paper is an important criterion, for as it dries, the paper gradually returns from a translucent wet state to its original opaque dry white, by which time it often is too late.[30] One can hasten drying with a fan, manual or electric, or a heater (see fig. 2.6). With the paper properly dry for the particular situation—environmental conditions, size and depth of line—one can apply the ink, a step no less important and painstaking than tamping. Authorities agree that one must work with particular concentration in inking, with the reward being an accurate and aesthetically pleasing rubbing; the irreparable "ink pigs" (blotches) and the need for rerubbing are the punishment for even a moment's inattention.

One can use four forms of ink to make rubbings: liquid, powdered, oil-based, and solid.

Liquid Ink

Liquid ink (*mozhi ta*) is the traditional form used to water-rub (*shui ta*). For objects in the studio, such as oracle bones, jades, or coins, one makes up a small batch by grinding stick ink directly on an inkstone. Otherwise, one can make up several batches and collect them in a saucer or small bowl.[31] The density will be greater than that for brush writing, varying with the width and depth of the line, the moistness of the paper, and the desired aesthetic effect, light or dark. For larger amounts of ink, necessary to rub steles, one must prepare a supply in a shallow bucket or tub (see figs. 2.3–2.4).[32] The ink in such cases is more viscous.

With materials and equipment ready, one removes the protective upper sheet, if used, lifting it gently so as not to disturb the rubbing paper. Finally, one must study the tamped rubbing paper to ascertain, first, the tightness of the apposition between the rubbing paper and the relief and, second, the amount of moisture in the paper. The apposition must be perfect, for only if the paper conforms to every minute detail of the surface can one obtain a faithful inked copy. Experience is essential, for it is very easy to overlook minute imperfections in apposition, which do not become apparent until one applies the ink, by which time it is too late to tamp further. A cross light helps to ferret out imperfections.

One often learns the hard way that once the paper has been laid and tamped, it must not move so much as a hair in the subsequent inking. Otherwise, the final image will be lacking in definition, and the rubbing will be worthless or of diminished value. Sometimes the rubbing paper will begin to lift before the inking is complete, the result of too dry a working environment, too weak a sizing solution, inadequate tamping, or too leisurely inking. One then often must repeat the entire process.

There also is need to ascertain the amount of moisture remaining in the rubbing paper. First, if the paper becomes too dry from sun or wind outdoors, high heat indoors, or low humidity in either place, it will contract and lift. The drying tendency can be slowed in the tamping as well as the inking stages by maintaining a lower temperature and higher humidity, misting the paper, or laying a lightly moistened cotton cloth or a sheet of plastic over the yet uninked areas. This is helpful, for once the paper shrinks and lifts, it is difficult to save the situation.[33]

Second, if the rubbing paper still is too moist, the ink dabber may stick on contact with the paper and pull it away from the relief: "In laying on the ink [one] must [wait until the] size [in the paper] does not stick to the hand, and then begin [to lay on the ink], and then the stickiness will not lift the [rubbing] paper."[34] If the paper still is too wet, one can draw out the unwanted moisture by additional tamping, in conjunction with an intermediate sheet.[35]

Third, the amount of moisture in the rubbing paper has a direct bearing on the sharpness of the inked reproduction, for if the paper is too wet, water-based ink will bleed, blurring the lines. This caution especially applies when the inscribed line is very fine or shallow. In such cases, the paper needs be almost dry, which implies the use of *baiji* to hold it to the surface. Jade, carnelian, glass, and other hard, smooth surfaces also all require strong *baiji* solutions. For steles with broader and deeper inscribed line and, often, eroded surfaces, one can begin laying on the ink while the paper still is damp, laying it on lightly at first and adding successive applications as the paper dries. The same basic principle applies in all rubbing situations, using "drier," lighter applications of ink when the paper is wet, and "wetter," heavier applications as it dries.

Fourth, the moistness of the paper has an effect on the final ink tone: "In laying on ink, one must observe the paper's dryness or moistness, [for] if it is too moist, then the [ink] tone will be a little lighter . . . . [Conversely,] when the paper is very dry, if in using the dabber . . . [one] pats and also rubs [strikes the paper obliquely], then the color of the ink will be bright."[36]

Apart from environmental conditions, one must consider the smoothness or glossiness of the surface of the host object and the fineness of the incised line before laying on the ink. When the host object is large and marked by a rough surface, such as a weathered stele, or has well-defined characters, often several centimeters wide and one or more deep, the rubbing paper can be quite moist. In such situations, there generally is no need for *baiji* solution unless strong wind or sun dictate. The combination of the textured surface and the glue in the ink helps to hold the rubbing paper down. As the characters on old steles generally are eroded, careful definition is essential in capturing small changes in strokes—highly important for dating rubbings.

When the object is small, and if it is smooth or glossy and the inscription or design is shallow and fine, as on oracle bones, polished jades and glass, bronze mirrors, and inkstones, one needs to take a different approach. First, a finer paper, such as *mianlian*, is necessary. Second, brushing *baiji* or another glutinous agent on the paper helps hold it to the surface until the work is done. Third, the paper should be 90 percent or more dry before one lays on the ink. Fourth, the ink again should be "drier," less moist, at the outset so that bleeding does not blur the fine line. One then can darken the tone with subsequent heavier applications of moister ink.

As general guidelines, first, the moister the rubbing paper and the ink, the more risk there is that the ink will bleed, blurring the inked line; second, the glossier the surface and finer the inscribed line, the more need there is for *baiji* or some other glutinous size to hold the rubbing paper tight during the rubbing process.

In judging the degree of dryness proper for applying the ink in rubbing bronzes, Rong Geng suggests that the paper be between 80 and 90 percent dry, while for working with shell-and-bone materials Jun Yu recommends that the rubbing paper be completely dry.[37] Jiang advises that the paper should be on the dry side but warns that it should not be too dry, and, advancing a different criterion, he suggests that if the paper has assumed its original opaque white color, it already is too dry, and it is too late to lay on the ink.[38] Conversely, if one can see the inscription or design through the translucent rubbing paper, it still is too wet. Atmospheric and other conditions play their parts, and one must judge the appropriate degree of dryness. Some specialists state that the degree of moisture also depends on the type of paper, with *lianshi* requiring that it be completely dry and *mian*, only 90 to 95 percent dry.[39]

There is a close relationship between the moistness of the paper and the quality and quantity of the ink as well as the timing of its application. One can begin lightly laying on lesser amounts of and more viscous ink while the rubbing paper still is quite moist, especially on larger line, working with quick, light pats. If the ink is too liquid, and if one applies it too heavily, it will bleed into the moist paper and dull the definition of the inscription or design. As the paper dries, one safely can lay on additional rounds, gradually increasing the amount, moistness, and density of ink.[40] There can be appreciable differences in drying time among working situations, and one must be sure that the paper is dry enough to prevent the ink from bleeding and the dabber from sticking, and yet not so dry that it contracts and lifts.

The tamping done, any intermediate sheet off, the exposed rubbing paper appropriately dry and free of hairs or other foreign objects, the dabbers moistened to soften them, and ink at hand, one is ready to apply it. One must carry the ink to the rubbing paper in prescribed manner, as Chen Jieqi describes for studio work:

> In inking the dabber, one uses a writing brush to pick up the ink and spread it on the inverted cover of a small porcelain bowl or saucer and then quickly rubs the dabber around in it. If it is too dry, then one adds more ink, but one should not dip the dabber into places where the ink has collected, for this will cause the cotton [dabber] to have wet places, and putting it to the paper will make ink spots. If there are ink spots, then one must change the cotton. Recently there has been the technique of causing the cotton to be completely wet, but this . . . is not a satisfactory method, for the ink readily will enter the [intaglio] characters. It is easy to accumulate [excess ink] on the sides of the dabber where the ink has not been used up, and if one inadvertently uses it, the ink is too heavy, and so one must wipe it off. When the silk outer covering of the dabber is worn out, change it, and if the dabber becomes loose, tie it up again right away. If the dabber is tight [and compact], then it will not enter the [intaglio] characters, while if it is loose, then it is easy for it to enter the characters [and deposit ink].[41]

Others repeat this advice on brushing the liquid ink onto a bowl cover or saucer; on the danger of taking up too much ink on the dabber, thus creating "ink pigs"; on the allied problem of gradual buildup of both liquid and dried ink on the sides of the dabber; and on the need to exchange the outer silk covering of the dabber when it becomes frayed, or to tighten it if it becomes loose.[42]

The care necessary in preparing the ink and in taking it up on the dabber also involves subtleties, especially with fine work: "The saucer with the layer of dried ink is made slightly damp by the breath, and the powder-puff pad is gently rubbed around the saucer, the adherent ink being delicately transferred to the high reliefs of the paper by quiet patting."[43] This technique of rejuvenating dried ink is useful in delicately inking small objects or fine relief, or when the rubbing paper still is damp and one is concerned about the ink bleeding.

All this relates to rubbing smaller objects. Steles require bolder methods of attack.[44] Instead of using a brush to smear a little ink on a saucer or palette and taking it up on a small dabber, one proceeds differently, with two approaches common. The first involves using two dabbers of appropriate size for the situation (fig. 4.4). One, the "male" (*xiong*), larger, is the dipping dabber. Made of pure cotton cloth for absorbency,

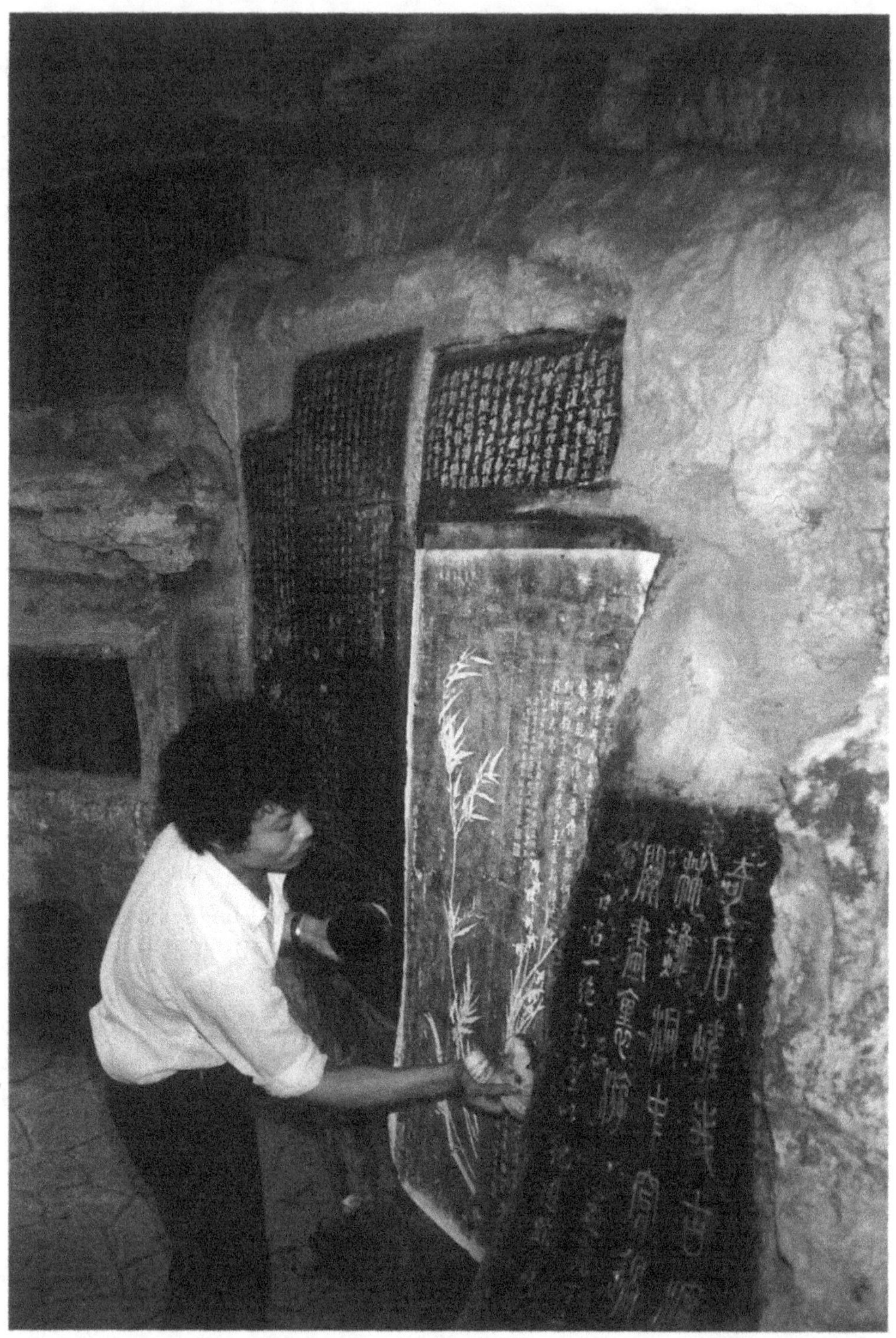

Fig. 4.4. Dipping and working ink dabbers. Guilin, Diecai Shan, 1994. Photograph by the author.

it is held in the left hand with the working surface up and dipped lightly into the ink supply. The dip should not be so deep as to make the dabber soggy, and so some artisans prefer to brush ink on it. The other dabber, the "female" (*ci*), smaller and of finer cloth, is the working dabber, held in the right hand with the working surface down. One inks the working dabber by rubbing or patting it against the dipping dabber, taking on an appropriate, even amount of ink, and quickly and rhythmically transferring it to the rubbing paper. One should moisten and soften both dabbers slightly with a little water before using them.

One can vary this method in rubbing very fine shell-and-bone inscriptions, using smaller dabbers:

> One can prepare two dabbers, one larger [the male], one smaller [the female], to lay on the ink. The larger one is used to carry the ink [from the supply], and the smaller one is used directly to lay the ink on the [rubbing] paper. The left hand holds the larger one, and the right hand holds the smaller one. Using a writing brush to dip ink on the left-hand dabber, one then left and then right mutually pats, continuously moving the wrist in order to turn . . . the dabber, causing ink to pass [from the larger left-hand dabber] onto the smaller right-hand dabber to distribute [the ink] evenly.[45]

The second approach uses the same type of working dabber, but instead of using a dipping dabber, one brushes ink on a wooden paddle. The artisan brushes the ink thinly and evenly on the paddle, held in the left hand, picks up the ink on the working dabber, held in the right hand, and transfers it to the paper (fig. 4.5). The movement of the dabber and the paddle is so rapid and so smooth that the viewer is not sure whether the dabber moves to meet the paddle or vice versa.

Whatever the manner of inking the dabber, it is important to do so lightly and evenly. This is especially important as one begins inking, for if the dabber is either too heavily or too moistly inked, the liquid ink "will penetrate the [damp] paper, causing the back of the paper to have places that are not white, and to have light and heavy, and dense and thin, places."[46] In extreme cases, the liquid ink may even flow into the intaglio areas or penetrate the paper and stain the underlying object. One sees countless steles, especially the popular inscriptions, blackened by centuries of rubbing.

Before starting to ink, one first should test the dabber in a blank or unimportant area of the relief, or on a separate piece of paper, to avoid an "ink pig" should the dabber be too heavily or too unevenly inked.[47] Finally, one must determine the sequence of application. In rubbing steles, artisans generally move from the top to the bottom of the stele. Some first ink the inscribed or decorated central areas of the stone and then move to the four edges, while others methodically move from left to right down

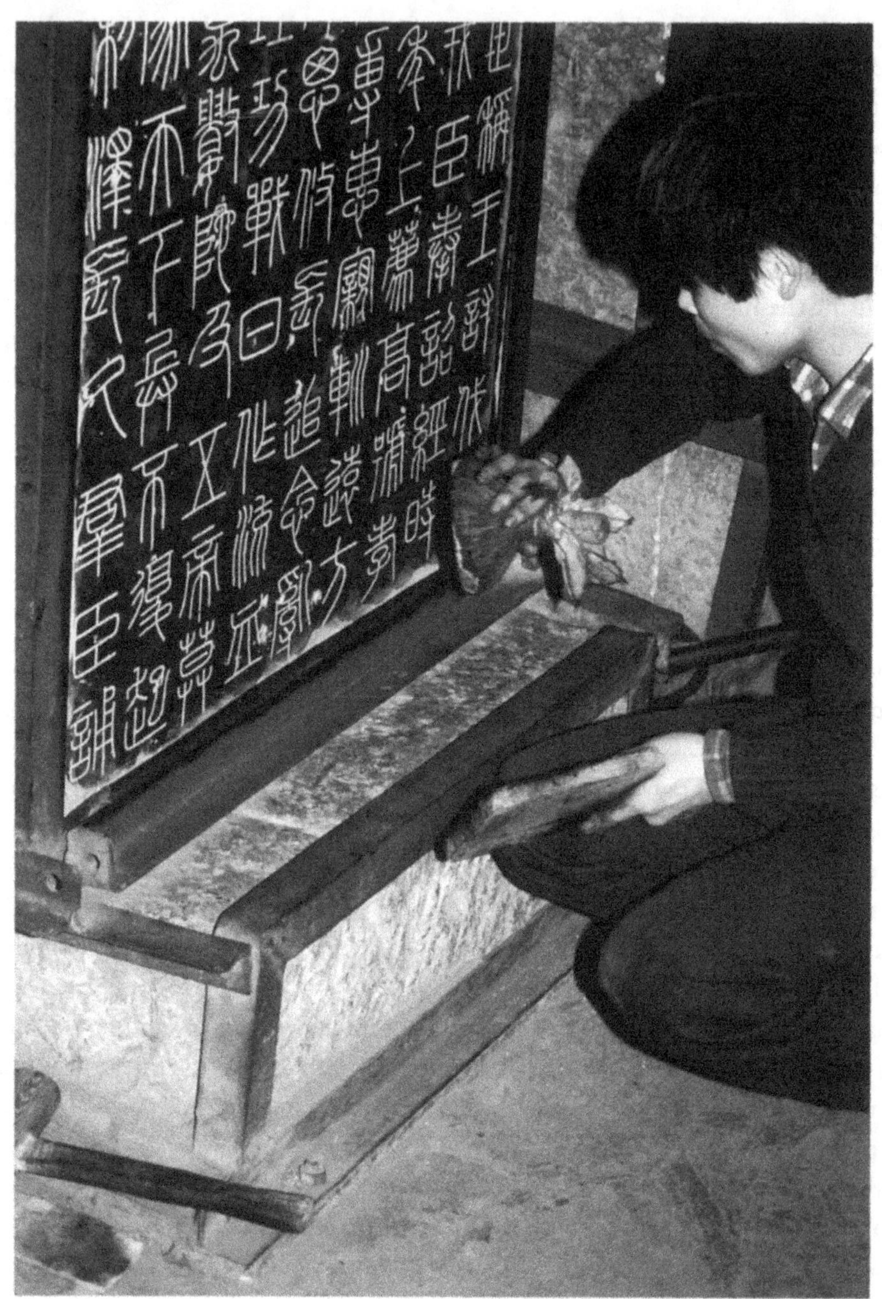

Fig. 4.5. Ink dabber and paddle. Xi'an Beilin Museum, 1993. Photograph by the author.

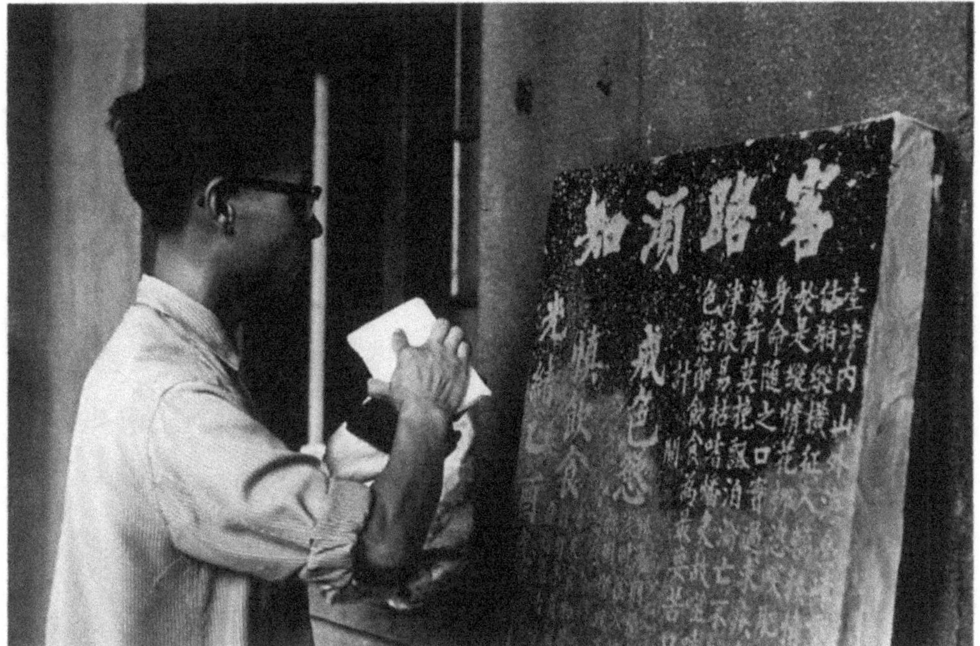

Fig. 4.6. Inking a stele inscription. National Historical Museum, Taibei, Taiwan, 1960. Photograph by the author.

the stone.[48] It is particularly important to ink the edges of the characters and designs, making them clear and sharp. Care is especially necessary with shallow, faint, or badly eroded inscriptions or designs, which, under the rubbing paper, can be difficult to distinguish from the surrounding surface. Preliminary photographs and sketches are useful, for once the rubbing paper is on the stone, and as it dries and begins to turn white again, it is increasingly difficult to make out eroded, irregular engraved lines beneath.

With the working dabbber inked in one of the prescribed ways, and the inking sequence well in mind, one begins laying on the ink (fig. 4.6). If the surface is eroded and the edges of the inscription are ragged, one can define them by initial outlining with a very small dabber. One can follow a similar procedure with fragmentary oracle bones, inking the edges sharply so that scholars can "rejoin" separated pieces (fig. 4.7).[49]

Two general considerations are important. First, if one is to achieve an elegant effect, it is essential to apply the ink lightly and evenly over the entire surface of the paper: "In laying on the ink, one must do it evenly, not first [laying it on] unevenly and then afterwards seeking to equalize it."[50] One should lay on the ink in an even pattern, moving back and forth as if one were sowing grass seed, first in one direction and then in another. Laying on the ink randomly, now here and now there, or with greater attention

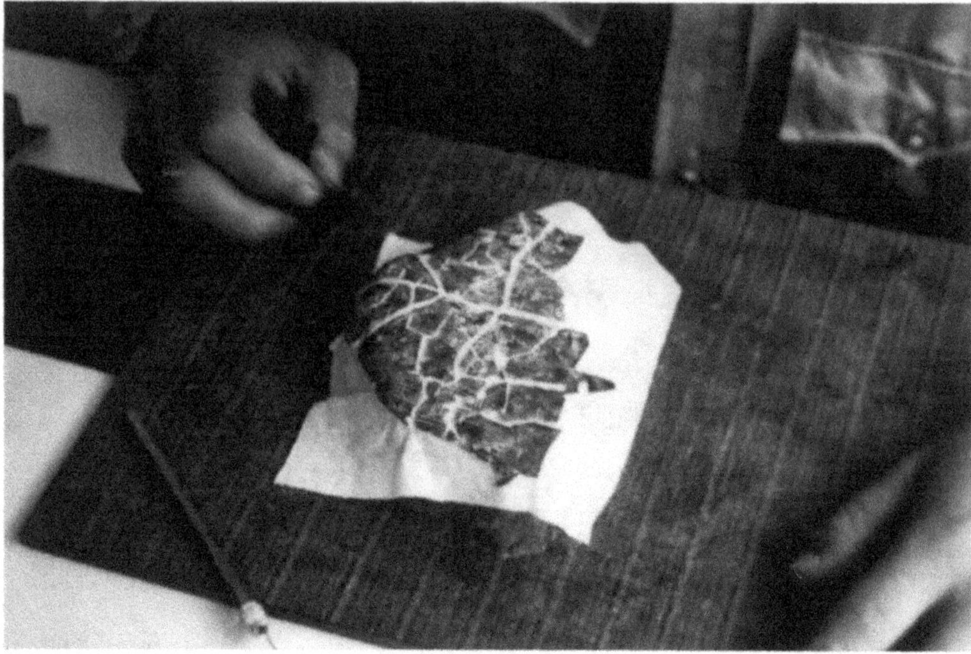

FIG. 4.7. Inking an oracle-bone inscription. Institute of History and Philology, Academia Sinica, Taiwan, 1960. Photograph by the author.

to certain parts of the relief, results in a mottled, "flower petal" effect that is difficult to equalize by subsequent dabbing.[51]

A second, related consideration is to build the ink tone layer by layer with successive rounds. At the outset, while the paper still is moist, one should lay on the ink lightly to bring out the lines of the inscription, applying the ink with many gentle pats of the dabber until the whole surface, inscribed or not, is lightly and uniformly covered.[52] Despite the primary interest in the inscription, one must not neglect the uninscribed spaces between the lines, for doing so results in uneven ink tone. Exceptions to this even inking are appropriate where aesthetics are a consideration, described in chapter 7.

The first round of inking completed and the ink dry, one applies another round, and after that yet others, equally even and ever more dense. In laying on these subsequent layers of ink, one pats fewer times with the dabber but gradually applies more and heavier ink with each pat, especially if one wishes to achieve heavy, matte inking called *chongmo,* "layered ink."[53] In a normal situation, one builds the ink layer on layer until one has obtained the desired degree of blackness, with the goal of achieving good contrast. One exception to these strictures about laying on the ink evenly and by successive rounds has to do with the edges of the stele. As the paper near the edges tends to dry more quickly and lift, rubbers sometimes ink these more heavily, using the glue in the ink for its adhesive, as well as its coloring, qualities. Clarity and evenness of tone also are important objectives: the inked line must be clear, and the ink tone, even. Above all, one must not try to apply the ink all at one time. Heavy inking before the rubbing paper is fully dry, and before one has built the density round by round, produces fuzzy lines and a dull, murky tone. In the case of very fine engraving, one also risks blotting out the line by laying on the ink too densely, too firmly, or too moistly.[54] In such situations, one must sacrifice strong contrast between black and white in favor of obtaining any representation at all. Evenness of tone also is important, and one must be especially watchful for irregular places that do not catch the ink evenly. Often the surface will manifest small convexities and concavities that will take too much or too little ink. One must give particular attention to such places, going lightly at the high spots and fashioning a special dabber of appropriate size and shape for the low. Aesthetics may suggest that the inking be uneven, to communicate the idea of the irregularity in the finished rubbing. Whatever the preference, one can test the evenness of the ink tone on a large rubbing by stepping back and studying the rubbing or by sighting at a low angle along its surface.

In knowing when to stop inking, one can use the general rule that the inked surface appears darker when the ink is wet and the paper still is on the object, while it appears lighter when the ink is dry and the paper is off. Although one should not overink, one also should take care to lay on enough ink, for one cannot compensate once the paper is off the object. With important objects, one should make an exploratory rubbing to determine the proper ink density.

Two final points of caution on inking are in order. First, the rubbing paper tends to lift off the object as it dries, especially if the glutinous size is lacking or weak, the tamping is insufficient, or the inking is too leisurely. Relatedly, if the ink, which contains glue, builds up thickly on the dabber, it may stick to the paper and pull it off the host. Second, as the result of repeated dipping and dabbing, ink builds on the outer sides of the dabber, and if a dabbing strike is ever so slightly off center rather than perfectly vertical, the accumulation will cause an "ink pig."[55] To prevent such a mishap, one periodically should wipe the sides and working surface of the dabber, removing dried ink and extending its life and ensuring its effectiveness. When the dabber surface becomes frayed and worn, one must replace the outer cloth.

In laying on ink, one must use the correct hand technique, especially for bronze inscriptions:

> Laying on the ink requires that the fingers not move but that one flex the wrist. If one flexes the wrist, then when the heart beats and causes movement, the wrist still will not move. Whether the force [of the stroke] is light or heavy, or whether one strikes or raises [the dabber], as soon as one comes to the edge of a character, the dabber rises. If one pats

> and lifts, with the wrist rising and falling, and with the paper giving off a sound, then one is achieving the [correct] technique.[56]

Augmenting, Jiang also emphasizes the need for a harmonious sound as the dabber strikes the rubbing paper, and he notes that an old term for rubbing was *xiang*[b]*ta*[b], "sound rubbing."[57] As in writing Chinese characters with a brush, wrist action is superior to finger action, for using the wrist allows more freedom of movement, yet more stability. The movement by a skilled rubber should consist of alternating up-and-down strokes, and one should lift the dabber when one reaches the edge of the character. Picturing the dabbing action poetically, Jiang states that "whether one is striking or lifting [the hand], it is a case of the dragon flying and the phoenix dancing."[58]

Inking relief requires special care: "In the case of intaglio inscriptions on [ritual] vessels, it is sufficient just to seek out the edges of the characters. In dealing with relief inscriptions, whether full-bodied or thin, one must control the dabber strictly, vertically dropping [the hand] and dabbing levelly. Not turning [the hand] is important, for if one turns off center, then [the resulting rubbing] will fail [to be like] the original."[59] If one pulls to one side in inking relief, the inked impression will be too "fat" (*fei*) and unfaithful.[60]

In sum, successful ink dabbing requires the following: waiting for the paper to be appropriately dry; moving the dabber vertically; inking lightly at first and then more heavily later, waiting for one round of ink to dry before laying on a successive round; not inking so heavily that the ink flows into the inscribed line; and "keeping the spirit" whether one inks lightly or heavily.[61]

In inking in places difficult of access, one can modify the ink dabber endlessly: "[For inscriptions] in deep vessels, use a piece of bamboo, tie the dabber to it, and rub them. [In the case of] obscure places [where one cannot readily see or reach], use pincers to hold the dabber. . . . [For inscriptions] on the insides of the loop handles of *jue* wine cups, use . . . a bamboo splint, add [wrap] a small bit of cotton and silk [to form the dabber]."[62] Extensions of this account describe modifications of the dabber in inking bronze vessels that are distinguished by their shape or the awkward location of their inscriptions or decor.[63] Inscriptions in deep-bellied *you* wine jars require fastening the dabber to the blunt end of a Chinese writing brush to reach them. Those on *jue* wine cups, opposite the close-lying, pitcher-type handles, require a thin splint, similar to a tongue depressor, fitted around its middle with the cotton core, interlayer, and silk covering, that one can slip through the opening between handle and body.

As exemplified by the strongly curving *Mao Gong ding* cauldron and the *Qi Hou lei* jar, particular individual vessels are known for their specific rubbing problems. In such situations, the rubber must adjust the rubbing paper, slit it, and use multiple sheets of paper to capture the inscription. One additionally can rub the lines one by one to compensate for any incompleteness in the overall rubbing. Despite such difficulties, an accomplished rubber of bronzes can manage handily in an average situation. Having described the various problems that one meets with in inking, Rong Geng reports that "experienced workers can rub two or three vessels [at a time, moving] from vessel A [to vessel B], without wasting time waiting for [the ink] to dry."[64] Finally, one best can ink highly irregular surfaces, such as those of rough-textured early potteries, by using a cut-off Chinese writing brush rather than a dabber to apply drier ink.[65]

Most of these techniques apply to typical situations, where the primary concern merely is to achieve a clear contrast between the paper and the ink. Some materials, types of relief, and subject matter require special inking. Such differing approaches are dramatically represented in two polar types of rubbings that go back to the Tang and the Song: layered ink (*chongmo,* plate 4), explained above, and black-gold rubbings (*wujin ta*, fig. 4.8), both used for calligraphic models (*tie*); and cicada-wing rubbings (*chanyi ta*, fig. 4.9). These two types, both used especially on smaller objects, represent diametrically opposite artistic and technical approaches to inking.[66]

The materials and methods used in making the two types are the determining factors in creating their distinctive effects. *Record of Superfluous Things* (Zhangwu zhi), by Wen Zhenheng (Ming), attributes the differences between black-gold and cicada-wing rubbings to those between paper and ink in north and south China: "Anciently, the grain of northern papers was horizontal, and it was loose-textured, thick, and did not take ink well. Northern ink was greenish in color and pale in tone, for it was not made with oil or wax. Therefore, the color [of the rubbings made from it] was light, and the grain showed, and so [the rubbings] are referred to as cicada-wing rubbings [*chanyi ta*[b]]. The grain of southern papers was vertical, and they used oil or wax [in making the ink], and so the color was deep black and very glossy, and thus [the rubbings] are called black-gold rubbings [*wujin ta*[b]]."[67]

Black-gold rubbings are characterized by the strong contrast between the white rubbing paper and the intensely black ink, and by the high sheen of the ink (fig. 4.8).[68]

> If the surface to be reproduced is exceptionally smooth and the design deeply incised, a spectacular result can be obtained by applying the method called *wu-chin-t'a* [wujin ta] . . . "black gold rubbing." For such rubbings one uses a thicker, sized paper, and a very superior ink. Before applying it to the surface, the paper is held over a bowl of boiling water, so as to make it soft and plastic without becoming too moist. It then is hung over the surface to be reproduced and tapped in the usual way with a stiff brush till it is securely glued on to it. Thereafter the surface is inked with a tampon, well soaked in thick ink. Because the paper is thicker than that ordinarily used for rubbings, it will not sag or tear

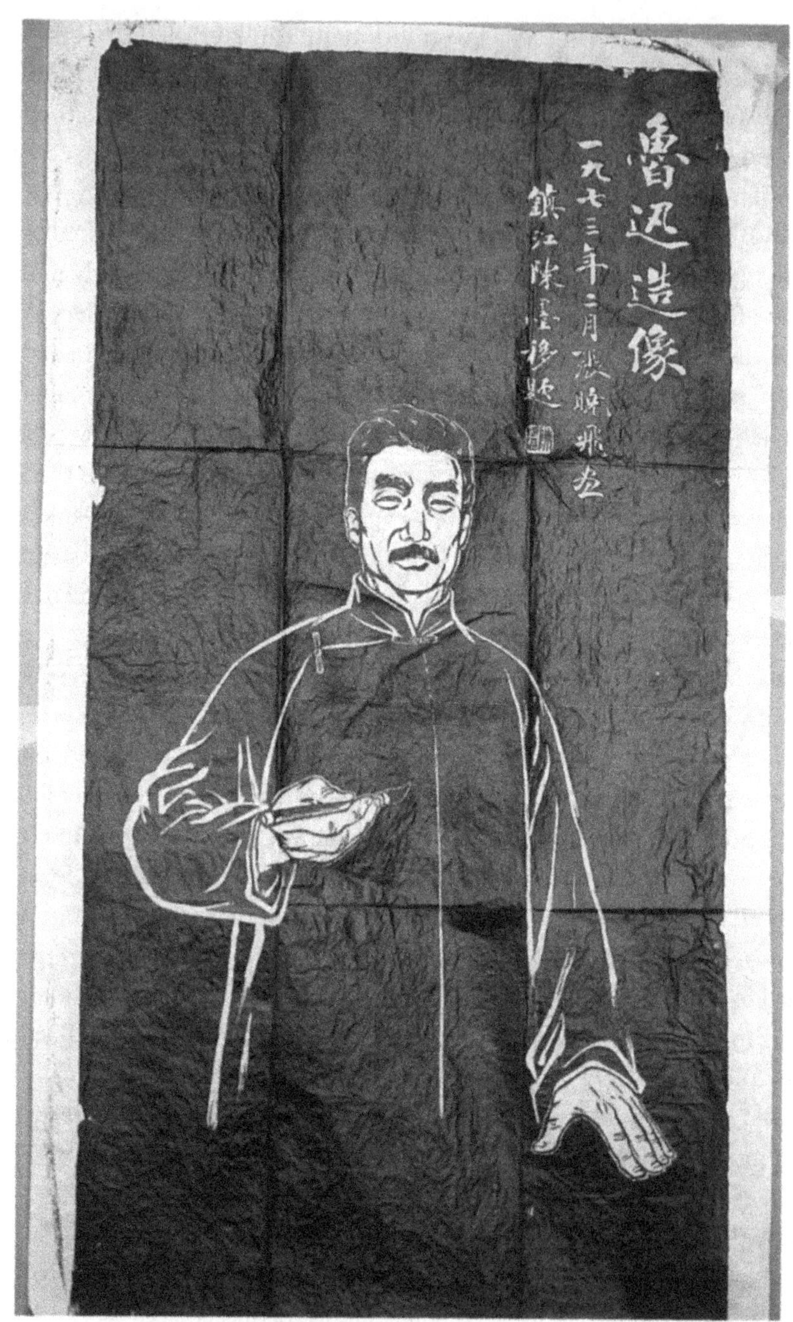

Fig. 4.8. Black-gold rubbing, portrait of Lu Xun, "China's [Maxim] Gorky." Author's collection. Photograph by the author.

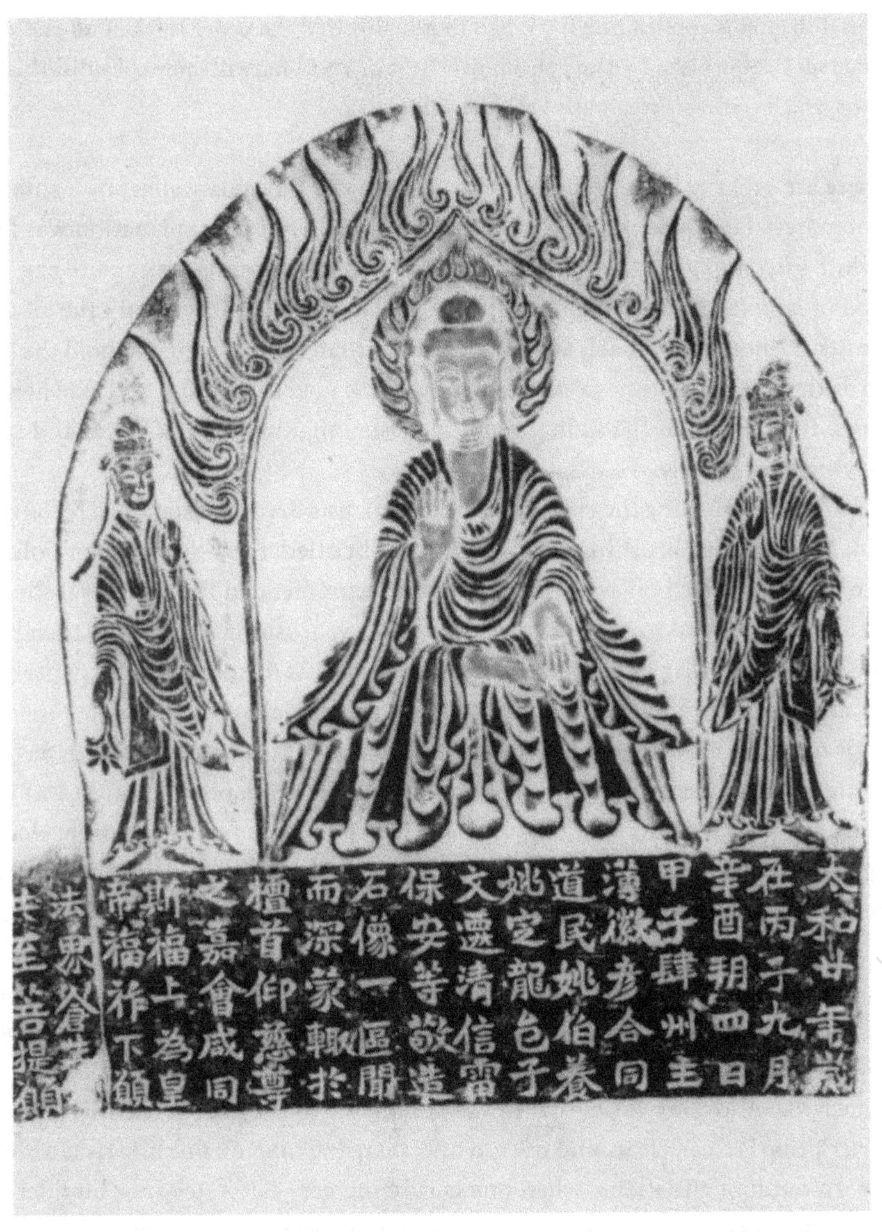

Fɪɢ. 4.9. Cicada-wing inking of a sculpture of the Buddha, cut by devotees. Northern Wei, 496. Shanxi. The Field Museum of Natural History, 233767.

> even if the ink is applied heavily. When thoroughly dry, the paper is taken off and the inked surface burnished with a polishing shell. Such a rubbing will show a beautiful black shine which contrasts pleasantly with the white design.[69]

There are other explanations about how to achieve this glossy effect by a combination of materials and techniques.[70] The most frequently heard explanation was to use egg white (*jidanqing*) in the rubbing process, with one formula using pure egg white instead of *baiji* to size the rubbing paper. A variant formula was to mix the albumen in the ink.[71] Another approach was to use heavier than normal sizing to hold the paper down during the longer time needed to make a black-gold rubbing, as well as to heighten its gloss. In addition to the sizing, some suggested making the ink dense and strong and laying it on heavily.

Brushing or polishing the rubbing once the ink was dry was a standard recommendation. Most advised brushing with a soft, short-bristled, thick-set brush or polishing it with a hard, smooth object. One informant recommended laying several sheets of paper atop the tamped paper when it was nearly dry, brushing it hard, and then laying on the ink. Yet another method of achieving a gloss was to lay on the ink densely, but "dry," and with a swiping motion, polishing it as it was laid on.

Artisans have used the two different dabbing motions through the dynasties.[72] From the Tang and extending to the Qing, the preferred dabbing motion was *cata*[a], oblique, at a low angle. In the Qing, artisans began to use a vertical motion, *chui*[d]*ta*[a], along with the *cata*[a] stroke. The argument over which of these two motions produces the better rubbing centers in which deposits less ink buildup at the edges of the intaglio characters—a particular challenge with fine and shallow line. The argument continues among both Chinese and Japanese specialists, with the nod toward the vertical motion, as seen at the Beilin, for it produces a sharper image.[73] In some circumstances, however, the swiping movement is more practical, as when the surface is large, smooth, and with no concavities and convexities that would contribute to the paper's tearing, and when the inscription is clear, clean, and not too fine, for using *cata*[a] on fine line risks a blurred image. In outdoor situations, when one is rubbing very large steles, or boulders and cliff faces, wind and sun may require the more rapid sweeping *cata*[a] motion to complete the work before the paper dries and lifts.[74] Along with the use of heavier ink, the swiping *cata*[a] movement also helps to achieve the glossy effect of black-gold rubbings.[75] According to Beilin authorities, oblique and vertical motions can be used for both black-gold and cicada-wing rubbings. Skilled workers master both movements.

Whatever the materials or techniques used to create the black-gold effect, one can heighten the contrast between paper and ink by inking the edges of the inscriptions or designs cleanly. Again, a stronger *baiji* solution holds the rubbing paper tight to the edges of the relief and produces sharp inking. Testimony for the strength of the solution is to be inferred from the suggestion that sometimes one must remove a completed rubbing by steaming it loose. Black-gold rubbings are more common for smaller objects and for smooth, even, inscribed surfaces, such as calligraphic models and line-drawn images. Calligraphers especially prefer deep-black, *wujin* rubbings because of the ease with which they can copy the rubbed inscriptions by the *shuanggou* outlining method.[76] Many, if not most, black-gold rubbings are from positive woodcuts rather than stone cuts.

Quite opposite in effect from black-gold rubbings are *chanyi ta,* cicada-wing rubbings, or, as a similar type is called, *xuehua jia sha,* "snowflakes between gauze."[77] Such rubbings appear like thin clouds and a misted moon, as characterized by Jiang, and like mist and clouds, as described by Chen Jieqi.[78] To make cicada-wing rubbings, one must use thin but strong paper, with *mianlian* paper specifically recommended; the ink must be dense but faint, and the dabber, bound very tightly.[79] The secret of the technique is to ensure that both the rubbing paper and the ink dabber are dry rather than moist.[80] One also must lay on the ink lightly in quantity and manner, dabbing gently and flatly, covering the ground and the relief in the same light, even tone. If the ink is too strong, one can add a little water, but not too much, or else the ink solution will be too thin and blur the line.[81]

Apart from its air of elegance, the cicada-wing technique is particularly suitable in several situations.[82] In terms of stone cuttings, it is good for copying either relief or, conversely, very shallow or faint intaglio. Hairline inscriptions, such as those on divinatory shells and bones or jades, invite cicada-wing treatment, for with normal inking the line may disappear, becoming one with the ground. One also can use the technique to heighten the air of antiquity with which an ancient object is invested, as were rubbings of the Palace Museum bronzes in Beijing.

One can ink various parts of decorated jades differentially for aesthetic purposes:

> If there are decorative elements, one must blacken the outline a little, then make the decor on the inside lighter, in the manner of a cicada-wing rubbing. As for parts such as birds' heads, fishes' eyes, and gills, one especially must rub them a little darker, and then the representation can be especially lifelike.[83]

One also can use the technique out of respect, inking the fleshly features—face, hands, and feet—of images of Buddha, Guanyin, or Confucius more lightly (fig. 4.9). As a variation, a vermilion rubbing, as of Zhong Kui, painted by Wu Daozi, may have the face done in some tone of black.[84]

Between these two technical extremes of black-gold and cicada-wing there is room for a fair measure of artistic freedom.

Powdered Ink

Some artisans, more interested in convenience and speed than in quality, use powdered ink (*mofen ta*). After affixing the dry sheet of rubbing paper, they wet it with a thin solution of glue (*jiao*), paste (*jianghu*), or *baiji*, and warm water. When they have brushed and tamped the paper, they pat the dry ink powder directly on the damp paper when it is 50 to 60 percent dry. An alternative method is to sprinkle the ink powder on a wet stamp pad and transfer the ink with a dabber.

The advantages of this method are that one does not have to carry liquid ink, mix it on the spot, or wait until the paper dries. For these reasons, the method is useful for traveling scholars. The disadvantages are that the resulting rubbing often is less clear and the ink tone is uneven. The ink also is more fugitive.[85]

Oil-Based Ink

As for oil-based ink (*youmo ta*), oil *sumi* (*abura zumi*), the Japanese oil-based inking compound, can be laid on while the rubbing paper still is quite damp, without the ink bleeding. This permits a worker to do a portion of an object at a time—wetting a part, tamping, and then inking it while it still is damp, and then doing another portion. Despite the saving of time, purists avoid this medium, for the oil in the compound penetrates the paper, spreads, never completely dries, and bleeds into neighboring stored rubbings.[86] It also is necessary afterward to wash the host object with soap and water, if its condition allows. In situations where time and convenience, rather than permanence, are primary considerations, the compound is useful.[87]

Wax-Based Ink

Rubbing with cakes made of wax mixed with carbon black uses the dry rubbing technique, described in chapter 5.

CLASSES OF RELIEF

Jiang Xuanyi defines five classes of relief common in Chinese pictures and describes techniques for rubbing them.[88]

Thread Cuts

Thread cuts (*xianke*) are the oldest class, characterized by the very fine intaglio line on ancient cultural objects of animal bone and deer horn, bronze, and jade, with grotesque zoomorphs. Gossamerlike, such line also occurs on Shang divination shells and bones.

The materials and methods for copying such fine intaglio largely are those for rubbing smaller objects. The paper should be thin and fine; the tamping, done carefully; and the dabber, made of very fine cloth and bound tightly, so as not to deposit ink in the faint line. A cicada-wing technique lessens the likelihood of laying on so much ink that it obliterates fine line.

Picture Stones

Picture stones (*huaxiang shi*) commonly are incised on fine, hard, polished stone and include copies of Tang and Song paintings of saints, worthies, literary figures, and artists (fig. 4.10). Such stone-cut copies are remarkably faithful, reflecting the original fine brushstrokes of beards and eyebrows and the heavier lines of clothing.

One also must use thin paper to capture the fine detail and should protect the paper with intermediate strike-stele paper (*qiaobei zhi*). The tamping should be adequate, and the dabber cover, fashioned of fine materials, tightly bound, and in several sizes for large and small line.

Picture stones also include paintings in fine relief, with the ground cut away, such as the Tang paintings of Guanyin and Buddhist saints (*yingzhen*). These relief pictures are harmoniously copied by inking the raised line more heavily and the blank ground, more lightly. In treating intaglio and relief, one must work carefully to capture every detail. The very fine lines, sometimes but a single delicate brushstroke that marks the sides of the nose or the corners of the mouth, require particular care if one is to capture the true spirit of the original. One uses the standard technique to rub the inscribed commentary, whether it is original or, as is common, added by later admirers.

Low Relief

Low relief (*foudiao*, "floating carving") includes four subclasses, each with distinctive characteristics and appropriate materials and methods.

SUBCLASS 1. The first subclass includes forms that slowly rise, with the relief slightly rounded, the ground flat, and with no markings, such as on stele sides, tops, and plinths, and on bronze mirrors and carved ceramics. Except for the mirrors, all are post-Han. For rubbing such relief, one should use a strong but pliable paper, such as *pi*. Tamping requires a looser pad of *ling* or *chou* silk filled with cotton waste, and one should press lightly with this pad to mold the rubbing paper around the relief.

One should lay on the ink a little obliquely, rather than vertically, but neither too much nor too little to left or right. As in all rubbing, one must study the relief closely to understand its meaning and spirit rather than rubbing aimlessly. Careless, hasty inking inevitably results in a reproduction that is either too thin and formless or too

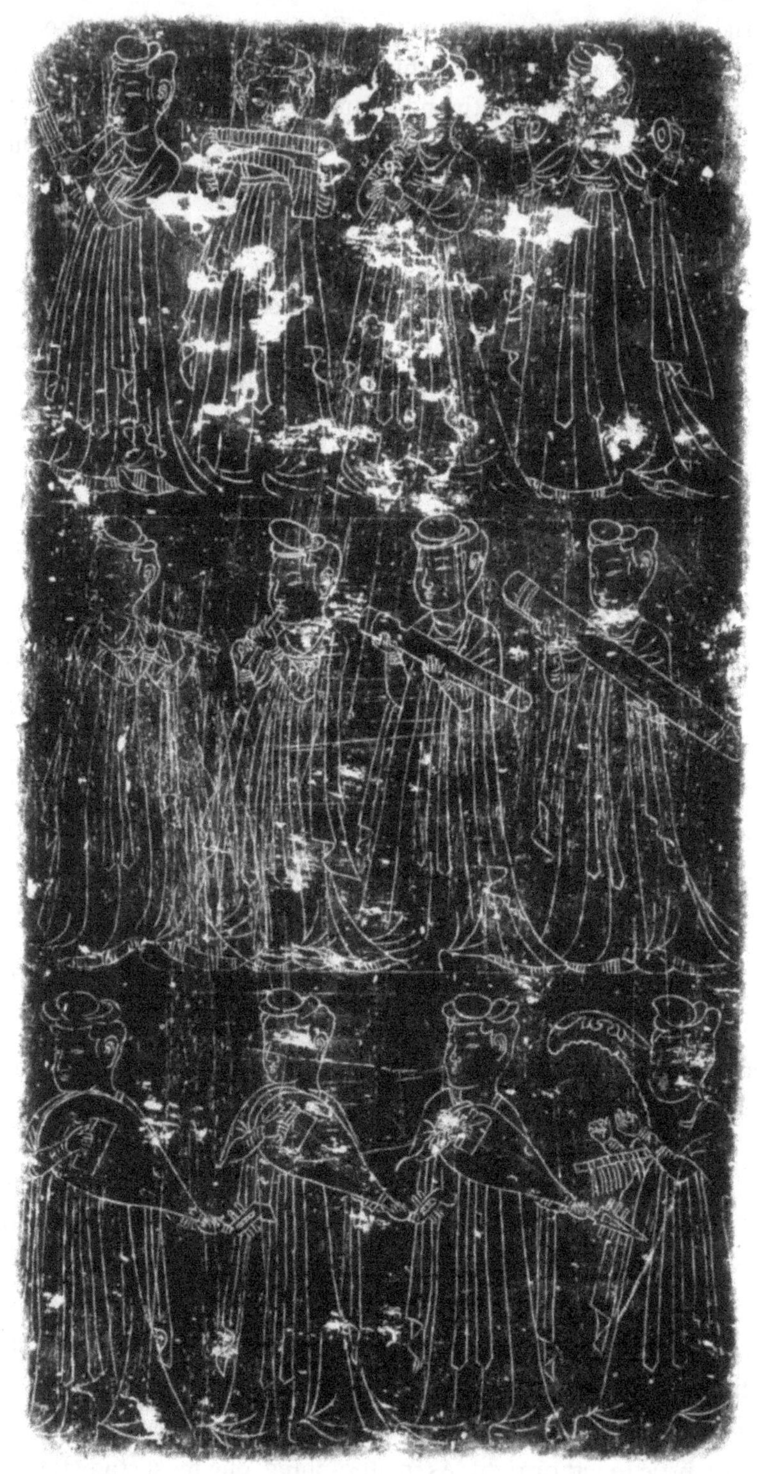

FIG. 4.10. Picture-stone figures of musicians, coffin of Li Shou (Tang). Courtesy Xi'an Beilin Museum.

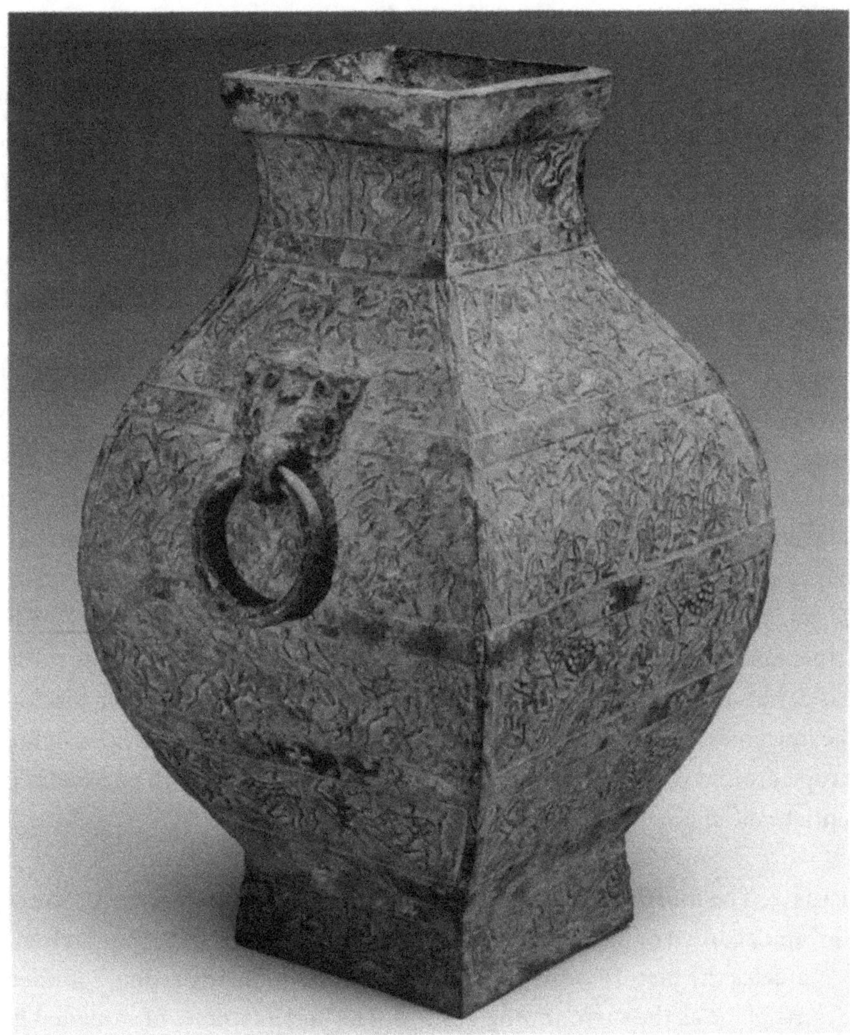

FIG. 4.11. Low relief, square *fang* vase, 5th century B.C.E. Freer Gallery of Art, Smithsonian Institution, F1956.15.

dark and swollen. Either way, the resulting inked image will not communicate the true spirit of the original.

SUBCLASS 2. The second subclass is *yangfou*, "relief floating," and is marked by fine intaglio figures and decorative motifs on relievo elements, with the ground chiseled away and showing a rope effect. This type of work flourished in the Later Han, with the best-known examples in the Wu Liang and Nanyang reliefs. Similar striking pictures occur on certain types of bronzes, such as round *hu* and square *fang* vases (fig. 4.11) with their hunting scenes, and on some kinds of ceramics.

Inking *yangfou* requires applying the ink heavily to the pictures, leaving the fine intaglio details in the white of the paper. On the rope ground one should use the cicada-wing technique, which gives an air of antiquity and provides contrast with the pictures. Unless one wishes to take on the daunting task of making a composite rubbing (*quanxing taben*), described in chapter 5, inking the relief on bronze or ceramic vessels requires rubbing the vessels a side, panel, or section at a time by the divided-paper method (*gezhi fa*), described below. One also should rub the ground and the edges of whatever part of the vessel one is copying. Finally, one can achieve particularly fine effects by giving different ink tones to the pictures, ground, and edges.

SUBCLASS 3. The third subclass includes picture stones whose decor is finely done in relief and whose ground again is cut away, leaving a ropelike effect. This also is a typical Han technique as represented in the mortuary reliefs at Xiaotang Shan and Nanyang, and on early bronze vessels, such as *hu* vases, where the pictures occur on the belly as disconnected scenes of people and things.

One can rub either the entire circumference, forming a long continuous belt or, easier, the separate scenes one by one. Rubbing such relief is very much the same as for subclass 2, but one must exercise caution in pressing the rubbing paper too far down into the low areas, for fear of its breaking. The ink tone should be a little lighter, and as the rope ground often carries an inscription, one must rub with particular care to differentiate the characters from the corded ground.

SUBCLASS 4. The fourth subclass consists of relief pictures that lie on the same plane as the ground, corded or plain, but are separated from the ground by an excised "line" that demarcates the picture, which then stands out in gradually rising, rounded relief on the same plane as the surrounding ground. The best examples of so-called floating carving occur in Han tomb and coffin decor, such as at Liangcheng Shan and Xilengyinshe.[89] One especially elegant approach to inking such relief is to make the edge or border sharp, the corded ground dark, the picture a bit lighter, and the edge-bulge deep black. To emphasize the rounded flavor, one gradually lightens the ink tone as one moves outward, ending with the border pure white. Metal-and-stone specialists, whose salient interest is in inscriptions cut into the ground, give the same ink tone to ground and pictures alike.

Han clay tomb tiles, mortuary bricks, and roof-tile heads (*wadang*) commonly feature fine pictures. These tiles and bricks generally carry relief carving of the kind just described, with details in intaglio. Pictures encompass an astonishingly rich and wide-ranging corpus of motifs, including hunting scenes, presentations of captives, strange animals and birds, emperors, and female beauties.

The rubbing method is the same as that described above. One often must apply a coating of white wax to such lower-fired tiles, or brush on a little alum water when one lays the paper; otherwise, the porous clay will absorb the water or sizing liquid so quickly that the tamping and inking processes are ineffectual. As these tiles and bricks often manifest burred edges from manufacture, the tamping and inking may take special care so as not to tear the paper or cause the burrs to take on too much ink.

Sculpture of the Six Dynasties carried on this Han tradition, with full scenes, such as offerings and Buddhas preaching, or individual images, such as the Buddha, Maitreya, and other holies. There were dedicatory inscriptions cut on stele heads and backs, mountain cliffs and grotto walls, pagoda waist slabs, scripture pillar bases, and tomb pagodas of Buddhist priests. Outstanding examples are the image of Cao Wangxi, the Longmen and Yungang cave sculptures, and others still extant in the middle reaches of the Yellow River (*Zhongyuan*). One either can copy an entire scene, using a whole sheet of paper, or, easier, make quality rubbings (*jingta*) of individual scenes or parts of scenes.

High Relief

High relief (*gaorou diao*) stands between low relief, or floating carving, and sculpture in the round. It is characteristic of the centuries following the Six Dynasties, with the Sui and the Tang manifesting particularly fine and delicate examples. Extant examples include the following: in the Sui, the lifelike quality of the Buddha preaching shown on the waist of the Sheli Ta (pagoda) at Xixia Shan, northeast of Nanjing; in the Tang, the limestone carvings of the Six Chargers of Emperor Taizong (figs. 4.12–4.13),[90] and the superb ornamentation in the Buddha niches at Xiangtang Shan, Yungang, and Longmen (fig. 4.14); in the Song, the cliff cutting at Feilaifeng, near Hangzhou, and the preaching Buddha on the twin pagodas at Quanzhou; and in the Five Dynasties period, scenes on the stone *chuang* pillars at Lingyin Si at Hangzhou, on the twin pagodas at Fantian Si, and in the niche decor at Ciyunling.

Representations of flying gods call for particular attention—marvelous details such as clasped hands, scattered flowers, long flowing skirts and wide sleeves, and a floating, ethereal quality, with the art of Wu Daozi exemplary. Such details pose many problems, but one must not neglect them.

Rubbing such high relief is more difficult to do than rubbing floating carving, and one becomes increasingly aware of the limits of the technique as the relief increases (fig. 4.15). The rubbing paper must be strong and pliable, with *pi* specifically recommended. Where bold relief demands, one should use *baiji* and a double layer of cushioning paper in tamping. As most high reliefs are in the outdoors, where there is no hot water to prepare the *baiji*, one should prepare it ahead, or else undissolved bits will show in the inking.

In brushing on the rubbing paper, one must be careful to lay it flat and without

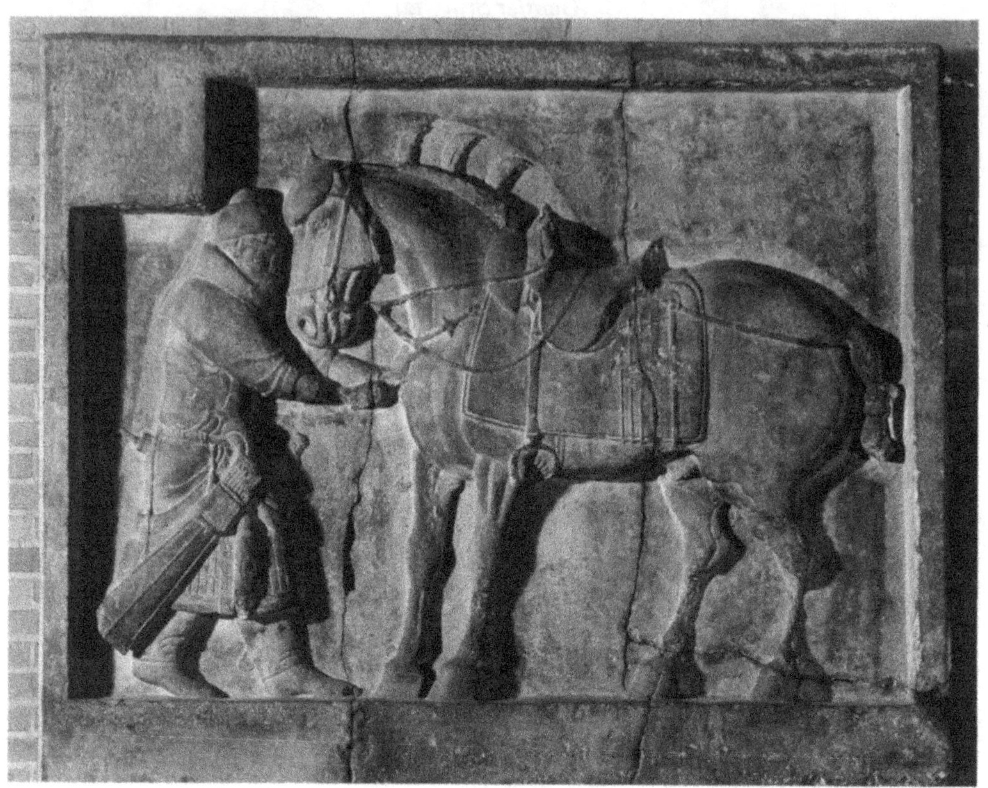

FIG. 4.12. High relief, *Whirlwind Victory*, 7th century. University of Pennsylvania Museum, S8.62844.

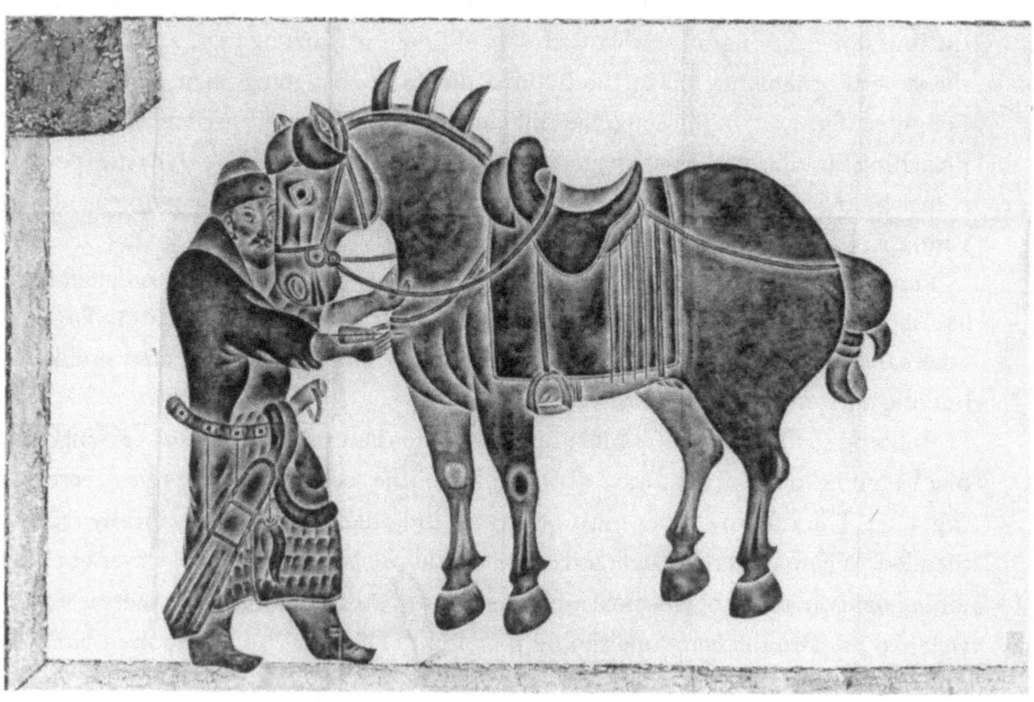

FIG. 4.13. Rubbing of a copy of *Whirlwind Victory*. Freer Gallery of Art Study Collection, Smithsonian Institution, FSC-R-404.

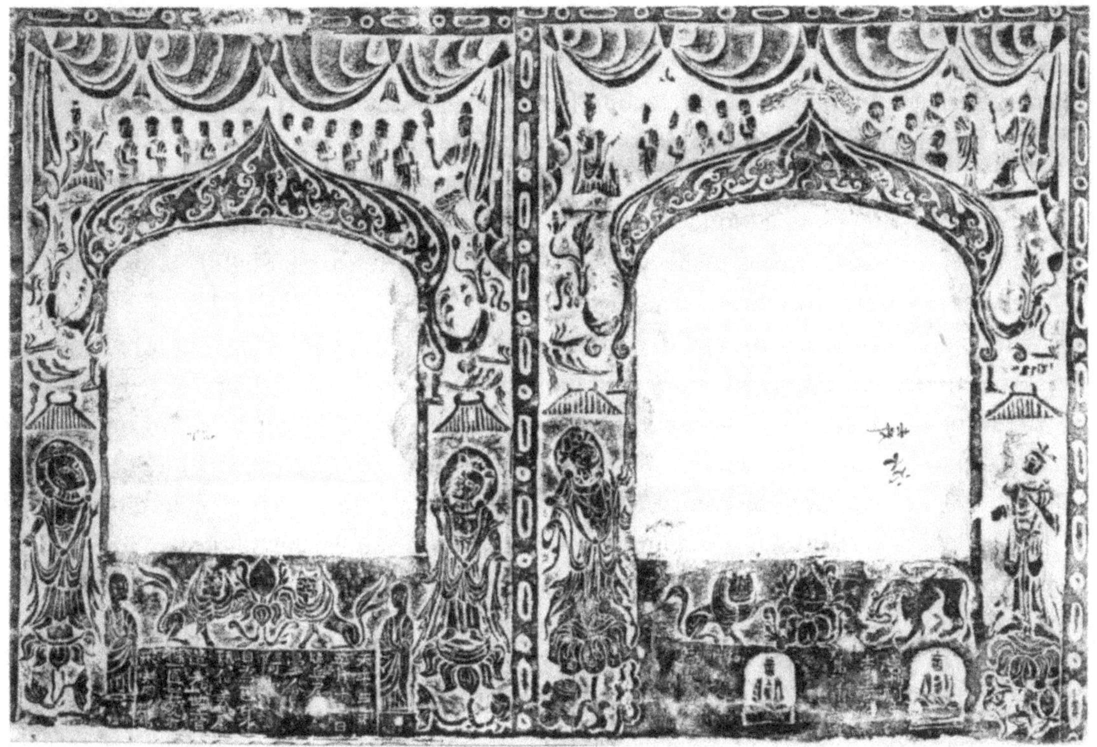

Fig. 4.14. High relief, Buddhist niche, Longmen. Eastern Wei, 537. Freer Gallery of Art, Smithsonian Institution, gift of Peking University, 1980.49.

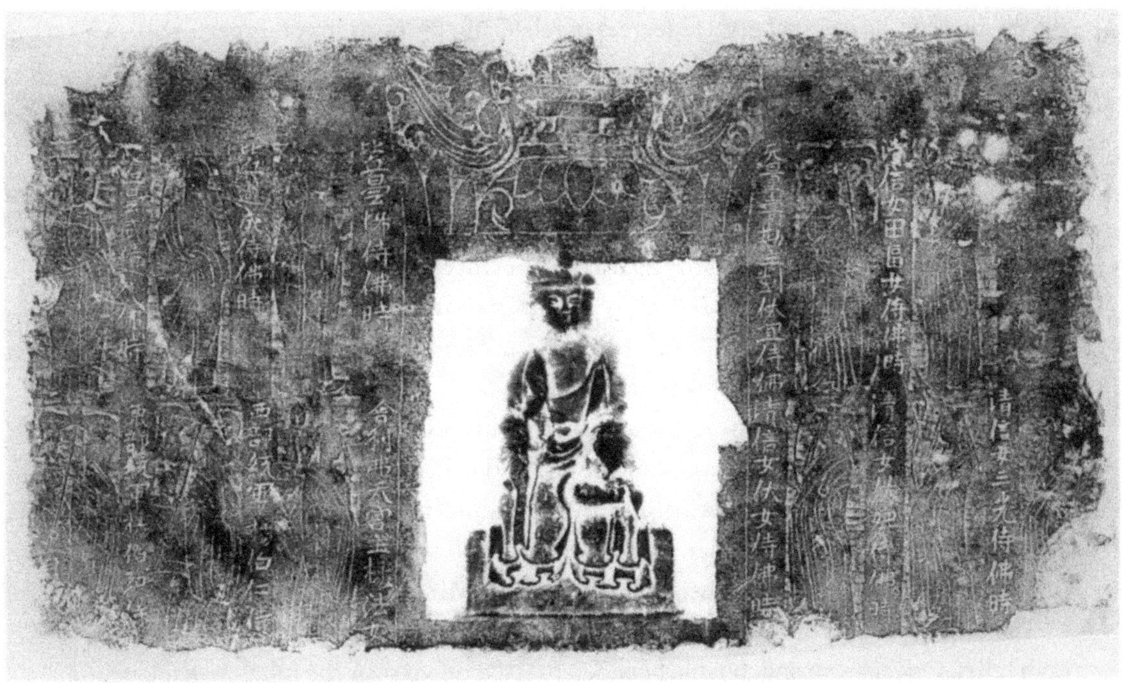

Fig. 4.15. Buddist high-relief sculpture, Northern and Southern dynasties or Tang, showing distortion in rubbing. Freer Gallery of Art, study rubbing no. 6, Smithsonian Institution.

creases, with special attention to the trailing portions of the "heavenly clothing" that characterizes mythological and religious figures. One must be careful not to wrap the paper too tightly, for fear of breaking it in tamping and creating too "fat" a representation in inking. One should use a wad of cotton waste wrapped loosely in *ling* silk to press the rubbing paper around the relief. Although a loose wad is preferred for the major elements of the relief, mallet and felt pad may be necessary for lightly tamping fine lines of whiskers, eyebrows, and clothing.

Inking calls for an artistic eye. In terms of a full 360 degrees, if the range of the relief is 120 degrees, one should rub only about 100 degrees, or else the inked representation will be too fat, distorted. If the range is only 100 degrees, one is limited to inking only about 80 to 90 degrees, and so on. Yet other aspects also must be considered if one is to achieve the maximum aesthetic effects. In rubbing the praying hands of images, one should not ink vertically, for by doing so one inks only the outer sides of the two little fingers. There is no way to represent such praying hands accurately, but the most satisfactory approach is to rub the entire back of one of the two hands. To represent ears effectively, one often must rub them separately, then cut them out and paste them on in a realistic manner.

The secret of rubbing high relief lies in postrubbing adjustment and mounting. One cuts the inked image apart and pastes the ears, hands, and arms together on a separate sheet to approximate the principles of painting and the proportions and balance of the human body. One then quickly takes the creation to the mounting shop while the memory of the original object, degrees of relief, and proportions of its parts still are clear in one's mind.

Sculpture in the Round

Sculpture in the round (*liti*) poses vastly heightened challenges, and one sees how the rubbing technique becomes severely strained and useful mainly as a supplement for photography to capture fine details, such as cutting marks and other evidence of workmanship common in Han stone carving. Exemplary are the stone cuts in memory of Qu Xiangbu and the bizarre animal sculptures in front of the tomb of Huo Qubing (d. 117 B.C.E.), an eminent military commander.

Examples of sculpture in the full round abound in Chinese art: Shang stone images; pre-Han bronze vessels, including *zun* wine jars in the form of wild animals; Northern Wei finely carved stone Buddhas; Sui and Tang Buddhist massive images, such as those at Yungang and Xinchang, Zhejiang; Song ceramic *luohan*; Yuan small Lamaist bronze Buddhas, only an inch or so in height; and excellent Ming bronze images.

The technique for rubbing three-dimensional objects is similar to that for rubbing high relief. One uses strong, pliable *pi* paper, pressed down over the relief with a loose wad of cotton waste and *ling* silk. Caution is especially necessary in dealing with the deeper parts of the relief, for if one presses the paper too far down, it will break, and so one must press it down just far enough that the ink dabber will not strike it. One must deal as best one can with the inevitable wrinkles by careful adjustment and judicious cutting of the paper.

Some differences of technique do occur, most of them in inking, the most important and difficult aspect of rubbing sculpture in the round. Here, there are two considerations, one relating to materials and techniques, and the other to aesthetics. First, the inking materials and the techniques must accommodate the demands of sculpture in the full round. The dabbers should be of several kinds and sizes to allow for types and degrees of relief that characterize such sculpture. Intaglio requires a very tightly bound dabber; relief, a more loosely bound one.

Second, from the standpoint of aesthetics, the inking must communicate the three-dimensional quality of the original. The technique comes under ever greater strain as the degree of curvature and amount of relief increase, and its limitations become eminently clear with full round. Such objects encompass the entire 360 degrees, but the viewer sees only 180 degrees, and that in theory only, for only some 140 degrees or so are clearly visible. Of this amount, one can rub only about 120 degrees, or else there is the problem of "fatness." As with high relief, one must consider the total effect and so should rub the back of one of the two praying hands rather than just the outer two little fingers, and only one of the two ears on a human figure, so that the image does not look like a double-eared vase.

All this suggests the need for careful planning in inking, to achieve a convincing representation. One must consider what effect one wishes to achieve and decide what ink tone to give the respective elements of the piece to gain that effect. One also must consider these differential inkings in relation to the sequence of dabber movement. In each case, the considerations differ greatly from those for inking flat, even steles or similar objects. The goal in inking such objects is to apply the ink evenly over the entire surface in quantity and, especially, quality, to emphasize the contrast between the white inscriptions or pictures and the black ground. The stele rubber follows a methodical dabbing pattern, commonly dictated by the columns of text, proceeding down and across the columns. The rubber of sculptures achieves the three-dimensional effect by zonal inking and differential toning. In zonal inking, the artisan considers the object in the round, mentally dividing it into ink-tone zones which he inks in turn, completing one zone before proceeding to another. A rubber whose main experience has been with steles will have difficulty in inking an object in the round because of the relief and different inking sequence.

In differential toning, one further must plan with particular care what shading to give each of the surface elements to heighten the three-dimensional effect. One must work out in one's mind well in advance which parts of the relief are to be dark and which light, and where the tone of the ink gradually should begin to darken, for it is only by differential shading that one achieves a convincing three-dimensional effect. If doubts exist about the tone of a given zone, one should lean toward a lighter rather than a darker tone, for corrections are easier.

These differential inking effects for rubbing in the round are quite different from the simple rubbing of light and dark effects, which are inspired by aesthetic taste or religious reverence. Here, the technique is much more sophisticated and is motivated by the desire to communicate a three-dimensional quality. The approach to capturing this quality is the divided-paper method (*gezhi fa*), which depends on differential toning and involves two aspects.[91] One is communicating the three-dimensional quality. This, one achieves by dividing the sculpture vertically down the midline in the mind's eye, and then laying the ink on the paper very lightly in the midline and ever more darkly toward the sides, ending with the edge line dead black. By such differential inking one can achieve the flavor of roundness. If one were to lay on the ink in the opposite fashion, with the midline dense and the sides gradually lighter, the resulting inked image would be shapeless.

The other aspect is the need for differentially toning the components of the sculpture. True differential toning is complicated and difficult, but there are a few general guidelines. First, as a fundamental rule, the more convex the relief, the darker the inking should be. Second, the head of a figure should be lighter than the rest of the body. The hair, particularly the typical Buddhist chignon, should be very dark, while the forehead should be left white. Third, the face is the most important emphasis, with clear differentiation among the forehead, eyebrows, eyes, tip of the nose, cheeks, lips, jaws, and chin. Moving from the area above the eyes, one gradually should lighten the ink toward the cheeks and lower face, with the desired effect likened to smoke lessening and clouds scattering. There is room for aesthetics, as in making the ink a little darker under the eyes for a natural effect. To heighten the effect of roundness one should darken the eyes, the end of the nose, and the lips, and using the cicada-wing technique to rub the facial parts enables one to achieve the marvelous effect of five different tones. Finally, as in rubbing high-relief sculpture, one must cut and paste to achieve the proper body proportions and most realistic results.

This affords insight into the great thought and skill that go into achieving a successful three-dimensional effect in rubbing objects in the full round. Ending on an exhortatory note, Jiang counsels: "Summing up, keep in mind the essential meaning of the pictorial quality, be bold but cautious, do not be afraid of complexities, put up with fatigue, examine and be sensitive [to the subtleties, and] adapt to the circumstances [of the situation]. [If one] follows these six rules, one will not have bad results."[92]

In inking, to an even greater degree than in other steps in the rubbing process, the essential factor is not to be too anxious or too hasty.[93] With inscriptions especially in mind, but with the observation equally valid in all rubbing situations, Chen Jieqi darkly forecasts the product of a poor technique: "An inferior and clumsy [technique] uses a soggy dabber and pounds directly down into the characters, does not observe whether the characters are wet or dry, does not question whether the ink on the dabber is even or uneven, does not strive for the [proper] hand technique, and does not consider the exactness or inexactness of the edges of the characters, and that's all there is to it!"[94]

One can make an adequate rubbing with relative ease and speed. To make an excellent rubbing, faithful and attractive, one must be prepared to give unsparingly of one's time, define one's intellectual and aesthetic objectives, concentrate one's mind, and carry out the work with painstaking care. One should not dally, but one also should not sacrifice quality for speed. If one follows this advice and proceeds in the prescribed manner, one will be able "to communicate [the spirit of] the writing-style of the characters, and by not rubbing too little and not rubbing too much, one moreover can [achieve it]."[95]

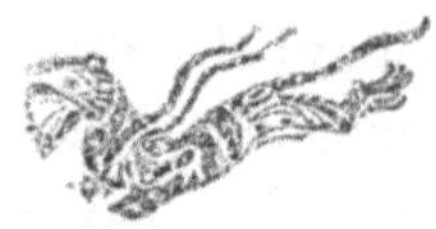

5 / Variations on the Theme

THE ACCOUNT thus far has dealt with simple, wet rubbings whose making involves wetting the paper, tamping it into or around the relief, and inking it with a dabber. They are two-dimensional, although zonal and differential toning of sculptures in the round can achieve a three-dimensional effect. Simple rubbings are most effective in rubbing flat or slightly curved surfaces, and they represent the standard rubbing and rubbing technique. Two variant forms are composite rubbings and dry rubbings.

COMPOSITE RUBBINGS

The making of composite rubbings, or "full-form rubbings" (*quanxing taben*), also called "three-dimensional rubbings" (*liti taben*), "vessel-form rubbings" (*qixing taben*), and "pictorial rubbings" (*tuxing taben*), uses the same wet technique as does a simple rubbing, but it involves supplemental graphic arts methods. Composite rubbings still are two-dimensional, but through clever techniques they more convincingly communicate three-dimensionality than do simple rubbings. An artistic and technical tour de force, the composite technique was devised to represent the ritual bronze vessels and is a relatively recent innovation, dating back to the last years of the eighteenth century:

> Rubbing ritual vessels in full form [*quanxing*] first was done by Ma Qifeng [Jiaqing period, 1796–1820] of Jiaxing [Zhejiang]. *Odds and Ends on Metal and Stone* (Jinshi xie) [by Bao Changxi] (1:*ce* 3) records a Han *xi* basin, and Mr. Ma annotated it: "Han *xi*, an old rubbing [*jiu*[a]*ben*], and on the eighteenth day of the sixth month of the *wuwu* [year], Fuyan Ma Qifeng records it." The *wuwu* [year], moreover, was the third year [1798] of Jiaqing. *Inscriptions on Ancient Objects in the Studio of Refined Manners* (Qingyi Ge suo cang gu qiwu wen), book 1, includes composite [*quanxing*] rubbings of four *zun* wine jars and the *Zhong fu fu dun* vessel, [but] none is of good work. Zhang Yanji annotated it in the second year [1822] of Daoguang. Xu Kang's *Record of Reflections of the Past* (Qianchenmeng yinglu) continues the story:
>
>> In Wumen [Suzhou] they made rubbings [*chui*[b]*ta*[b]] of metal and stone [objects], but until then they did not know how to make composite rubbings. By the first years of Daoguang [1821–1850], Ma Fuyan [Ma Qifeng] of He [Jiaxing], in Zhe [Zhejiang],

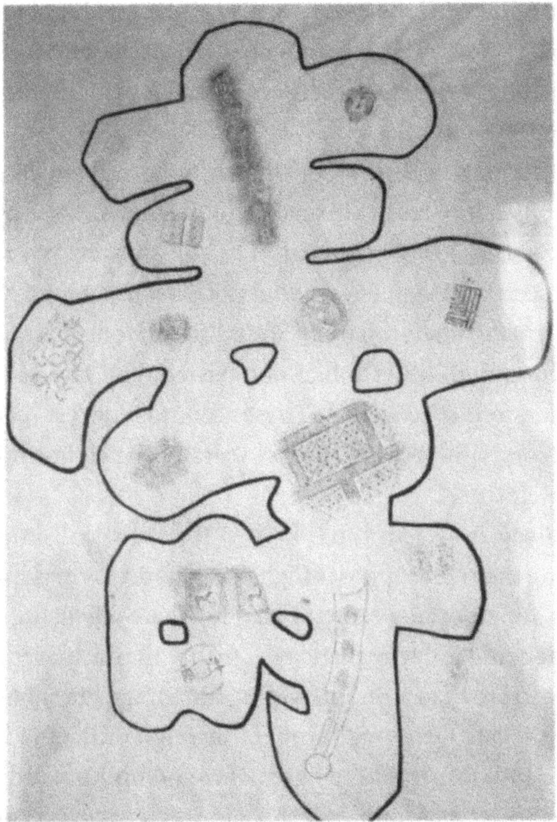

FIG. 5.1. Outline "longevity" character, filled with disparate small rubbings. Rubbings and photograph by the author.

> was able to do it. Liu Zhou [literary name of Da Shou (1791–1858), Buddhist monk at White Horse Temple (Baima Si), Haining, Zhejiang] was his student, and subsequently he made a "longevity picture" [*Baishou tu*] for Ruan Wenda Gong [Ruan Yuan] at the Jade Buddha Temple [Yufo An]. Using a 6–foot sheet of paper, he wrote a large outline longevity character in "grass style." Then he selected many kinds of metal and stone [objects] and took rubbings [of parts of them], a corner, the top, or the bottom, and although one did not see the objects in their entirety, nevertheless, as it was laid on [them], the rubbing paper sometimes must have been dry and sometimes wet, and after thus having moved it five or six times, he first succeeded in obtaining a finished representation [showing the disparate rubbings inside the outline].[1]

Although Liu Zhou did not use the technique to represent a whole vessel, he used the basic principle of shifting the paper to rub parts of different objects on a single sheet, as in figure 5.1.[2] The account adds that Ruan Yuan, one of the most esteemed scholars of the time, greatly appreciated the new type of rubbing and highly rewarded Liu Zhou with gold for his artful work. He also presented Liu Zhou with a stone seal inscribed "Metal-and-Stone Monk" (*Jinshi seng*). Thereafter, it is said, others copied Liu Zhou's technique.

Rong continues, quoting *Register of Metal and Stone, Calligraphy and Painting in the Studio of Precious Simplicity* (Baosu Shi jinshi shuhua bian nianlu, by Weng Fanggang) for the sixteenth year (1836) of Daoguang: "The sub-prefect, Wu Kangfu, visited me and said there was a certain Hong Pu, secretary of Cheng Muan of Xin'an, who saw his teacher rub [*shouta*[a]] a *ding* cauldron in the round, and [Hong Pu] said [that his teacher] had created something that hitherto had not existed, and had initiated a marvelous model for metal-and-stone specialists."[3] These accounts suggest that making composite rubbings began sometime during the last years of the eighteenth century and the first years of the nineteenth.

Scholars and collectors esteem those known for their skill in making composite rubbings, for making them presupposes high competence in making simple rubbings. Several individuals are especially remembered for their talents in making composite rubbings and for the remarkably realistic effects that they achieved.

Ma Qifeng has been credited with innovating the composite rubbing technique, and he was active from the late Qianlong through the reign of Jiaqing into the Daoguang period, from 1790 to 1830. Ma is said to have passed on his knowledge to Da Shou (Liu Zhou), the "Metal-and-Stone Monk." Of this pioneer work with composite rubbings, little remains: "Nowadays, save for that [1798 rubbing in the *Jinshi xie*], there is not a single [extant] example of Mr. Ma's work. Through transmission we still have examples of Liu Zhou's rubbings, and they very closely approximate the *yinyang* [three-dimensional] quality of the original objects."[4]

In turn, Liu Zhou passed on his knowledge to Li Jinhong of Yanghu [Changzhou, Jiangsu]. In more recent times, Zhou Xiding (personal name, Kangyuan [1891–1961]) of Jinqi, Jiangxi, a renowned cutter of seals, also achieved fame as a maker of composite rubbings. Although Zhou Xiding's work is said not to be quite as fine as that of Chen Jieqi (1813–1871), his work convincingly captures the illusion of three dimensions. Zhou's skill is represented in Sun Zhuang's *Illustrations of Auspicious Metals in the Clear Autumn Studio* (Chengqiu Guan jijin tu), which features composite rubbings of bronzes in the collection of Chen Baochen (1845–1935). There are many of Zhou's wonderfully realistic rubbings in the National Central Library, Taiwan (figs. 5.2–5.3). The seals associated with the square *ding* cauldron are those of Luo Zhenyu and Zhou Xiding. Luo's seal reads, "Vessels from the Three Ancient Dynasties in the Xuetang [Luo's courtesy name] collection" [*Xuetang cang San Dai qi*]. Zhou's seal reads, "Xiding hand-rubbed metal-and-stone inscription" [*Xiding shouta*[a] *jinshi wenzi*]. One other *quanxing*

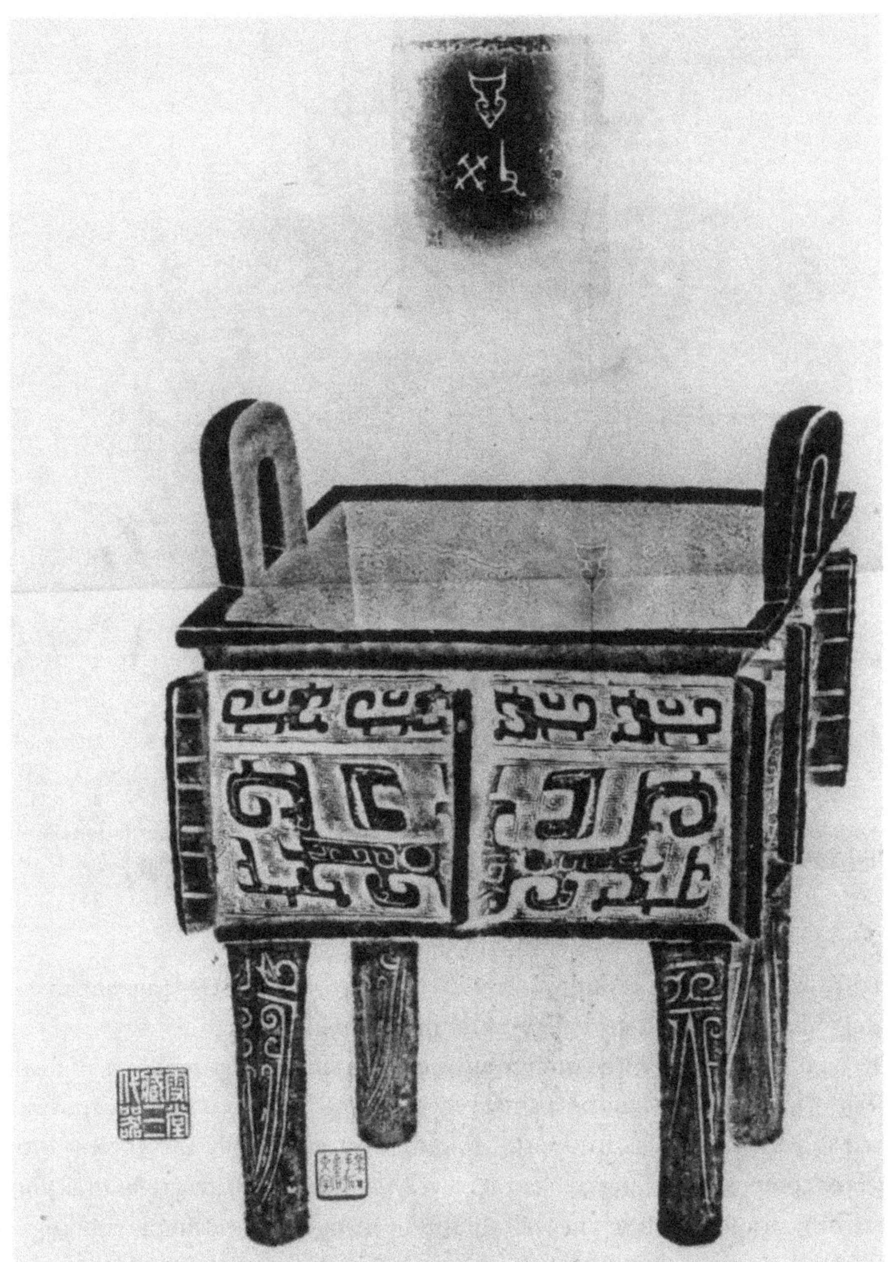

FIG. 5.2. Composite rubbing by Zhou Xiding of the Shang *Fugui* square *ding* cauldron, seals of Zhou and Luo Zhenyu. Collection of the National Central Library, R.O.C.

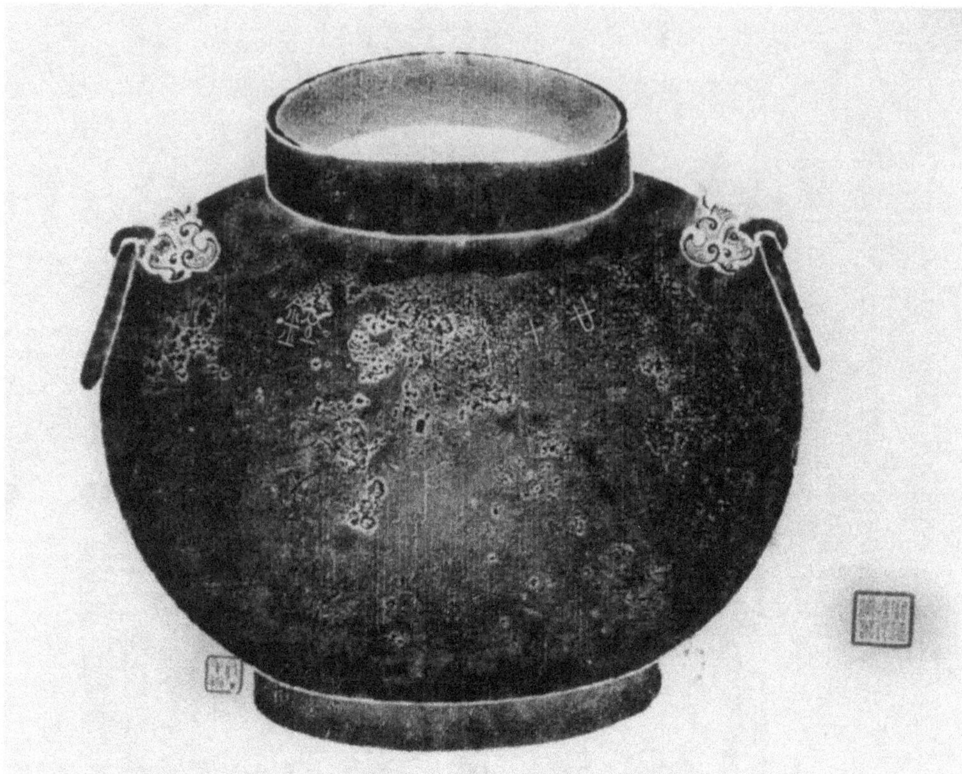

Fig. 5.3. Composite rubbing by Zhou Xiding of a Han *pou* jar. Collection of the National Central Library, R.O.C.

specialist in the modern period was Ma Ziyun (1903–1986) of Heyang, Shaanxi. Ma's rubbings are preserved in the Palace Museum in Beijing.

The technique began with combining a series of simple, wet rubbings of disparate small inscriptions or designs on a single sheet of paper for decorative purposes. That evolved to rubbing objects in the full round, most commonly the ancient bronzes. Makers of composite rubbings seek to achieve what Chinese writers refer to as *yinyang*, a three-dimensional quality. They obtain this by using standard simple rubbing materials and techniques, augmented with preliminary conjunctional graphic arts methods, manipulation of the rubbing paper, and differential inking to achieve the illusion of depth.

Five descriptions of the technique afford insights into the careful planning and demanding work. Four are written; one is oral. The oldest written account, that on which the other two are based, is in *A Separate Record on Transmitting Antiquity* (Chuangu bielu), by Chen Jieqi. It consists of but five cryptically succinct lines:

> In "rubbing a picture" [*tatu*], recording measurements is important—top, middle, and bottom [of the vessel], high and low. In determining its curvatures, use a horizontal string between wooden boards. If the string represents the outline and substitutes for the vessel, then [one] can achieve accuracy. Further, by tipping [the vessel] forward to see the mouth, [one] can obtain a perspective [*yinyang*] view of the vessel, using cardboard to cut it out. Lastly, for designs, ears, and feet, rub them and piece them together, removing them and combining them. For undecorated areas, use the flat surface of an old vessel, and rub them. One cannot do the rubbing on a tile or a board. For disconnected areas, shift the paper, and rub them. The technique of rubbing by adjusting the paper seems clever, but it is a vulgar and inelegant trifle.[5]

Apart from his initial elitist opinion of the composite technique, Chen assumes that his readers will be familiar with the method, in addition to which he perhaps shows his scholarly reluctance to involve himself in craft details. Finally, as Rong Geng suggests below, Chen may not have fully understood the technique himself. These aspects, plus the esoteric quality of the subject, the spare nature of the language, and the passage of more than a century, with all the loss of cultural content that such passage implies, combine to make the account so arcane as to be unintelligible to the uninitiated.

Although he, too, is concise, Rong Geng amplifies:

> Composite rubbing [*quanxing taben*] involves manipulating the paper, and during the time of Mr. Chen [Jieqi] they simply still had not acquired the knack. Fleetingly observed, the composite rubbing technique is not easy to understand. . . . [1] One first calculates the measurements [of the vessel] and then either sketches it . . . in the manner of *Illustrated Catalogue of Antiquities* [in the Song imperial collection] [Xuanhe bogu tu, by Wang Fu, d. 1126] or takes a photograph and makes a one-to-one enlargement, and then it is easy to approximate the original. [2] Next, lay down a thick piece of oiled [ink-resistant] paper [on the sketch or photograph], and, following the drawn ink line [or photograph underneath], cut it [the oiled paper] out [in stencil fashion], dividing it into an appropriate number of pieces [according to the parts of the vessel]. If one wishes to rub a particular part, one lays down the oiled paper [stencil] representing that part. [3] Next, fashion a zinc or iron plate, whose surface should not be too smooth, and [4] lay [a sheet of] blank [rubbing] paper on it. Then [5] take the [stencil-type] representation cut out of the oiled paper and lay it on the blank [rubbing] paper. If one is rubbing a *ding* cauldron, one lays down the oiled paper [stencils] for the mouth, handles, belly, and feet and rubs [inks] their outlines [on the rubbing paper]. [6] Finally, lay the rubbed outlines [by turns] on [the corresponding parts of] the original vessel and, one by one, [simple, wet] rub their decorative elements, corrosions, and interior inscriptions. Then the representation can be considered complete.[6]

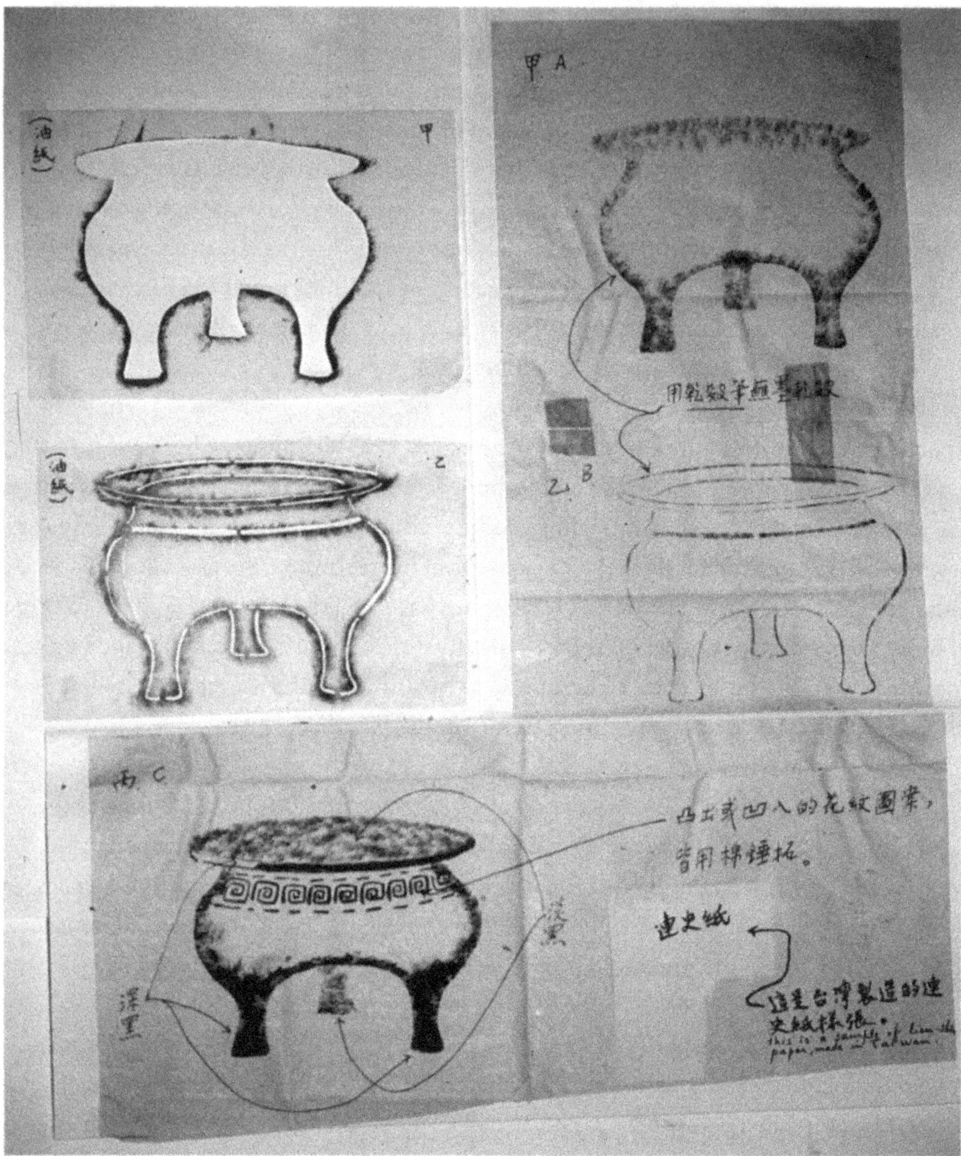

Fig. 5.4. Sketching, stenciling, and inking techniques. Sketch by Su Yinghui; photograph by the author.

Su Yinghui further clarifies the process:

According to the new method of making a composite rubbing, as explained by Rong Geng . . . , the *first step* is to sketch the size and shape of the vessel in full size (that is, a *shuanggou* [outline] stencil) on a sheet of rubbing paper. The *second step* is to spread a same-size sheet of [translucent] thick oiled paper on top of the outline representation of

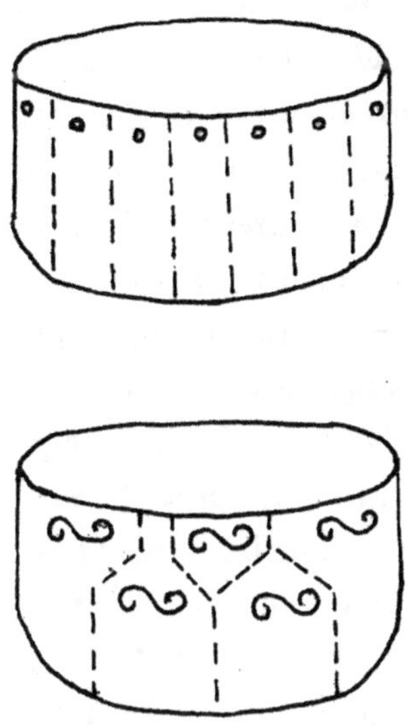

FIG. 5.5. Zone division for a composite rubbing. Sketch by the author.

> the vessel. Then use scissors to cut out the black line on the oiled paper (that is, the drawn outline of the vessel). That is to say, the outline on the original sheet of paper then becomes a negative line [stencil] on the oiled paper. The *third step* is to fashion a zinc or iron plate of the same size as that of the vessel's representation. The *fourth step* is to spread a sheet of white *lianshi* [rubbing] paper on the zinc plate (flat and not too smooth). The *fifth step* is to lay the cut-out oiled-paper [stencil] on the blank [rubbing] paper. Use a rubbing tool [dabber] (the best is to use fine *chou* silk, inside of which is cotton, to make a dabber; if not that, then using a worn-down [Chinese] brush pen will do). Ink-rub the negative [stencil] lines [representing the vessel outline]. The *sixth step* is to lay the [rubbing paper with its stenciled] ink-rubbed outline on the original vessel to rub [by turn] its decorative elements, corrosions, and interior inscriptions. In this manner, the composite [rubbing] then is complete.
>
> If there are projecting parts of the vessel (such as ears, rings, feet, et cetera), then one must use the oiled-paper [stencils] and, in sequence, rub their outlines, [repeating the entire process for each part].[7]

Figure 5.4 illustrates these sketching, stenciling, and inking techniques, and figure 5.5 illustrates zone division.

Further amplification came from a demonstration by Zhang Xuan of rubbing an iron gong (fig. 5.7).[8] Before starting, one must decide which face of the vessel carries the most important inscriptions or designs. The most common view is from the front, with the vessel standing flat or tipped slightly forward. In the latter case, only part of an interior inscription will show, and one then makes a separate simple rubbing of the full inscription. The vessel also can be turned slightly to show flanges, or "ears." When possible, one should select a face with a dividing "line," such as characterizes *taotie* (monster mask) motifs on Shang bronzes that divide vertically into two mirror-image halves, with vertical lines to divide the rubbing work into working zones. One also must determine how best to divide the inscription or design to create a perspective effect. Some inscriptions or designs are regular and easily divided, and one can shift the rubbing paper without adversely affecting the perspective. The *Mao Gong ding* tripod is an example, for its external border band consists only of spaced rosettes between which one can run the zone lines (see fig. 3.5 and fig. 5.5, top). Vessels with complicated overall designs are more challenging, as are many Shang and Zhou bronzes, especially those from the Warring States, which are covered with fluid designs (fig. 5.5, bottom; fig. 5.6). To avoid problems with perspective, the zone lines will be irregular, so as not to pass through the motifs. Each type of vessel has its distinctive characteristics and challenges: square *ding* cauldrons are difficult to capture in side-angle view, and *zhong* bells with bosses pose difficulties. The more one tips vessels forward, the more pronounced the arc becomes, and the more difficult the perspective is to represent. Finally, heightening the challenge, the larger the vessel and the more complex its designs, the larger the paper must be, and the more difficult its manipulation.

Making a composite rubbing involves two phases, each with several steps (numbered below 1–5 in the first phase, and 6–10 in the second), and two graphic arts techniques: that of sketching and stenciling, and that of simple wet rubbing.

Phase 1

The first phase consists of five steps that involve sketching and stenciling.

STEP 1. When one has decided on the point of view, the first step is to sketch or photograph the vessel and its parts precisely and in full scale, for making stencils. There is a direct relationship between the accuracy of the sketch or photograph and that of the resulting rubbing. If the sketch or photograph is inaccurate, or not a one-to-one representation, it will be difficult to match the stenciled line on the rubbing paper with the corresponding areas on the vessel when the rubbing work begins. The sketch or photograph must include the overall outline of the vessel and that of each part—ears, handles, feet, covers, and inscribed or decorated zones. Accurate measurements are crucial: across the mouth, from the top to the surface of rest, around the top and the middle bands (especially important), and the lower band.

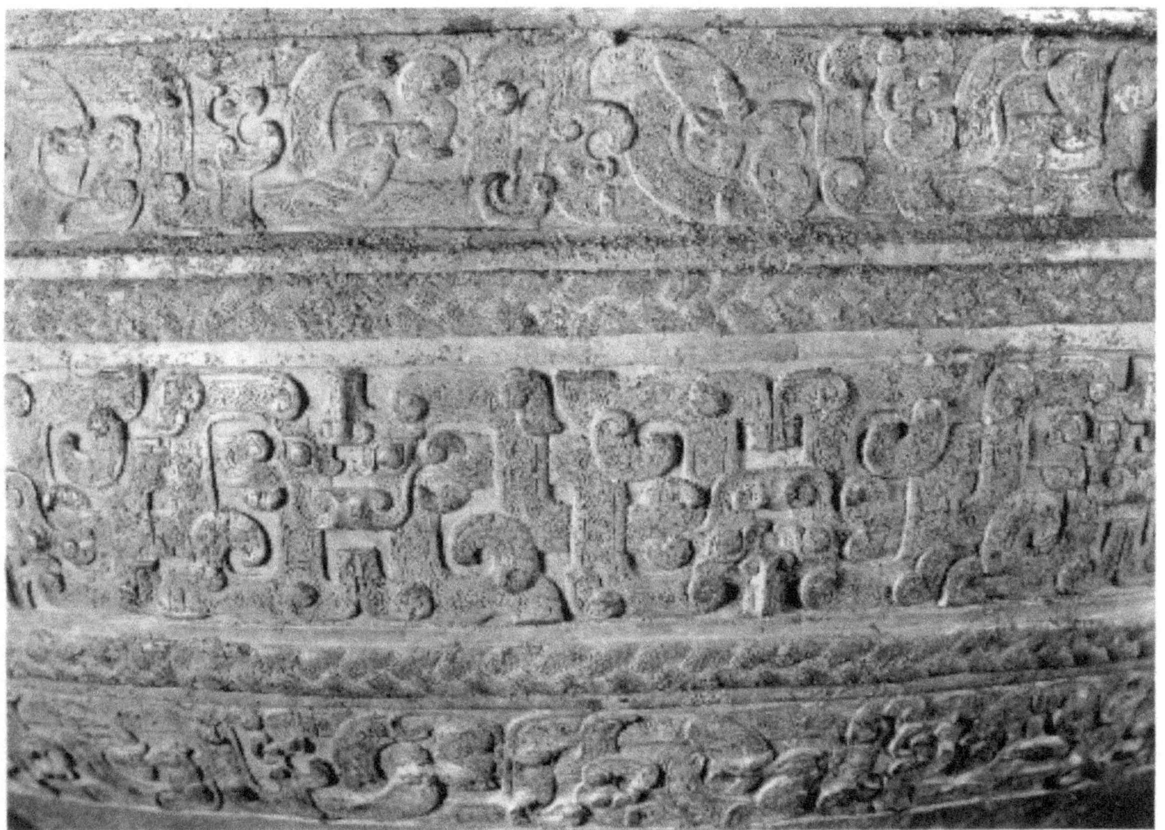

FIG. 5.6. Detail of an inscribed Warring States bronze *jian* basin. Shanxi, Houma. Freer Gallery of Art, Smithsonian Institution, Washington, D.C. F1939.5.

STEP 2. The second step involves making stencils for the vessel, its component parts, and the boundary lines of the zones of inscriptions and designs. These stencils must be ink-resistant and can be of two types, depending on the artisan's preference and the complexity of the vessel. Some artisans use a series of simple positive cutouts (fig. 5.7, top; fig. 5.8, B), while others prefer negative stencils (fig. 5.8, C). One must experiment to obtain the most convincing results.

If one uses a simple cutout, one cuts out the overall form of the vessel that one has sketched or photographed (fig. 5.7, bottom; fig. 5.8, A). One then cuts out from it other pieces for the individual parts and zones, which one then uses to break down the subsequent rubbing work (fig. 5.7, top; fig 5.8, B). Zhang noted that in making a composite rubbing of a vessel with many component parts and a complex design, there may be twenty separate cutouts for an ear alone, and as many as two hundred shifts of the rubbing paper in the ensuing rubbing phase. One must plan and try to foresee how one's decisions will contribute to three-dimensionality.

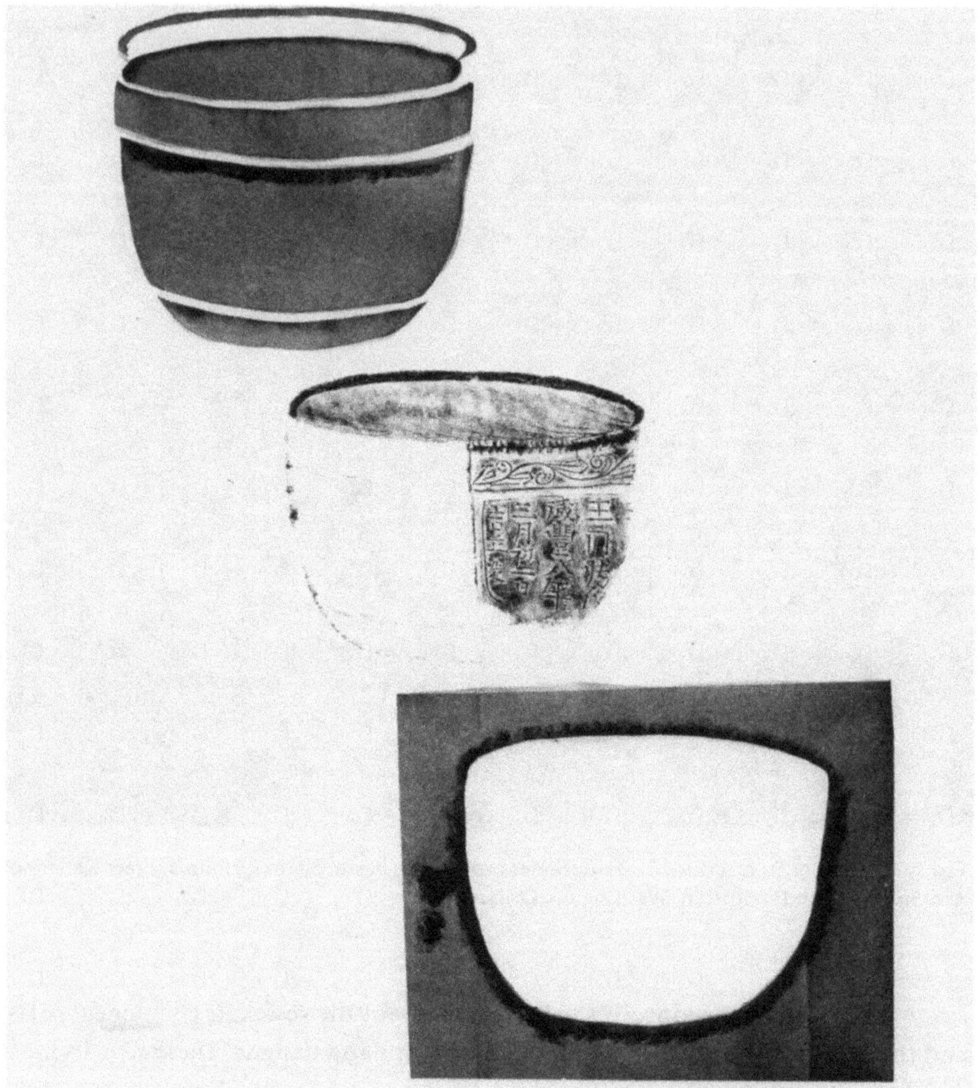

FIG. 5.7. Stencils for and composite rubbing of a Qing-dynasty iron gong. Stencils, rubbings by Zhang Xuan; photograph by the author.

STEP 3. The third step involves using the stencil to ink the overall outline on a sheet of rubbing paper. One uses a flat metal plate (fig. 5.9, C) whose surface texture approximates that of the undecorated surfaces of the vessel. One lays the rubbing paper (fig. 5.9, B) on the plate, and the stencil on the paper (fig. 5.9, A).

STEP 4. In the fourth step, one dabs ink very lightly around the edges of the outline stencil to form a faint outline of the vessel on the rubbing paper. This stenciling is done

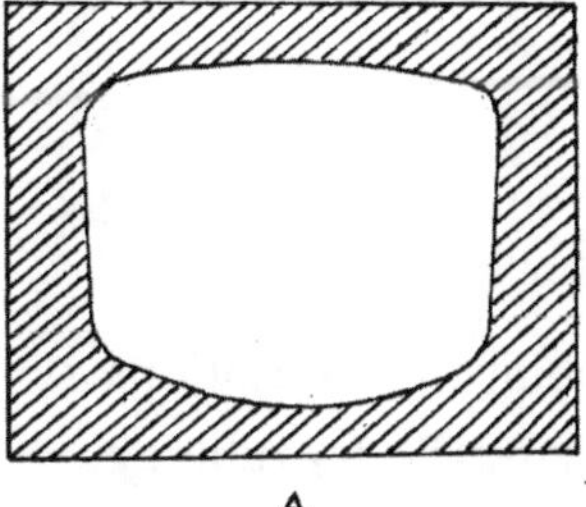

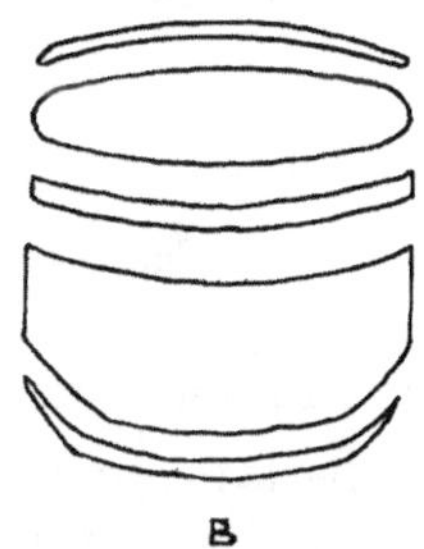

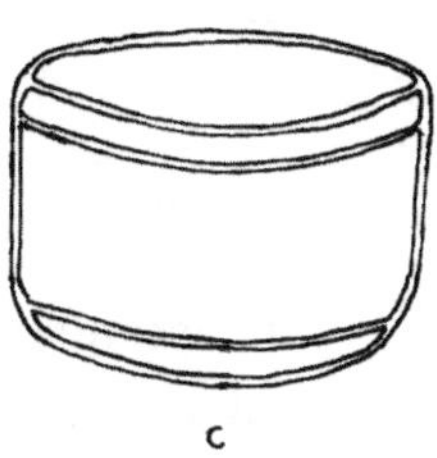

FIG. 5.8. Stencils for a composite rubbing. Sketch by the author.

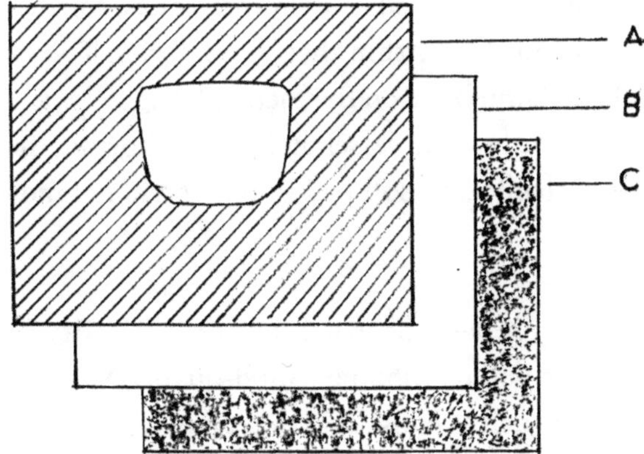

FIG. 5.9. Inking of undecorated surfaces. Sketch and photograph by the author.

so that only the outer edge of the vessel is well defined while the inner plain portion is treated to blend with the inking of the undecorated surfaces. If the vessel is plain and undecorated, or is tipped forward and the visible part of the interior rear wall is plain, one can lay the rubbing paper on the metal plate and rub it to achieve a textured effect, inking differentially to represent perspective, as described below. If the surfaces, either exterior or interior, have zones of inscriptions, designs, or corrosions, then one must rub them one by one by the simple wet rubbing technique. This method consists of dividing the rim or inside into a number of arbitrary segments that can be easily managed in the rubbing process. Each segment, especially of the rim, because of its curvature, may measure no more than a couple of centimeters.

STEP 5. The fifth step repeats the stenciling process for the outlines of each component part—ears, handles, feet, cover, and the boundary lines of the inscribed and decorated zones.

Phase 2

The second phase consists of five additional steps that involve rubbing the inscriptions and designs on the vessel and its parts by simple wet rubbing—laying the dry rubbing paper, wetting it with *baiji,* tamping it, and dabbing on ink. Whereas one rubs the textured plate to represent the plain surfaces of the vessel, such as the interior back wall, one rubs the actual inscribed, decorated, or corroded areas by the simple wet rubbing technique. Some modifications are necessary to heighten the perspective effect. Before rubbing the inscribed and decorated zones on the gong, one studies the stenciled lines demarcating those zones as well as the other zones, for the rubbed inscription and decorative elements must fit within their boundaries. The stenciled lines on the rubbing paper should be faint, done on the metal plate.

For ease of working, one lays the vessel on its side, showing the working face. One must support the vessel firmly on a soft pad so that it will not move or be damaged in the ensuing work.

STEP 6. In the sixth step, one lays the matching area of the dry rubbing paper on the area of the vessel that one will be rubbing. Good-quality Xuan paper will do, but for fine detail, thinner paper, such as *liansi,* is better. One aligns the paper so that the faint stenciled line matches the corresponding central ridge of the vessel.

STEP 7. One then begins the simple wet rubbing process, starting along the central vertical line and moving outward to the side, on the censer, toward the right (fig. 5.7, middle). With the rubbing paper perfectly aligned with the matching area on the vessel, in the seventh step one wets it with *baiji,* the strength of the solution depending on the smoothness of the surface—the smoother it is, the stronger the solution. In rubbing bronzes, one generally lays on the dry rubbing paper and then wets it with a brush, wetting only the portion on which one is working. Where the stenciled line and the matching line on the vessel begin to diverge, one stops wetting, leaving the next section for subsequent treatment.

STEP 8. Depending on the curvature of the line, the length of the section that one wets may be only 2 or 3 centimeters. The eighth step involves tamping that short section of wetted paper till it is suitably dry.

STEP 9. The ninth step, dabbing on the ink, requires careful toning to enhance the illusion of depth, shading darker those parts of the object that lie nearer the viewer and shading lighter those that lie farther away (figs. 5.2–5.3): "When making the rubbing, [one] must use dark and light [ink tones] to differentiate the *yin* and *yang* [three-dimensional quality], so that [the result] is not flat."[9] The use of light and dark ink in making composite rubbings thus differs from that in simple rubbings, where it commonly serves only aesthetic ends.

STEP 10. In the tenth step, one peels the rubbing paper and shifts it ever so slightly to the next segment outward toward the periphery and repeats the process, just as Da Shou did in a rudimentary way in making the longevity picture for Ruan Yuan. One proceeds in this fashion, rubbing a feature or an area, jiggling and shifting the paper ever so little, to match the features with those of the next line or section of the vessel—rewetting, retamping, and reinking until one has rubbed the entire vessel, its component parts, and their inscriptions, designs, and corroded areas. As the author knows from his own modest experience, all this is devil's work.

One must be careful that the ink is dry in one area before moving on to an adjoining area or else it will bleed and create a fuzzy image. A skilled artisan can save time by working on another area of the vessel while one area dries.

For a vessel that is about 25 centimeters wide, one would move the paper eight or nine times. In moving from section to section from the center outward, one must allow for the upturning of horizontal lines near the periphery, studiously following the line on the vessel, wiggling the rubbing paper ever so little upward to create the perspective effect. In adjusting the rubbing paper from one small section to the next, one must match the elements of the motif, as well as the lines on the vessel and any inscriptions. In creeping along this way, one must be particularly careful at the periphery, for it is there that errors in perspective are the most difficult to compensate for, and that mistakes are most obvious.

On the gong, the inscribed zone (fig. 5.7, middle), is the most important. It also is the most challenging, for its vertical depth makes the perspective problem the greater. One must divide the panel or zone into manageable horizontal segments. It is helpful to find natural demarcation lines, especially central ones, such as those on Shang *taotie* masks. If there are no natural demarcation lines, then one must make arbitrary ones, and the more complex the inscription or design is, and the more densely filled the area, as with the Warring States designs, the more difficult the challenge. In some cases, the design is so intricate and dense that there is no place to run a demarcation line, no matter how irregular it might be. Figure 5.5 shows a simplified representation of the difference between dividing regular and irregular designs. Figure 5.2 shows a Shang square *ding* with regular designs; figure 5.6 is a detail of a Warring States bronze *jian* basin with irregular designs.

Whether zones are regular or irregular, after having rubbed each portion of a line or zone, one shifts the rubbing paper ever so little toward the periphery to rub the next section, moving the lower part of the paper, corresponding to the lower part of the line or zone on the vessel, minutely more than the upper part. The rubbing paper thus gradually twists ever so slightly counterclockwise, if one is rubbing the right side, or clockwise, if one is rubbing the left side. In this way, one achieves the perspective effect. Here, the reason becomes apparent for not having the vertical division line pass through a design or inscription.

Where lines of characters are involved, if there are dividing lines or ridges on the vessel itself, one rubs the characters first and inks the lines last. If one instead inks the lines or ridges as one goes along, one finds that these inked lines are off center in relation to the rows of characters. This results from having shifted the paper a little for each succeeding row of characters to achieve a perspective effect (fig. 5.10). In achieving a matching maneuver, one must watch carefully, shifting and adjusting the rubbing paper so that, although one moves the paper, the demarcation lines, the inscriptions, and the designs all match as closely as possible. The perspective effect will be more successful if as many of the shift lines as possible occur in undecorated or uninscribed areas. In achieving a match, the most challenging areas are the upper and lower corners. The upper corners should be filled as much as possible; the lower, left as empty as possible.

Finally, an article by Zheng Shanshan et al. further clarifies the composite technique. The account gives a detailed description, complete with illustrations of each of the seventeen steps in the process and of rubbings of bronzes in the Palace Museum, in Beijing.[10]

These descriptions help in understanding how a composite rubbing transfers inscriptions and designs from a three-dimensional object to two-dimensional paper and how it allows foreshortening of the inscriptions and designs on the curved, receding outward edges. The artisan resolves these challenging problems by painstakingly manipulating the rubbing paper, shifting it as the demands of realistic representation require.

Summing up, making a simple rubbing is a *one-phase* operation: laying, tamping, and inking the paper. Making a composite rubbing is a *two-phase* operation, consisting of initial sketching (or photographing) and stenciling, and then laying, tamping, and inking, as in making a simple wet rubbing. The need for the first phase, and variations in the second, differentiate simple and composite techniques and their effects. Careful planning is essential, for corrections often are not possible, especially in the advanced stages of the work.

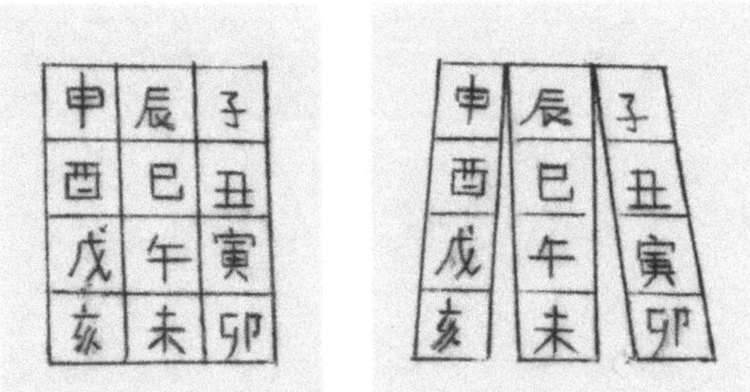

FIG. 5.10. Division of inscriptive zones. Sketch and photograph by the author.

The simple rubbing technique is effective for rubbing flat or lightly curved surfaces but cannot represent objects in the round. Makers of a composite rubbing achieve this effect by conceiving an image of an object in three-dimensional form and then devising the means of representing that image on two-dimensional paper. This conceptualization and the means of representing it on paper characterize the making of a composite rubbing.

The composite technique is a tour de force, with numerous stencils and up to two hundred shifts of the rubbing paper for rubbing a vessel with many parts and complex designs.[11] Even a very simple vessel requires a surprising number of stencils and shifts (fig. 5.11). Infinite care and skill are requisite in executing the technical details, with two particular challenges: the sequence in stenciling and rubbing the vessel and its component parts; and manipulation of the rubbing paper and application of the ink to simulate depth, overcome problems of foreshortening, and faithfully render curving or receding portions of the vessel. The rubbings in Wang Fu's *Illustrated Catalogue of Antiquities* depict the handling of such problems. The artisan must possess a keen aesthetic sense, a strong visual quality, and great manual dexterity. There is a highly creative factor, and composite rubbings of the same vessel done by different artisans, or even by the same artisan at different times, will differ in their perspective, details, and shading.

The advantages of this artful technique are apparent. When skillfully done, composite rubbing creates surprisingly realistic three-dimensionality, capturing peripheral decorative elements as well as those in the center, all in proper relationship. Even with square or rectangular objects, one does not have to torture the designs on the side panels unduly in altering the square into a rhomboid to attain perspective. Aesthetically, composite rubbings satisfy in that one can see the whole vessel and its decorative treatment and can visualize the relation of the various parts to each other and to the

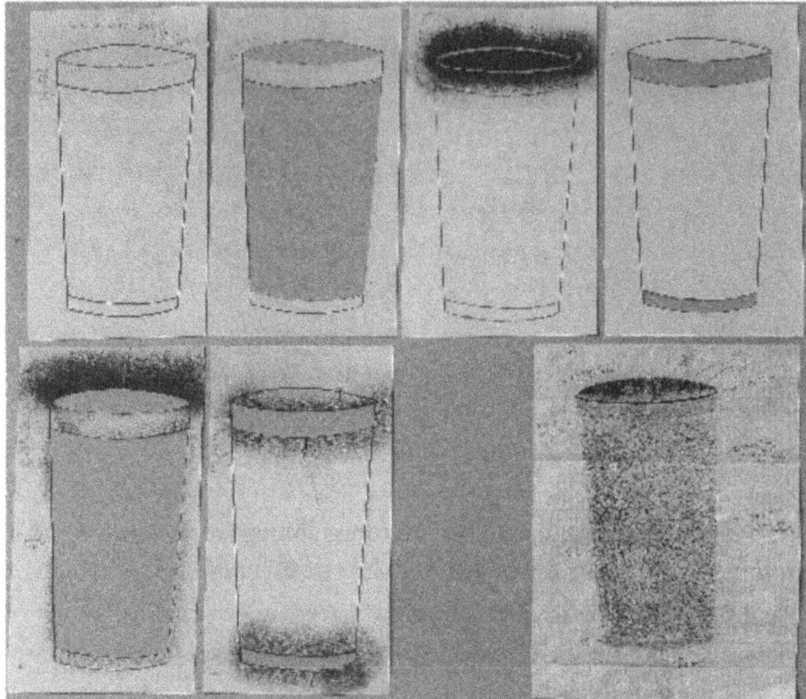

Fig. 5.11. Stencils for and composite rubbing of a glass tumbler. Sketch and rubbing by the author.

overall shape. Carrying realism to a high degree, and despite his initial elitist reservations about the technique, Chen Jieqi's household created rubbings in five colors, including simulated patination. When skillfully executed, composite rubbings achieve truly admirable effects, the more remarkable when one considers that the technique originated in China before the formal invention of photography in Europe and well before photography became common in China. Composite rubbings have constituted only a minuscule part of the great world of rubbings since the inception of the composite technique two hundred years ago, but recent years have seen a renewed interest in this ingenious art form.[12]

DRY RUBBINGS

The second variant involves making simple rubbings by the dry technique. The origins of the technique in China are clouded because of the lesser role it played by comparison with the wet technique, the lack of clarity about terms in early sources, and the temporal relationship between the initial making of dry rubbings in China and in Europe. One Chinese informant stated that the dry technique came to China from Europe only in the late nineteenth century, but it is likely that the diffusion was in the reverse direction. It is intriguing to note a scene in *The Interior of the Old Church at Delft* (fig. 5.12), a painting by Hendrick Van Vliet (1611–1675) in the Baltimore Museum of Art. It shows a group of four children and a small dog at the base of a massive pillar. One of the boys is on his hands and knees, with both hands on a small sheet of paper spread before him. The older girl holds a sheet of paper with two irregular red blotches on it.

The museum file included a letter in which the writer, a member of the Monumental Brass Society, noted that the scene, which suggests the dry rubbing of a mortuary slab, "confirmed my earlier impression that there are indeed some brass rubbers at work."[13] The secretary of the society was "sure" that it would "prove to be the earliest known record of rubbing." Although uncertain, the situation does suggest dry rubbing.

One can speculate that Europeans were making dry rubbings of covers in the mid-seventeenth century, but it is likely that the diffusion of the technique was from China to Europe.[14] As described earlier, Chinese tradition recorded the use of "stone ink" (*shimo,* graphite?) in Zhou times, but paper was not invented till the Later Han, and the rubbing technique, circa 500. The Chinese early used graphite or a similar substance for various purposes, perhaps including rubbing, well before Europeans used the method to rub tomb covers. In *Extension of the String of Pearls on the Spring and Autumn Annals* (Yanfan lu), written in the Song, Cheng Dachang uses the parallel phrases, *keshi wei bei, lamo wei zi,* "engrave stones to make stele (inscriptions), moisten with ink to make characters (writing)."[15] *Lamo* here seems to mean "moisten with ink," but, although less likely, it may refer to wax (the primary meaning of *la*) admixed with carbon powder to dry rub. Pursuit of the answer is beyond the reach of this study, but it would be intriguing to document the origins of dry rubbing.

The dry technique involves much simpler materials and methods than does the wet technique. They consist only of paper, less varied in type and less demanding in quality than that for wet rubbing, and a solid coloring agent. One uses the paper dry (thus the term "dry technique"), does not tamp the paper, and colors it with the solid agent. Many of us remember using the technique to rub embossed book covers in dull school classes.

The dry technique allows for a wide range of paper, Xuan or other. The traditional Chinese coloring agent is an ink cake made of hard wax (*baila*) and lampblack, described earlier. Before making the rubbing, one studies the surface that one is copying to remember the details of the relief, with preliminary sketches or photographs helpful. One lays the dry paper smoothly on the object to be rubbed and, depending on its nature, size, and shape, holds the paper down with one's hand or fastens it with weights, an adhesive, or tape to prevent it from shifting. One then presses the paper gently into or around the relief with a pad, or with the fingers or heel of the hand to relax the paper and shape it to the relief, broadly comparing with tamping in the wet technique.

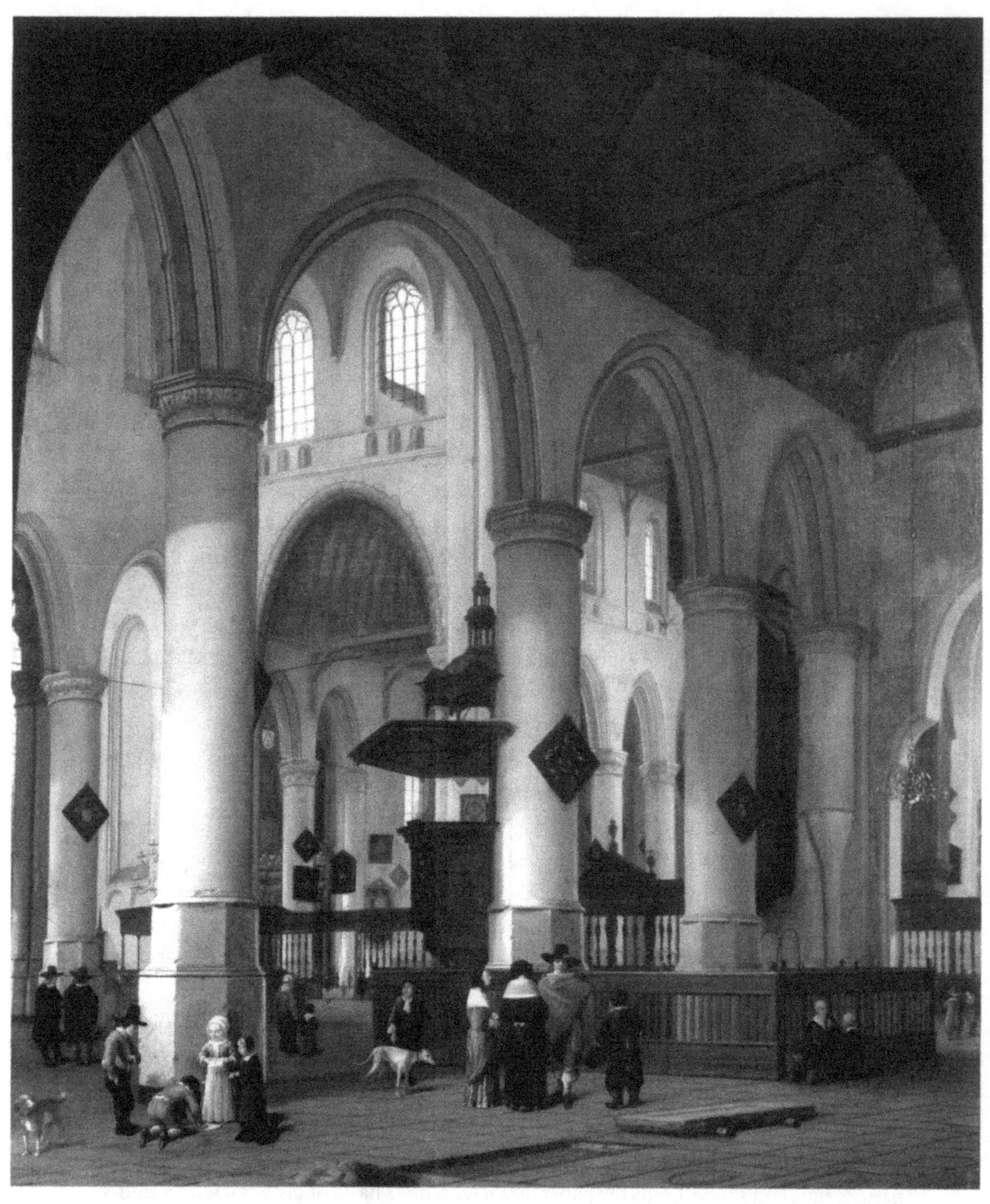

FIG. 5.12. Hendrick Van Vliet (1611–1675), *The Interior of the Old Church at Delft.* The Baltimore Museum of Art, bequest of Ellen Howard Bayard, BMA 1939.185.

Aided by remembering the surface and by running one's fingers across the paper, one lays on the coloring, rubbing the rounded side of the heelball back and forth across the paper, laying wax evenly on the high surfaces.

The dry technique requires simpler materials and methods and is more convenient and rapid than the wet technique. In general, however, it is less accurate and more limited in its use. The dry technique is most useful for copying smaller objects with flat and relatively smooth and even surfaces whose relief is sharp and clean, such as Chinese seals.[16] It also is effective for rubbing engraved wooden boards, especially if they are lacquered or gilded, or for copying porous or fragile materials that wetting would harm. The method is less effective for curved or uneven surfaces. Figure 2.1 illustrates wet and dry rubbings of a Warring States hollow bronze architectural element. Figure 2.7 includes inks for making dry rubbings.

DEFINITION OF "RUBBING"

Over fifteen centuries since they invented the rubbing technique, the Chinese have used Xuan and other papers to make rubbings, especially of bronze and stone inscriptions. For coloring they have used Chinese ink in several forms and, in lesser measure, other colors.

In the modern period, Westerners adapted and broadened the range of subject matter, materials, and techniques. Among serious artists, Surrealists, especially Max Ernst, used soft pencil or crayon to rub paper laid on textured surfaces, creating frottages (from French *frotter*, "to rub"). Amateur artists as well as antiquarians, anthropologists, and paleontologists have experimented with a wide variety of papers, cloths, and coloring agents, especially oil paints, to swipe or bray colors on a multitude of reliefs, including tombstones, Native American and other petroglyphs, and such mundane objects as manhole covers.

The term "rubbing" is appropriate for the dry technique, for one actually rubs the heelball over the paper. An alternative name for rubbing is "squeezing," but a squeeze is "a moulding or cast of an object obtained by pressing some plastic substance around or over it," with wax as an example.[17] Earlier scholars used papier-mâché to copy reliefs at Borobudur and other sites, with latex a modern molding material.[18] Paper is minimally plastic but does not accommodate strong relief and does not maintain its form well. Squeezing fits neither the wet nor, particularly, the dry technique.

The term "rubbing," in one of its several Chinese forms, truly applies to dry rubbings, less so to wet rubbings, but its wide currency, going back in the West at least to 1845, recommends it as a generic term.[19] For clarity, one can differentiate among simple and composite rubbings, wet and dry rubbings, and texts (*bei*) and calligraphic models (*tie*).

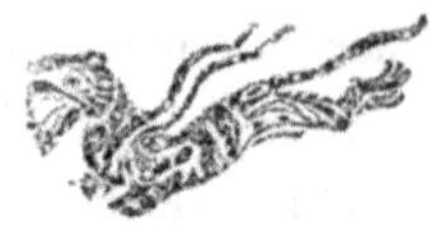

6 / When the Work Is Done

AFTER the inking is done, one must examine the rubbing minutely to ensure that it has captured every detail of the relief. When one is content with the sharpness of line, the contrast of light and dark, and the aesthetic quality of the inking, one can remove the finished rubbing. Normally this is easily accomplished, but as the paper still is moist and tears easily, one must carefully peel it off (fig. 6.1). The resulting rubbing shows a white, uninked image for intaglio (*yinwen*) and a black, inked image for relief (*yangwen*).[1]

Removing the rubbing may require special attention, for it may stick to the surface if the glutinous size or the ink, which contains glue, has been applied too heavily. One usually can avoid this by removing the rubbing while the paper still is moist, but if one has been slow and the paper sticks, one must use special methods to release it.[2] If the adhesion occurs but here and there, one can free the paper by lifting it gently and blowing it loose. If it sticks over larger areas, one can release it by moistening it with a damp towel when the paper and ink are sufficiently dry; otherwise, the added moisture will blur the inked line.[3]

Sometimes a rubbing sticks with particular tenacity: "If one sizes too heavily and rubs [inks] too densely, one can use boiling water to steam it loose."[4] Steaming is more common with black-gold rubbings, which require heavier sizing and inking.[5] Once removed, the rubbing, which because of the combined effects of the size and the tamping still conforms to the relief, should be left to dry exactly as it came off the surface. Particular care must be taken not to stretch it, for doing so expands those parts of the paper that have been tamped into or around the relief, distorting the characters and causing them to become "fat" and lose their subtle aesthetic qualities. With the same concern in mind, one immediately should press the wrinkled rubbing flat.

The work done, one should clean the equipment, especially the dabber, rinsing its surface with a little water to remove accumulated ink.[6] One also should scrape off ink buildup on the sides of the dabber with a dull knife; otherwise, the dabber will make ink rings on the next rubbing. Periodically, as it wears thin, one also must replace the dabber's outer covering, along with the interior wadding.

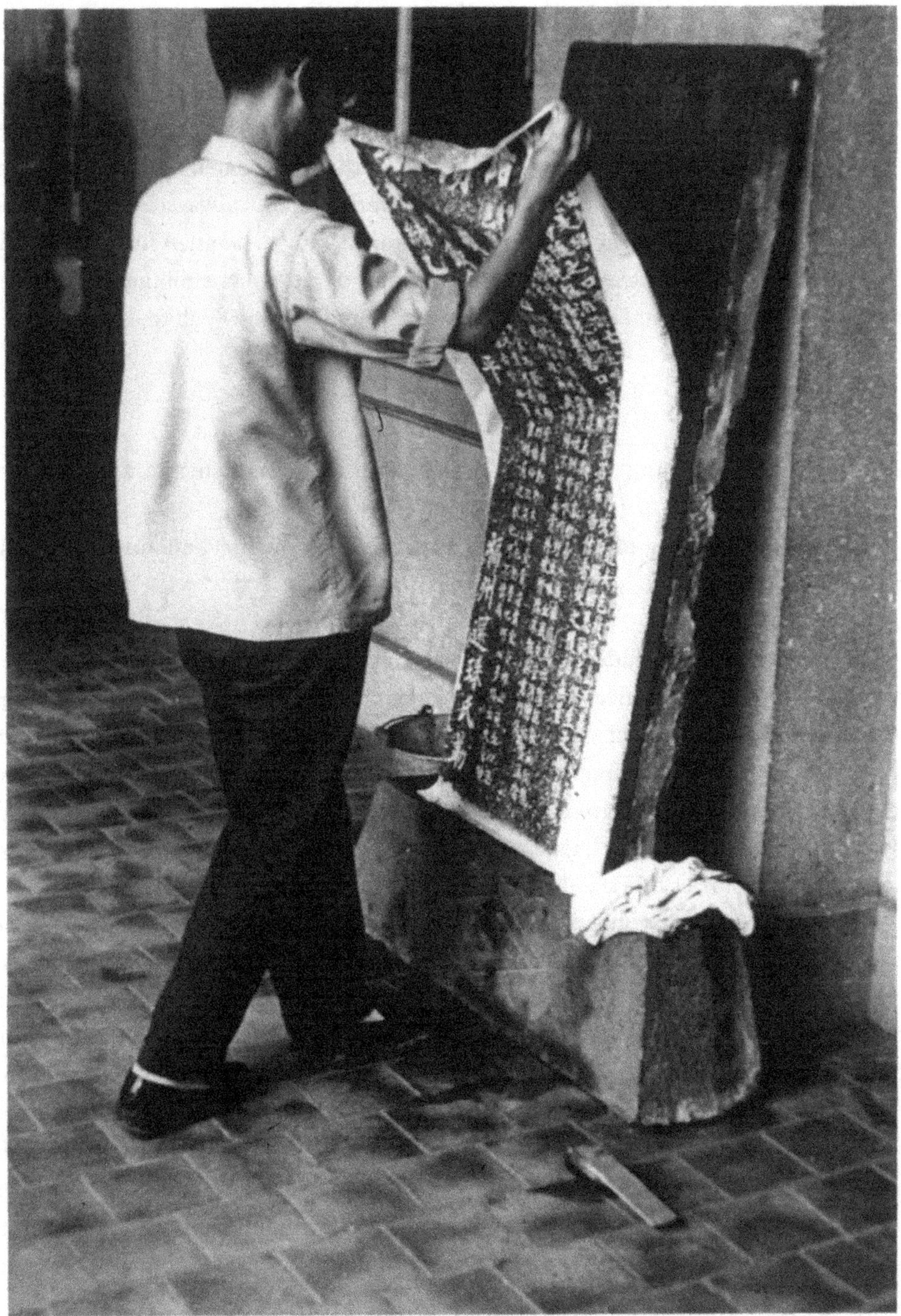

FIG. 6.1. Peeling a finished stele rubbing. National Historical Museum, Taibei, Taiwan, 1960. Photograph by the author.

DOCUMENTATION: KINDS AND CATEGORIES OF DATA AND WHERE THEY ARE RECORDED

A full record on the host object is essential, for the value and usefulness of rubbings are directly related to the quality and quantity of their associated data. Information about an object often can be found in reference works, but not always. Even when it is, the information may be difficult to track down and lacking in detail. A little additional care at the time saves extra work later. Discussion of data on a rubbing and its host requires consideration of *kinds* of data to record and *places* in which to do so.

Kinds of Data

Four kinds of data are important: numbering, location, measurements, and content.

NUMBERING. Assigning a field number to the rubbing is the first and most important requisite after naming it.

LOCATION. Location includes provenance, site, and position. The term "provenance" refers in this case to political divisions, such as the province, county, city, town, or village. If the location is a city or town, one should record the section and the name of the temple or public building. In China, the written record is millennia long, and changes of dynasties and reigns commonly brought corresponding changes in political organization and place names. One must consult geographical dictionaries, gazetteers, and dynastic histories to trace the changes.

If the object is small, rubbed indoors, one should note the name and address of the institution or private collection, and the catalogue number or other identification. If it is outdoors, one must specify the exact site, such as where on the temple grounds a monument stands with reference to the temple door, which customarily faces south, the usual point of reference.[7] This is especially important with pairs of Buddhist scripture pillars, which, being almost identical, must be identified with reference to their respective positions at the right or left of the temple door. If the stone is in a wilder location, one should define its position in relation to permanent natural features as well as by compass bearings or, nowadays, global positioning. Specifics are important, and so one also should provide a written description, photographs, and a sketch map showing the location and orientation of the stone.

Finally, one should record information on the object and its inscription or decor. For multisided, usually octagonal scripture pillars, one should assign subnumbers to the faces according to their relationships to the temple door, giving the south face of the pillar the first subnumber and proceeding counterclockwise.[8] If the stone has only two faces, one designates them "front" (*qian, zheng*) or "rear" (*hou, bei*). Steles, pictorial reliefs, and other large objects frequently have multiple levels and require one to use separate sheets of paper for each level, with subnumbers for each, and to relate the sheets with descriptive notes and sketches so as to show their relationships, such as the many levels and scenes in the Later Han mortuary reliefs.[9] Vessels may require differentiation of the elaborate designs that appear on the bands of their different faces and levels. With *hu* and *fang* vases, one identifies the rubbing as being of such-and-such a vase and level for a round *hu,* and of such-and-such a vase, face, and level for a square *fang* (see fig. 4.11).[10]

MEASUREMENTS. The rubber also must provide careful measurements, for precise measurements are vital in distinguishing two highly similar objects.

CONTENT. One needs to classify the content of the inscription or picture. There is no set formula, but one should set down as full a record as possible. Formal museum classifications have highly detailed descriptions, as at the Institute of History and Philology, in Taiwan, with numerous classes and subclasses of cultural objects, such as shells and bones, ceremonial bronzes, ceramics, and other categories, with subdivisions by function and date.[11] The Taiwan Cultural Committee (Taiwan Wenxian Weiyuanhui) organizes its rubbings simply by county (*xian*) and village (*xiang*), date (dynasty and reign), and subject. An informal approach divides materials into inscriptive or pictorial.[12] Antique shops in Beijing's Liulichang section shelved stele rubbings (*bei*) on one side and model books (*tie*) on the other, and these were further organized by dynasty and reign of the original objects. Earlier rubbings of the same object were shelved on top, with inserted slips giving their names and dates, a practice also common with private collectors. Subdivisions of primary classes can be endless, depending on the interests of the classifier.

Categories of Data

No matter what the classificatory system, one should include several essential categories of data and perhaps additional information.[13]

TITLE OR NAME OF THE OBJECT. The title or name of the object or its inscription or picture is essential. One identifies a particular bronze vessel or stele by its actual caption, such as the *Zhang Qian stele* (Zhang Qian bei), or by its name, such as the *Duke Mao ding* cauldron (Mao Gong ding). If there is no name, one gives the first several legible characters of the text and the name of the person, group, or event. One must never give the same name to another object or rubbing—a standard cataloging rule worldwide. Early coins and bronze mirrors also have distinctive identifying inscriptions.

DATE OF THE OBJECT. The date of the object is important. Stele inscriptions commonly carry a date, usually at their ends, and inscribed metal, ceramic, and other kinds of material sometimes also are dated. The date should be as complete as the text or other information permits, including especially the dynasty but also the reign period, the year, the month, and such further specifics as the season, the day, and cyclical signs.

CALLIGRAPHIC STYLE. With stele inscriptions (*bei*), the calligraphic style or styles always are given. One should list the caption, commonly inscribed either in large seal (*dazhuan*) or clerical (*li*) script on the tablet head (*bei'e*), or in smaller characters, usually clerical or standard (*zheng, zhen, kai*) script, at the upper right. The latter often is inscribed at the beginning of the text in a script that is slightly larger than, but of the same style as, the text. If there is no formal heading or title, or if the text is fragmentary, one should record the first several characters of the text, or remaining text. *Tie* take their names from their titles, such as the *Preface to the Orchid Pavilion Collection* (Lanting ji xu), or from several initial characters in their first lines.

DATE OF THE RUBBING AND NAME OF THE ARTISAN. One should record the date of the rubbing work and who made it. The date is particularly important, for it permits the sequencing of successive rubbings, reflecting minute degradation of the inscription or design over time.

ADDITIONAL INFORMATION If one has well-defined interests, one can add additional information about the object, its setting and condition, the artisan, and the rubbing materials and techniques. One also can include the names of donors to the erection of a stone, relevant bibliographical references, and information gleaned from local historical museums or inhabitants.[14] One should set down all of this data hard upon completing the rubbing, for time erodes the memory as well as the object.[15] Pale ink is better than the best memory.

Places for Recording Data

The other aspect of documentation is the places in which one sets down data, with four places, different in nature and purpose, common.

FIELD NOTEBOOK. The first and most vital place to record data is in a field notebook, where one immediately sets down a full record on the object and rubbing. The notes

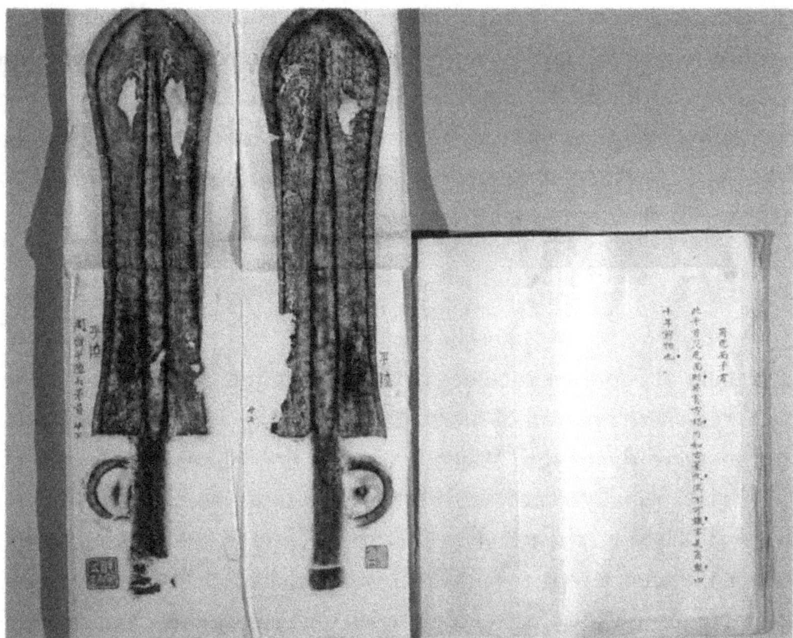

Fig. 6.2. Personal rubbing catalogue of Zou Shouji. The Field Museum of Natural History, 245600.

that Huang Yi, the early Qing geographer, made on the Wu Liang offering shrines are representative.

SURFACE OF THE RUBBING. The second place, common with commercial rubbings or those at temples with famous steles or calligraphic models, is on the rubbing itself. The maker or seller brushes basic information, usually the name, date, and perhaps the location of the stele or other object, directly on a side margin of the rubbing or on a simple paper label at the upper left of the folded rubbing or its envelope.

PERSONAL CATALOGUE OR HANDBOOK. A third place, especially for smaller objects, such as ancient jades or coins, is in a collector's personal catalogue or illustrated handbook, both simple and usually handwritten. Broad classification commonly is by the substance of the object, bronze or stone, and then by date, with the reverse order equally common. Personal catalogues are stitch-bound books with lined columns. Handbooks are stitch-bound books whose blank pages carry pasted-on rubbings and associated data, such as *Ancient Weapons in the Pleasurable Studio* (Shilu suo cang gu bingqi), a catalogue of rubbings of antique military devices belonging to Zou Shouji, a modern collector (fig. 6.2).[16] One should not confuse such catalogues with cut-mounted editions, described below.

LIBRARY AND MUSEUM CATALOGUES. A fourth place is in library and museum catalogues, the two most common repositories. One record includes registration forms and catalogue cards for individual rubbings or sets of rubbings.[17] Another consists of formal, printed catalogues, such as *Calligraphic Art in the Xi'an Beilin* (Xi'an Beilin shufa yishu) and *Catalogue of Stone Rubbings from Successive Dynasties in the Beijing Library* (Beijing Tushuguan cang Zhongguo lidai shike taben huibian).[18]

PRESERVATION

Initial treatment of rubbings includes drying, flattening, and cleaning. The rubbing still may carry a small amount of moisture and must be dried and flattened, without stretching, to avoid distortion. When it is fully dry, one should brush off foreign matter.[19] This is especially important for stele rubbings, which commonly carry bits of sand, dirt, and lichen on their reverse that cause tears in the ensuing handling. One also should make needed repairs to the rubbing, which often breaks in capturing large, deeply cut intaglio inscriptions and high relief. One pastes a patch of self paper on the reverse, orienting its grain with that of the rubbing. The adhesive agent traditionally is rice paste—thin, or else the dried paste will be stiff, and the paper will be inflexible and crack. One should make the paste several days ahead to ensure full absorption of the water. The advantage of water-soluble rice paste is that the process is reversible; the disadvantage, that it attracts vermin.

If the rubbing is of high relief or full round, the cutting and pasting of body parts, such as ears, is necessary for three-dimensionality.[20] Finally, one must finish the composition by patching, trimming, and pressing at the time, for the memory of the image fades, and with it subtleties of the relief.

The great majority of ordinary rubbings receive no further treatment. If the paper is thin, one can back it with tougher stock, again without stretching it. *Discussing Stone Inscriptions* (Yu shi) names *pi* paper as best for this purpose but also names *mianlian* and *zhulian*.[21] The backing should be slightly larger all around; the paste, properly prepared and applied rice paste. Old and rare rubbings, new rubbings of valued objects, or those made for presentation are mounted so as to be preserved and enhanced, but, as with other aspects of rubbings lore, there is less information on mounting rubbings than on mounting paintings: "Zhang Yanyuan describes mounting calligraphy and painting in great detail . . . unfortunately he does not describe mounting calligraphic rubbings [*tie*]."[22]

Mounting occurs in two forms, whole-mounted editions (*zhengbiao ben, zhengzhuang ben*) and cut-mounted editions (*jianbiao ben, jianzhuang ben*). Whole mounting carries the rubbing along in its original, whole state; cut mounting cuts the rubbing

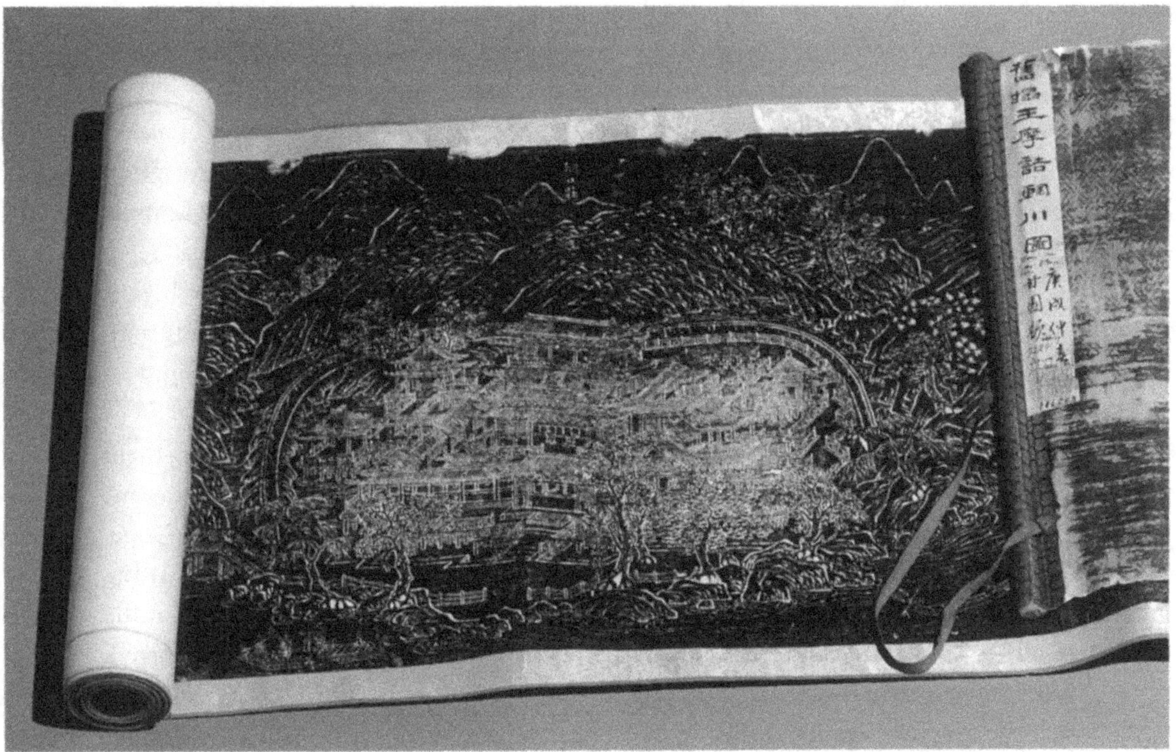

Fig. 6.3. Scroll-mounted "old" rubbing of the *Wang River Picture* (*Wang chuan tu*). The Field Museum of Natural History, 116203.

into pieces of appropriate shape and size and rejoins them in a new format. Whole mounting usually results in a scroll; cut mounting, in an album or book. In the Ming and the Qing, the best mounting is said to have been done in Jiangnan, modern Anhui, and Jiangsu. With Beijing, east central China continues to be known for mounting, including Suzhou and Yangzhou, Jiangsu, and Hangzhou, Zhejiang.[23]

Our initial concern will be with whole mounting as a scroll, the earliest of the three formats.[24] As scroll mounting leaves the rubbing uncut, it lends itself to subject matter that requires being kept in its original state (fig. 6.3): "Generally speaking, rubbings are mounted according to the same principles as paper scrolls. As . . . the paper used is mostly very thin and heavily inked, it will expand considerably when moistened and in general is difficult to handle. Thus, for mounting rubbings, exceptional skill is necessary."[25] Mounting paintings requires that the paper or silk be stretched tight in attaching the support paper; mounting rubbings demands that the paper be fixed exactly as it came off the relief, preserving every tamping wrinkle, pressed flat. Even the slightest stretching will destroy the aesthetic qualities of the inscription or design, a sobering challenge, for backing and mounting require that the rubbing be wetted. Chinese connoisseurs of rubbings thus categorically state that good rubbings should be given over only to craftsmen specially trained in mounting rubbings.

Rubbers sometimes add egg white to the ink to heighten the glossy effect of black-gold rubbings, or as a binder in vermilion and other colors. To provide protection against insects that feed on the albumen, mounters add vermifuge to the paste or apply a solution of borax, camphor, and alcohol, thinned to proper strength with water.[26]

The materials and workmanship used in mounting prized rubbings are of higher quality and, in the case of old rubbings (*jiu taben*), often older as well, in keeping with the age of the rubbing. Sometimes a new or relatively new rubbing may be set into an old mounting, through intentions good or ill, to lend an aura of age.

Collectors also preserve and protect fine, old, and rare rubbings by mounting them as accordion albums or Chinese stitch-bound books. Both formats, especially albums, accommodate inscriptive and picture rubbings that can be segmented to fit on a page, and thus their name, cut-mounted editions (*jianbiao ben*). The process involves cutting the rubbing into rectangular or, less often, square pieces of appropriate size that the mounter reorganizes and pastes onto backing paper in modified sequence to form a more convenient new format. This requires careful planning, cutting, and pasting so that the mounted edition faithfully preserves the intellectual and aesthetic character of the original. Collectors chose mounters of their prized rubbings thoughtfully, often bringing them into the household, so that the owner could monitor the work. The date of an old rubbing can hinge on the condition of a few characters, a key character, a single stroke, or part of a stroke:

> I particularly take pains with [rubbings of] metal-and-stone inscriptions. Each time that I select a stele rubbing to hand over for mounting, my heart is anxious. First, I record its text, determining that each column is composed of such-and-such a number of characters, and that each character is formed of such-and-such a number of strokes. I further note elevated characters [*taitouzi*] that indicate respect, date, initial and final [portions of the text], associated inscriptions and colophons, and any supplemental sheets at front and rear. For each, I select quality paper and, one by one, sketch the format. Then, with courteous manner and pleasant words, I give it over [to the mounter].
>
> The mounters's skill strictly lies in cutting [the rubbing into the appropriate pieces]. The cutting first and last must be regular, and throughout must evidence no traces [such as snipped off parts of characters]. If the cutting is expertly done, then the matter [the successful mounting] can be concluded.
>
> I have spoken of stele-rubbings [*bei*, but] it is the same with calligraphic models [*tie*].[27]

The most common form of cut mounting for albums is raincoat mounting (*suoyi biao*), from the resemblance of the overlapping rubbing strips to a Chinese grass raincoat.[28] There are variant styles. Three-leaf mount (*sanye biao*) sets three columns of characters on an album page, with surrounding borders. The variant scattered-leaves mount (*sanye biao*) is a metaphor occasioned by the resemblance of the cut pieces of the rubbing to fallen leaves. Folded-cloth mount (*jinzhe biao*) allows for continuous flow of the rubbing text by eliminating the side and internal borders, retaining only top and bottom borders: "Such albums . . . are especially suited for . . . *ching-chuang* . . . , rubbings of long inscriptions of comparatively small height, such as those taken from the eight-cornered socles of Buddhist steles (*shih-chu* . . . , colloquially *pa-lêng-pei*). Such texts may . . . also be mounted as horizontal hand scrolls."[29]

Spread-awning mount, or transverse mount (*tuipeng shi*), accommodates very large characters, one or two per album page. The mount is horizontal, with the text read from right to left instead of from top to bottom:

> People's tastes and objectives are not the same, and so their [mounting] styles also are not one. Nowadays, the current style is the cut-mounted edition [*jianbiao ben*]. This style involves initially counting the characters and lines, and its [pattern of] raising [certain] characters and leaving a blank space above a name [to show respect] must follow that on the original stone. . . . Because it is done by dividing [the rubbing] into strips and pasting [in keeping with the original vertical and horizontal spacing of the lines and characters], [this style] commonly is called "raincoat mounting."[30]

Whatever the type of cut mounting, the mounter sets the cut segments of the rubbing onto what will be the new pages. The top border, "heaven" (*tian*), is the widest; the bottom border, "earth" (*di*), is narrower. Side borders are of equal width and commonly slightly narrower than the *di*.[31]

Albums are continuous or discontinuous. Continuous albums have only the two vertical external borders, with the text running uninterrupted across the double page (fig. 6.4 A). Discontinuous albums are similar to a Chinese book, with top and bottom borders and four vertical borders, two external, right and left, and two internal, on each side of the central fold (figs. 6.4 B, 6.5). Whirlwind folded leaves (*xuanfeng zhe ye*), or simply whirlwind-mount (*xuanfeng zhuang*) accordion albums, have been vehicles for mounting rubbings since the Song.[32]

After backing the rubbing, the mounter calculatingly cuts the columns of text into vertical strips, and these in turn are cut into lengths appropriate for the intended album. The artisan must keep in mind the format of the original text and the envisioned album, noting the number and spacing of columns and the characters in each, according to

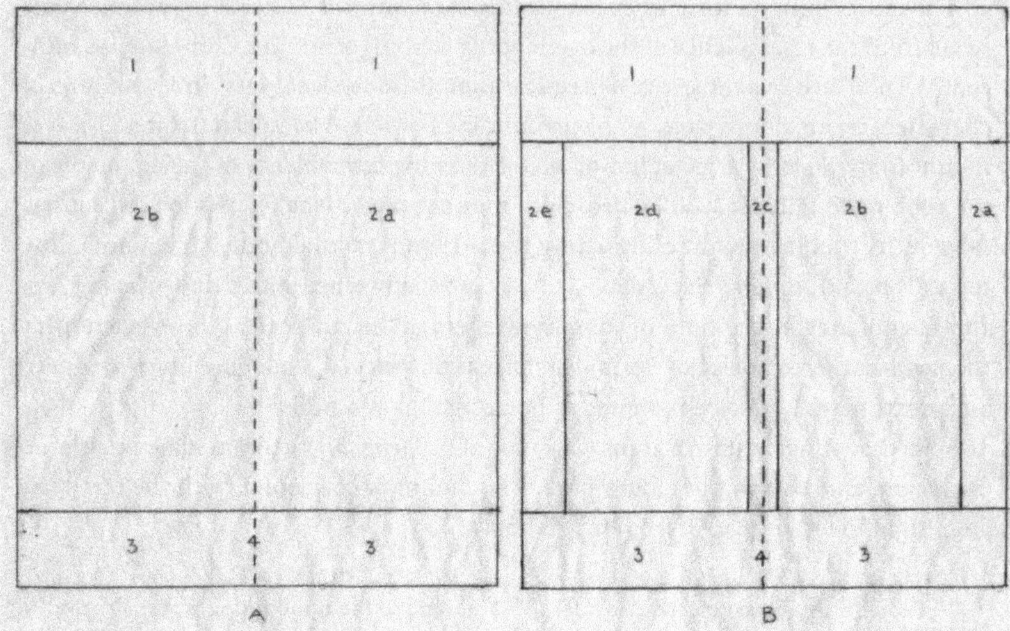

FIG. 6.4. Continuous and discontinuous albums; horizontal zones and vertical panels. Sketch and photograph by the author.

their size and style. He also must remember the start of new columns, characters raised above the top margin out of respect (*taitouzi*), empty spaces (*kongge*) before the names of exalted persons, and colophons. The caption (*bei'e*), in seal or other script, also must be in its proper place in relation to the text.

The mounter then organizes the strips into groups to form the album pages, backs each group, maintaining all the original proportions and relationships, and pastes them in sequence on a long strip of backing paper. Folded borders (*zhebian*) are added at top and bottom, and the long strip is folded vertically, accordion-style. Finally, the mounter presses and dries the album and adds front and back covers of sturdy, pressed cardboard faced with silk, often padded with cotton wool. Covers also can be separate boards or attached wood covers, often engraved, as with a boxed and bagged rubbing of the *Lanting tie,* a calligraphic album (*beitie, shutie, zitie*) with silk-covered pasteboards. Said to be from the Southern Song, it is a fine example of a quality rubbing, well mounted by You Si, its then owner, in his characteristic style, with blue and buff papers (plate 6). Figure 6.6 shows an album-mounted rubbing of the Han *Zhang Qian Stele* (Zhang Qian bei), a good-quality old rubbing, shoddily mounted, with transposed lines two and three, and crude tape repairs.

Mounters follow a similar procedure in preserving a rubbing as a stitch-bound book, similar to a printed book except that the text, instead of being printed, consists of

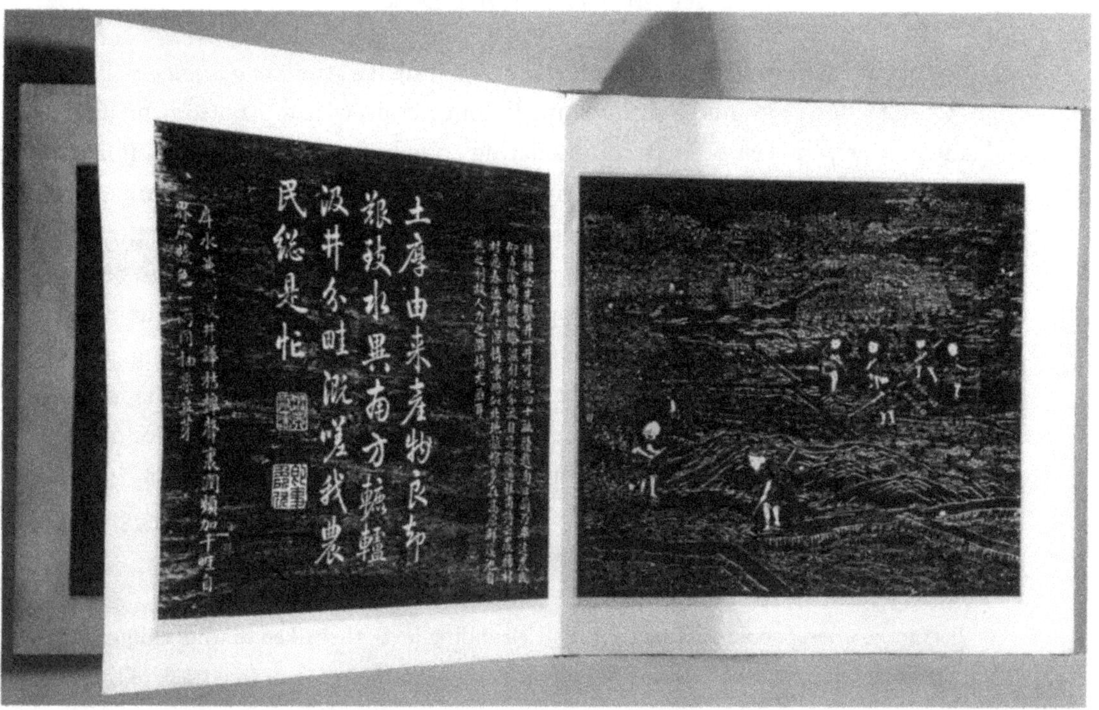

Fig. 6.5. Discontinuous album-mounted rubbing of *Illustrations of Cotton Production* (*Mianhua tu*). The Field Museum of Natural History, 117094.

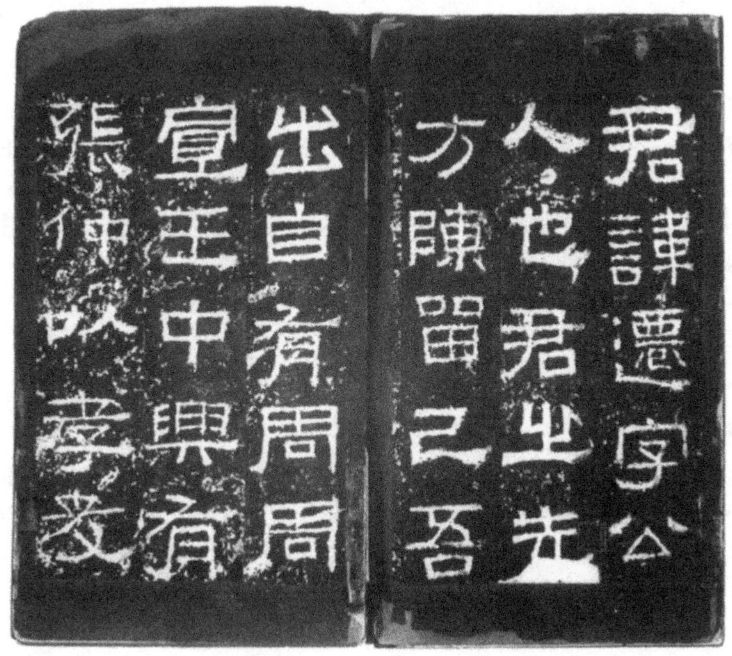

Fig. 6.6. "Old rubbed" album, *Zhang Qian Stele* (*Zhang Qian bei*, 186 C.E.), poorly mounted, with transposed lines (two and three) and tape repairs. The Field Museum of Natural History, 244122.

columns of cut rubbing strips pasted onto the pages, such as the *Kong Zhou bei* (plate 7, figs. 6.7–6.8). Book mounts commonly are discontinuous, with top, bottom, median, and side borders, the last often accommodating colophons and seals. The unfolded sheet (*ye*) of the book typically shows three horizontal zones and five vertical panels but may have fewer (fig. 6.4). Book covers, the front one (*fengmian*) carrying the title strip (*shuqian*), commonly are paper but may be faced with native blue cotton or, for fine books, silk. Book mounting is appropriate for old and rare inscriptive rubbings, and, as with album mounting, it involves two phases: first, backing the rubbing, planning the desired format, and cutting the rubbing into pieces of appropriate shape and size; and, second, mounting the pieces on the pages. It also is a form of cut mounting, and again, the most common form is raincoat mount.

The advantage of mounting rubbings as albums or books lies in its convenience, but its disadvantage, a serious one, is that when the paste lets go, the pieces fall:

> Formerly, when people obtained a fine stele rubbing [*bei*], they liked to whole mount it, thus avoiding [the risk of pieces] falling off. Moreover, they did not lose track of the original dimensions of the tablet. It certainly is a good method, but unless one spreads it out on a table or hangs it on the wall, it is not easy to open out and study. I say that to collect stele rubbings properly, one must have two copies, with the master copy whole mounted to preserve the format of the original stone, and with a duplicate copy cut mounted . . . for convenience in handling.[33]

Jiang poetically echoes this advice, writing that "although cut-mounted editions are convenient for study, they have a disadvantage, for as the years pass, the adhesive loosens, and then [the pieces] flutter down like butterflies and very easily are lost."[34] Many incomplete albums and books of rubbings verify this, and thus the need for uncut security copies.

ELEMENTS OF CONNOISSEURSHIP

Ordinary sheet rubbings are stored just rolled or folded. Rolling results in smudging; folding, in creasing, and usually is with little exactitude, despite Ye Changchi's comment to the contrary.[35] Folded rubbings can be slipped into paper wrappers or sandwiched between *jiaban* boards. Scrolls, backed and often edged with silk, are rolled (figs. 6.3 and 7.15). Fully mounted scrolls are self-contained, with staves and rollers, but collectors lavish attention and money on enhancing their old and quality mounted rubbings. Scrolls have figured-silk facings and ivory or jade *zhu* roller knobs; albums, covers of high-quality pasteboard, faced with embroidered silk, or padded with silk-

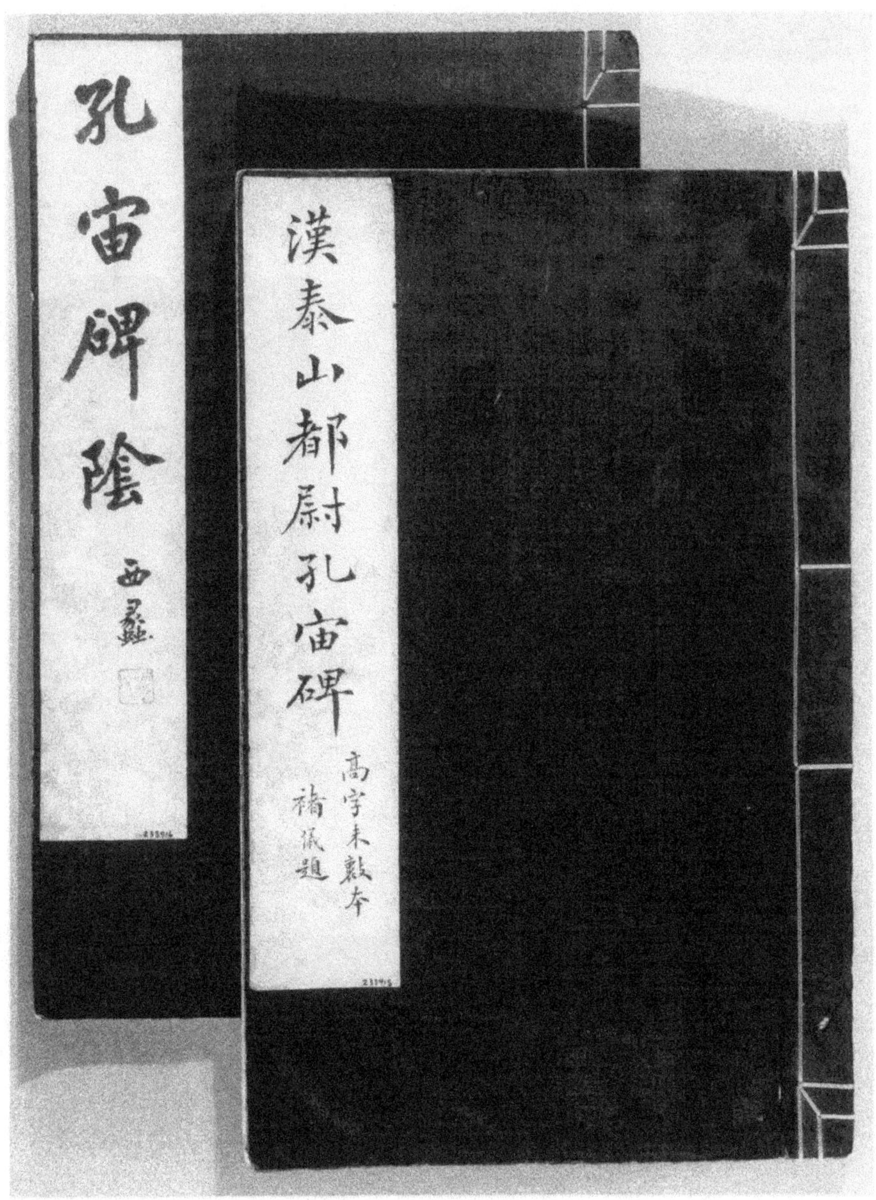

FIG. 6.7. Book-mounted "quality" rubbings of front and rear faces of the Later Han *Kong Zhou Stele* (*Kong Zhou bei*, 163 C.E.). The Field Museum of Natural History, 233915, 233016.

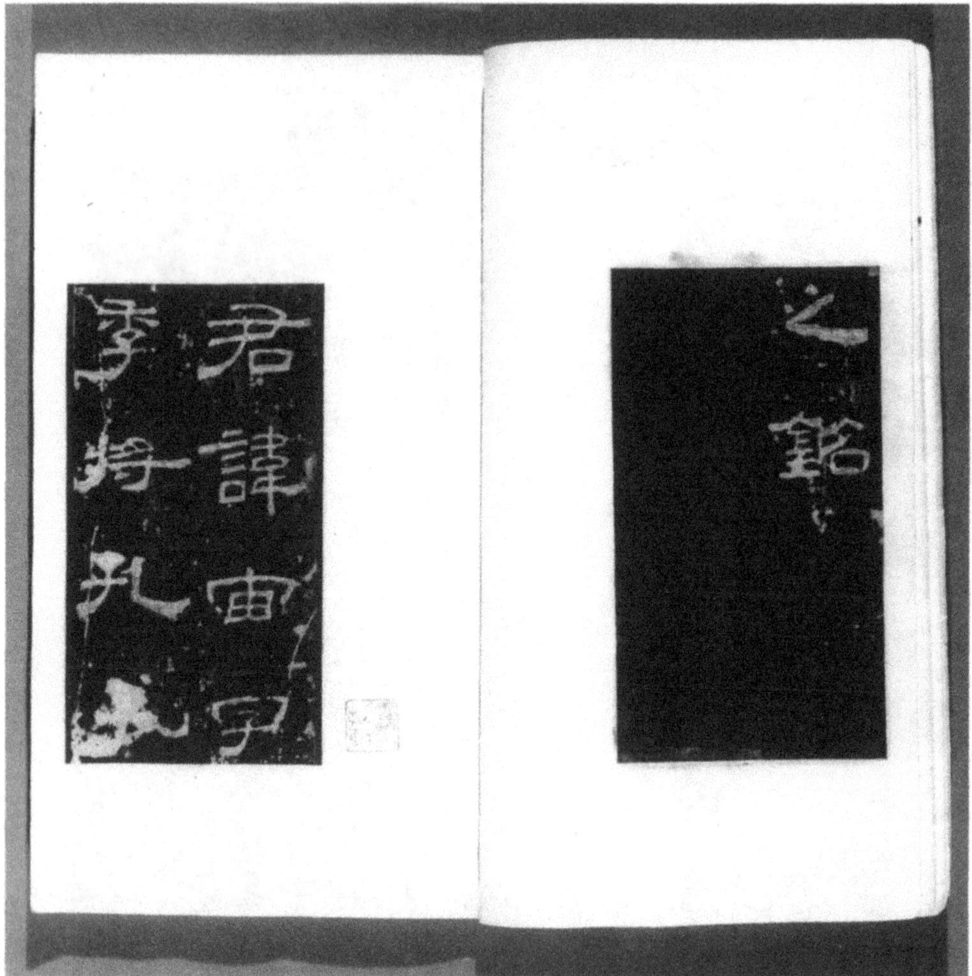

FIG. 6.8. Two pages of a book-mounted "quality" rubbing of the Later Han *Kong Zhou Stele* (*Kong Zhou bei*, 163 C. E.): left side, two initial rubbing strips of the text; right column, *hui* "avoidance character." The Field Museum of Natural History, 233915.

covered cotton for greater sumptuousness; and book-mounts, blue silk facings stitch-bound with tan silk thread.

Zhou Jiazhou describes the importance of good pasteboard album covers, which purists made themselves from detailed recipes:

> The good results seen in attractive rubbings albums [*beitie ceye*] that do not deteriorate over many years are the product of hard [pasteboard] covers. The labor is great, and the materials are numerous, and so one does not dare trust [the work to] the mounter. The rubbings that I [personally] have mounted number more than a hundred, and the albums

> [that I have made number] between ten and twenty. All had handmade paperboard covers. . . . Calligraphic albums rely on this outer protection, for the contents will suffer no misfortune, and the good results will be boundless. It is appropriate, then, to add various kinds of thin *ling* or *juan* silk as [facial] ornamentation.[36]

The suspicion of commercial mounters continues.

Plate 5 illustrates a rare Lanting album. The dense pasteboard covers are covered with worn, old, pale ivory silk brocade with a geometric pattern in muted tones of buff, tan, yellow, gray-green, and blue. As with the other mounting materials, the silk is said to be of Song origin.

Wood album covers could be wood alone—pine for ordinary albums, lacquered wood or rare woods for better ones—or they could be embellished with embroidered silk padded with cotton wool. In *Record of Prolonged Gratification of the Simple Heart* (Shangyan suxin lu), Zhou Erxue advises on facing albums:

> For the faces, genuine Song-period *jin* brocade is best. Next best are either mottled *nan* wood [*douban nan*] or fragrant *nan* [*xiang nanmu*] to make the boards, or [boards painted with] matte black lacquer. One should prize album covers that are properly squared, without crooked corners. For the title strip [*mianqian*] on the cover, use either *cangjing* paper [*cangjing jian*] or white Song paper [*bai Song jian*]. Then write the caption in seal [*zhuan*], clerical [*li*], standard [*zhen*], or correspondence [*xing*] style. One should not engrave the inscription, [as that is in poor taste].[37]

Writing a century later, Ye Changchi amplifies:

> If one uses fragrant *nanmu* for the covers of the rubbing, one can avoid weevils. In the south, such wood is quite satisfactory, but in the north the climate is very dry, and the wood easily cracks like a tortoise shell or ultimately splits in two. Red sandalwood is too heavy. If one selects a thin, clear piece of ginkgo wood and polishes it, one can use that, and, being common, ginkgo wood is convenient. Otherwise, one can use pasteboard covers, but abrasion easily damages them, and they readily absorb oily substances. Old brocade is elegant and beautiful, and the best for mounting. Next best, new brocade imitative of fine old brocade also is satisfactory. Nowadays, people use imported printed cotton, but such cloth definitely does not have the simplicity and strength of [domestic] blue cotton. There also are those who use wood boards. The four edges are raised [by hollowing out the central area or by adding edging strips]; the central area is slightly sunken and is filled with brocade [for decoration]. This, however, is but seeking to embellish the exterior, and nothing more. For the title label, *zangjing* paper is best, [with] white *ling* silk next best. Gold-flecked paper [*nijin jian*] is quite decorative, but in time the gold

powders and falls off, and the strokes of the characters also are damaged. The end result is dark and lifeless.[38]

Label content varies widely, with the value of the rubbing again determining its quality and quantity.[39] Ordinary rubbings have simple labeling, just the name of the object, written on the side margin or on a simple written or printed paper label (*shuqian*), often in archaic script, pasted on the folded rubbing. Labels on prized rubbings are more expansive: dates of the object and the rubbing, prior owners, features that differentiate it from other rubbings of the same object, or that authenticate it, place it in time, or mark it as an old or quality rubbing (plate 5; figs. 6.3, 6.9, 6.10).

Connoisseurs preferred particular papers for their labels. Huizong, the Song emperor and patron of the arts, and Zhang Zong, the Tartar Jin emperor, favored porcelain-blue paper (*cilan zhi*), with Jinsu paper (*Jinsu zhi*) from Hangzhou the second choice.[40] There are countless statements of personal choices, with the most frequently cited being white Xuan paper (*Xuan zhi*), white Song paper (*bai Song jian*), and Buddhist sutra paper (*zangjing zhi, zangjing jian*).[41] Colored papers also occur, including pink and red, often flecked with gold. Label papers containing alum do not take ink well and often fall off in a few years.[42]

Cloth labels, cotton for ordinary rubbings or silk for fine ones, often are stitched on protective outer cloth covers (fig. 6.9). Label tags are common for scrolls, tied to their knobs, and paper slips (*jiajianzi*) identify album- and book-mounted rubbings, inserted in their ends on shelves. Although purists disapprove, titling can be engraved, often with paint infill, on the front covers of boards and wood albums.[43] Labels can be written in any calligraphic style, with grass script less common. The choice depends on the age of the object (such as clerical [*li*] for a Han stele inscription), the calligrapher's forte, or the owner's preference. Collectors preserve old labels from earlier mountings, authenticating and affirming their age and quality (fig. 6.10). Collectors also save the former surface of attachment of a label, such as an earlier cover or box top.

Collectors protect and enhance their fine rubbings by enclosing them in *baofu* wrappers, *nang* bags or *tuo* sleeves, and boxes, with their own pasted, carved, or sewn labels, or tags (fig. 6.9).[44] Scrolls are preserved in individual boxes, *xia* (colloquially, *he*). Made of sturdy pasteboard, they have blue cotton or silk facing, with silk padding. Fine rubbings command wood boxes, with pine, cedar, redwood (*hongmu*), southern wood (*nanmu*), lacquer-tree wood, and red or white sandalwood the most common: "Use red or white sandalwood to make the *xia* box, and line it with Xuande-[period (1426–1435)] white *ling* satin with a small-clouds-and-phoenixes [pattern]. Mixing sandalwood powder with new cotton to make the padding not only produces a fragrance when one unrolls [the scroll] but also repels worms."[45] Separate sachets also are used.

Double boxes for scrolls are not uncommon, with an unassuming outer box made

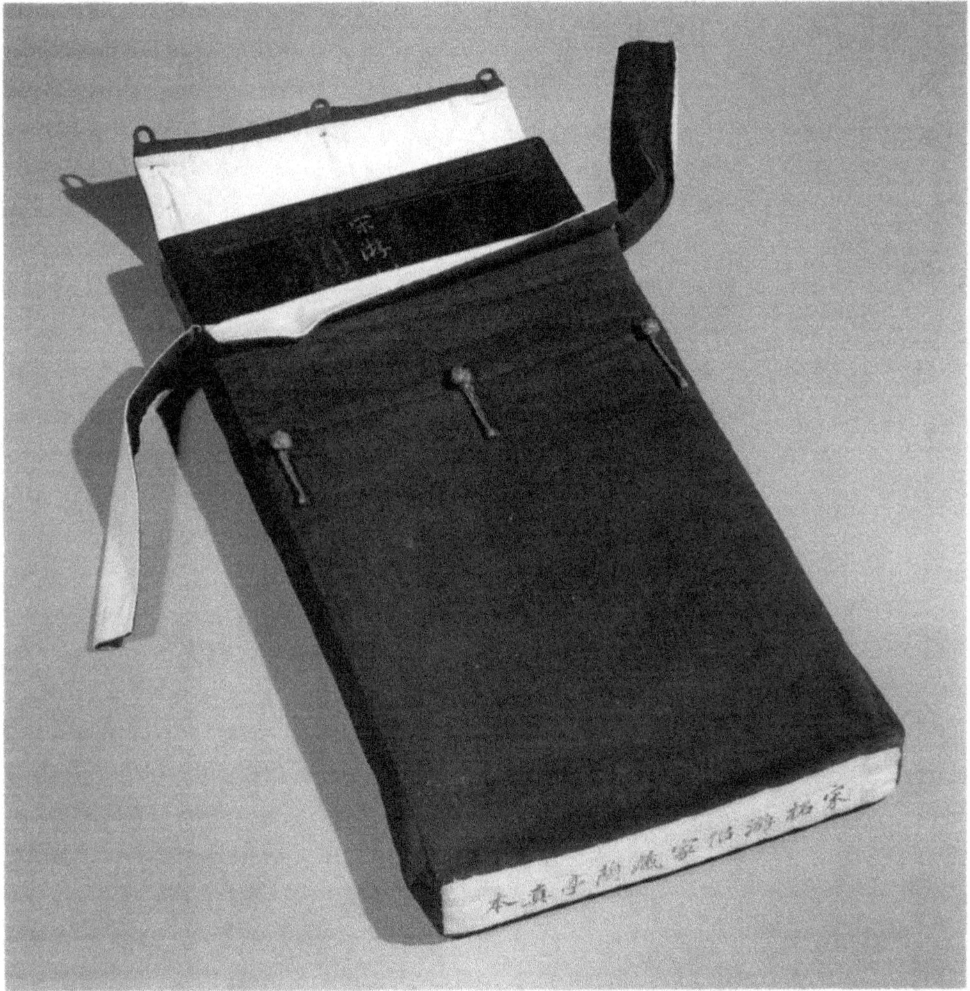

FIG. 6.9. You Si, *True Lanting* (Lanting zhenben), no. 52, in bag with cloth label. Song. The Field Museum of Natural History, 233914.

of pasteboard faced with blue cotton, or of an ordinary wood, left plain with no effort to draw the eye, and an inner box is of finer wood, superior craftsmanship, and painted or lacquered. A sliding top or end panel carries an identifying label or a painted or carved inscription, and it may be protected by a fitted bag of patterned fine cotton, with an end flap, a sewn label, and *kouzi* knot fasteners. Finally, the scroll itself may gain further protection from a silk wrapper, sleeve, or bag. Double boxes are partitioned lengthwise, with one side holding the silk-wrapped scroll and the other side, earlier accoutrements, such as boxes and inscribed lids, to preserve fine craftsmanship along with previous title strips and authenticating documents.

Album- and book-mounted rubbings go into flat *xia* boxes of fine wood with sliding

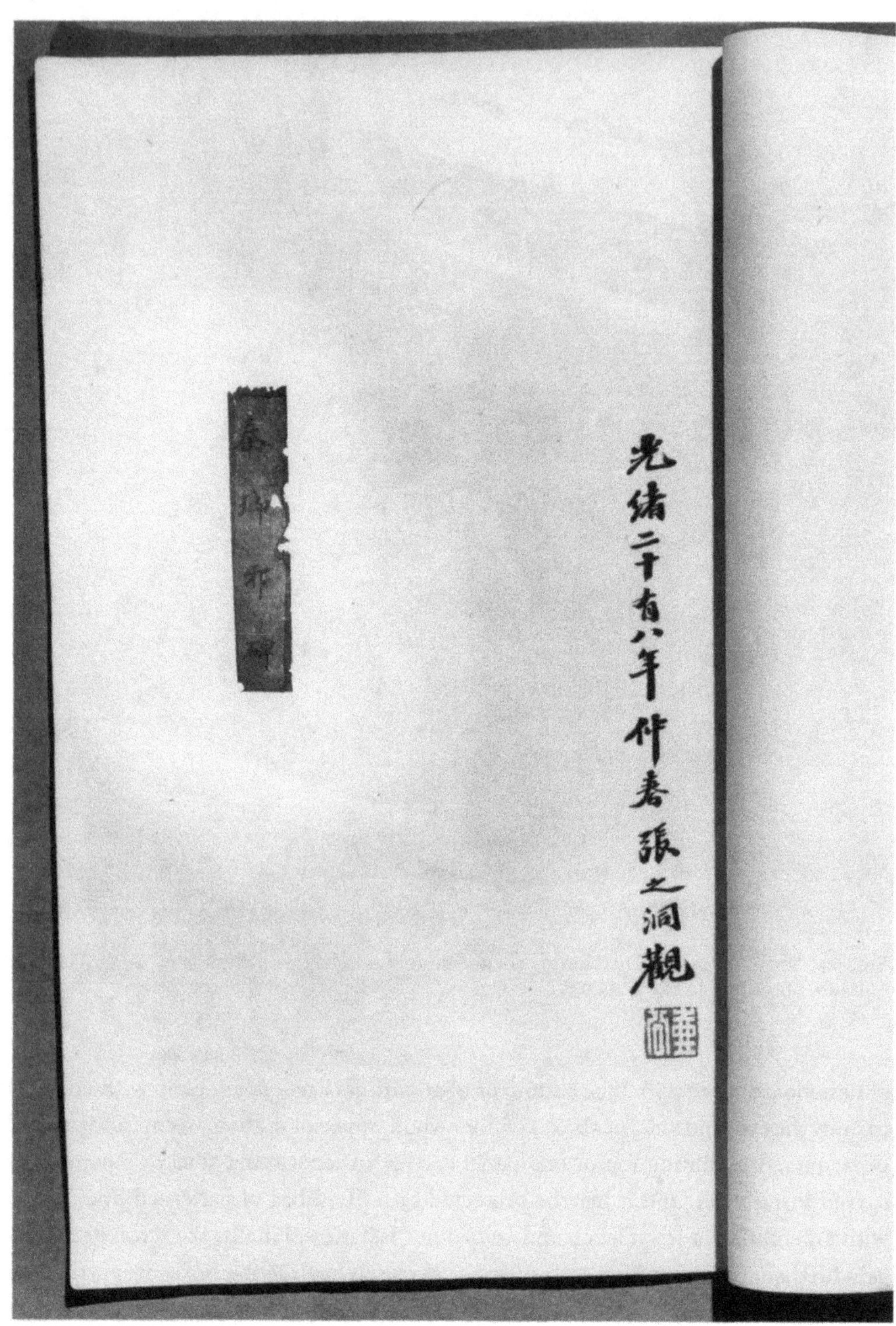

FIG. 6.10. Label from an earlier mounting of a *Langya Tai* rubbing, 1902 colophon by Zhang Zhitong (1837–1909). The Field Museum of Natural History, 233919.

top lids, often with engraved titles. A classic example of both a prize rubbing and its redwood box is an album-mounted old and quality rubbing of Wang Xizhi's Lanting inscription in the collection of one hundred editions assembled by the Song collector You Si (plate 5). The carved label on the sliding top reads, "Lanting edition number fifty-two in the collection of Song You Si" (*Song You Si cang Lanting di wushier ben*). A smaller inscription below and slightly to the right reads, "Yijin Zhai," studio name of Yongxing, Prince Cheng (1752–1823), Qianlong's eleventh son, from whose collection it came. Particular collectors attached great importance to *xia* boxes, their materials, construction, and use.[46]

Book-mounted rubbings are protected by cloth wrappers, *jiaban* boards, *xia* boxes, *tao* wrappers, and *han* cases. Old and quality book mounts are preserved, as are album mounts, in fine *xia* boxes. The most common means of storing single or multiple book-mounted rubbings, as with printed books, is in *tao* wrappers or *han* cases. The two are similar in materials and construction, made of well-pressed pasteboard faced with blue or, less often, black cotton cloth, but they differ in form. *Tao* are hinged panels of varying complexity that wrap around the enclosed books. *Han,* a more recent form, have a simple three-paneled folding wrapper that surrounds the books, and a boxlike container, open on one long side, into which they slide (see fig. 7.4).

Connoisseurs are exacting about the construction of *tao* and *han.* Jiang Xuanyi recommends making them from "horse-manure paper" (*mafen zhi*), from the flecks of rice or wheat straw in it.[47] He cautions against having the mounting shop make *han* cases and advises using a Western-style bindery and its heavy-duty press to ensure proper bonding.[48] Finally, connoisseurs often insert between the pages of their albums and books sheets of vermifugal papers—sulphur paper (*xionghuang zhi*) or Guangdong paper (*Guangdong zhi*)—whose active agent is arsenic sulphide.

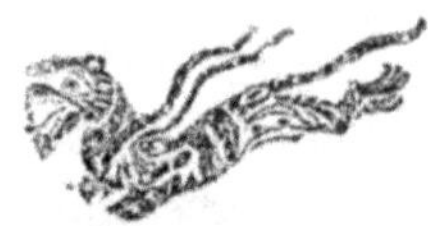

7 / The Rice and the Chaff

CONNOISSEURSHIP of rubbings is demanding. It involves careful, sometimes exquisite, judgments based on scholarship and personal taste as well as on the whole underlying system of traditional Chinese cultural values. Collectors seek individual rubbings and build collections with two considerations in mind: intellectual or aesthetic content, and connoisseurship. The two aspects are bound; for purposes of discussion, however, one can gently separate them.

INTELLECTUAL AND AESTHETIC CONTENT

From the inception of the technique, the Chinese valued rubbings as reliable and convenient vehicles for copying a wide variety of culturally meaningful inscribed, cast, or molded inscriptions or pictures. Initially, they prized rubbings as carriers of intellectual content, serving in the first centuries as surrogates for stone-cut texts, especially the Confucian classics. For a society founded on Confucian writings, accurate copies of authorized texts were a requisite, and rubbings provided scholars and aspiring government officials with such copies. Subsequent centuries saw the further cutting of editions of the classics, as well as historical and commemorative inscriptions, and their rubbing.

The Chinese also continued to rely on rubbings of stone-cut religious texts. Despite their significant part in developing woodblock printing, the Buddhists kept on cutting and rubbing their stone canons. While acknowledging the element of chance, one notes that the three best-known extant rubbings generally accepted as Tang—the *Hot Springs Inscription,* the *Huadu Temple Pagoda Inscription,* and the copy of the *Diamond Sutra*—all came from the great Buddhist center at Dunhuang. Other rubbings thought also to be Tang are of Buddhist scripture pillars. The Daoists also continued to cut and rub their classics, *The Classic of the Way and Its Power* a particular favorite.

By the Qing dynasty, cuttings of the classics were few, mainly a nod to tradition, but commemorative inscriptions continued strong, from official edicts to those honoring prominent officials to more modest subjects. In the modern period, scholarly interests have broadened, with a corresponding extended use of rubbings. In historical studies, scholars have widened their focus beyond traditional subjects and sources to include archaeological and paleographic data. In addition to their role in the latter, "crucial," texts on bronze, stone, and bone "are the very lifeblood of studies in early Chinese literature, history, and philosophy—all three aspects of China's tripartite classification of the human sciences."[1]

These materials provide data that corroborate, supplement, or differ with standard written sources. Archaeology and history complement each other endlessly.[2] Divination and bronze inscriptions constitute unique resources for early Chinese history, language, and culture, with Chinese interest in the bronzes running uninterruptedly from pre-Han times to the present, and with Western interest active in recent decades. Han steles and epitaphs from the Northern and Southern dynasties provide historical and biographical information that is more detailed, reliable, and geographically focused than that in the orthodox sources, which often are later and subject to revision as well as copying errors, an original spur in cutting the Xiping Stone Classics. They also manifest distinctive calligraphic styles. Stone inscriptions offer insights into official organization (*guanzhi*) and political jurisdictions, especially for pre-Qing history. Taiwan researchers use epitaphs to supplement historical records with information about individuals (*chuanji*) and the official system.[3] They also rely on Ming and Qing steles to document arrivals of immigrants; the building of roads, bridges, and canals; and relations with the aborigines. There are eighty-three stele inscriptions on Penghu Island alone, with the earliest dated 1603 but discovered only in 1919, recording the event. Inscriptions in non-Chinese languages, many long extinct, mark the flow of peoples and cultures in the borderlands, as the discoveries in the northwestern marches manifest (fig. 7.1). All these materials provide a rich corpus of comparative data through the millennia, all of it conveniently available through rubbings.[4]

From early on, the Chinese also prized rubbings for their aesthetic content. Calligraphy, often combined with poetry, has been the primary focus, as both extant rubbings and bibliographic references attest. Extant Tang rubbings include Ouyang Xun's *Huadu Si stele* and Liu Gongquan's stone-cut *Diamond Sutra*. Literary references add to the evidence, for the two nonclassic rubbings listed in the *History of the Sui*—Li Si's small-seal Kuaiji inscription, and his small seal, copied in the 993 recut of the Yi Shan inscription—almost surely were included more for their aesthetic value than for their historical content. Devotees continued to rub the latter even after its overturning and destruction and cut the inscription imitatively in wood, in the positive, for rubbing. The Tai Shan and Langya Tai stone cuts also are admired Li inscriptions.

The Northern Song *Chunhua Ge fatie* is the best-known example of the continuing high emphasis on rubbings for their aesthetic content. Three of the seven galleries at the Beilin are devoted to famous calligraphies, with one featuring the 1646 edition of the original 992 cutting. The strong interest of present-day Chinese visitors clearly manifests their continuing devotion to calligraphic art.

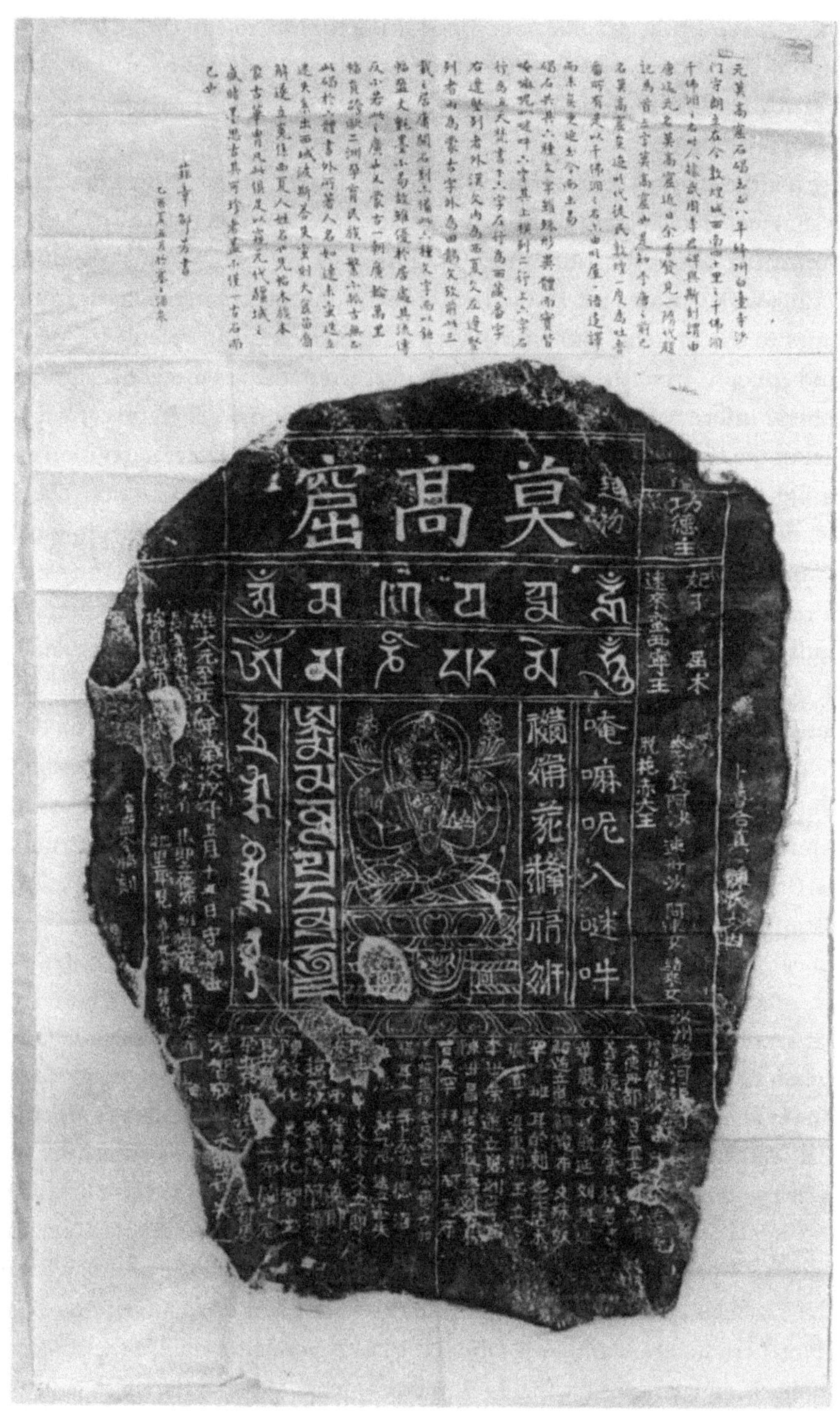

FIG. 7.1. Fragmentary Sui Buddhist votive stone in Chinese, Sanskrit, Tibetan, Xixia, Mongol, and Uigur. Dunhuang. The Metropolitan Museum of Art, gift of Mrs. Shao Fang Sheng, 1956 (56.34), image 160792 tf.

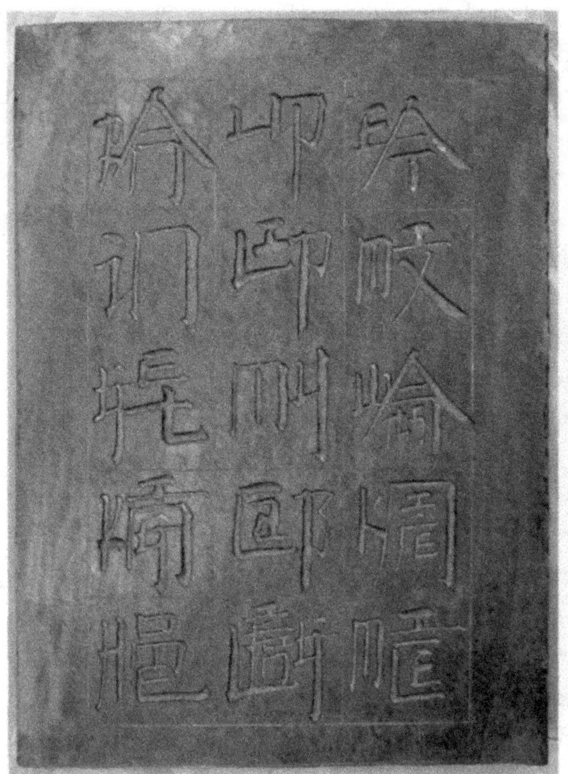

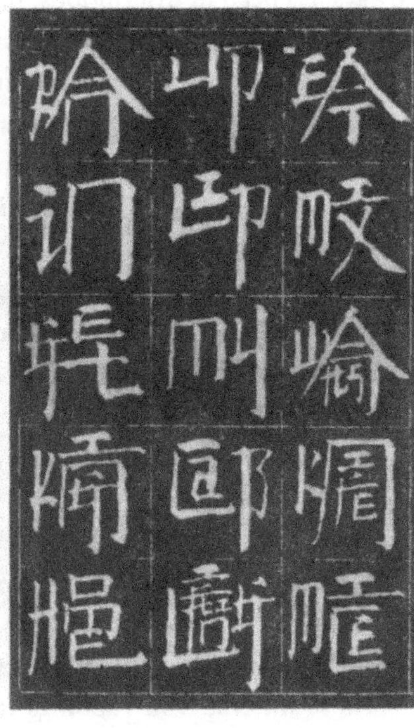

FIG. 7.2. Rubbings of Xu Bing's "Square Word Calligraphy": *left*, stone cut; *right*, rubbing. Courtesy of Xu Bing.

The interest in calligraphic rubbings continued in the Ming, remained keen in the Qing dynasty, and endures strongly today on both sides of the Taiwan Strait, despite the suppressions of the Cultural Revolution. Exemplary of the enduring vitality of calligraphy and its continuing evolution is the innovative work of the contemporary Chinese artist Xu Bing, who uses traditional brush writing to compose Chinese-looking words formed of a sinicized English alphabet, creating an amalgam of Chinese brush-work and English words.[5] *Word Play: Contemporary Art*, an exhibit of Xu's work, included a twenty-foot-long accordion album of rubbings with board ends of Xu's "Square Word Calligraphy," a contemporary *tie*, and the stone-cut blocks from which the rubbings came (fig. 7.2).

Students of calligraphy most highly prize *zhenji* (true traces) of early calligraphies, valuing rubbings from original or recut stones as well as from woodblocks cut in the positive and woodblock prints of calligraphies. The abundance of both traditional and modern calligraphic models, alongside current magazines and music tapes in shops in China and wherever Chinese culture has moved across the world, speaks clearly of this phenomenon.

In all these areas of intellectual and aesthetic content, the salient Chinese interest always has been in inscriptions, reflected clearly in the high proportion of such rubbings. It is common for a picture rubbing, such as that of a stele or Buddhist votive piece, to include the inscription but, to save paper, not the bordering motifs. Rubbings provide ready access to inscriptions and designs that no longer exist, whose intelligibility time has degraded, or that are in inaccessible sites or distant repositories. Referring to the Stone Drum inscriptions, Gilbert Mattos makes the point:

> As can be seen from ink rubbings taken from the stones early in this [the twentieth] century, in only one of the [ten] stones does its inscription approach completeness, while in one of the others [number 8] not a single character remains. . . . Those who have studied them . . . increasingly have had to rely on ink rubbings taken centuries ago, when considerably more characters were still extant.[6]

Finally, rubbings are convenient vehicles in practical ways, for "rejoining" fragmented cultural objects. Paleographers join separated shell-and-bone, pottery, or bronze fragments, and art historians compare rubbings of similar bronze mirrors or clay tiles to see if they came from the same mold.

Those interested in rubbings fall into three groups: metal-and-stone specialists (*jinshijia*), few in number and until recent decades largely limited to Chinese scholars; connoisseurs (*jianshangjia*) and collectors (*shoucangjia*); and dealers (*gudongshang*). The range of cultural materials represented in rubbings is great, and the range of interests of individual collectors is no less so, and, according to their personal intellectual or aesthetic predilections, they assemble various types of collections.

General collections are the most common, representing all types of content, materials and objects, time periods, and provenances. Other collections are specialized, some highly so, built with one or more considerations in mind.

They may concern themselves with *content*, with inscriptions by far the main focus, and with interests, very broad or highly specific. Inscriptions relating to history and language are the main intellectual foci; calligraphy, the predominant aesthetic focus. Among pictures, Buddhist and, in lesser measure, Daoist art, along with Han mortuary reliefs, are important interests. Each content area is susceptible of almost infinite subdivision. The dichotomy of content, intellectual and aesthetic, is reflected in the division that collectors make between those interested in rubbings of stele inscriptions (*bei*), cut primarily for intellectual reasons, and those interested in rubbings of calligraphic models (*tie*), prized for their aesthetic appeal. Terms relating to stone monuments, stone inscriptions, and rubbings of them include *li shi, jie, ke shi, bei, tie, fatie, zitie, beitie, shike,* and *moyai.*[7]

Qin used *li shi,* "to erect a stone," in referring to those that the First Emperor planted.

Called *jie*, they were irregularly conical boulders.[8] *Ke shi*, "to engrave a stone," also was a Qin term used in connection with commemorative inscriptions.

The term *bei*, stele, was known in the Qin, and the character, in Zhou small-seal script, appears in the *Shuowen jiezi*.[9] Brashier notes that "before the erection of stelae in the second century C.E., the term *bei* is surprisingly rare and is completely absent in the *Shi ji* and *Han shu*. . . . The earliest known stone tablet to refer to itself as a *bei* does not predate 128 C.E."[10] The Han used *bei* for the familiar monuments that over the centuries have been the standard public medium to perpetuate classical and religious texts, commemorate people and events, proclaim edicts, venerate worthies, praise achievements and heroic deeds, and laud loyalty, filial piety, and virtuous widows who did not remarry, to name some standard subjects. *Bei* were most abundant in the Later Han, notably in the reigns of Huandi (147–167 C.E.) and Lingdi (168–189 C.E.). They commonly are tall and massive, stand on tortoise bases (*guifu*), and are tabular to accommodate long, recordative texts.[11] Their backs often include names of relatives or donors, or later, supplemental inscriptions. They commonly manifest a caption (*bei'e*) at the top, and more elaborate steles have encircling mythical animals (*qishou*), especially the favored dragon. They occasionally manifest human figures, as on the *Zhang Qian Stele*, where the figure at the top may be Zhang Qian himself.[12] Their inscriptions, formal in content and format, typically are in restrained clerical (*li*) or standard (*zhen, zheng, kai*) scripts in orderly columns, with captions often in decorative seal script (figs. 1.9, 7.3, 7.25). *Bei* dominate temple grounds and public buildings, and they stand out in urban and rural landscapes across China.

Although they often have a collateral aesthetic function when inscriptions are in an admired hand, *bei* and rubbings of them, by extension also called *bei*, are important mainly for their intellectual content. They have continued strong over the centuries, primarily in their commemorative and edictal functions, but with calligraphic values often combined, such as Li Si's small seal and Cai Yong's *li*/*bafen* script. Modern examples include the *Monument to the People's Heroes* (Renmin yingxiong jinian bei), an obelisk with gold-filled characters that towers over Tiananmen Square. Its primary function is commemorative, but it carries a short inscription by Mao Zedong, whose brushwork during his tenure was omnipresent, and a longer and rarer example of the more admired calligraphy of Zhou Enlai.

Anciently, *bei* were said to have had noninscriptive, functional uses.[13] In the Han, they became ground for inscriptions and began to vary in shape and decor.[14] In part for economic reasons, *bei* yielded to memorial epitaphs (*muzhi ming*) immediately after the Han but continued in later dynasties.[15]

Tie had pre-Han beginnings, when writing was on silk, bamboo, and wood *jian* slips.[16] Admired calligraphy was copied on stone and wood for durability and, with rubbings from them, took on the names *tie*, "models"; *fatie*, "calligraphic models"; and

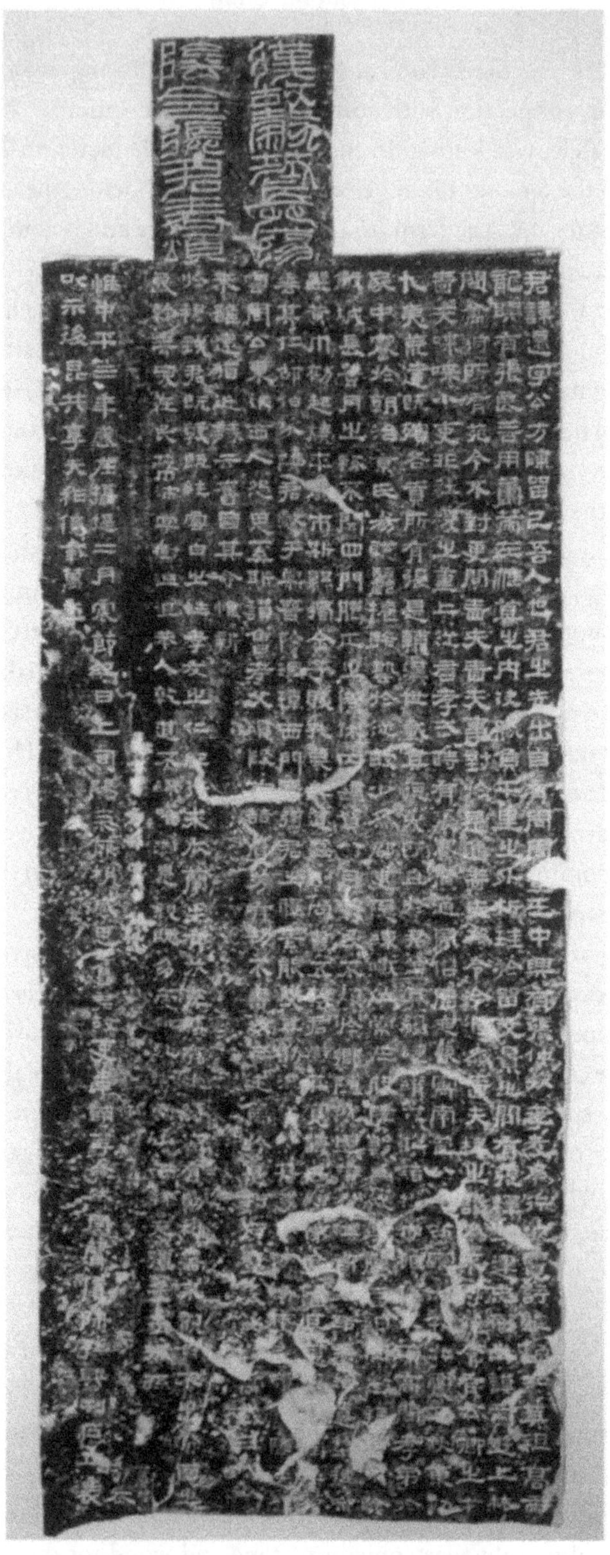

Fig. 7.3. Rubbing of the inscription only of the *Zhang Qian Stele* (*Zhang Qian bei*, 186 C.E.), to save paper. The Field Museum of Natural History, 244122.

zitie, "character models." *Tie* are informal, personal compositions, valued for their artistry, and typically are in a less restrained script—such as *xing*, "running," and *cao*, "grass"—and in small, horizontal, relaxed format. *Tie* came into greater favor in the Six Dynasties, following the Han, with their cutting in stone probably not until the Northern Song, with the *Chunhua Ge Model Book* (992) suggested as the earliest example.[17] *Tie* flourished in the Southern Song, dropped in popularity in the Tartar Jin and the Yuan, flowered again in the Ming and the Qing, and remain a core part of Chinese culture today.[18]

Collectors differentiate *tie* by type. A single-path model (*danxingtie*) is a work by one artist or poet, such as the *Dingwu Lanting tie* in the running script (*xingshu*) of Wang Xizhi. Collected models (*jitie, congtie*) are collections either of one artist or poet, such as Yan Zhenqing or Su Shi, or of many, such as the *Chunhua Ge Model Book*.[19]

Ye Changchi differentiates *bei* from *tie*, stating that a *tie* is not a *bei*, and he bluntly criticizes his contemporaries for not distinguishing between them.[20] In the Qing, there were two very different approaches to stone inscriptions. Ye emphasized metal-and-stone studies (*jinshi xue*), the analysis of early inscriptions on metal and stone for their intellectual, especially historiographical, content. That approach, harking back to the Song neo-Confucian tradition, came alive anew in the late Ming and flourished in the Qing, notably in the Qianlong (1736–1795) and Jiaqing (1796–1819) periods. The other approach emphasized aesthetics, the appreciation of fine calligraphy, commonly as copybooks (*tie*).[21] According to Percival David, "*Pei* [*bei*] and *t'ieh* [*tie*] are difficult to render precisely into English. *Pei* can refer either to a stone tablet, its inscription, or the rubbing of the inscription. . . . *T'ieh* could be an inscription on stone or on wood or the rubbing from it."[22] Although both are used as "copy slips" for calligraphy, "there is . . . an important difference. *Pei* invariably commemorates an event, while *t'ieh* never does."[23] Because *bei* generally record contemporary events, their scripts usually reflect current writing style.[24] The Qin used seal; the Han, the Wei, and the Jin preferred clerical; and the Northern and Southern dynasties favored standard. Running style was less common, and grass, cursive, was rare. *Tie* generally manifest running, grass, and small-standard scripts.

Tie, fatie, and *zitie* are copies of the ink traces (*moji*) or true traces (*zhenji*)—the latter term often indefinite—of celebrated calligraphers. Such copies occur in stone, wood, and other materials; the function, not the material, makes them *tie*. *Beitie* is an umbrella term that encompasses both types of inscriptions and, by extension, rubbings of them. The distinction is traditional.[25] When one meets a fellow rubbings collector, a common initial inquiry is whether one's interest is in *bei* or *tie*, and one often notes a subtle but clear tone of condescension on the part of those who collect *tie* when they learn that another's interest is in *bei*. Ye and others interested in content hold a different view.

Smoothed cliffs (*moyai*) are inscriptions cut on smoothed boulders or cliff faces. Depending on its definition, the practice began in the Qin or the Han, became popular in the fifth and sixth centuries, and continues today. *Shike* is a comprehensive term that includes all types of stone inscriptions. Ye Changchi enumerated more than forty in the *Yushi* but did not include *tie,* causing devotees of calligraphy to suffer "incomplete appreciation."[26] *Shike* are ubiquitous all across China. In the early 1930s, there were more than eight thousand stone cuts in Beijing.[27] On sacred Tai Shan, there are fourteen hundred *shike* from the Qin to the Qing, and on to the present.[28] One estimate is that there are more than one hundred thousand extant stone inscriptions, with rubbings of thirty thousand of them.[29]

Collections can be based on the *material* and the *type of object*: stone (steles, boulders, and rock faces; sculptures and jewelry of jade and other precious and semiprecious stones); metal (vessels, weapons, tools, mirrors, coins, and seals made of bronze, iron, and pewter; gold and silver objects; lead tallies); fired clay (funerary tiles, roof tiles, and pots); shell, bone, and ivory (oracle bones, carved hairpins), glass, lacquer, and other substances. Collections of rubbings of steles and other stone objects are most common, with both stone and bronze together following. Some collectors interest themselves solely in stone rubbings, as did Miu Quansun, a late Qing–early modern scholar whose collection of ten thousand rubbings was privately published as *Catalogue of the Studio of Artistic Taste* (Yifeng Tang mulu) and went to Beijing University. Ye Changchi specialized in rubbings of scripture pillars, his collection numbering a thousand. Others favor rubbings of the ritual bronzes and their inscriptions, as did Ruan Yuan, or of mirrors.

The *age* of the host may be of primary interest. Most collections are general, spanning time, but many feature rubbings of objects from a single dynasty, such as Han stele inscriptions or reliefs, Wei epitaphs, or Buddhist sculptures.

Collections may focus on a specific *provenance.* The older historical areas, especially those in the middle and lower reaches of the Yellow River, are of greatest interest, with Shandong and Shanxi the two provinces whose bronze and stone inscriptions antiquarians have collected with particular zeal.[30]

Collectors may seek rubbings that have *special qualities,* or that were made by a particular artisan or use a particular technique, such as cicada-wing rubbings, black-gold rubbings, or composite rubbings. They frequently combine several criteria, such as Sui and Tang stone inscriptions from Shanxi. Only the more sophisticated connoisseurs have such specific collecting foci. Most collectors are not so discriminating, and general collections are the most common type, representing a wide range of content, materials and objects, time periods, provenances, and connoisseurship qualities. Even in such broad collections, the central interest traditionally has been in inscriptions, primarily stone.

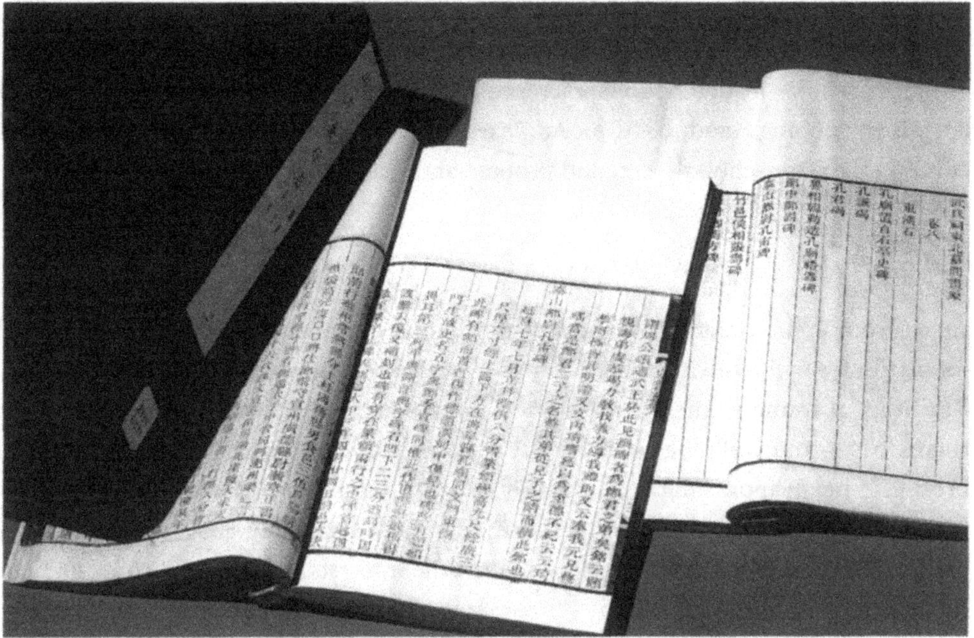

Fig. 7.4. Entries in Bi Yuan and Ruan Yuan, *Record of Shandong Metal and Stone* (Shanzuo jinshi zhi).

CHINESE RUBBINGS IN THE WEST

There are very few areas of knowledge on which the Chinese have not touched in their carved and cast records, and, by reflection, in rubbings of them. One can find these records, especially on stone, in every corner of the country, from major cities to small villages to mountain fastnesses, and in temples, museums, and libraries. Catalogues document them, organized by province or region, such as Bi Yuan and Ruan Yuan, *Record of Shandong Metal and Stone Inscriptions* (Shanzuo jinshi zhi, fig. 7.4), or by dynasty, such as Weng Fanggang's *Record of Metal and Stone from the Two Han* (Liang Han jinshi zhi).

These inscriptions and pictures and their surrogate rubbings have utility for research into literally every facet of Chinese life in every district of China from prehistoric times forward, as exemplified in figures 7.16–7.26, with Western scholars having made only limited use of them.[31] "Minor inscriptions" on pottery, tiles, seals, and weights and measures especially have been neglected: "Unfortunately, these inscriptions have attracted little notice in Western-language scholarship."[32] Several reasons come to mind. First, many Western scholars have not been fully cognizant of the existence and research potential of rubbings. Second, some materials, such as divination and bronze inscriptions, are so specialized in form and content as to have been more effectively exploited in the past by Chinese scholars. Such materials compose but a small portion of the vast quantity of inscriptive materials whose forms are modern and whose content is clear. Third, information on rubbings seldom has been included in university "tool courses" or bibliographies. Fourth, published reproductions exist for but a fraction of the total corpus of rubbings, and, until recent years, collections have not been organized or computerized for scholarly use, and proper catalogues have been rare.[33]

RUBBINGS AS OBJECTS OF VALUE

Apart from their content, rubbings are objects for cumulation in themselves, prized for attributes with which time, circumstance, and their qualities have infused them. The heart of connoisseurship, the appreciation of rubbings as fine and rare objects in themselves—and, lest it be overlooked, as vehicles for financial investment and social prestige—lies in appraising individual rubbings through keen knowledge, long experience, and sometimes costly mistakes in judgment. A rubbing can be evaluated for certain characteristics, absolute or relative to the interests or tastes of a collector. The first consideration is its type, with three most important: quality rubbings, old rubbings, and unique rubbings.

The term "quality rubbing" (*jing taben*) carries a complex of connotations relating to the excellence of the original object and its rubbing, including mounting and preservation. The original object should be significant in some culturally valued way, intellectually or aesthetically. Its nature, age, and condition are essential considerations, with sharpness of line particularly important. Ideally, a quality rubbing should be a copy of an early and valued inscription or picture, when it still was in good condition. A quality rubbing also may be a more recent copy of the same inscription in worn state, or it may even be a copy of a relatively new inscription. It must be a decided cut above average and in good condition. Paper and ink should be of good quality, and the work should be technically sound, with the reproduction complete and fully faithful, for accuracy is a quintessential attribute of a rubbing and often a determinant in dating (plate 7; fig. 7.5). Finally, it should be aesthetically pleasing, with connoisseurs having preferences regarding techniques and effects.

As with other aspects of rubbings lore, there is little early information about the makers of rubbings or the effects that they achieved. Even in the Tang and later, when the technique was well established, makers of rubbings were considered artisans rather than artists, as seen in references to rubbing artisans (*ta*[a]*shu shou*) in the *Codes and Regulations of the Six Boards of the Tang Dynasty* (Tang liudian) and Tang histories. Consequently, their names normally were not handed down as were those of calligraphers and painters.

The work of some later artisans was recognized as superior, and their rubbings were sought after; among them were Da Shou and Chen Jieqi (cited below), Liao Yingzhong,

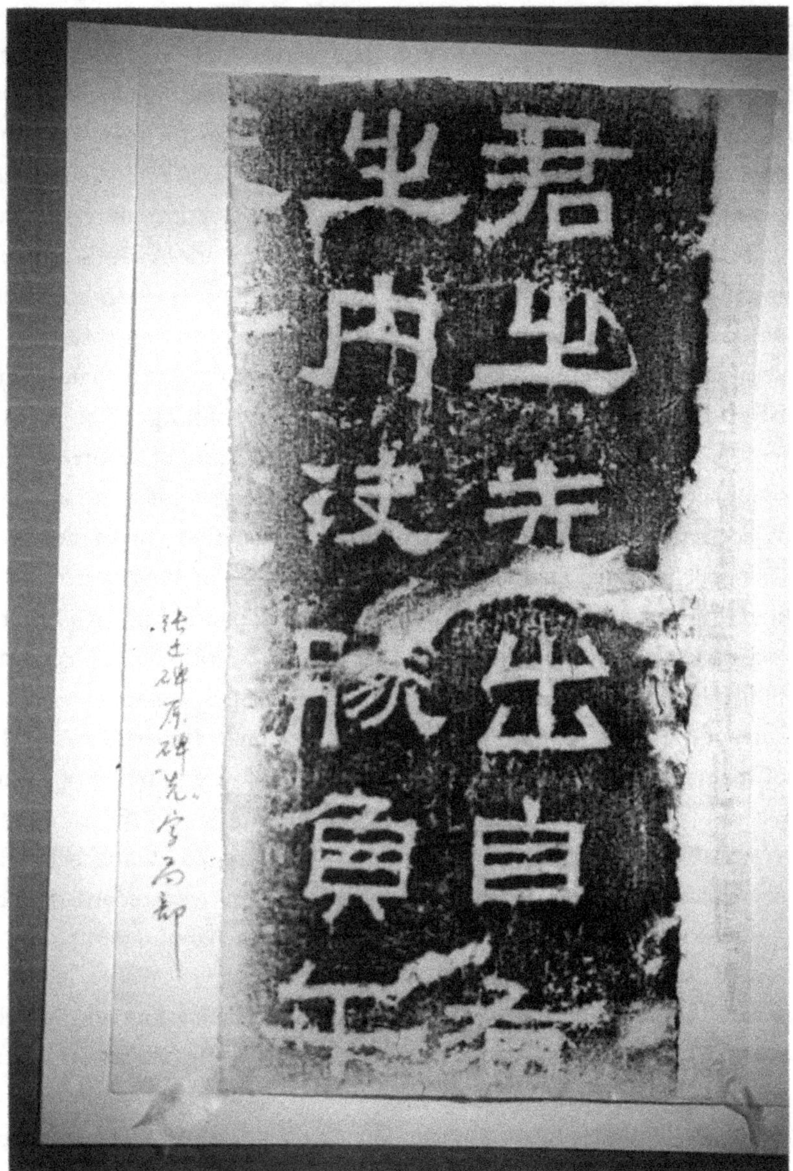

FIG. 7.5. Rubbing of part of the *Zhang Qian Stele* (*Zhang Qian bei*, 186 C.E.), showing the eroded *xian* character, critical for dating. Author's collection. Photograph by the author.

Che Yongzhao, Wang Xiting, and Zhou Xiding.[34] Liao lived in the mid-thirteenth century, at the end of the Southern Song. A retainer of Jia Sidao (d. 1276), a military official, Liao is known for recutting the *Chunhua Ge Model Book*. There is no information about Che Yongzhao, save that Jiang heard the name in his travels through Shaanxi in the 1930s, and that provincials "still spoke of 'Che rubbings.'" Che may have lived and worked in the late Qing or early Republican times. There also is no information about Wang Xiting, save that he was widely respected for rubbing the Stone Drums.

The differential skills in making stone and bronze rubbings are reflected in the terms for those who make them. The term "rubbing artisan" (*tagong*) refers to a person who rubs steles and other ordinary objects. Rubbing artisans commonly receive travel expenses, subsistence, and pay by the square foot for their work. A specialist (*zhuanjia*) is one who rubs bronzes and other more demanding objects, with commensurate financial rewards. Because stone rubbings are more common and generally require relatively less skill to make, they less often carry seal signatures or dates, with such evidence of pride of workmanship usually reserved for rubbings of objects that are more difficult to rub, or of materials having greater intellectual or aesthetic value. Seal signatures more often occur on composite rubbings of bronze vessels, and sometimes on rubbings of jades, mirrors, weapons, seals, old coins, and Han tiles. One of the best-known of the modern specialists who signed and sealed their bronze rubbings was Zhou Xiding, who lived and worked in Shanghai before World War II. Zhou was known for his remarkable rubbings of ancient bronzes, whose inscriptions and motifs he copied and whose forms he skillfully represented in composite rubbings (see figs. 5.2, 5.3).[35]

At the turn of the eighteenth century into the nineteenth, in part through the publications of scholars such as Ruan Yuan and Qian Dian, the popularity of rubbings increased. It also was then that scholars and collectors began to accord attention to those who were especially sophisticated in rubbing and began to define technical skills and aesthetic effects. Even then, the names of skilled artisans were recorded more often if they also were known for their scholarship. Two such men are remembered, one for his technical skills, the other for his aesthetic sensitivities.

The first was Da Shou (literary name, Liu Zhou), a Buddhist monk with a high name for his composite rubbings. A religious at White Horse Temple (*Baima Si*) in Haining, Zhejiang, Da Shou lived in Qianlong, Jiaqing, and Daoguang times, spanning the late eighteenth and early nineteenth centuries. The scholar-monk was versed in the study of inscriptions on ancient bronzes and stone tablets and particularly was recognized for his skill in rubbing them. Ruan Yuan, the renowned scholar of the time, called Da Shou "the metal-and-stone monk" (*Jinshi seng*).

> The most famous person making rubbings [*ta*[a] *mo*[a]] at that time was the Buddhist monk Da Shou. [In Daoguang times, 1821–1850], Wu Rongguang governed Wu [the Hunan region], and he had him make rubbings of the finest bronzes and steles for inclusion in the *Record of Metal and Stone in the Hall of Clear-Skinned Bamboo* (Yunqing Guan jinshi zhi) [by Wu Rongguang]. . . . Da Shou's rubbings all were [done in] light ink like cicada wings.[36]

The second individual was Chen Jieqi, a Daoguang (1821–1850) scholar-official from Wei County, Shandong. Author of *Chuangu bielu*, Chen was a renowned collector of stone rubbings, bronzes (including the *Mao Gong ding*), bronze rubbings, and coins. He particularly is remembered for the quality of his rubbings.[37]

> [Among rubbings] marked by heavy ink like black lacquer, [authorities] consider those from Chen Jieqi as the finest. Now, he gave specific instructions to his fellow provincial, Chen Peigang, about making rubbings. In correspondence with Pan Zuyin [Xianfeng period, 1851–1861], Mr. Chen discusses rubbing in detail. In *Collectanea from the Studio of Abundant Happiness* (Pangxi Zhai congshu), cut by Mr. Pan, the best-known [piece] is [Chen Jieqi's] *Separate Record on Perpetuating Antiquity* (Chuangu bielu).[38]

Chen's capture of the long inscription on the curved interior of the *Mao Gong ding* was the result of skillful manipulation of the paper, and he was able to capture it on just two sheets of paper instead of four, as less skilled workers are forced to do. Because of the reputation of the Chen family, many others in Shandong, a province famous for its antiquities and antiquarians, emulated Chen's technique. Some consider that of all those who made or collected rubbings, Chen Jieqi was foremost.[39]

Over and above the attributes of the rubbing proper, its mounting and preservation are connoisseurship considerations. The quality of the materials and workmanship in the mounting, and its condition, are highly important to the discriminating collector, for the work faithfully must preserve the integrity of the original inscription, including spacing, elevated characters, and even faults, and must do so in pleasing manner (plates 4 and 7). Equally important is the preservation of the mounted rubbing and its accoutrements. Lastly, the quality and quantity of the documentation associated with the rubbing and its mounting, in the forms of colophons, seals, and associated correspondence, are of signal importance.

The designation "quality rubbing" connotes the interplay between the excellence of the original subject matter and that of the rubbing, its mounting, and its preservative components. Ideally, the relationship should represent a balance, with both subject matter and rubbing praiseworthy, but, as the term implies, the quality of the rubbing is the main consideration. Finally, enhancements, age, and rarity are not necessarily requirements for a quality rubbing.

Old rubbings (*jiu taben*) constitute a second type of prized rubbing. "Old" is an indefinite, relative term, meaning only that the rubbing is not recent. To be counted as old, a rubbing generally must date from a time no later than the Qing, with conservative scholars setting the Qianlong (1736–1795) as the division line, and the more liberal choosing the Daoguang (1821–1850). As with all antiques, the date advances with time. When evidence permits, scholars assign dynastic dates, as "Song rubbing" (*Song ta*) or "Ming rubbing" (*Ming ta*). The rubbings of the *Kong Zhou Stele* (Kong Zhou bei) represent both, with that of the front face being Song, and that of the rear face, Ming (see fig. 6.7). The Song date of the front face is confirmed by the presence of an eroded but still legible *gao* (tall) character that had spalled by the Yuan dynasty (plate 7). Often such specific evidence is wanting, in which case it is possible only to designate a rubbing simply as an old rubbing.

The term "old rubbing" refers primarily to the age of the rubbing but implicitly also often refers to that of the original object. Some collectors categorize a rubbing of a newly discovered old stele as an old rubbing, as with one of the *Stele of the Thrice Venerable* (San lao bei), also called the *Zhao Kuan Stele* (Zhao Kuan bei), a Han stone discovered only in 1943. Ideally, however, an old rubbing is an old rubbing of an old object, with the primary emphasis on the age of the rubbing. Although collectors value recent rubbings of old objects, it is the old rubbings that they most highly prize and avidly seek. Apart from the fact that older copies are rarer than newer ones, all things being equal, an earlier rubbing is sharper and clearer than a later one, or, sometimes, than the object itself is today. It is possible, however, for a later rubbing to be clearer, as the result of superior rubbing paper and technique. A well-made newer rubbing that more sensitively manifests the accuracy and essence of the original also may be of greater value than an older one that fails to capture that spirit.[40] Thus there is often a close and meaningful relation between the age and the quality of a rubbing. Quality is always desirable, despite the fact that it is not requisite in an old rubbing.

Connoisseurs also seek unique rubbings (*guben*). The term connotes that the rubbing is the only one in existence, with the obvious implication that the original object no longer is extant. Unique rubbings may be quality rubbings and generally also are old rubbings. In theory, however, quality and age are not necessarily criteria. A unique rubbing may be a crude rubbing of an undistinguished inscription on a newly erected monument dedicated at ten o'clock on Thursday morning, hastily rubbed once at eleven o'clock, and demolished by a runaway truck at high noon.

In addition to quality rubbings, old rubbings, and unique rubbings, connoisseurs value other special types. A complete rubbing (*zuben*) lacks none of its characters. The term "without-defect editions" (*buduanben*) refers to faultless rubbings of stones that are not cracked or split. A first rubbing (*chuta*) is an initial rubbing of a newly found object. Periodically, an ancient bronze vessel or stone tablet will be unearthed, and as parts of the inscription may spall in the initial cleaning, scholars may make a rubbing on the spot. A first rubbing also may be an early rubbing of an object. First rubbings are rare, with old ones particularly so, and collectors prize them, even though their other rubbings all are quality, old, or unique. The *Epitaph of the Prince of Lu, Heir to the Imperial Ming* (Huang Ming Jianguo Lu Wang kuangzhi), or *Epitaph of the Prince of Lu* (Lu Wang muzhi ming), is an example. Cut in 1663 on the death of a Ming prince regent who had fled the mainland to escape Qing armies, the stone was unknown until 1959, when road workers unearthed it on Quemoy Island. Collectors covet rubbings of the original inscription (fig. 7.6) but also seek those of the modern recut (fig. 7.7) that was left with the Quemoy office of the Taiwan Cultural Commission when officials removed the original to Taibei.[41]

There is a small percentage of rubbings in red, so called red rubbings (*zhu*[a]*ta*[a]) or vermilion rubbings (*zhu*[b]*ta*[a]), in contrast to those in black (*mo*[a]*ta*[a]). Makers and collectors of rubbings favor red in auspicious situations, among them for the making of a first rubbing (*chuta*[a]) or the copying of some particularly valued object (plate 8). Blue, green, and purple also are used but do not have the frequency or cultural potency of red. Another category consists of rubbings that one lacks. Here, there is no suggestion of quality, age, or rarity—indeed, the rubbing may be quite common—but the collector needs it to complete a particular series or collection.

A single rubbing may combine all these categories of rubbings, especially if the rubbing is categorized as a quality, old, or unique rubbing.

DATING

A second major consideration in appraising a rubbing is determining its age. Connoisseurs prefer old rubbings, with a twelfth-century rubbing of a second-century stone inscription prized above one made in the sixteenth century, and with that in turn valued over a twentieth-century copy. The following comments on dating apply particularly to rubbings of stone inscriptions, the most abundant and amply documented objects that the Chinese rubbed.

The dating of a rubbing can be absolute or relative. Absolute dating, especially of old rubbings, is rare. The great majority of rubbings seldom are even signed, let alone dated, for rubbing traditionally was a craft, not considered worthy of signature or date. The makers of rubbings, especially rubbings of smaller objects, often have been girls, as was said to be the case in the household of Chen Jieqi.[42] Young boys have also served in the same role (see fig. 4.1).

Rubbings occasionally are signed, such as those by specialists, and thus datable, either precisely or within narrow limits. Among the best-known modern artisans who signed or sealed their rubbings was Zhou Xiding, mentioned above. Apart from the rare instances when a piece can be dated absolutely or narrowly, one can but assign it a relative date, connecting it to a dynasty or reign, or to another rubbing of known date. Various evidences are used to assign a relative date, including the elimination of other possibilities.

Physical characteristics are criteria. The ages, type, and characteristics of the paper and ink are important, and sophisticated collectors pay close attention to whether they

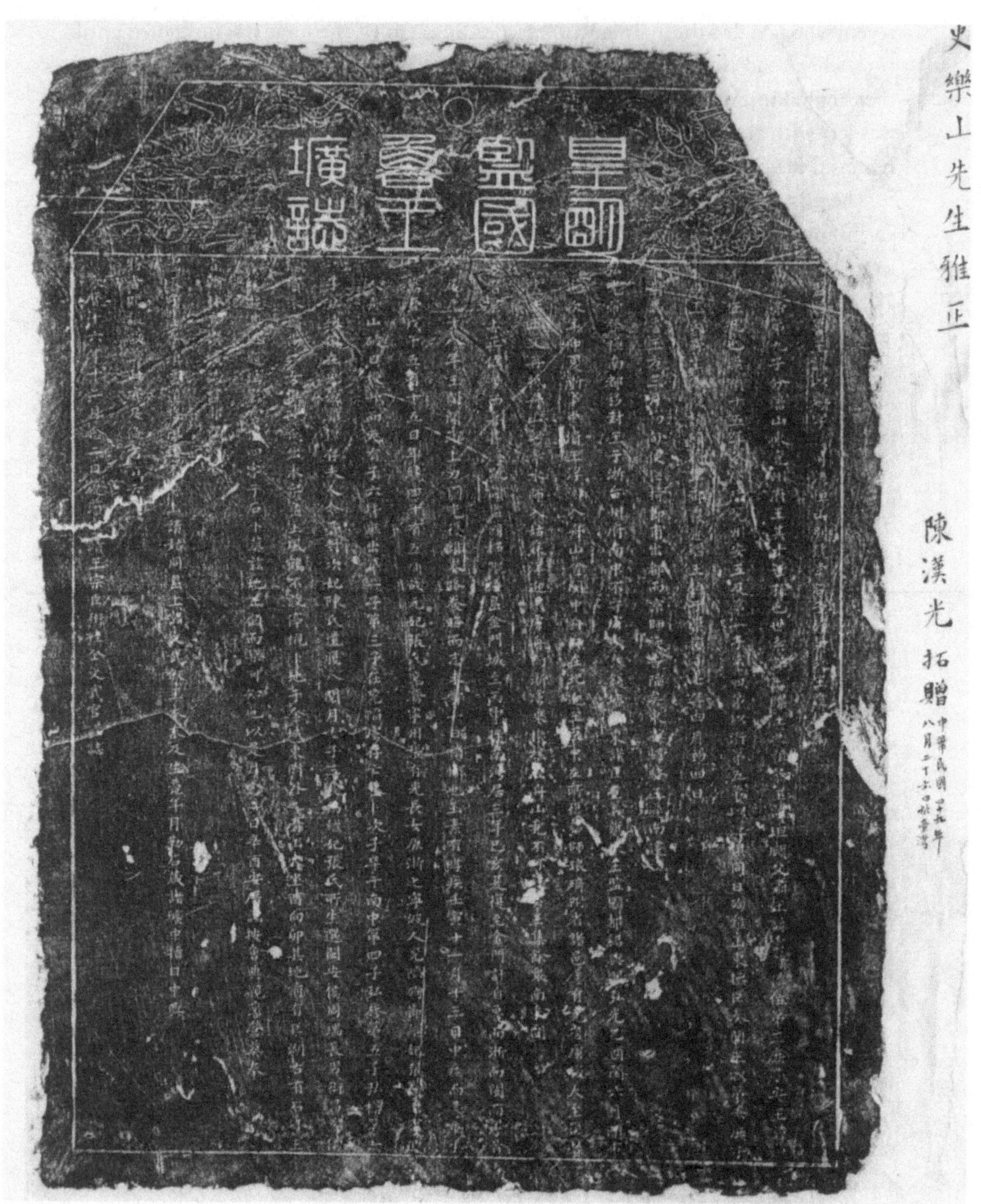

Fig. 7.6. Original Lu Wang epitaph (1663). The Field Museum of Natural History, 264204/1.

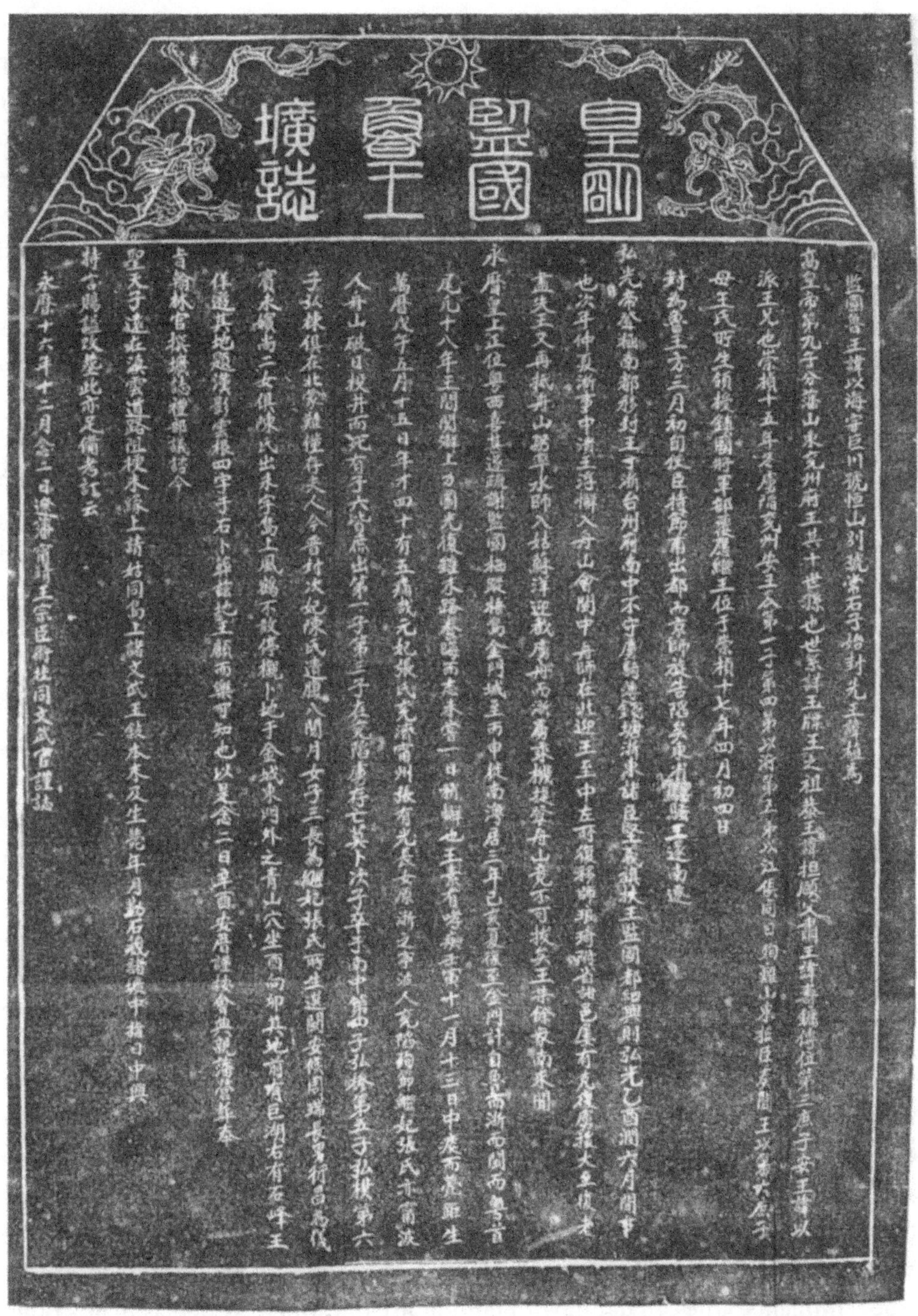

Fig. 7.7. Recut (1960) of the Lu Wang epitaph. The Field Museum of Natural History, 264204/2. Rubbing and photograph by the author.

are from the time supposedly represented by the rubbing, especially those said to be from the Tang and the Song. Older rubbing papers are said to be grayish, through long exposure to the ink and the effect of the paste in repeated mountings. Among the special rubbing papers in the collection of Jiang Gusun in Taiwan in 1960 was red-thread *luowen* paper (*hongsi luowen zhi*), used for colophons on the *Song-Rubbed Classic of the Yellow Hall* (Song ta Huangting Jing), a Daoist classic thought to have been written by Wang Xizhi. The paper was light buff, with very fine darker horizontal lines, and had ever so faint a rose tint, thus its name. Both Jiang and Qu Wanli stated that red-thread *luowen* was a Ming paper.[43] The paper alone is no absolute criterion, however, for, as with manuscripts and paintings, one can make new rubbings on old paper or treat new paper to give it aura of age.

Sometimes characteristics of the rubbing itself are criteria. Qu and Jiang pointed out one of Jiang's rubbings of a type that they called "partitioned-hemp rubbing" (*kema ta*). The rubbing manifested a slightly irregular grid pattern, as though the rubbing had been made through a fine, very loosely woven cloth, with warp and woof captured in the rubbing. Neither Qu nor Jiang could explain whether the effect was a result of the paper, the ink, or the technique, but they agreed that only Song rubbings manifested it.[44] Another criterion is the shape of the incised characters, for cutting styles have varied with temporal and regional factors and with the cutter's preferences. It is sometimes possible to draw inferences about cutting style from the rubbings themselves, and such inferences, though difficult to draw, can serve as one more criterion for dating. Characteristics of the materials used in the mounting are important criteria, as are those evidenced in the making and decorating of fittings, enclosures, and other accoutrements.

Associated documentation and corroborative data are essential dating keys. Central in judging the age of a rubbing, as well as its quality, are colophons, signatures, seals, associated correspondence, and other additions by successive owners and knowledgeable scholars and collectors who have seen the piece. Apart from carrying helpful dates, these complements also often include specific statements about the history and significance of the rubbing that permit its placement in time. Frequently, however, the documentation is limited to a note that the undersigned has "seen" (*guan*) the rubbing and so explicitly or implicitly has confirmed its genuineness, age, and quality (see fig. 6.10). One must know the qualifications of the documenter and, even when the credentials are excellent, be able to read between the lines to determine the writer's true sentiments. One can damn with faint praise in Chinese as well as in any other language.

Seals further identify those who have owned or seen the rubbing. One individual may have several dozen seals of different materials, with a variety of scripts and names—the personal name (*ming*), the literary name (*hao*), the courtesy name (*zi*),

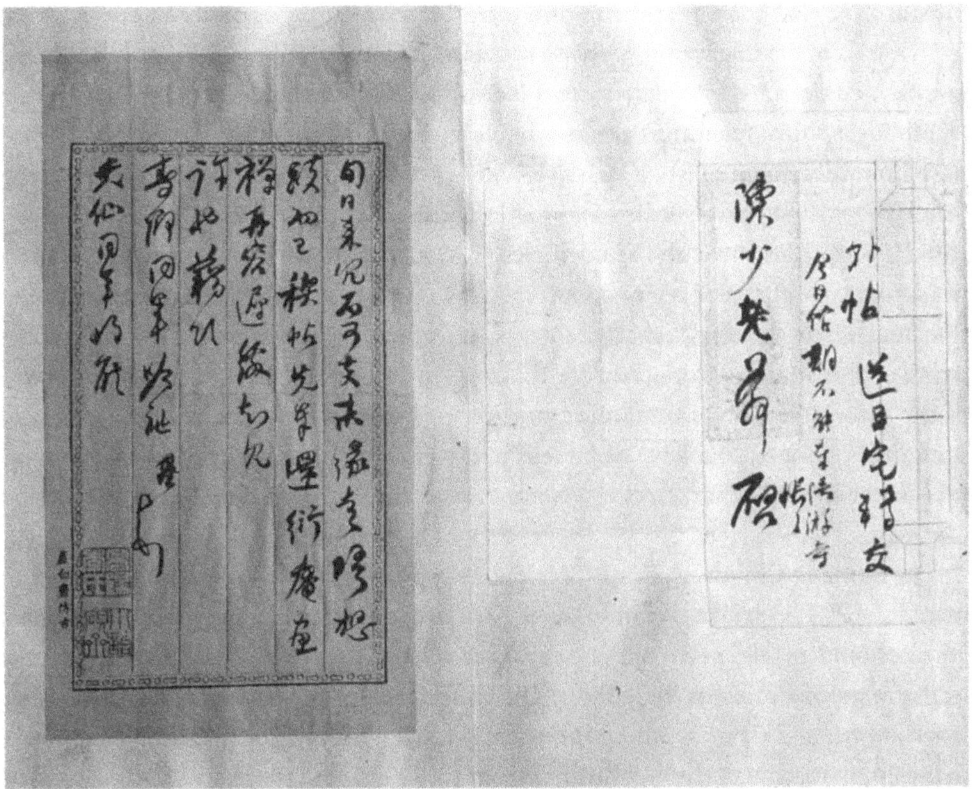

Fig. 7.8. Letter from He Zizhen to Chen Jieqi (1813–1844) about the rubbing of the *Lanting calligraph* (Lanting tie). The Field Museum of Natural History, 233914.

and the studio name (*shiming*). Sometimes a seal will identify the artisan or, more often, the specialist. Physical characteristics of seal impressions sometimes are corroborative, as with a water seal (*shuiyin*) made with ink that has water rather than oil as a vehicle. Such impressions, paler red, are said to characterize earlier dynasties. Opinion diverges about when the use of the water seal ended, with some setting the terminal date at the end of the Song, as did Li Zongtong, but with others holding that its use continued through the Ming, as did Qu Wanli. The opportunities for falsification of such a simple compound are obvious. In commenting on colored seal impressions, one needs to mention the traditional Chinese practice of using blue seal ink for a period of months—twenty-four or twenty-seven, varying with the informant—following the death of a parent.[45]

Relevant correspondence from recognized authorities often accompanies a prize rubbing as part of the preservation assemblage. Exemplary is a letter from He Zizhen to Chen Jieqi, both eminent Daoguang (1821–1850) scholars and collectors, in reference to a Lanting rubbing (fig. 7.8). In considering these authenticating components, one must realize that such documentation is not necessarily a guarantee of authenticity. Individuals of flexible moral fiber use spurious documentation, or documentation by unqualified persons, to add luster to a fake or mediocre rubbing.

Bibliographical references are invaluable in dating. Within the vast corpus of Chinese literature there exists a massive body of works on inscriptions and pictures. Scholars zealously have studied and meticulously documented bronze and especially stone inscriptions through the centuries. Catalogues may be general or limited to a particular type of object, region, or period, and they often provide a wealth of information: location of the object, measurements, and commentary on its history, commonly citing earlier sources. Important for dating, the statements also often include a copy of the inscription, or of remaining portions, as well as an account of the changes, sometimes minute, that have occurred in it over the centuries. Scholars also provide missing or illegible characters by reference to earlier descriptions, or by speculation (see fig. 1.3).

The Stone Drum inscriptions (*Shigu wen*) provide a classic example of such documentation.[46] The drums, a name dating back to the Tang, are ten irregularly rounded granite boulders (*jie*), each carrying a rhymed verse in large-seal script recording events in the reign of a predynastic duke of Qin. They are one of the earliest Chinese stone inscriptions, and Chinese interest in them has been unflagging since their discovery in the upper reaches of the Wei River, early in the Tang, with the exact original location unrecorded. Views on their date have varied from traditional assignments to the twelfth century B.C.E. down to the fourth century B.C.E.[47] Gilbert Mattos concludes that "their specific date . . . cannot be determined as yet [but] . . . we might tentatively place the S[tone] D[rum inscriptions] in the 5th century B.C."[48] The Beijing Library catalogue gives a date of 475 B.C.E.[49]

Originally, each boulder held about seventy characters, totaling some seven hundred. By the Song, as known from extant rubbings, there were fewer than five hundred. Today fewer than three hundred remain, with one stone nearly complete and the inscription on number eight completely gone.[50] Save for brief modern wartime removals, the stones have been in Beijing since the Tartar Jin took them to Yanjing (Beijing) in 1126 and placed them in the Imperial Academy.[51] They are one of China's greatest treasures, and it is unlikely that any other inscription in the world has been so well tended and so much studied over so long a time (fig. 7.9).[52] According to Li Yingji of the Palace Museum [Gugong Bowuyuan], "The rubbing is a Ming period rubbing, and it is one of the finest rubbings now in the collections of the Palace Museum."[53] Manifesting its rarity, the rubbing carries eleven seal impressions, one marking a completely spalled character in the fifth line. Similar records exist for tens of thousands of bronze and stone inscriptions, helping to date old rubbings.

In lieu of assignment to a dynasty or a reign, one can place a rubbing in a chrono-

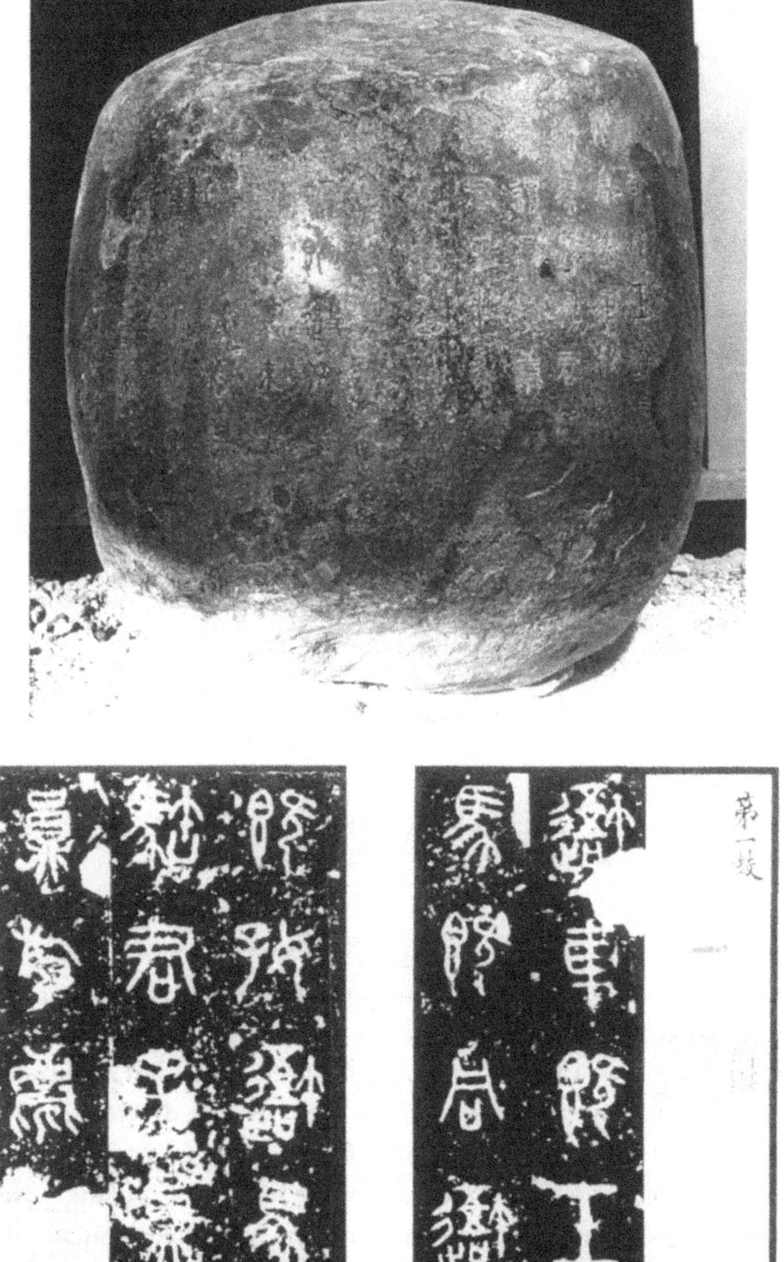

Fig. 7.9. Stone Drum no. 1 (ca. 475 B.C.E.) and Ming rubbing. Collection of the Palace Museum, Beijing.

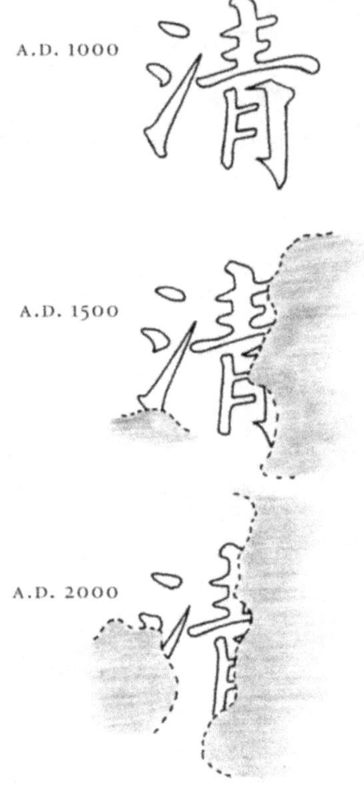

Fig. 7.10. Relative dating: characters and strokes. Sketch and photograph by the author.

logical sequence relative to other rubbings of the same inscription. Along with analysis of paper and ink, relative dating is based on the number of remaining characters and their completeness, as with the Stone Drums. As the rate of attrition is not regular but depends on a stone's history—as when it has been buried, left in the open, or kept under cover—there is no way to determine the precise age differential between two rubbings, only that one is earlier. Moving to finer analysis, one can place rubbings of the same inscription in a temporal sequence on the basis of parts of the characters and strokes remaining (fig. 7.10). Exemplary is a rare *jiu taben* (old rubbing) of the *Kong Zhou Stele* (Kong Zhou bei), memorializing Kong Zhou, a second-century descendant of Confucius and chief official of Tai Shan prefecture, Shandong. Ascribed to the Song, the rubbing is dated by a fragmentary *gao* character (tall, exalted), said to have spalled entirely by the end of the Song. This significant fact is recorded cryptically on the title strip of the book-mounted quality rubbing—"The-*gao*-character-is-not-ruined edition" (*gao zi wei huai ben*)—and more fully where the character occurs in the text (plate 7; fig. 6.7). The gradual disintegration, from the Song period to the modern period, of the *yu* character on the admired *fenshu* (*bafen*) script of the Later Han *Ritual Vessel Stele* (Li qi bei) also illustrates the phenomenon.

The proportions of the remaining characters, strokes, and parts of strokes also are a consideration, for their broadening, which is sometimes microscopic, is progressive, subtly changing them in successive rubbings. Exquisite care is necessary in copying calligraphy (whether from an original or from a rubbing), cutting it in stone or wood, and rubbing it, for even minute divergences at any step result in loss of fidelity. As divergences continue with successive cuttings, in time a calligraphic drift, parallel to genetic or linguistic drift, occurs. The vital importance of faithful rubbings is obvious; not all rubbings are equal.

There also can be human changes, as when a scholar or cutter reworks an old stone and mistakes a character, as with the *Xia Cheng bei,* a Han stele of which a rubbing was made in the Song. The stone was lost but was rediscovered in the Ming, by which time the lower part of the inscription was unclear. In reworking it, the cutter misinterpreted *yue* as *shao,* and so rubbings with the latter character date from the Ming or later. A similar misinterpretation occurs in a Song rubbing of the *Lanting Preface.* Such mistakes are not uncommon.

Surface faults also are a criterion. These can be natural or human, and they include scratches, cracks, spalls, or nicks, in the case of stone objects, and scratches, pitting, or corrosion, in the case of metal ones. In this vein, one is moved to refer to a practice darkly said to be followed by unprincipled collectors. Having made a rubbing of a stone inscription, and in order to ensure its relative position in time, a collector may then deface the stone in some small way, minutely nicking the surface between the lines, or, infinitely more execrable, chipping the edge of a stroke. To a scholar or collector of conscience, such a practice is a mortal sin.

A constellation of evidences—physical, corroborative, and bibliographical—is the best guarantee of an accurate determination of authenticity. Even so, a faint shadow of doubt can hang over a piece for centuries.

DUPLICATES AND FORGERIES

What has been said thus far applies to genuine rubbings of original objects. Other kinds of rubbings include genuine rubbings of duplicate cultural objects, and forged rubbings. Legitimate duplicates are copies, recuts, or reprints (*mo[d]ben, chongmoben, chongkeben,* and *fankeben*). Forgeries opprobriously are fakes or counterfeits (*weiben* and *yanben*). Chinese tradition has allowed for legitimate duplication of cultural objects. In the context of rubbings, the most common such objects are stele inscriptions; and, when duplicated, they are recut for two reasons, both manifestations of the high cultural value of the originals. First, the original stone has been lost or has deteriorated badly, and a copy may be cut, with the model commonly being an old rubbing. The Song recut of the Qin Yi Shan tablet is such a case. One must be careful in purchasing rubbings in such situations. As an example, all else being equal, a Ming rubbing of a weathered Han stone will differ from a Song rubbing of the same stone. Song rubbings of a Han stone and of a Song recut of that stone both are Song rubbings, but the two original stones are very different, and the rubbings will differ in cultural and monetary value. Second, a stone may be duplicated to protect and preserve the original, or because antiquarians desire additional copies at other locations.

The recutting of the caption of the Nestorian Stele (Da Qin Jingjiao liuxing Zhongguo bei, 781) at the Beilin is an example of protecting and preserving the original, including for purposes of reproduction (fig. 7.11). That of the *Goulou Stele* (Goulou bei) is a novel example of making additional copies. According to legend, there anciently was an inscribed stone tablet on Goulou Shan, highest peak of Heng Shan, one of China's five sacred mountains, in Hunan.[54] The inscription on this "original" tablet, also known as the *Stele of Yu* (Yu bei), described the efforts of the legendary Xia emperor Yu to control the waters of China. In the late Song, one He Zhi climbed the peak, where he claimed to have seen the tablet and to have copied the inscription, purportedly written by Yu himself in an eccentric wriggly script known as *ketou wen* (tadpole script). In 1212, He commissioned the cutting of the inscription on the rock wall in the courtyard of the Yuelu Academy (*shuyuan*) in Changsha, Hunan, at the foot of Yuelu Shan. The inscription now is only of historical interest, generally acknowledged to have been a figment of He's imagination.

In Ming and Qing times, however, there was high interest in the inscription. In the Ming, Yang Shen wrote a commentary on the stone, and over the two dynasties, based directly or indirectly on the He version, some half dozen copies were erected around China (fig. 7.12).[55] As the script is highly fanciful, scholars and collectors annotated their copies, often setting down in standard (*zheng*) script their interpretations beside the tadpole characters.

Rubbings of duplicate stone cuts sometimes are difficult to distinguish from those of the originals, for a recut may follow the original quite faithfully, even dutifully reproducing imperfections. Beilin scholars study rubbings of new recuts minutely and rubricate strokes and parts of strokes in need of corrective recutting. A dated colophon often will distinguish a recut, but sometimes no such indicator exists, and one must make detailed comparisons of content, form, and style. Careful scholars pride themselves on being able to distinguish a rubbing of a recut from one of the original by subtle differences in the styles of the characters and the ages of the paper and ink used for the rubbing. Rubbings of recuts are not as highly valued as those from the original.

Allied to duplicates cut in stone are copies in wood, cut with the tracing of the inscription laid face up on the block, rather than in the reverse orientation, with the

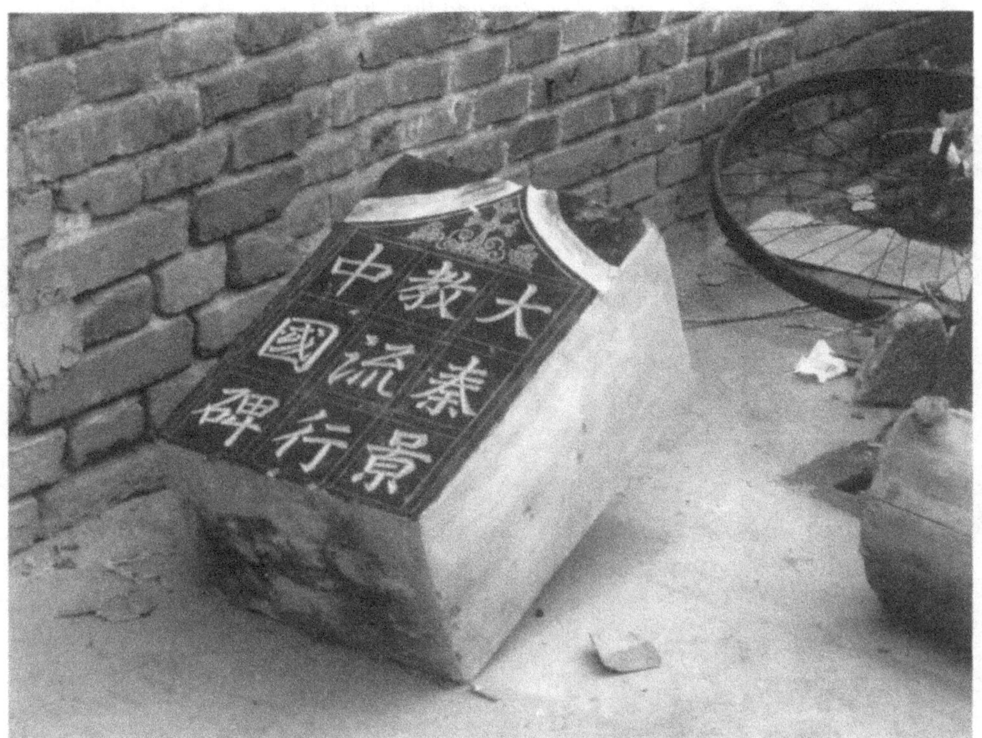

Fig. 7.11. Recut of the caption of the *Nestorian Stele* (*Da Qin Jingjiao liuxing Zhongguo bei*, 781). Xi'an Beilin Museum. Photograph by the author.

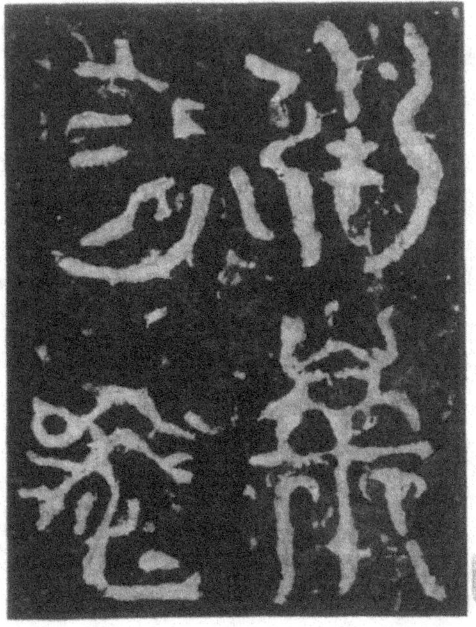

Fig. 7.12. Book-mounted "quality" rubbing of a Jiajing-reign (1522–1566) Yunnan recutting of the *Goulou Mountain Stele* (*Goulou Shan bei*), Yunnan, Anning. The Field Museum of Natural History, 244844.5.

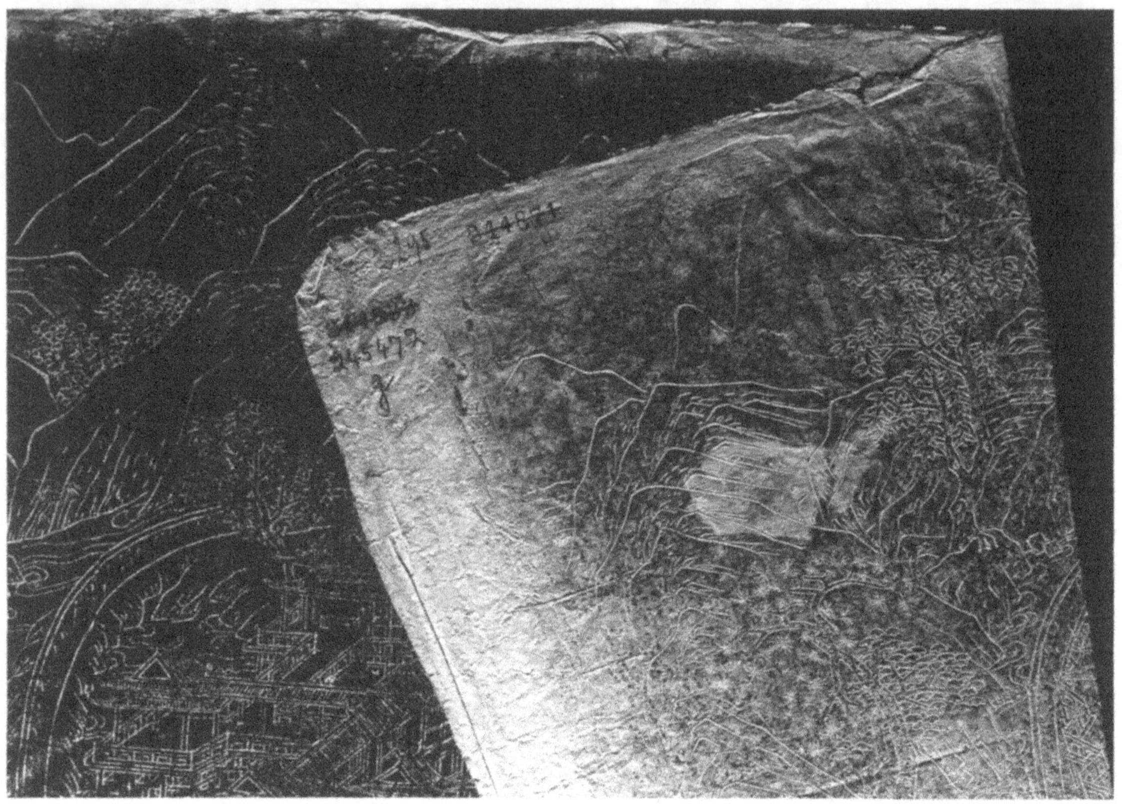

FIG. 7.13. "Old rubbed" *Wang River True Footsteps* (*Wang Chuan zhenji*): tamping wrinkles and patch on back of a rubbing of a 1617 stone edition. The Field Museum of Natural History, 245472g.

tracing laid face down, as in cutting woodblocks. It is not uncommon for missing members of a set of stones to be replaced in wood, a fact that is relevant for the resultant rubbings. Although such woodcuts may follow the original stone inscription with great fidelity, knowledgeable specialists can distinguish a rubbing of a positive woodcut from one of a stone, and that in turn from a woodblock print. The presence of wrinkles from laying and tamping the paper serves as the most reliable indicator of technique. Well-made rubbings retain clear tamping bulges, and when they are pressed flat, the wrinkles are readily apparent (plate 7; figs. 7.12, 7.13). Woodblock prints show few such traces (fig. 7.14).

Evidence of surface texture also can be a useful diagnostic in differentiating rubbings of stone cuts, woodcuts, and woodblock prints. Wood blocks typically are smoother and more even, barring wear, splits, vermiculations, or other faults, although when they do occur, they may be difficult to simulate. Surfaces of metal and stone objects, especially ancient ones, show corrosion in the case of metal, and weathering, pitting, cracks, and spalls in the case of stone, all of which appear in rubbings. Rubbings of

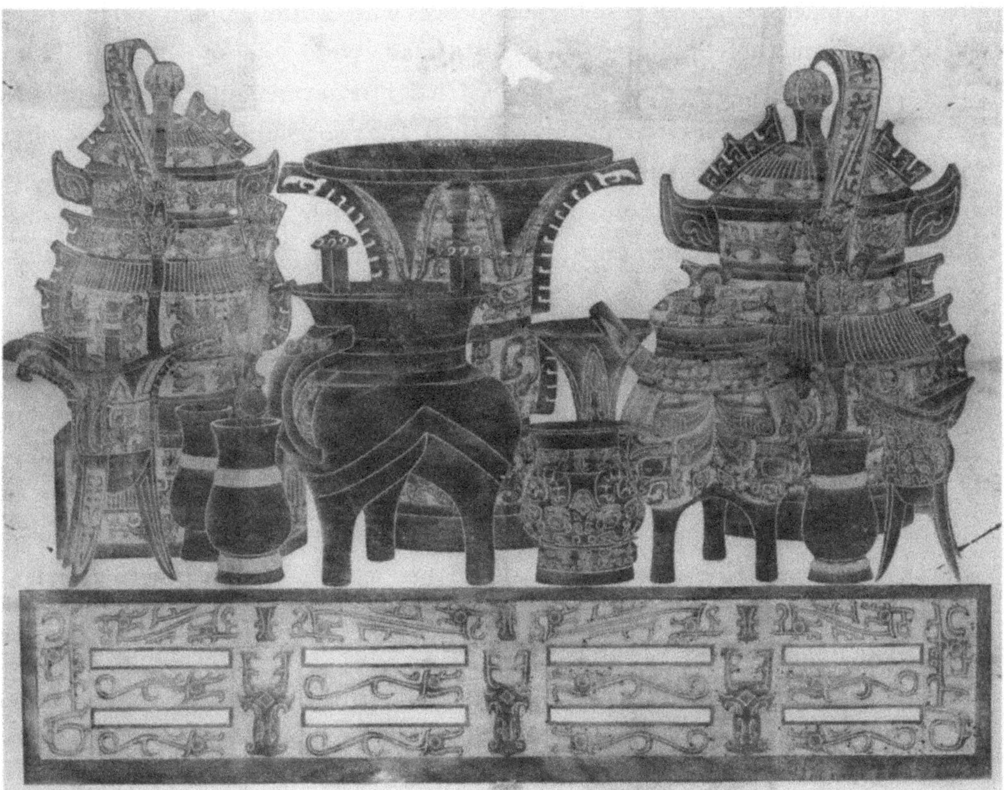

Fig. 7.14. Woodblock print of an altar set. Freer Gallery of Art Study Collection, Smithsonian Institution, FSC-R-67.

pottery and tiles show small uninked spots that reflect holes or other firing imperfections, with such irregularities hard to copy in wood.

Inking on woodblock prints generally is more even, whereas the inking of rubbings is often uneven. This is especially true with worn old stones or hastily made rubbings, and ink may appear in intaglio areas, particularly if the relief is shallow or the work is careless, or on creases in the rubbing paper if it was poorly laid. If the inking is not too heavy, one sometimes can discern the grain of the wood, as against that of the rubbing paper, and distinguish between a stone and wood host. It also is said that marked regularity of line in a rubbing, especially small, tight curves in copies of paintings, indicates a stone rather than a wood original, the rationale being that the knife is led astray by the wood grain and that such faults are reflected in the rubbing. Another view, however, holds that some woods, such as pear, are soft, lack strong grain, and do not show such faults. Woodblock prints generally are more complete, more regular of line, and more evenly and heavily inked, without smudging in the white areas, than are rubbings. As noted earlier, many black-gold rubbings and calligraphic models are from wood blocks. One must use these evidences with caution, and in combination, in differentiating rubbings from woodblock prints.

Simulated composite woodblock prints of archaic bronze ceremonial vessels similarly can be distinguished from true rubbings (*zhenta*). The two techniques, woodblock and rubbing, can be used separately or in combination, with both a bronze vessel and its inscription sometimes being true composite rubbings—devil's work—and sometimes both being easier woodblock prints. Other times, the vessel is a woodblock print, easier to make than a composite rubbing, and its inscription is a simple rubbing, separately pasted on. Some situations especially invite the woodblock technique, such as a square *ding* cauldron, tipped forward and seen from a side angle. Such a perspective is difficult to achieve with composite rubbing and often is done by wood block. There has been continuing interplay between stone and wood, and between rubbings and woodblock prints over the centuries.

The emphasis above has been on evaluating rubbings whose legitimacy is not a concern, but which require study to determine their age, quality, and other attributes. Implicit is the fact that a rubbing, or its host, may not be genuine, for rubbings also are susceptible to forgery. Aside from passing off a rubbing of a genuine, but later, stone copy, there are other common types of deception. A seller may pass off a rubbing of a wood block done in the positive to simulate a stone cut. Hustlers make molds from original stone inscriptions, produce casts, including ones in cement, and rub them.[56] They also may touch up worn or illegible inscriptions with cement. The resulting rubbing may be clearer and thus seem earlier. Outline copies (*shuanggouben*) and collotype copies of genuine old rubbings are other deceptions, especially for calligraphic rubbings. Other contemporary reproduction techniques also lend themselves to trickery.

Other than passing off a rubbing of a recut or other duplicate as being from an original object, or selling an incomplete rubbing, another form of fraud is misrepresenting the age of a rubbing, doctoring it to give it a semblance of age that it does not rightfully possess. Staining the paper is a common deception, and one must look at the back of the rubbing paper, for natural yellowing of the paper through long exposure to light and air is more pronounced on the obverse, while artificially induced discoloration commonly affects both sides. The effect also is achieved by artificially heightening the impression of the age of the materials and of the mounting of the fraudulent rubbing, which enterprising copiers embellish and sell as old or quality rubbings. Spurious colophons, seals, and supporting documentation play an evil but effective role, as do old facings and simulated spalls and vermiculations (fig. 7.15).[57] As also occurs with volumes of prints and maps, greedy merchants break up sets of rubbings and sell the components singly.

Such deceptions count upon the ignorance and the cupidity of the buyer. In purchasing rubbings, the surest guarantee of getting what one is paying for is to possess a close

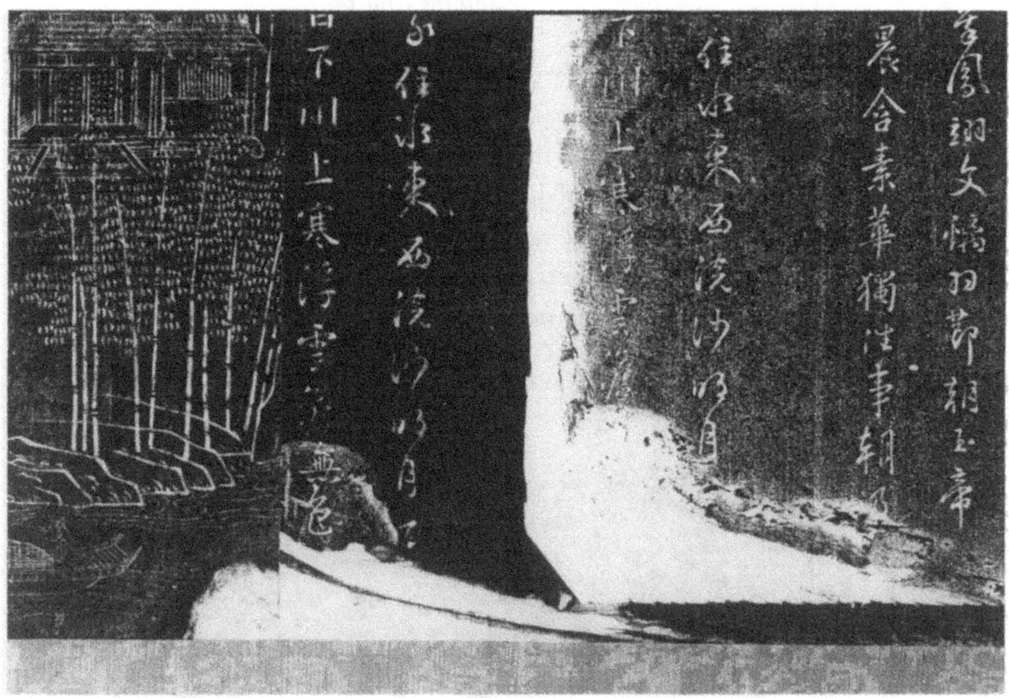

Fig. 7.15. Right: rubbing of part of a sheet rubbing (245472b) of the *Wang Chuan True Footsteps* (*Wang Chuan zhenji*), showing spall. Left: scroll-mounted copy (116203) with "fingerprint" simulation of the spall and added missing characters. The Field Museum of Natural History.

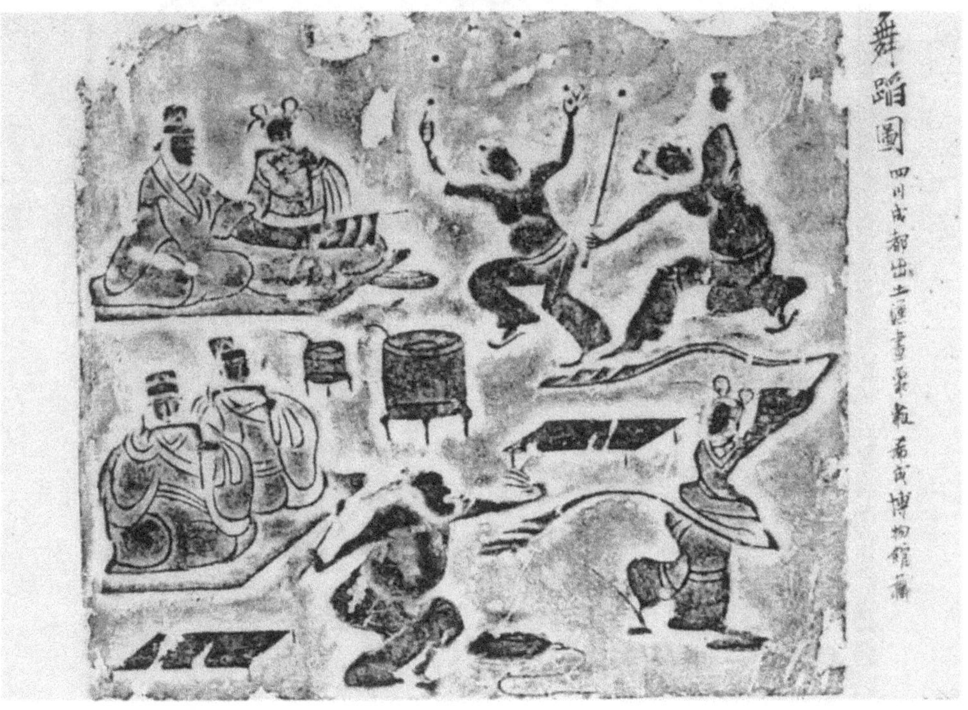

Fig. 7.16. Performing arts, costume, floor seating. Tomb tile, Sichuan, Later Han. The Field Museum of Natural History, 233469.

knowledge of the history and characteristics of the original object and successive rubbings of it, and to make minute comparisons with other rubbings of known antecedents. The connoisseurship involved in the study and appreciation of fine rubbings can be nice and demanding. Rare old and quality rubbings can command princely sums, and mistakes in judgment about their authenticity, age, and quality, resulting in hasty, ill-informed, and uncritical purchases, can devour collectors and their money. Thus collectors have the term for rubbings, *hei laohu*, "black tigers."[58]

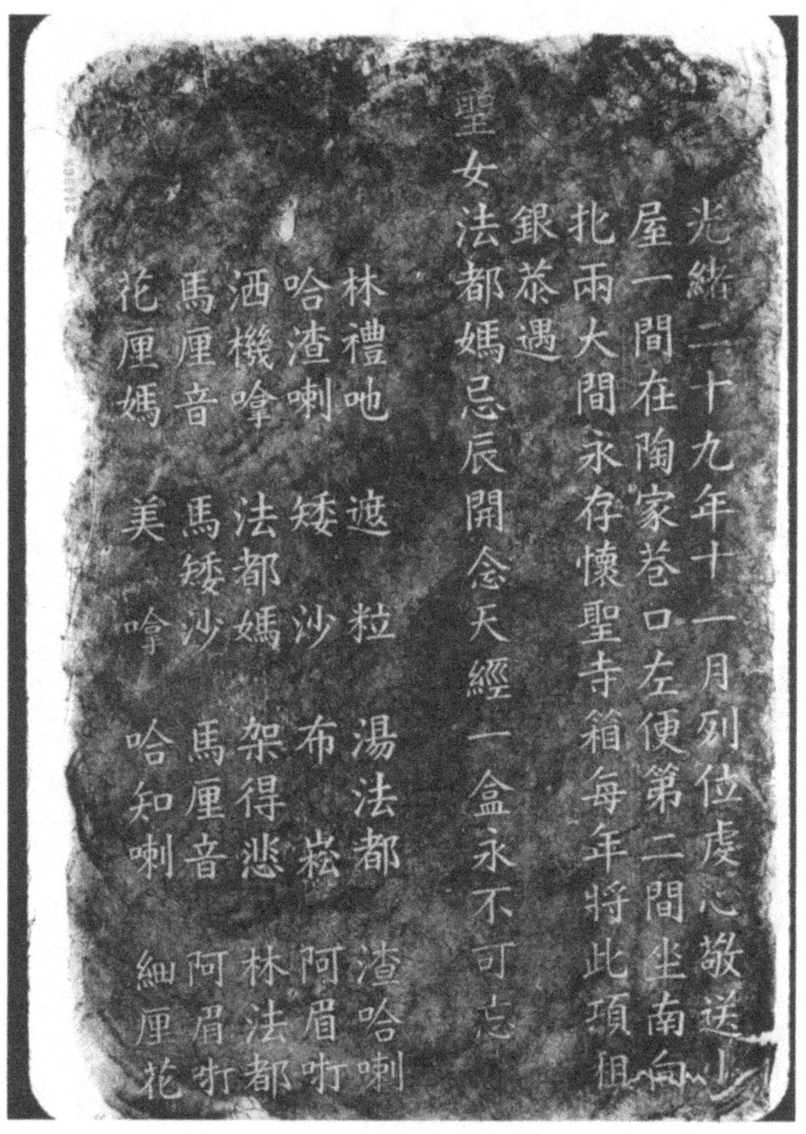

FIG. 7.17. Muslim ladies' purchase of a small house in Canton, honoring Fatima, Mohammed's daughter. Guangzhou, 1903. The Field Museum of Natural History, 244968.

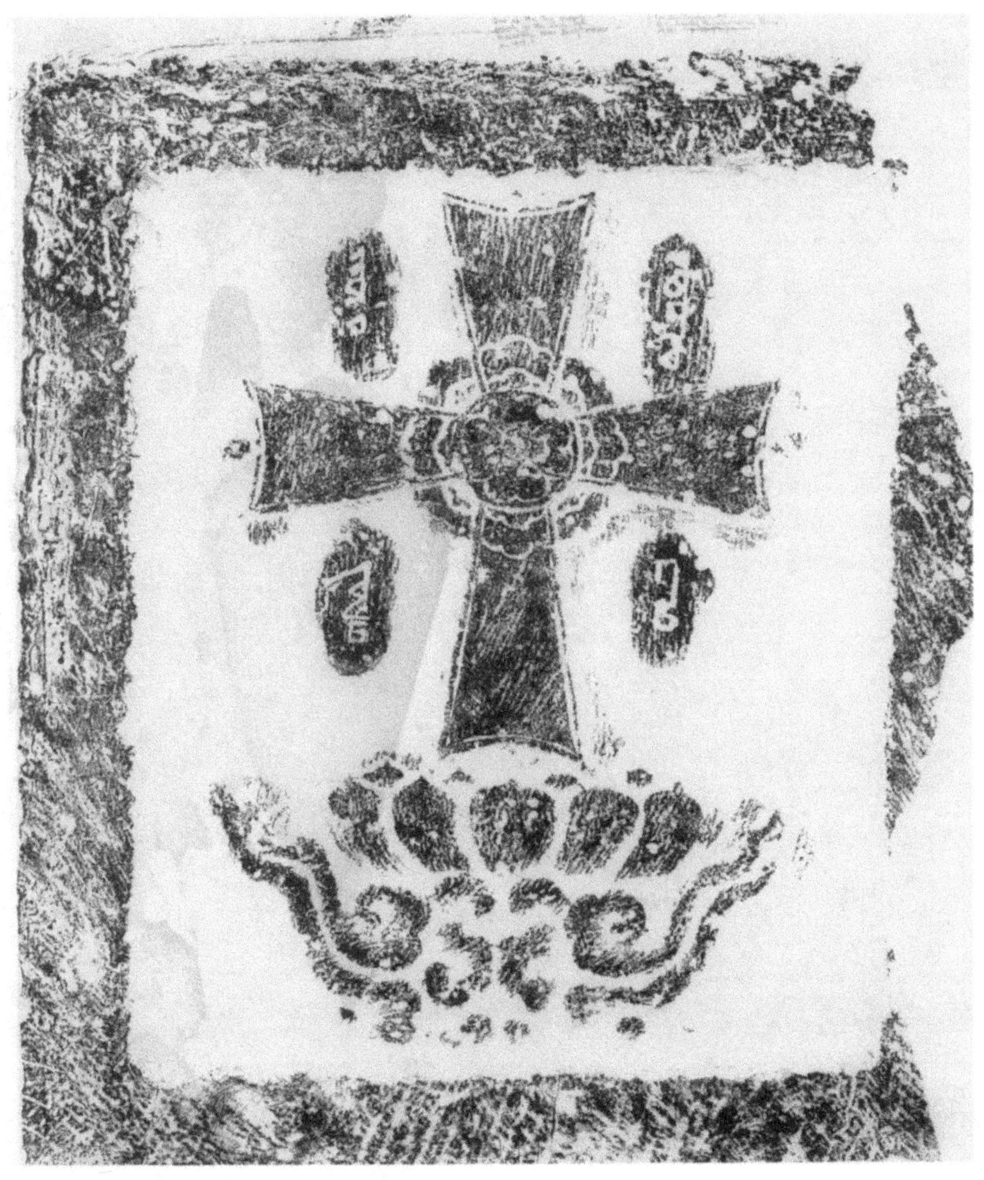

FIG. 7.18. Cross atop a lotus on an architectural piece, Hebei, Fang Shan, Yuan dynasty. Freer Gallery of Art, Smithsonian Institution, gift of Peking University. F1976.28.1.

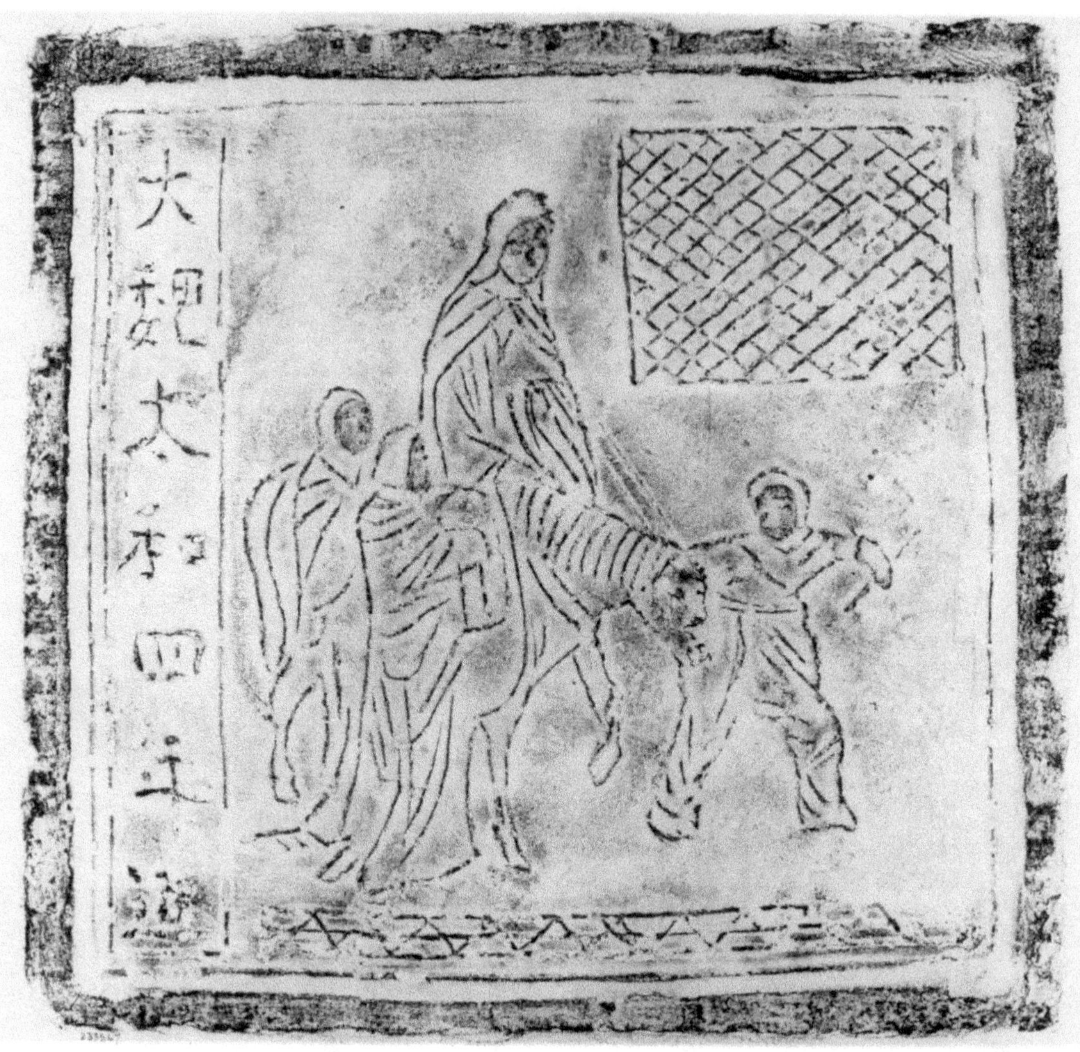

Fig. 7.19. Tile, scene reminiscent of the "flight from Egypt." Northern Wei, 480. The Field Museum of Natural History, 233567.

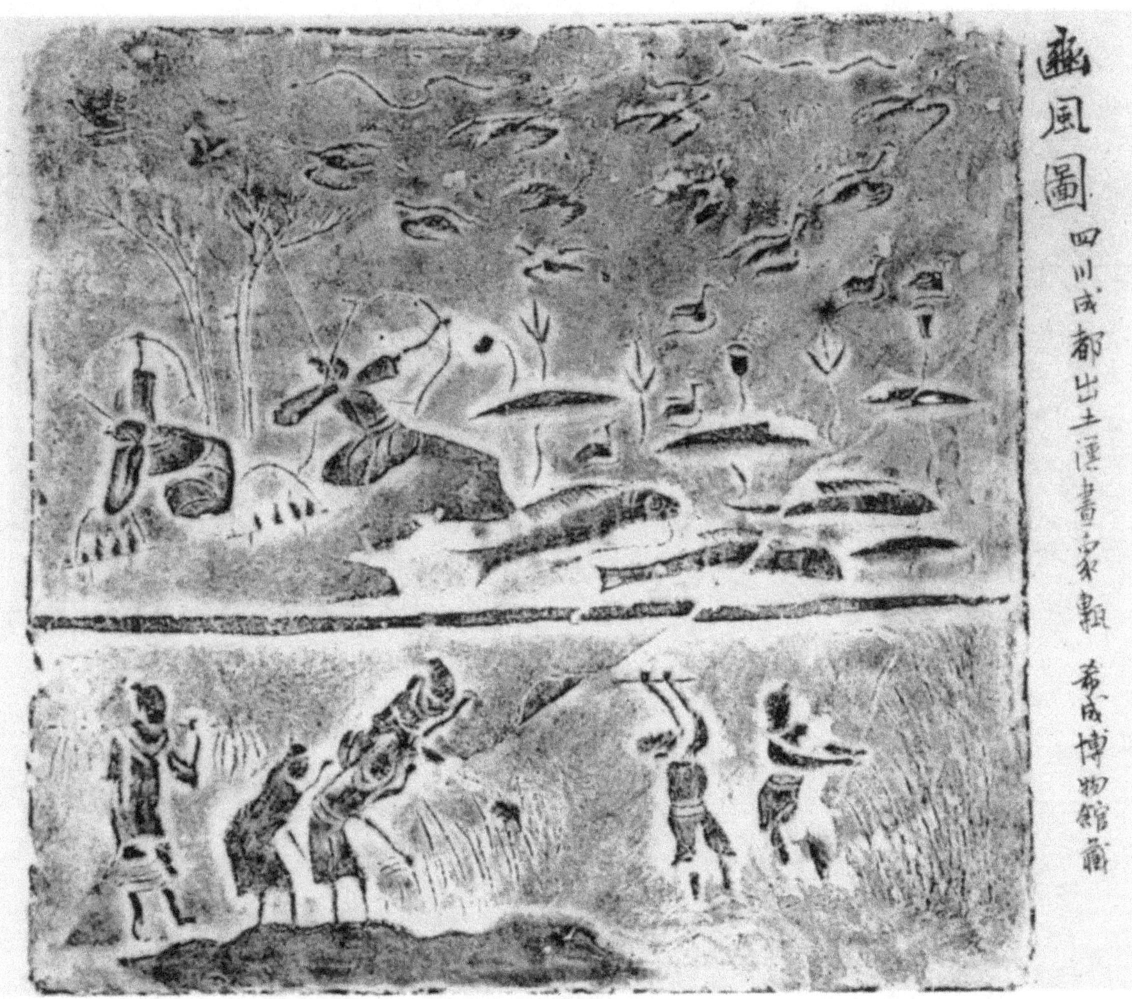

FIG. 7.20. Harvest; hunting with composite bow; carp with barbels, early pictorial evidence of Pangaea. Tomb brick, Sichuan, Later Han. The Field Museum of Natural History, 233477.

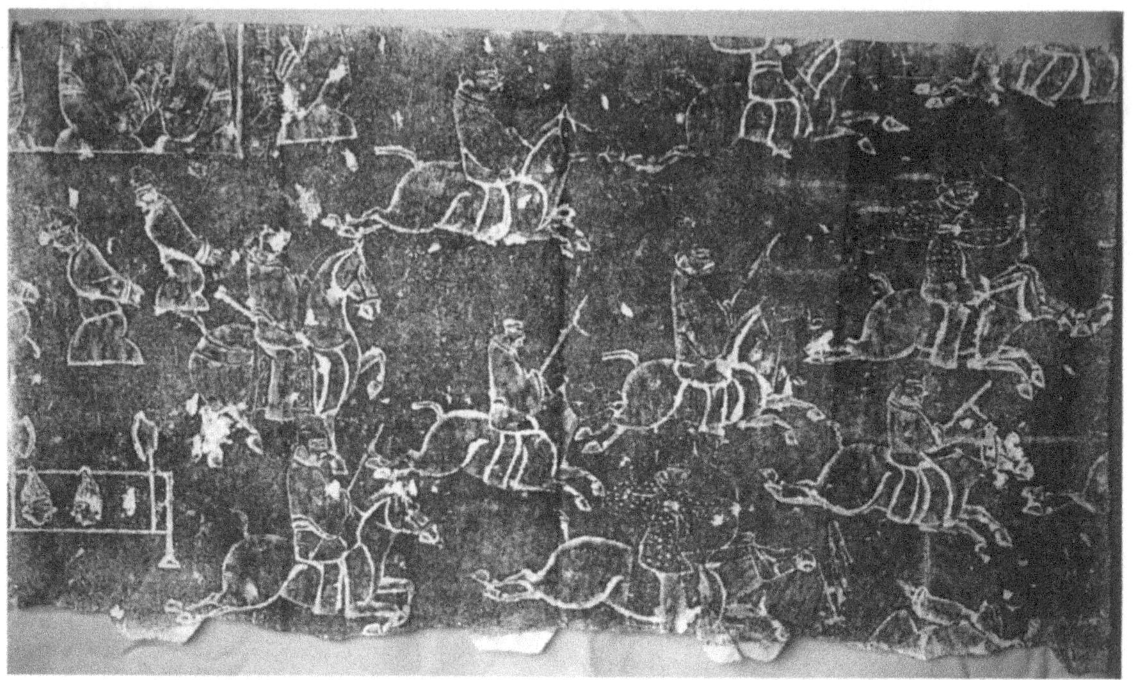

Fig. 7.21. Warfare: *ge* dagger ax, composite bow, beheading of captives. Shandong, Xiaotang Shan, shrine of Guo Ju, Later Han dynasty. Author's collection. Photograph by the author.

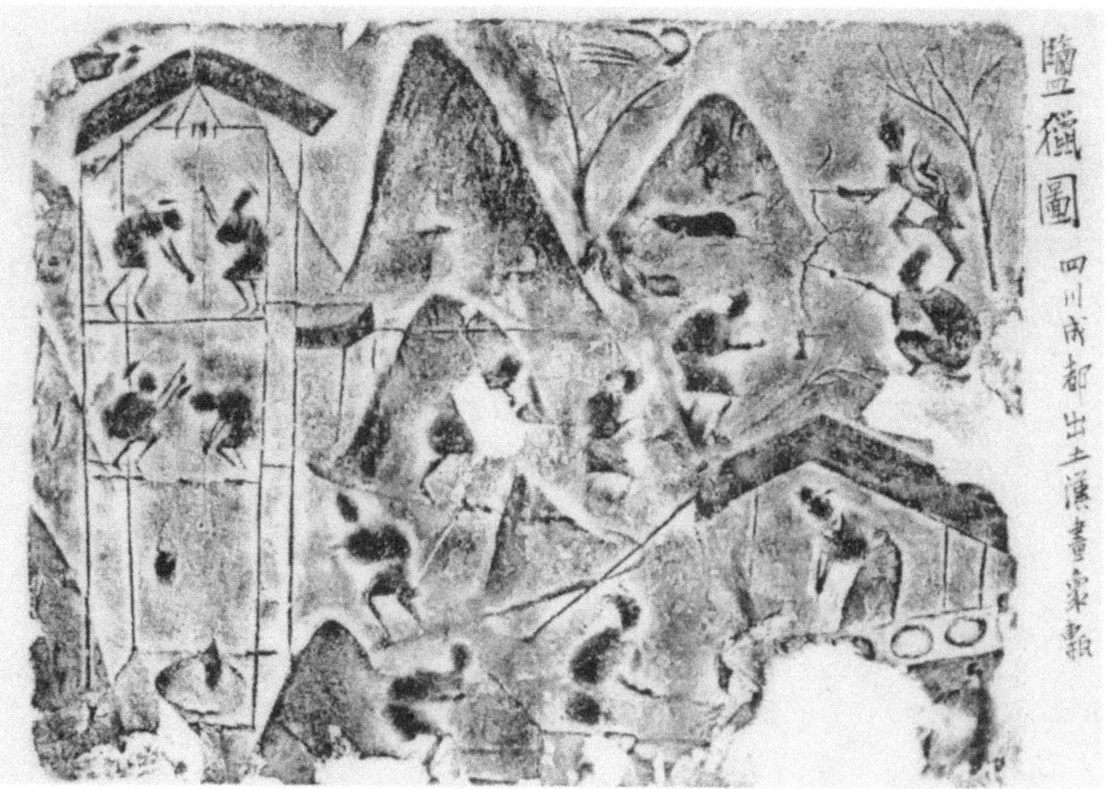

Fig. 7.22. Salt-well technology, with pulleys and drying ovens. Tomb tile, Sichuan, Later Han. The Field Museum of Natural History, 233471.

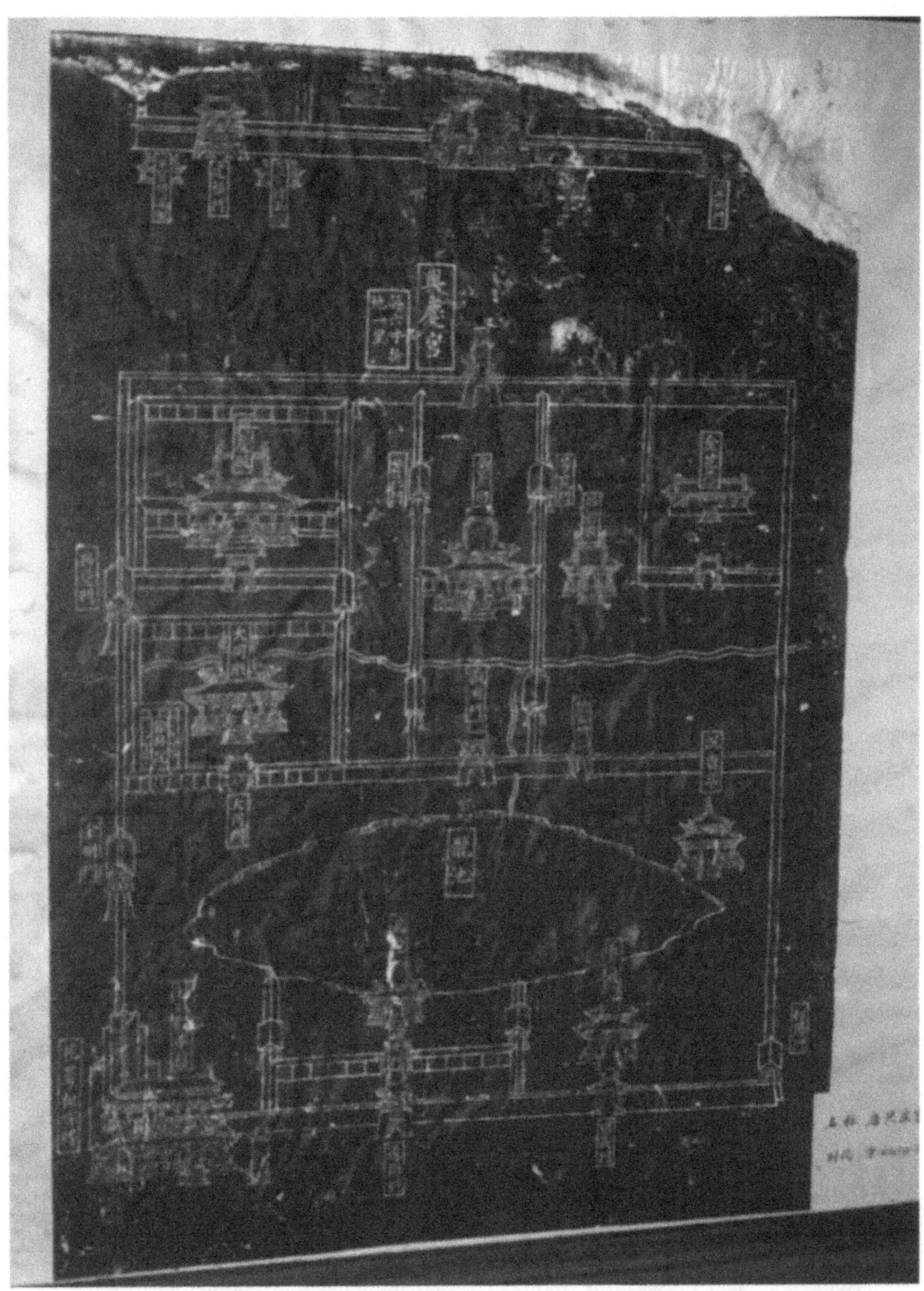

Fig. 7.23. Map of Xingqing Gong, Tang Buddhist temple, no longer extant. Xi'an. Author's collection. Photograph by the author.

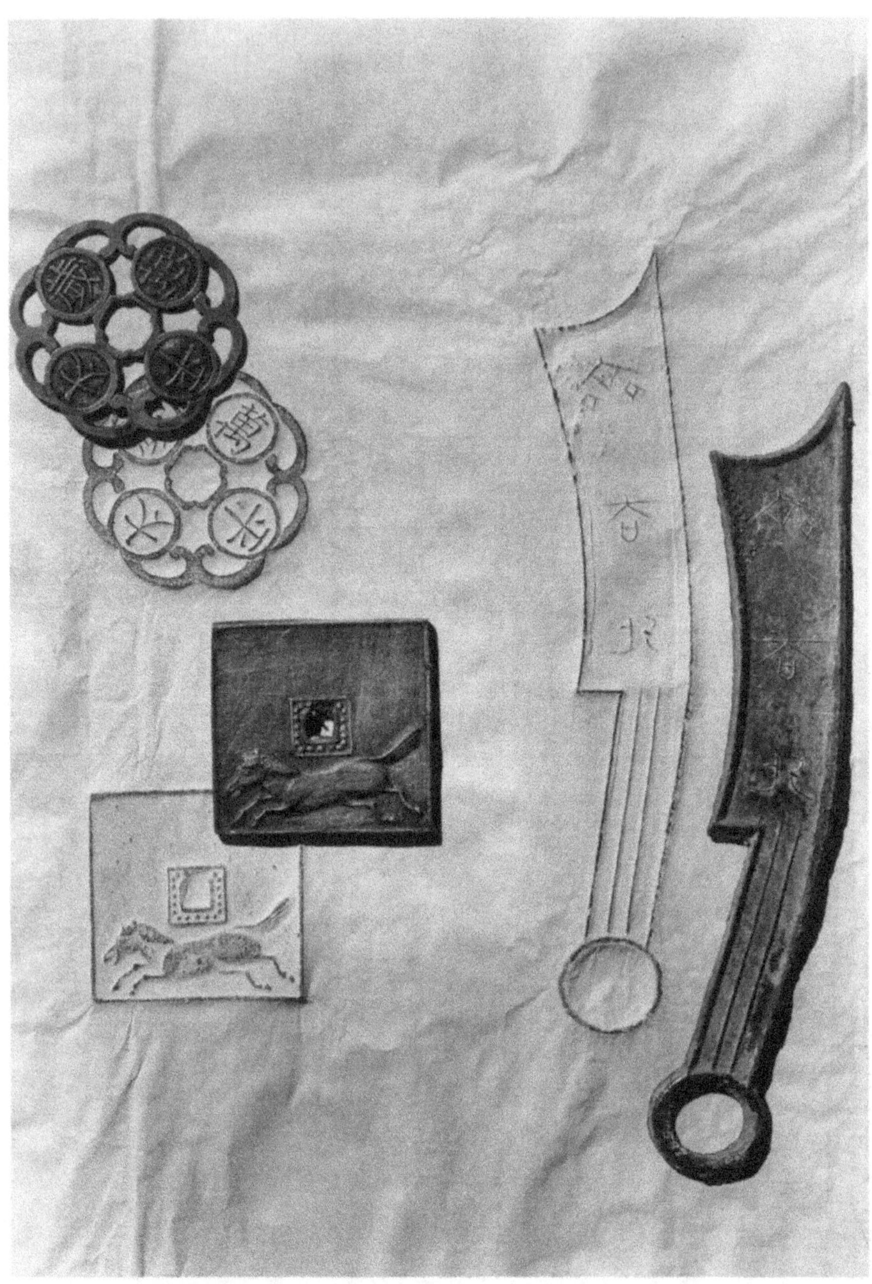

Fig. 7.24. Knife coin (124587), State of Qi, Zhou dynasty; modern coin charms (181551, 181590). The Field Museum of Natural History. Rubbings and photographs by the author.

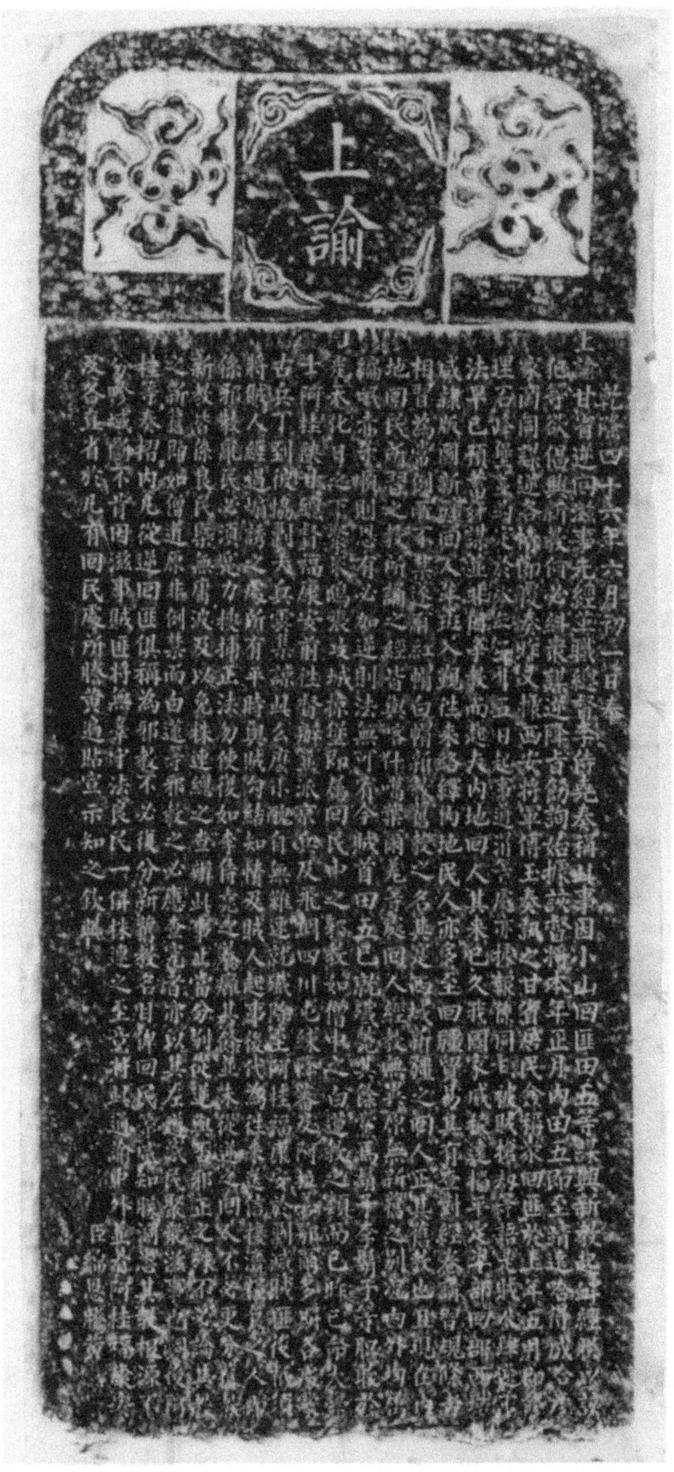

FIG. 7.25. Suppression of rebellious Muslims and protection of loyal Muslims in Gansu (1781). The Field Museum of Natural History, 244343.

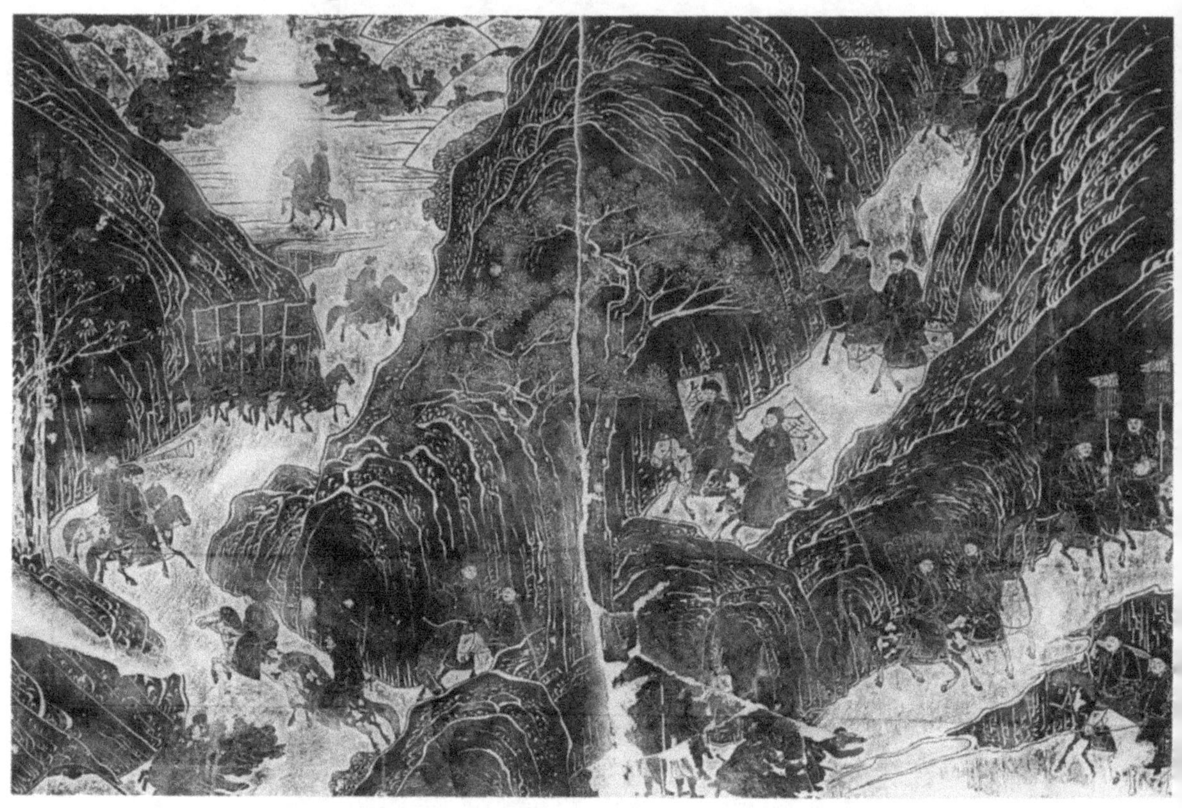

FIG. 7.26. Imperial expedition against the Red Miao, shown with black faces (1740). Xi'an, Cien Temple. The Field Museum of Natural History, 245119.1.

Appendix 1

Historical Periods

Paleolithic	
Zhoukoudian (Upper Cave)	c. 15,000 B.C.E.
Neolithic	c. 8000–16th century B.C.E.
Shang (Shang–Yin)	c. 16th–11th centuries B.C.E.
Zhou	
Western Zhou	c. 11th century–771 B.C.E.
Eastern Zhou	770–221 B.C.E.
Spring and Autumn	770–476 B.C.E.
Warring States	475–221 B.C.E.
Qin	221–207 B.C.E.
Han	
Former (Western) Han	206 B.C.E.– 8 C.E.
Later (Eastern) Han	25–220
Six Dynasties	
Three Kingdoms (Wei, Wu, Shu–Han)	220–265
Jin (Western, Eastern)	265–420
Northern and Southern Kingdoms	420–589
Northern Wei	386–534
Qi	479–502
Liang (Xiao Liang)	502–556
Sui	581–618
Tang	618–907
Five Dynasties	907–960
Liao	916–1125
Song (Zhao Song)	
Northern Song	960–1127
Southern Song	1127–1279
Jin (Tartar)	1115–1236
Yuan	1271–1368
Ming	1368–1644
Qing	1644–1911
Republic of China	1912–
People's Republic of China	1949–

Appendix 2

Terms for Rubbings, the Rubbing Technique, and Related Processes

This appendix includes two lists, one of sources and the other of terms. The list of sources gives authors' or informants' names as well as their dates (or other indications of the periods in which they were active) and titles of relevant works. The list of terms associates authors' surnames (and, when a surname is shared, given names as well) and works of other identifying information with terms that authors or informants have used, giving abbreviated titles when there are multiple titles by the same author, and sample page references. Full source information is given in the bibliography.

Some terms are homophones, different in form but pronounced and romanized the same; the meaning of these may vary. Examples include five forms of *chui*, (1) "mallet," "beat" or (2) "vertical"; six forms of *mo*, with varying meanings; three forms of *ta*, "rub" or "rubbing"; and two forms of *xiang*, with different meanings. Some texts use different forms of the same homophone in the same work. Finally, different dictionaries, Chinese and Western, old and new, give different romanizations, and sometimes different translations. I have distinguished the different homophones with superscript letters.

SOURCES

Bai Qianshen (modern), "The Artistic and Intellectual Dimensions of Chinese Calligraphy Rubbings"
Beijing Tushuguan cang Zhongguo lidai shike taben huibian (modern)
Cao Zhao (Ming), *Gegu yaolun*
Thomas Francis Carter (modern), *The Invention of Printing*, 1st and 2nd eds.
Edouard Chavannes (modern), "Les Inscriptions des Ts'in"
Chen Jieqi (1813–1884), *Chuangu bielu*
Chen Yuanlong (1652–1732), *Gezhi jingyuan*
Cheng Dachang (1123–1195), *Yanfan lu*
Cihai (modern; Chinese dictionary)
Daijiten (modern; Japanese dictionary)
Percival David (modern), *Chinese Connoisseurship*
Dong Juewei (modern), Zeyang tabei, parts 1 and 2
Dou Ji (Tang), *Shushu fu*

Ennin (Jikaku Daishi, 739–864), *Dai Nihon Bukkyō Zensho*; *Ennin's Diary: The Record of a Pilgrimage to China in Search of the Law*; *Nittō guhō junrei gyoki no kenkyu*
Fan Ye (398–445), *Hou Han shu*
Fang Yizhi (Ming–Qing), *Tongya*
Feng Yan (fl. 756), *Feng shi wenjian ji*
John C. Ferguson (modern), "Wang Ch'uan"
Robert E. Harrist Jr. (modern), "Copies, All the Way Down: Replication in Chinese Calligraphy"; "Record of the Eulogy on Mt. Tai"
Charles O. Hucker (modern), *A Dictionary of Official Titles in Imperial China*
Jiang Xuanyi (modern), "Mota shu," parts 1 and 2
Jun Yu (modern), "Tan taben"
Kangxi zidian (Qing; Chinese dictionary)
Li Shuhua (modern), "The Early Development of Seals and Rubbings"; "Yinzhang yu mota de qiyuan ji qi duiyu diaoban yinshua faming de yingxiang"
Liu Xu (Tang–Song), *Jiu Tang shu*
Lu Shihua (1714–1779), *Shuhua shuoling*
Luo Zhenyu (Qing–modern), "Mogaoku shishi milu"
Ma Ji, assistant to the director, Xi'an Beilin
Ma Xulun (modern), *Shuowen jiezi liu shu shuzheng*
Robert Henry Mathews, *Chinese-English Dictionary*
Yūjirō Nakata (modern), *Chūgoku no bijitsu*; *Chūgoku shoronshū*; *Chinese Calligraphy* (vol. 2 of *A History of the Art of China*)
Ouyang Xiu (Song), *Xin Tang shu*
Paul Pelliot (modern), *Les débuts de l'imprimerie en Chine*
Qu Wanli and Chang Bide (modern), *Guoshu banbenxue yaolüe*
Rong Geng (modern), *Shang Zhou*
Ruan Yuan (1764–1849), *Jigu zhai zhongding yiqi kuanshi*
Sang Shen (modern), "Quanxing ta zhi chuangcheng yu liubian"
Sang Shichang (Song), *Lanting kao*
Sima Qian (former Han), *Shiji*
Sima Zhen (Tang), *Shiji suoyin*
Su Yinghui (modern), "Tushuguan cang tapian de bianmu gongzuo"
Sun Xingyan (Qing) and Xing Zhu (Qing), *Huanyu fangbei lu*
Sun Yuxiu (modern), *Zhongguo diaoban yuanliu kao*
Tang Xuan Zong, ed., *Tang liudian*
Tsuen-hsuin Tsien (modern), *Written on Bamboo and Silk*; *Zhongguo gudai shu shi*
Tu Long (Ming), *Kaopan yushi*
R. H. van Gulik (modern), *Chinese Pictorial Art As Viewed by the Connoisseur*
Wang Chang (1725–1806), *Jinshi cuibian*
Wang Chi-chen (modern), *Reproductions of Chinese Rubbings Taken from Inscriptions Cut in Stone, Wood, and Also from Bronzes, Monuments and Other Bas-reliefs*
Wang Guowei (modern), *Mao gong ding kaoshi xu*; "Shuowen suowei guwen shuo"
Wang Houzhi (Song), *Wang Fu Zhai zhongding kuanshi*
Wang Zhuangwei (modern), *Shufa zongtan*
Wei Zheng (580–643), *Sui shu*
Wen Zhenheng (Ming), *Zhangwu zhi*
Weng Fanggang (Qing), *Baosu shi jinshi shuhua biannian lu*; *Liang Han jinshi zhi*

Weng Kaiyun (modern), "Beitie mantan"
Xu Kang (Qing), *Qianchenmeng yinglu*
Xu Shen (Later Han), *Shuowen jiezi*
Ye Changchi (1849–1917), *Yu shi*
Zhai Qinian (Song), *Zhou shi*
Zhang Guangyuan (modern), "Shigu wen de renshi"
Zhang Yanyuan (ninth century), *Lidai ming hua ji*
Zhang Zuyi (late Qing), colophon, book-mounted rubbing of the *Kong Zhou bei*
Zheng Shanshan et al. (modern), "Zhimo liuxiang—chuanta jifa, quanxing ta; chuanji shou de rongyao"
Zhu Feng (Qing), *Yongzhou jinshi ji*

TERMS

Term	Definition
bei 碑	Stele, stele inscription, stele rubbing. Common term through the dynasties. Xu Shen, 9 *xia*:4b. For amplification, see Ma Xulun, 18:55.
beiban 碑版	Stone edition or rubbing of it. Luo, 33.
beike 碑刻	Stone inscription. Fang, 31:11b.
beitie (ceye) 碑帖 (冊葉)	Calligraphic rubbing, model. Fang, 31:11b.
buduanben 不短本	Rubbings of stones not deficient in any way.
camo 擦墨	Dab with a swiping motion. Dong, part 1, 41.
cata[a] 擦拓	Swiping motion in inking. Ma Ji (informant), Xi'an Beilin.
chanchi ta[b] 蟬翅搨	Cicada-wing rubbing. Wen, 5:182. Cited by van Gulik, 90.
chanchi ta[c] 蟬翅榻	Cicada-wing rubbing. Fang, 31:15b.
chanyiben 蟬翼本	Cicada-wing edition. Fang, 31:13a.
chanyi ta[a] 蟬翼拓	Cicada-wing rubbing. Jiang, part 1, 75; Dong, part 1, 41.
chanyi ta[b] 蟬翼搨	Cicada-wing rubbing. Van Gulik, 90.
chanyi ta[c] 蟬翼榻	Cicada-wing rubbing. Fang, 31:15b.
chaoxie 抄寫	Copy by hand. Tsien, *Bamboo and Silk*, and Tsien, *Zhongguo gudai*, 80.
chongke (ben) 重刻 (本)	Recut (edition). Sun and Xing, 2a.
chongmo[a]ben 重墨本	"Layered ink (edition)," successive heavy, matte applications of oil-smoke ink, similar to *wujin ta*, "black-gold rubbing." Dong, part 1, 41.
chongmo[c] (ke) ben 重摹(刻)本	Copy, recut, reprint. Common.
chuanke 傳刻	Recut. Li, "Yinzhang," 116.
chuanta[a] (zhi ben) 傳拓 (之本)	Transmitted-rubbing (edition). Wei, 32:36b; Luo, 33; Qu and Chang, 17 passim (citing Wei); Su, 25 passim (citing Wei).
chuanta[b] (zhi ben) 傳搨 (之本)	Transmitted-rubbing (edition). Dou, *shang*:3a; Li, "Yinzhang," 115; Qu and Chang, 16 passim.
chui[a] 捶 (搥,鎚)	Hammer, beat.
chui[b] 槌 (椎)	Hammer, beat.
chui[c]bei 鍾碑	Using mallet and pad to make a rubbing. Fang, 31:11b; Wang Yuqing (informant), National Historical Museum, Taibei.
chui[d] 垂	Vertical.

chui[e] 錘	Hammer.
chui[a]ta[a] 捶拓	Mallet-rub. Ma Ji, Xi'an Beilin.
chui[b]ta[a] 椎拓	Mallet-rub. Chen Jieqi, 8a.
chui[b]ta[b] 椎搨	Mallet-rub. Zhu, *xu*:1a; Rong, 1:180; Qu and Chang, 16.
chui[b]ta[a] (jinshi) 椎拓 (金石)	Mallet-rub (metal and stone). Xu Kang, 234; Chen Jieqi, 8a; Rong, 1:180 (citing Xu Kang); Jiang, part 1, 72 passim; Dong, part 1, 41.
chui[b]ta[a] (zhi mo[a]ben) 椎拓 (之墨本)	Mallet-rubbed (ink edition). Xu Kang, 234; Rong, 1:180 (citing Xu Kang); Jiang, part 2, 50; Dong, part 1, 41.
chui[b]ta[b] (zhi) (mo[a]ben) 椎搨 (之) (墨本)	Mallet-rubbed (ink edition). Zhu, *xu*:1a; Qu and Chang, 16 passim (citingWei); Su, 25 (citing Wei).
chui[d]ta[a] 垂拓	Vertical inking motion. Ma Ji, Xi'an Beilin.
chui[e] . . . zhenji 鍾 . . . 真蹟	Beat . . . true footsteps (calligraphy). Fang, 31:11b.
chuta[a] (ben) 初拓 (本)	First rubbing of a stone.
ci 雌	Female dabber; common usage.
da 打	Strike, lay on, rub; eighth–tenth centuries.
da bei (wen) 打碑 (文)	Strike, rub such-and-such a stele (inscription). Sima Zhen, 8:2b; Xu Kang, 149.
da lamo 打蠟墨	Lay on ink rub. Cheng, 7:6a.
daben 打本	Strike-edition, rubbing. Sima Zhen, 8:1b; Dou, *juan shang*:4a; Zhu, 9:3b; Su, 25, referring to Tang sources (Sima Zhen; *Na Luoyan jian zun sheng jingchuang* stele); Zhu, 9:3b, 9:4a; Qu and Chang, 17 (citing Tang sources, including Sima Zhen and *Na Luoyan jian zun sheng bei*); Li, "Yinzhang," 116 (equated with *ta[b]ben*, citing Wei), and Li, "Seals and Rubbings," 78 (equated with *ta[b]ben*); Su, 25 (citing Sima Zhen); van Gulik, 86.
dade . . . beiwen 打得 . . . 碑文	Strike-obtain stele-inscription. Sima Zhen, 3:2b.
data 打拓	Strike-rub. Li, "Seals and Rubbings," 80 (citing Chen Yuanlong).
datoku (Japanese) 打得	Strike-obtain (a rubbing). Ennin, "Nittō guhō junrei gyōki," *kan* 3:115, and Ennin, *Ennin's Diary*, 255.
dazao (beiwen) 打造 (碑文)	Strike-make (stele inscription). Sima Zhen, 8:1b; Su, 25 (citing tenth-century Song inscription).
de zhiben 得紙本	Obtain a paper edition. Qu and Chang, 17 (citing Sima Zhen, 8:1b).
fanben 翻本	Copies, recuts. Li, "Yinzhang," 115, and Li, "Seals and Rubbings," 77 ("reduplications on stone").
fang (ben) 仿 (本)	Imitating, freely interpreting the style of another, usually earlier, artist. Ferguson, 58.
fanggu 仿古	Imitate an earlier work. Ferguson, 59. Also, visiting ancient sites.
fanke (ben) 翻刻 (本)	Recut edition, copy. Ye, 299; Li, "Seals and Rubbings," 77 ("reduplication on stone").
fashu 法書	Calligraphic model, rubbing or woodblock print. Common. Also, Tang, 8:17b.

fatie 法帖	Calligraphic model, rubbing or woodblock print. Chen Yuanlong, 39:6a; Fang, 31:11b; Jiang, part 2, 51; van Gulik, 40; Nakata, *Chinese Calligraphy*, 117, "copybook"; Bai, 84–85, "model book."
fenlin 粉臨	Transfer method of copying. Van Gulik, 397.
fenta 粉拓	Rubbing with powdered ink.
gou 勾	Trace character outlines. Ferguson, 58.
guben 孤本	Unique rubbing. Common.
guta[a] (guben) 古拓 (古本)	Old rubbing. Li, "Yinzhang," 116.
gutie 古帖	Old calligraphic model, rubbing. Used as heading by Chen Yuanlong, *juan* 39; referred to by Carter, 1st ed., 199; Jiang, part 2, 51.
hei laohu 黑老虎	"Black tigers," collectors' name for rubbings.
hei zi 黑字	Black, blacken characters. Rong, 1:181, describing a method Percival Yetts used to represent bronze inscriptions.
ishizuri (Japanese) 石摺	Stone rubbing. *Daijiten*; van Gulik, 87.
jijing jiuta[a] (ben) 極精舊拓 (本)	High quality old rubbing (edition).
jingta[a] (ben) 精拓 (本)	Quality rubbing (edition). Chen Jieqi, 8a. *See ta*[a].
jingta[b] (ben) 精搨 (本)	Quality rubbing (edition).
jiu ta[a] 舊拓	Old rubbed, rubbing.
jiu ta[a]ben 舊拓本	Old rubbing edition.
jiu ta[b]ben 舊搨本	Old rubbing ediion.
jiuben 舊本	Old edition.
ke ban 刻版	Cut in wood. Pelliot, 115.
keben 刻本	Engraved edition, often used for a stone-cut text. Van Gulik, 87.
kema ta[b] 隔麻搨	Rubbing, effect of loosely woven cloth, described by Qu Wanli and Jiang Gusun (informants).
ketie 刻帖	Nakata, *Chinese Calligraphy*, 118, "printed copybook."
lamo[a] (ta) 蠟墨 (拓)	Moisten with ink (rub).
lamo[a] (wei zi) 蠟墨 (為字)	Moisten with ink (to make characters). Cheng, 7:6a ("cut stones to make steles; moisten with ink to make characters"); Su, 25 (citing Cheng).
lin (ben) 臨 (本)	"Reproduction copy," free-hand copy of a nearby original, with some freedom. It may include tracing, but that is not the primary means of copying. Ferguson, 58; van Gulik, 397, "free copy"; Nakata, *Chinese Calligraphy*, 117, "copybook," and Nakata, *Chūgoku shoronshū*, 255; Harrist, "Copies," 181, "to look down over."
linmo[c] 臨摹	(1) Outline (*shuanggou*) with ink fill. Nakata, *Chinese Calligraphy*, 117, "copybook," 118, loosely includes among "various

	copying techniques." (2) Copy; "copy by rubbing." Fang, 31:15a; Ferguson, 59, copy; Dong, part 1, 41; Zhang Guangyuan, 7. An album in the author's collection translates as "rub." See *Cihai*, *linmo*, for difference between *lin*, copying from a nearby original, and *mo*, "rubbing" (*ta*[b]) a stone or wood *tie*.
linmo[c] gutie 臨摹古帖	Copy/trace an old calligraphic model. Lu, 28:11a; Nakata, *Chūgoku shoronshū*, 122, and Nakata, *Chinese Calligraphy*, 118; *Cihai*.
linta[c] 臨搨	Trace a rubbing. Fang, 31:13a (for cutting in pear wood).
lintie 臨帖	Copy free hand, imitate, with the calligraphic rubbing (*zitie*) alongside (*Cihai*).
liti ta 立體拓	Three-dimensional rubbing. Jiang Xuanyi, part 2, 148; Sang Shen, 52.
meita[a] 煤拓	Charcoal, soft-coal rubbing. Dong, part 1, 42.
miaomo[c] 描摹	Copy. Ferguson, 59.
mo[a] 墨	Ink, blacken, rub. Zhai, *shang*:10.
mo[b] 摩	Feel, rub. Trace, copy, facsimile. Fang, 31:11b, 14a–b (equates with *mo*[a]*ta*[c]); Li, "Seals and Rubbings," 75–76, copy "by following the text." Carter, 1st ed., 197, and Carter, 2nd ed., 23, "make exact copies" (Han equivalent of *ta*[b] ?); van Gulik, 397, trace; Wang Zhuangwei, 119, copy by tracing, cutting in stone. Harrist, "Copies," 181, trace (no Chinese). *See mo*[b]*xie.*
mo[c] 摹	Model, pattern, replica. Fang, 31:11b, equals *mo*[a]*ta*[c]; Li, "Yinzhang," 115, and Li, "Seals and Rubbings," 77; van Gulik, 397, trace; Wang Zhuangwei, 120, trace; Nakata, *Chūgoku shoronshū*, 255, equates with *ta*[b]. *See mo*[b]*xie.*
mo[d] 模	Feel, rub. Zhu, 1:1b; Li, "Seals and Rubbings," 77, replica.
mo[e] 摸	Trace. Same as *mo*[d]. Mathews.
mo[f] 磨	Rub (a stele). Fang, 31:12b. *See mo*[f]*bei.*
mo[a] laohu 墨老虎	"Ink tigers," name given by some collectors to rubbings; by others, to calligraphy. See chapter 7, n. 57, this volume; Wang Chi-chen, 4.
mo[a] qi (kuan) 墨器 (款)	To ink, rub bronze (inscriptions). Zhai, *shang*:10; Rong, 1:176, and Su, 25 (both citing Zhai).
mo[a]ban 墨版	Ink-block, woodblock (print). Li, "Yinzhang," 117, and Li, "Seals and Rubbings," 82.
mo[a]bao 墨包	Ink dabber. Chen Jieqi, 2b.
mo[d]bei 模碑	Copy, rub a stele (inscription). Li, "Yinzhang," 115 (citing Feng), and Li, "Seals and Rubbings," 77; Mathews, 4590.
mo[f]bei (shi gong zhi) 磨碑 (石供之)	Rub a stele (to copy it). Fang, 31:12b.
mo[a]ben 墨本	Ink edition, rubbing. Wei, *juan* 32; Fang, 31:16a; Rong, 1:176; Qu and Chang, 16 (citing Wei); Su, 25; van Gulik, 86–87.
mo[c]ben 摹本	Copy, trace an original. Zhu, 1:1a; Ye, 1:1; Li, "Yinzhang," 115, and Li, "Seals and Rubbings," 77; Ferguson, 58, copying by tracing the original, with "no originality or interpretation"; van Gulik, 397, "tracing"; Wang Guowei, *Mao Gong ding Kaoshi xu*, 275; *Beijing Tushuguan*, 1:8, "Yi Shan keshi."

mo^{d}ben 模本 — Replica, hand copy, rubbing. Fang, 31:14a; Chavannes ("rubbing"); Pelliot ("replica"); Li, "Seals and Rubbings," 77, "replica," citing Xu Xuan, d. 991, getting a *moben*, "hand copy," of the Yi Shan text. Nakata, *Chinese Calligraphy*, 118, gives as "copybook," as also he does for *linben* and *fatie*.

mo^{e}ben 摸本 — Copy by feeling, stroking-rubbing. Zhu, 1:1b. Also, trace, same as *mo*^{c} (*Cihai*; Mathews).

mo^{f} (bei) 磨 (碑) — Fang, 31:12b.

mo^{a}fen (ta) 墨粉 (拓) — Rubbing with powdered ink.

mo^{c}gu 摹古 — Copy an earlier work. Ferguson, 59.

mo^{a}ji 墨蹟 — "Ink traces," "ink footsteps," especially original calligraphy. Chen Yuanlong, 39:6b; Li, "Yinzhang," 116, and Li "Seals and Rubbings," 80.

mo^{c}ke (ben) 摹刻 (本) — Copy-cut (edition). Fang, 31:13b; Chen Jieqi, 3b; Wang Zhuangwei, 117 passim; Pelliot, 111; *Beijing Tushuguan*, 1:8, "Yi Shan keshi"; Zhang Guangyuan, 7.

mo^{d}(ke) (ben) 模 (刻) (木) — Copy-(cut) (edition). Fang, 31:13a, 14a.

mo^{c}ke (yu shi, yu ban) 摹刻 (于石,于版) — Copy-cut (on stone, wood). Fang, 31:13b; Pelliot, 111 ("cut in facsimile" in wood, stone).

mo^{c}le 摹勒 — Copy-engrave. Chen Yuanlong, 39:6b; Wang Zhuangwei, 120.

mo^{a}shu 墨書 — "Samples written in ink." Nakata, *Chinese Calligraphy*, 118.

mo^{a}ta^{a} 墨拓 — Ink rubbing, black rubbing. Carter, 1st ed., 13, and Carter, 2nd ed., 20; Li, "Yinzhang," 114 passim; Jiang, part 1, 69 passim; Su, 25 (citing Zhai, rubbing bronze vessels); Dong, part 1, 41.

mo^{a}ta^{b} 墨搨 — Ink-rub. Nakata, *Chinese Calligraphy*, 118, "rubbings."

mo^{a}ta^{c} 墨榻 — Ink-rub. Fang, 31:11b (equates with *mo*^{c}).

mo^{c}ta^{a} 摹拓 — Copy-rub. Feng, 8:2b; Jiang, part 2, 51; Li, "Yinzhang," 115, and Li, "Seals and Rubbings," 76, "rubbings."

mo^{c}ta^{c} 摹榻 — Copy-rub. Fang, 31:11b passim.

mo^{b}ta^{b} 摩搨 — Inked rubbing. Li, "Yinzhang," 117, and Li, "Seals and Rubbings," 73, equate with *ta*^{a}*ben*, rubbing.

mo^{a}ta^{b} 墨搨 — Ink-rub. Ye, 9:298; Sun, 1; Carter, 1st ed., 13, and Carter, 2nd ed., 20; Jiang, part 1, 75; Li, "Yinzhang," 113 (equals *mo*^{c}*ta*^{b}?), and Li, "Seals and Rubbings," 73, "inked rubbings," equates with *ta*^{a}*ben*, *mo*^{b}*ta*^{b} 75 (Li cites the translation of Sun, "taking rubbings"); Dong, part 1, 41.

mo^{c}ta^{c} 摹榻 — Copy-rub. Fang, 31:12b passim.

mo^{b}xie 摩寫 — Carter, 1st ed., 197, and Carter, 2nd ed., 23, "make exact copies" (equals Han *ta*^{b} ?); Li, "Seals and Rubbings," 75, "copy by following the text."

mo^{d}xie 模寫 — Nakata, *Chinese Calligraphy*, 118, "various copying techniques," "copy," "sketch."

mo^{c}xie 摹寫 — Copy by hand, imitatively transcribe. Fan, 90 *xia*:9a; Fang, 39:9a; Feng, 8:2b; Sun, 1 (equated with *mo*^{c}*ta*^{b}); Carter, 1st ed., 13, and Carter, 2nd ed., 20, "to make exact copies" (rubbings?); Qu and Chang, 16; Li, "Yinzhang," 114 (citing *Han shu*), and Li, "Seals and Rubbings," 75–76, uses *moxie* in referring to the Han

	term for copying the stone classics. Although some translate *moxie* as "taking rubbings," Li, "Seals," 76, prefers "making copies by following the text," presumably transcribing. Su, 25 (citing Fang). These differences mark a continuing overlap and confusion in terms.
mo[c]yai (ta[a]) 摩崖 (拓).	Cliff-smoothing (rubbing). Dong, part 1, 41, and Dong, part 2, 47–48; Harrist, "Eulogy," 68; Tsien, *Bamboo and Silk*, 1962, 72.
mo[a]yin 墨印	Ink impression. Li, "Yinzhang," 118.
mo[c]yin (beitie) 摹印 (碑帖)	Rub (an inscription). Wei, 32:36; Ye, 10:320; *Cihai*, under *ta*[b], "rubbing."
mo[a]ying 墨影	Rubbing. Jiang, part 2, 52.
mo[a]zhi(ta[a]) 墨汁 (拓)	Liquid-ink (rub)
mo[c]zi 摹字	Copy characters. Fang, 31:14a.
mo[d]zi 模字	Copy characters. Fang, 31:13b.
pu (bao) 擈 (包)	Ink dabber. Common.
pu (ta) 擈 (拓)	Ink dabber. Jun, 74.
qixing ta 器形拓	Vessel-form rubbing, composite rubbing. Sang Shen, 52.
quanti 全體	Composite rubbing. Rong, 1:180.
quantu 全圖	Composite rubbing. Rong, 1:180 (citing Weng Fanggang, *Baosu shi jinshi shuhua biannian lu*, *xia*:1).
quanxing (taben) 全形 (拓本)	"Full-form," composite (rubbing). Rong, 1:181; Su, 26.
quzheng 取正	Capture accurately. Li, "Yinzhang," 114, and Li, "Seals and Rubbings," 75, "took these inscriptions as standard." Li cites some translating as "taking rubbings from stone inscriptions" and notes that Sun equates the term with *mo*[c]*ta*[b], copying by rubbing.
sheying 攝影	Photograph. Rong, 1:181.
shiben 石本	Stone edition, rubbing. Fang, 31:13a; Luo, 32; Qu and Chang, 17 (citing Tang sources); Su, 25.
shimo[a] 石墨	"Stone-ink," graphite (?). Zhu, *xu*:5b; Tsien, *Bamboo and Silk*, 1962, 171; 2004, 189; and Tsien, *Zhongguo gudai*, 161.
shimo (zhi tapian) 石墨 (之拓片)	Apply-ink (rubbing). Rong, 1:181; Su, 25.
shita[a] 施拓	Apply-rub. Jiang, part 2, 48.
shouta[a] (jinshi) 手拓 (金石)	Hand-rub (metal and stone). Xu Kang, 159, 226; Rong, 1:176; Li, "Yinzhang," 176.
shouta[a] quantu 手拓全圖	Hand-rub full picture (composite). Weng Fanggang, *Baosu shi jinshi shuhua biannian lu*, *xia*:1; Rong, 1:180 (citing Weng Fanggang, *Baosu shi jinshi shuhua biannian lu*).
shuaben 刷本	Brushed edition, rubbing. Van Gulik, 87.
shuanggou (ben) 雙鉤 (本)	Outline (edition), tracing outlines, sometimes with ink infill. Van Gulik, 397; Nakata, *Chūgoku shoronshū*, 254.
shuanggou kuotian 雙鉤廓填	Trace, outline, and fill in. Harrist, "Copies," 181. Same as *shuanggou ben*, *shuanggou motian*.

shuanggou mo[a]tian 雙鉤墨塡	Harrist, "Copies," 181. Same as *shuanggou ben, shuanggou kuotian.*
shuata[a] 刷拓	Brush-rub. Jiang, part 2, 43.
shuiben 蛻本	Exuvial edition, comparing a rubbing to a cast-off insect skin. Dong, part 1, 41. *See also* tuoben.
shuita[a] 水拓	Rubbing made with liquid ink.
shutie 書帖	Calligraphic album. Van Gulik, 40.
ta[a] 拓	Most common modern form for rub, rubbing. Fang, 31:13a; Xu Kang, 157 passim; Chen Jieqi, 1b passim; Ye, 1:1, 5:160, 9:298 passim; Luo, 33; Wang Guowei, 7:6a; Rong, 1:176 passim; Jiang, part 1, 72 passim; Li, "Yinzhang," 113 passim; Wang Chi-chen, 2, synonymous with *ta* (no Chinese) and with *yin*, a general term for printing at some periods; Su, 25 passim. See also Dong, part 1, 40–41, for comments on *ta*[a] and *ta*[b]. *Cihai*, "use hand to press."
ta[b] 搨	Basic but less common form for *ta*[a]. Ennin, "Nittō guhō junrei gyōki," 113; Wen, 5:182; Wang Chang, 41:23a; Weng Fanggang, *Liang Han*, 15:1a passim; Zhu, *fu*:6b; Chen Yuanlong, 39:6b; Carter, 1st ed., 197 n., and Carter, 2nd ed., 23 n., not used until Tang (Han equivalent of *mo*[c] uncertain); Ruan, 1b; Wang Chi-chen, 2 (synonymous with *ta*[a] and *yin*, with no Chinese characters); Li, "Yinzhang," 117; van Gulik, 99, 516; Hucker, 475, no. 6125. See also Dong, part 1, 40–41, for comments on *ta*[a] and *ta*[b]. Nakata, *Chūgoku shoronshū*, 255, equating *ta*[b] with *mo*[c], "replica," "trace," suggests that it means "ink copies," not rubbings. See also *Cihai*, both *ta*[b] and *yinghuang*, which relates it to *shuanggou*, tracing.
ta[c] 榻	Least common form for rub, rubbing. Sang, 3:17; Fang, 31:11b passim; Tu, 3:26a–b; Wang Houzhi (central fold); Lu, 13:5b. See *Cihai*; *Kangxi zidian*.
ta[a] bei 拓碑	Rub a stele (inscription). Jiang, part 1, 72.
ta[c] beijie (wei moben) 榻碑碣(為墨本)	Rub a tablet (make ink edition, rubbing). Fang, 31:16a.
ta[c] getie 榻閣帖	Rub a calligraphic model. Fang, 31:12a.
ta[a] quanxing 拓全形	Rub "full-form," composite rubbing. Rong, 1:179–80 passim; Su, 26.
ta[b] shi 搨石	Rub a stone (inscription). Ye, 9:298 passim; Li, "Yinzhang," 115.
ta[c] shi 榻石	Rub a stone (inscription). Fang, 31:15b.
ta[a] yiqi 拓彝器	Rub ritual vessels. Wang Guowei, 7:6a; Su, 25.
tabao 拓包	Ink dabber. Jiang, part 1, 71.
ta[a]ben 拓本	Most common term for a rubbing. Sun and Xing, 1b passim; Xu Kang, 127; Chen Jieqi, 1 passim; Ye, 1:1, 9:298; Wang Guowei, 7:6a; Luo, 31 passim; Wang Guowei, *Mao Gong ding kaoshi xu*, 275; Rong, 1:176 passim; Jiang, part 2, 51 passim; Li, "Yinzhang," 117 (same as *ta*[b]*ben*), and Li, "Seals and Rubbings," 73 (equates with *mo*[b]*ta*[b]); Su, 26; Dong, part 1, 41; Nakata, *Chūgoku no bijitsu*, 2:123, 2:184; Nakata, *Chinese Calligraphy*, 118.

ta[b]ben 搨本 — Rubbing. Ruan, 2a; Li, "Yinzhang," 116 passim (equates with *daben* and *ta[a]ben*), and Li, "Seals and Rubbings," 78 (equates with *daben*); Dong, part 1, 41; Zhang Guangyuan, 7.

ta[c]ben 榻本 — Least common form for rubbing. Sang, 3:17; Lu, 13: 5b; Zhang Guangyuan, 7.

tada 拓打 — Rub-strike. Chen Yuanlong, 39:6b.

tafa 拓法 — Rubbing technique. Ye, 10:315.

tagong 拓工 — Rubbing artisan, especially a stele rubber. Ye, 9:298 passim; Jiang, part 1, 73 passim, and Jiang, part 2, 51.

takuhon (Japanese) 拓本 — *ta[a]ben*, rubbing; van Gulik, 87; *Daijiten*.

ta[a]mo[a] (zhi fa) 拓墨 (之法) — Rub-ink (technique); Chen Jieqi, 2b; Wang Guowei, 7:6a; Rong, 1:176 passim, rubbing bronze vessels; Jiang, part 1, 73 passim; Su, 25 (citing Wang Guowei and Wei); Zhang Zuyi, book-mounted rubbing of Kong Zhou bei, colophon.

ta[b]mo[c] 搨摹 — Copy? Nakata, *Chūgoku shoronshū*, 264.

ta[b]mo[d] (ben) 搨模 (本) — "Copy," "collections of rubbings," "*tamo* reproductions." Nakata, *Chūgoku no bijitsu*, 2:123, and Nakata, *Chinese Calligraphy*, 118, "a type of rubbing."

ta[a]pian 拓片 — Rubbing. Rong, 1:181; Su, 26; Jiang, part 2, 51 passim; Dong, part 1, 41.

ta[b]pian 搨片 — Rubbing. Li, "Yinzhang," 116.

ta[a]pu 拓業 — Ink dabber. Jun, 74.

ta[a]qu 拓取 — Rub-take. Feng, 8:2b (Li, "Yinzhang," 115); Rong, 1:181.

ta[a]shu 拓書 — Outline, ink infill. Nakata, *Chinese Calligraphy*, 168.

ta[b]shu (ren) 搨書 (人) — Rub-writing person. Nakata, *Chūgoku shoronshū*, 255–56, gives as "copyist" (ink copy).

ta[c]shu (ren) 榻書 (人) — Rub-writing (person). Sang, 3:17; Fang, 31:11b.

ta[b]shu (shou) 搨書 (手) — Rub-writing (artisan). Tang, 8:3a, 9:11a; Liu, 43:36a, 40a; Ouyang, 47:5b, 47:8b, 49 *shang*:13b; Carter, 1st ed., 197; Qu and Chang, 17 (citing Liu Xu, *Jiu Tang shu*, and Ouyang Xiu, *Xin Tang shu*, "Baiguan zhi" section); Li, "Yinzhang," 116. Nakata, *Chūgoku shoronshū*, 255, gives as "copyist" (ink copy).

ta[c]shu (shou) 榻書 (手) — Rub-writing (artisan). Tang, 8:17b, 9:2b, 26:3a.

ta[c]tie 榻帖 — Rub calligraphy. Fang, 31:11b.

ta[a]tu 拓圖 — Rub a picture, composite rubbing. Chen Jieqi, 3b.

ta[b]xie 搨寫 — Rub-write, rub. See *tōsha*.

ta[c]xie 榻寫 — Rub-write. Fang, 31:11b.

tayin 拓印 — Rub-print. Wang Chi-chen, 2; Tsien, *Zhongguo gudai*, 80; Weng Kaiyun, 70; Dong, part 1, 41.

ta[c]ying 榻影 — Rub-image. Fang, 31:11b.

tazi 拓字 — Rub characters. Chen Jieqi, 1a passim; Rong, 1:176.

tie 帖 — Calligraphic model, cut in stone or wood; the resulting rubbing or print. Nakata, *Chinese Calligraphy*, 118, gives as "album," "model book."

tōsha (Japanese) 搨寫 — *ta[b]xie*, rub-write. Ennin, *Dai Nihon Bukkyō Zensho*, 114, no. 563.

tuoben 脫本 — Molted-skin edition, rubbing. Dong, part 1, 41. *See* shuiben.

tuxing ta[a] 圖形拓 — Pictorial rubbing. Sang Shen, 52.

weiben 偽本	Counterfeit, fake.
wujin ta[a] 烏金拓	Polished, black-gold rubbing. Jiang, part 1, 75; Dong, part 1, 41.
wujin ta[b] 烏金搨	Polished, black-gold rubbing. Van Gulik, 87.
wujin ta[c] 烏金榻	Polished, black-gold rubbing. Fang, 31:15b.
xiang[a]ta[b] 嚮搨	Facing-rubbing, opposite-rubbing. *Cihai* describes it as placing a manuscript or rubbing against a light source, outlining the characters with a fine brush pen, and filling them in with ink; *Cihai* refers the reader to *xiang[b]ta[b]*, the homophonous and more common term for "tracing," despite its base meaning, "sound rubbing." See also Harrist, "Copies," 181.
xiang[b]ta[a] 響拓	Tracing a rubbing. Wang Guowei, 7:6a; Jiang, part 1, 73; Su, 25 (citing Wei); David, 36, 344. Jiang describes this as "a sound rubbing," from the sound in the tamping and inking stages. This *xiang[b]* character actually means "sound," although the usual translation in this context is "copying" or "tracing." A homophonous form of *xiang[b]*, "sound," is *xiang[a]*, "facing" or "opposite," more appropriate for tracing.
xiang[b]ta[b] 響搨	Tracing. *Cihai* directs one to *xiang[a]ta[b]*; Dong, part 1, 41, equates with *ta[a]ben*, *ta[b]ben*, and *yingxieben*. Nakata, *Chinese Calligraphy*, 118, and Nakata, *Chūgoku shoronshū*, 262, includes among "various copying techniques."
xiang[b]ta[c] 嚮榻	Tracing characters in a rubbing against a light source, then filling them in with deep-black ink. Cao, 2:1a–b, and Fang, 31:15a, explain the technique.
xiong 雄	"Male" dabber. Common usage.
xuehua jia sha 雪花夾紗	"Snowflakes between gauze," an effect in making rubbings. Jiang, part 1, 75.
yanben 贗本	Counterfeit, fake.
yin 印	Print, seal. Li, "Seals and Rubbings," 73. General term for printing in earlier times. Synonymous with *ta* (no Chinese given), according to Wang Chi-chen, 2.
yingxie(ben) 影寫 (本)	"Reflected-writing (edition)." Dong, part 1, 41, equates with *ta[a]ben*, *ta[b]ben*, and *xiangta[b]ben*. Nakata, *Chūgoku shoronshū*, 261.
you(mo[a])ta[a] 油 (墨) 拓	Rubbing with oil-based ink. Common.
yuanji 原蹟	Original. Nakata, *Chinese Calligraphy*, 117.
zhanla (zhi fa) 氈蠟 (之法)	Felt-wax (method). Luo, 33.
zhanmo 氈墨	Felt tamping-inking. Wang Guowei, 7:6a; Jiang, part 2, 54 (appendix); colophon on a Dunhuang stone rubbing (see plate 7.1, this volume).
zhenben 真本	"Genuine copy," vertical and long. Li, "Seals and Rubbings," 77, "rubbing copy from the original stone inscription," "true footsteps"; Seals, 77.
zhengben 正本	Original copy, authentic.

zhenji 真蹟 — "True footsteps"; "original." Fang, 31:11b; Nakata, *Chinese Calligraphy*, 117; Lu, 28: 112.

zhenta[a] 真拓 — True rubbing.

zhiben 紙本 — Paper edition, rubbing. Sima Zhen, 8:1b; Qu and Chang, 17.

zhu[a]ta[a] (ben) 朱拓 (本) — Red rubbing (edition). Dong, part 1, 41.

zhu[b]ta[a] (ben) 硃拓 (本) — Vermilion rubbing (edition). Ye, 316; Jiang, pt. 2, 50–51.

zhu[b]ta[a] guben 硃拓古本 — Vermilion unique rubbing.

zhuanjia 專家 — Rubbing specialist, rubber of bronzes.

zhuoben 摭本 — A rubbing. Mathews.

zhuoqu 摭取 — Take a rubbing. Mathews.

zise 字冊 — Calligraphic album. Van Gulik, 40.

zitie 字帖 — Calligraphic rubbing. Van Gulik, 40.

zong (laohu) 棕 (老虎) — Coir (tiger), brush.

zuben 足本 — A complete rubbing.

zuo quanxing 作全形 — Make a composite (rubbing). Rong, 1:180.

zuota[a] 作拓 — Make a rubbing; equals *mo*[c]*ta*[b]. Li, "Yinzhang," 113.

Appendix 3

Terms for Papers Used to Make Rubbings

bai jing jian 白經牋	White sutra paper; see Tsien, *Paper and Printing*, 86.
bai lianqi zhi 白連七紙	*See* lianqi zhi.
bai Song jian 白宋箋	"White Song paper."
baidie zhi 白褶紙	"White lining paper" for labels.
bi zhi 壁紙	See van Gulik, *Chinese Pictorial Art As Viewed by the Connoisseur*, on *pi zhi*; see also comments at the end of this appendix.
cabai zhi 擦白紙	"White wiping paper," general term for absorptive tamping paper; *see* xishui zhi.
canjian zhi 蠶繭紙	"Cocoon paper," cited by Tu Long, *Kaopan yushi*, under Song papers. Said to have been made from silkworm cocoons, reputedly used by Wang Xizhi in writing the *Lanting xu*. See also Tsien, *Paper and Printing*, 63–64.
celi zhi 側理紙	*See* tai zhi (jian), "intricate filament" or "oblique grain paper."
celi zhi 側黎紙	*See* tai zhi (jian), "oblique black paper."
chen zhi 襯紙	"Liner paper," nonspecific, intermediate paper to cushion tamping. *See* qiaobei zhi; xishui zhi.
Chengxin Tang zhi 澄心堂紙	"Chengxin Tang paper," "paper from the Hall of the Pure Heart," a fine, thin, smooth, strong paper used to rub the *Chunhua Ge tie*.
chu (shu) 褚(樹)	Paper mulberry (tree).
cilan zhi 瓷藍紙	"Porcelain-blue paper."
dan Xuan 單宣	*See* Xuan zhi.
er Hsuan 二宣	*See* Xuan zhi.
gaofei pi zhi 高飛皮紙	*See* Xuan zhi, definition 4.
Gaoli pi zhi 高麗皮紙	*See* Xuan zhi, definition 4.
gou (shu) 构 樹	A variety of mulberry.
Guangdong zhi 廣東紙	Vermifugal paper.
hongsi lowen zhi 紅絲羅文紙	*See* Xuan zhi.
hupi zhi 虎皮紙	*See* zangjin jian (zhi).
jiagong Xuan 夾貢宣	*See* Xuan zhi.
jian zhi 繭紙	*See* Xuan zhi, definition 4.
jingji zhi 經籍紙	Book paper, as for the classics.

jingpi (lian, zhi) 淨皮 (連,紙) — *See* Xuan zhi, definition 4.

Jinsu Shan zangjing zhi 金粟藏經紙 — *See* zangjin jian (zhi).

Jinsu zhi 金粟紙 — *See* zangjin jian (zhi).

lianqi zhi 連七紙 — "Continuous-seven paper," *bai lianqi*, "white continuous-seven paper," from Jing County, Anhui, near Xuancheng Xian. *Lianqi* of good quality, comparable to good modern *pi* paper, is mentioned as being made at Xi Shan, Jiangxi, in the Ming Yongle–reign period (1403–1424). Heavy, it comes in large sizes. See Tu Long, *Kaopan yushi*, 2:37; van Gulik, *Chinese Pictorial Art As Viewed by the Connoisseur*, 296.

lianshi zhi 連史紙 — "Continuous-history paper," northeastern Jiangxi and northwestern Fujian. *Lianshi* paper, variant types of which include *liaoban lianshi*, is made of bamboo and noted for its resistance to color change. Valued for calligraphy, painting, and rubbings, and for books, letter paper, and fans. An earlier name was *liansi zhi*, "connected- (continuous-) four paper."

liansi zhi 連四(泗)紙 — *See* lianshi zhi.

liaoban lianshi zhi 料半連史紙 — *See* lianshi zhi.

liu chi te jingpi (lian) 六尺特淨皮 (連) — *See* Xuan zhi, definition 4.

Liuji te jingpi (lian) 六吉特淨皮 (連) — *See* Xuan zhi, definition 4.

Liuji (mianlian) zhi 六吉 (棉連) 紙 — *See* Xuan zhi, definition 3.

luowen Xuan (jian, zhi) 羅紋 (箋,紙) — *See* Xuan zhi, definition 1.

mafen zhi 馬糞紙 — "Horse-manure paper," made with rice or wheat straw; for cardboard boxes and stiffening book covers and *han* cases.

maobian zhi 毛邊紙 — Bamboo paper from Jiangle County, Fujian, and Taihe County, Jiangxi. Fine, soft, smooth and glossy, and yellowish; used for correspondence, calligraphy, and woodblock printing, and rubbing. There are different grades; Tsien, *Paper and Printing*, 51, describes it as wrapping paper.

maotai zhi 毛泰紙 — A Fujian specialty, fine but slightly dark. Jiang Xuanyi recommends it as intermediate paper in tamping.

maotou zhi 毛頭紙 — "Hair paper," made in Hobei and Shansi, where, as in Beijing, it is used for papering windows and for commercial-grade rubbings.

mian zhi 綿 (棉) 紙 — Made from the paper mulberry.

mianjian zhi 綿繭紙 — "Cocoon-threads paper," made from silkworm cocoons. *See* canjian zhi.

mianlian zhi. 棉連紙 — *See* Xuan zhi, definition 2.

nijin jian 泥金牋 — Decorative gold-flecked paper.

pi zhi 皮紙 — *See* Xuan zhi, definition 4.

qiaobei zhi 敲碑紙 — "Strike-stele paper," nonspecific intermediate paper for tamping. *See* chen zhi; xishui zhi.

sajin jian 洒金箋 — "Gold-sprinkled paper," imitative of Song paper, made in Xin'anzhen, Jiangxi. Cited by Tu Long, *Kaopan yushi*, under Ming papers.

sangpi zhi 桑皮紙 — Mulberry-bark paper, generic term.

shidao tou 十刀頭 — *See* Xuan zhi.

shifa zhi 石髮紙 — *See* tai zhi (jian).

shiqi dao 十七刀 — *See* Xuan zhi.

shuang Xuan zhi 雙宣紙 — *See* Xuan zhi.

shupi zhi 樹皮紙 — "Tree-bark paper," generic term.

tai zhi (jian) 苔紙 (牋) — Paper made from seaweed, especially by southern coastal people. Also called *celi zhi*, "intricate-filament paper" (Tsien, *Paper and Printing*, 62) or "oblique-grain paper," and *celi zhi*, "oblique black (?) paper," *shifa zhi*, "stone-moss paper," and *zhili zhi* (meaning unclear).

Wang Liuji zhi 汪六吉紙 — *See* Xuan zhi, definition 3.

xiangyan xizhi 香煙錫紙 — Cigarette paper.

xionghuang zhi 雄黃紙 — Insecticidal paper.

xishui zhi 吸水紙 — "Absorb-water paper." Nonspecific, intermediate paper to draw excess water from the rubbing paper in tamping. *See* cabai zhi; chen zhi; qiaobei zhi.

Xuan zhi 宣紙 — "Xuan paper" comes from its original source, Xuancheng County, Anhui. It is made chiefly from the bark of the *chu shu* (*gou shu*), the paper mulberry (*Broussonetia papyrifera*). Li Ch'iao-p'ing, *The Chemical Arts of Old China*, 164, also names the bark of the *tanmu*, the *huangtan*, or yellow sandalwood tree (*Dalbergia hupeana*). The Chinese from at least the Tang have favored Xuan for calligraphy, painting, rubbings, bookmaking, and mounting, valuing its quality and resistance to insects and color change. See van Gulik, *Chinese Pictorial Art As Viewed by the Connoisseur*, 155; Tsien, *Paper and Printing*, 61–62, 90; and Zhang Yanyuan, *Lidai ming hua ji*, 2:75. Xuan covers a wide range of papers of varying quality. It is a standard high-grade paper, widely produced and sold in China and overseas. It comes in several weights: single weight (*dan Xuan*, which Dong Juewei, "Zeyang tabei," part 1, 42, equates with *liaoban*); double weight (*shuang Xuan*, or *jia* [*gong*] *Xuan*, which Dong equates with *shidao tou*); and triple weight (*yuban jian*). Special varieties cited in the context of rubbings include the following:

1. luowen (Xuan, jian, zhi) 羅紋 (宣,箋,紙) *Luo* means "gauze" or "net"; *wen*, vein or grain. "Net-grain Xuan paper" is high-quality cream-white paper, with older examples greatly prized. Tu Long, *Kaopan yushi*, 2:37, refers to *luowen jian* as one of the papers made in Shaoxing, Zhejiang, in Yuan times. Tsien, *Paper and Printing*, 90, calls *luowen* "silk stripe." *Luowen* paper was the only paper specifically named by Jean Baptiste Du Halde, who described it as prized in the Qing Kangxi (1662–1722) and Yongzheng (1723–1735) periods; see Du Halde, *Description Géographique, Historique, Chronologique, Politique, et Physique de l'Empire de la Chine*, 2:288; Du Halde, *The General History of China*, 2:418. Van Gulik, *Chinese Pictorial Art As Viewed by the Connoisseur*, appendix V:7–8, illustrates two weights made for the palace in Qianlong times (1736–1795). The caption states that "already at that time [*luowen* paper was] much sought after by painters and calligraphers" and is "now prized as an antique." He adds that *luowen Xuan* paper shows crisscross mold marks; thus, one surmises, the name *hongsi luowen zhi*, "red-thread *luowen* paper."

2. mianlian (zhi) 棉連 (紙) "Cotton-continuous (paper)," very thin and fine, yet strong. From Xuancheng, Anhui, the best grade is made entirely from the inner bark of the paper mulberry tree; lesser grades, such as *zhulian*, from northwest Fujian, include bamboo pulp. It also is known as *mian zhi*, *zhulian mianlian* (*zhi*), and "bamboo-continuous, cotton-continuous (paper)." Van Gulik, *Chinese Pictorial Art As Viewed by the Connoisseur*, 74, notes that "*mianlian* and similar papers are often collectively referred to as *hsüan-chih*, . . . 'Hsüan-ch'eng paper.'"

3. (Wang) Liuji mianlian (or Xuan) (汪) 六吉棉連 (宣) Named after Wang Liuji, an early maker of fine paper. Chen Jieqi refers to it but notes that in his day (1813–1884) it no longer was available. Its popular name was *shiqi dao*, "seventeen knives." The paper, or one using the same name, was available in the earlier half of the twentieth century. Jiang Xuanyi, "Mota shu," part 1, 71, calls it "fan paper" and recommends it for rubbing small articles.

4. pi zhi 皮紙 Widely made in China, "bark paper" is a specialty of Jiangxi, Zhejiang, Guizhou, and Yunnan. *Pi* is made from a variety of materials, including particularly the barks of the *chu shu* or *gou shu* (paper mulberry, *Broussonetia papyrifera*), *sang shu* (white mulberry, *Morus alba*) *sanya* or *huang rui xiang* (paper bush, *Edgeworthia papyrifera*), and bamboo shoots. Variants include *sang pi*, from the white mulberry; *gaofei pi*, of reddish cast and used in Beijing for commercial-grade rubbings; and *Gaoli pi*, "Korean *pi*," characterized as coarse, with poor color and low absorbency. Jiang Xuanyi, "Mota shu," part 2, 51, names *Gaoli pi* as the *jian* paper that Wang Xizhi used to write the *Lanting xu*. This relates to the fact that the Chinese prize some kinds of *Gaoli zhi*, "Korean paper," said to be made from the threads of the silkworm cocoon, or *mian jian*, whence the name "*jian* paper." Jiang also adds that this is the *jian* paper to which Ye Changchi refers. Tu Long, *Kaopan yushi*, 2:37, after noting the qualities of *jian zhi*, observes that it does not exist in China and that *Gaoli* paper "is a wonderful thing."

Fibers of silkworm cocoons were said to be one of the components of the quasi-paper made in the Former Han. Given Tu's comments, one might speculate that sometime after the diffusion of papermaking to Korea, in the fourth century, the Chinese either lost or discarded the method of making paper from cocoon fibers so that by Ming times Tu found the imported Korean *mian jian* a novel and wonderful thing not to be had in China. *Pi* paper is widely produced in China. It comes in large sheets and is soft, smooth, and absorbent but tough and pliant, which recommends it for copying large inscriptions and relievo. It also resists insects. The paper comes in various qualities, with many modern variants, including *liu chi te jingpi* (*lian*), "six-foot special *jingpi* (*lian*)," a high-quality paper for rubbing fine inscriptions.

5. yuban (jian, zhi) 玉版 (箋,紙) "Jade-tablet (paper)" is a high-quality white paper, large and heavy but soft and fine Xuan.

yinghuang 硬黃 — Also, *huangying*. Mentioned by Yūjirō Nakata, *Chūgoku shoronshū*, 261; Yūjirō Nakata, *Chūgoku no bujitsu*, 122; Yūjirō Nakata, *A History of the Art of China*, 118. *Cihai* names it for tracing, copying old calligraphic models (*linmo gu tie*), and *shuanggou*. Van Gulik calls it "hardened yellow paper," from its wax coating, 137, 518. *Daijiten* calls it a Tang paper, as does Van Gulik.

yuanshu zhi 元書紙 — For absorbing water in tamping. This paper comes from several districts in the Hangzhou area. Made from "stone bamboo" (*shizhu*, *Dianthus chinensis*), it is yellowish and commonly is used for account books and wrapping.

yuban jian — *See* Xuan zhi, definition 5.

zangjin jian (zhi) 藏金箋 (紙) — A Ming product imitative of Song paper, from Xin'an, Jiangxi; see Tu Long, *Kaopan yushi* 2:37.

zangjing jian 藏徑箋 — Jiang Xuanyi, "Mota shu," part 1, 71, gives the source of "Buddhist-path paper" as Xin'an, Jiangxi, and refers to it as imitative of Song paper of that name. Five hundred years earlier, Tu Long, *Kaopan yushi*, 2: 7, referred to it as *zangjin jian zhi*. The *jing* character here may be a typographical error.

zangjing jian (zhi) 藏經牋 (紙) — Zhou Erxue, *Shangyan suxin lu*, 45:6b, refers to "Buddhist sutra paper," a mottled yellow paper used by calligraphers for labels for scrolls, albums, and books and their outer cases. Other names include *hupi zhi*, "tiger-skin paper"; *Jinsu jian*, *Jinsu Shan zangjing zhi*, "Jinsu Mountain sutra paper"; and simply "Jinsu paper," from its purported place of origin at Jinsu Temple, near Haiyan, on the north coast of Hangzhou Bay. Tsien, *Paper and Printing*, 88, calls it "golden-grain paper," an imitation of *Jinsu Shan zangjing zhi*.

zangjing zhi (jian) 藏經紙 (牋)	Buddhist sutra paper. See Ye Changchi, *Yu shi*, 318; van Gulik, *Chinese Pictorial Art As Viewed by the Connoisseur*, 301n.
zhili zhi 陟釐紙	*See* tai zhi (jian).
zhulian zhi (mianlian) 竹連紙 (棉連)	"Bamboo-connected" paper is a cheaper paper made from young bamboo shoots. *See* Xuan zhi, definition 2.

Some of the above-mentioned papers, although historically associated with a particular town, district, or province, are widely imitated, as is Xuan. Van Gulik, *Chinese Pictorial Art As Viewed by the Connoisseur*, appendix V, provides swatches of the most common Chinese and Japanese papers and textiles in his text. Of relevance here are *luowen* Xuan (7–8), *mianlian zhi* (5), *pi zhi* (12), *Wang Liuji zhi* (11), *yuban jian* (10), *zangjing zhi* (19) and *zhulian* (6). He gives the character, *bi*, for *pi* paper. The usual character is the *pi* in *shupi zhi*, "book-cover paper," used on the cover of his appendix.

Glossary of Chinese Characters

For specialized terminology related to rubbing materials and processes, see Appendixes 2 and 3.

abura zumi 油墨
ai 艾
Anhui 安徽

bafen 八分
bai (silk) 帛
Baiguan zhi 百官志
baiji 白芨
baila (shu) 白蠟 (屬)
Baima Si 白馬寺
Baishou tu 百壽圖
Baiyun Dong 白雲
baizhi 白芷
baleng bei 八棱碑
Ban men nong fu 班門弄斧
baobei zhuang 包背裝
baofu 包袱
baoku 寶庫
bei (rear) 背
bei (stele, inscription) 碑
Bei Xue 碑學
bei'e 碑額
Beilin 碑林
beitie (ceye) 碑帖 (冊葉)
beiyin 碑陰
bi 壁
biane 匾額
bieming 别名
Bifu 祕府
Bige (tie) 祕閣 (帖)
bu (cloth, money) 布

Cai Lun 蔡倫
Cai Yong 蔡邕
cao 草
Cao Wangxi 曹望僖
Chang'an 長安
Changzhou 常州
Che Yongzhao 車永昭
Chen Baochen 陳寶
Chen Jieqi 陳介倛
Chen Peigang 陳佩綱
Cheng Muan 程木庵
Chengxin Tang 澄心堂
Chengziyai 城子崖
chensha 辰沙
Chenzhou 辰州
chi 尺
chishou 螭首
chong 重
Chongwenguan 崇文館
chou 綢
chu shu 褚叔
Chu Suiliang 褚遂良
chuang 幢
chuanji 傳記
Chunhua (bi) Ge (fa) tie 淳化 (祕) 閣 (法) 帖
Chunyu ji 春禹集
Cien Si 慈思寺
Ciyunling 慈雲嶺
congtie 叢帖
cuyan 粗煙
cun 寸

Da Qin Jingjiao liuxing Zhongguo bei 大秦景教流行中國碑

Da Shou 達受
Da Tang san zang sheng jiao xu bei 大唐三藏聖教序碑
Dai 軑
Dai Miao 岱廟
daizhe shi 代赭石
danxingtie 單行帖
daobu 刀布
Daode Jing 道德經
Daoguang 道光
dazhuan 大篆
di 地
Diecai Shan 疊彩山
ding (character) 丁
ding (cauldron) 鼎
Dingwu Lanting 定武蘭亭
dingyi 鼎彝
Dong Qichang 董其昌
Dongyue Tianqi Rensheng Di bei 東嶽天齊仁聖帝碑
dou 豆
douban nanmu 豆玟楠木
Du Fu 杜撫
duan 緞
Duanfang (siyin) 端方 (私印)
Dunhuang (shiku, shishi) 敦煌 (石窟, 石室)

Ennin 圓仁
Er Shi (Huangdi) 二世 (皇帝)

fan 礬
Fan Wo 范諤
fang 鈁
Fang Liang Gong (bei) 房梁公 (碑)
Fang Shan 房山
Fang Xuanling (bei) 房玄齡 (碑)
fangbei 訪碑
fanggu 訪古
Fantian Si 梵天寺
fei 肥
Feilaifeng 飛來峰
fen 分
fengbei 豐碑
Feng Dongyue Tai Shan zhi shen bei 封東越泰山之神碑碑
Fengman Lou jitie 風滿樓集帖
fengmian 封面
foudiao 浮雕 (之屬)
fu (approaching) 傅, 附
fu (tray) 簠
Fugui ding 福貴鼎
Fuji Zenzaburo 藤井善三郎

gao 高
gao zi weihuai ben 高字未壞本
gaorou diao zhi shu 高肉雕之屬
Gaozong 高宗
Gaozu 高祖
ge 戈
gezhi fa 隔紙法
gou shu 構樹
goudiao 句掉
Goulou (Shan) bei 岣嶁 (山) 碑
gu 觚
guan (seen) 觀
guang 觥
guanzhi 官制
Guanzhong 關中
gudongshang 古董商
Gugong Bowuyuan 故宮博物院
gui 簋
guifu 龜趺
guwen 古文

Haining County 海寧 縣
haitai 海苔
Haiyan County 海鹽 縣
han (case) 函
Han (dynasty) 漢
Han Zhenquan xi 漢偵泉洗
hao (*bi*, hole) 好
hao (literary name) 號
he (box) 盒
He (place) 禾
He Zhi 何致
He Zizhen 何子貞
heixin 黑心
Heng Shan 衡山
Hong Pu 洪溥
hongmu 紅木
Hongwenguan 宏文館
hou 後
houma 後馬

hu (*ge*, dagger ax) 胡
hu (vase) 壺
Hua Shan 華山
Huadu Si (*bei*) 化度寺 (碑)
Huadu Si gu seng Yongzhan Shi sheli taming 化度寺古僧邕禪師舍利塔銘
Huairen 懷仁
huan 環
Huandi 桓帝
Huang Ming Jianguo Lu Wang kuangzhi 皇明監國魯王壙誌
Huang Ming Shijing Zheng shi fenzhiming 皇明石井鄭氏墳誌銘
Huang Yi 黃儀
Huangting Jing 黃庭經
Huangyou 皇祐
huaxiang shi 畫像石
Huayi tu 華夷圖
hudie zhuang 蝴蝶裝
hui 諱
Huo Qubing 霍去病
husao 糊掃

inshō 印象

Ji Wang (*Xizhi sheng jiao xu*) *bei* 集王 (羲之聖教序) 碑
jia 斝
Jia Sidao 賈似道
jia you qi qi, ren shi qi wen 家有其器, 人識其文
jiaban 夾板
Jiading 嘉定
jiagu(wen) 甲骨 (文)
jiajianzi 挾簽子
Jiajing 嘉靖
jian (slip) 簡
jian (silk) 縑
jian (basin) 鑑
jianbiao(ben) 剪裱 (本)
Jiang Gusun 蔣轂孫
jianghu 漿糊
Jiangle 將樂
Jiangnan 江南
jianshangjia 鑑賞家
jianzhuang (ben) 剪裝 (本)
Jiao Shan (Zhenjiang) 焦山
Jiao Shan (Wuxi) 膠山
jiao (shui) 膠 (水)
Jiaqing 嘉慶
Jiaxing 嘉興
jiazhi 假紙
jidanqing 雞蛋青
jie 碣
Jikaku Daishi 慈覺大師
jin (weight) 斤
Jin (Tartar) 金
Jin (dynasty) 晉
jin (brocade) 錦
Jing Shan (pai) 金山(派)
jing (classics, sutras) 經
Jing County 涇縣
Jingang Jing 金剛經
jingchuang 經幢
jingji (zhi) 經籍(志)
Jin'ge Si 金閣寺
Jinglong Guan 景籠觀
Jinmen (Island) 金門島
jinshi (scholar) 進士
jinshi (bu, xue) 金石(部，學)
Jinshi seng 金石僧
jinshijia 金石家
Jinshi xie 金石屑
jinzhe biao 巾摺裱
jitie 集帖
Jixiandian shuyuan 集賢殿書院
jizibai 雞子白
Ju 莒
Ju dao 莒刀
juan (roll, chapter) 卷
juan (silk) 絹
jue (wine cup) 角
jue (wine goblet) 爵
junma 軍馬

kai 楷
Kaicheng 開成
Kaiyuan 開元
Kangyuan 康元
Kankarō kikin zu 冠斝樓吉金圖
ke shi (wei bei, lamo wei zi) 刻石 (為碑, 蠟墨為字)
ketou wen 蝌蚪文
Kong Zhou (*bei*, *beiyin*) 孔宙 (碑, 碑陰)

kongge 空格
Kongzi Miaotang (zhi) bei 孔子廟堂 (之) 碑
kouzi 釦子
Kuaiji (keshi) 會稽 (刻石)

Langya Tai (bei, keshi) 琅邪臺 (碑, 刻石)
Lantian 藍田
Lanting (taben) 藍亭 (拓本)
Lanting (ji) xu 藍亭 (集) 序
Lanting (xi) tie 藍亭 (禊) 帖
Lanting xu 藍帝序
Lanting zhenben 藍亭真本
Lao Shan 勞山
Lee Tung-fang (Orient Lee) 黎東方
lei 罍
li (mile) 里
li (measure) 225
li (script) 隸
Li Baiyao 李百藥
Li Bian 李昪
Li Jinhong 李錦鴻
Li Lincan 李霖燦
Li Peng 李鵬
Li qi bei 禮器碑
li shi 立石
Li Shou 李壽
Li Shuda 李叔達
Li Si 李斯
Li Tinggui 李延珪
Li Yingji 李英基
Li Zongtong 李宗侗
liang (measure, money) 兩
Liang (dynasty) 梁
Liang Wenzhao Gong Fang Xuanling bei 梁文昭公房玄齡碑
Liangcheng Shan 兩城山
Liao 遼
Liao Yingzhong 廖瑩中
Lie Zu 列祖
ling 綾
Lingdi 靈帝
Lingyin Si 靈隱寺
Liquan 醴泉
liti 立體
Liu Gongquan (*Kaishu jingang jing*) 柳公權 (楷書金剛經)
Liu Hui 劉慧
Liu Yuanjian 劉淵監
Liu Zhou 六舟
liubo 六駁
Liulichang 琉璃廠
Longmen 龍門
Longshanzhen 龍山鎮
Longshuo 龍朔
Longxing Guan 隆興觀
Lu Ban men neng fu 魯班弄斧
Lu Wang muzhi ming 魯王墓誌銘
Lu Xun 魯迅
lü 律
lun 論
Luoyang 洛陽

Ma Fuyan 馬傅嚴
Ma Ji 馬冀
Ma Qifeng 馬起鳳
mao 矛
Mao Gong ding 毛公鼎
Mawangdui 馬王堆
Menxiasheng 門下省
Mi Fei 米芾
mian 面
Mianhua tu 棉花圖
mianqian 面籤
Ming (dynasty) 明
ming (personal name) 名
mingfan 明礬
Miu Quansun 繆荃蓀
mofa 末法
Mogaoku 莫高窟
moshi 墨豕
moshui 墨水
mozhi 墨汁
muchui 木鍾
muzhi (ming) 墓誌 (銘)

Na Luoyan jian zunsheng bei (jingchuang) 那羅延建尊勝碑 (經幢)
nan (mu) 楠 (木)
nang 囊
Nanyang 南陽
nei 內
ni 呢
niantu 粘土

Ouyang Xiu 歐陽修
Ouyang Xun 歐陽詢

pan 盤
Pan Zuyin 潘祖蔭
Penghu Dao 澎湖島
pou 瓿
Puyuanzhen 濮院鎮

Qi 齊
Qi hou lei 齊侯罍
qian (front) 前
qian (weight) 錢
Qianfo Dong 千佛洞
Qianlong 乾隆
Qianyuandian 乾元殿
Qianzhou 乾州
Qimingdui 鴟鳴垍
qin (tree) 梣
Qin (dynasty) 秦
Qin Shihuang 秦始皇
Qing 清
qinglü 青綠
qingtong 青銅
qishou 麒首
qu 瞿
Qu Wanli 屈萬里
Qu Xiangbu 瞿相圃
Quanzhou 泉州
Qufu 曲阜

ren (human) 人
Renmin yingxiong jinian bei 人民英雄記念碑
Rongbao Zhai 榮寶齋
rongbu 絨布
rou 肉
Ruan Yuan 阮元
Ruan Wenda Gong 阮文達公
Rui Zong 睿宗

Saluzi 颯露紫
San Dai 三代
San lao bei 三老碑
San (shi) pan 散 (氏) 盤
San Zang 三藏
San zi shijing 三字石經

sang shu 桑樹
sanya 三椏
sanye biao (three-leaf mount) 三頁裱
sanye biao (scattered-leaves mount) 散葉裱
Shang shu (youcheng) 尚書 (右丞)
Shang(-Yin) 商 (殷)
Shanggu Zhai 賞古齋
Shanyou 山右
shanzha (zi) 山楂 (子)
Shanzuo 山左
shao 紹
shasuo mu 杉杪木
Sheli Ta 舍利塔
Shenlong 神龍
shi (instead of *jing*) 溼
Shigu (wen) 石鼓 (文)
Shihuang (di) 始皇 (帝)
Shijing Shan 石經山
shike 石刻
Shilu suo cang gu bingqi diyi zu 適廬所藏古兵器 第一組
shiming 室名
shimo 石墨
shizhu 石柱
Shodō Hakubutsukan 書道博物館
shou 壽
shoucangjia 收藏家
shuiyin 水印
Shunzhi 順治
shuqian 書籤
si bao 四寶
Sima Guang 司馬光
Song You Si cang *Lanting* di wushier ben 宋游似藏蘭亭第五十二本
Songxue (daoren) 松雪 (道人)
Songxue shu *Daode jing* 松雪書道德經
Su Dongpo 蘇東坡
Su Shi 蘇軾
Su Yinghui 蘇瑩輝
Sui 隋
sumi 墨
suoyi biao 蓑衣裱

Tai Hang 太行
Tai Shan (*keshi*) 泰山 (刻石)
Taian 太安
Taichang 太常

Taihe (reign) 太和
Taihe County 泰和
Taiping Si 太平寺
taitouzi 擡頭字
Taiwan Wenxian Weiyuanhui 臺灣文獻委員會
Taiwudi 太武帝
Taiyue 太樂
Taizong 太宗
Tang 唐
Tang Ouyang Xun Huadu Si Yong Chan shi taming 唐歐陽詢化度寺邕禪師塔銘
Tangyin Zhang Qian biao (song) 蕩陰張遷表 (頌)
tanmu 檀木
tao 套
taotie 饕餮
Tchen Hoshien 陳和銑
Telepiao 特革驃
tian 天
tianqing jinyin (duan) 天青金銀 (緞)
Tie Xue 帖學
tsurigane zumi 釣鐘墨
tu 圖
tuipeng shi 推篷式
tuo 橐
Tuoli 坨里
Tuoluoni jing (chuang) 陀羅尼經 (幢)
tuzhu 土硃

Umehara, Sueji 梅原末治

Wanfo Tang 萬佛堂
Wang Chuan tu 輞川圖
Wang Chuan zhenji 輞川真蹟
Wang Liuji 汪六吉
Wang Wei 王維
Wang Xianzhi 王獻之
Wang Xiting 汪郎亭
Wang Xizhi 王羲之
Wei (river) 渭
Wei County 淮縣
Wei (dynasty) 魏
Wei Dan 韋誕
Wei Wendi 魏文帝
wen 紋
Wende 文德
Weng Fanggang 翁方綱
wenli 紋理
Wenquan ming 溫泉銘
Wu (surname, state, region) 吳
Wu (surname; shrine) 武
Wu Daozi 吳道子
Wu Kangfu 吳康甫
Wu Liang (Ci) 武梁 (祠)
Wu Rongguang 吳榮光
wu wang zai Ju 毋忘在莒
Wumen 吳門
Wutai Shan 五台山
wuwu 戊午

xi 洗
xia (box) 匣
Xia (dynasty) 夏
Xiacheng bei 夏承碑
xian (character, Zhang Qian inscription) 先
xian (county) 縣
Xi'an 西安
xian(feng) zhuang 線 (縫) 裝
xiang (village) 鄉
xiang (box) 箱
xiang nanmu 香楠木
xiangmo 香墨
Xiangtang Shan 響堂山
xianke 線刻
Xianning 咸寧
xianzhuang 線裝
Xiao Liang 蕭梁
Xiaotang Shan 孝堂山
xiaoxue 小學
xiaozhuan 小篆
Xiding shouta jinshi wenzi 希丁手拓金石文字
Xie Jin 解縉
Xilengqiao 西冷橋
Xilengyinshe 西冷印社
Xin'an(zhen) 新安 (鎮)
Xinchang 新昌
xing (shu) 行 (書)
Xingqing Gong 興慶宮
Xiping 熹平
Xixia 西夏
Xixia Shan 棲霞山
Xu Bing 徐冰
Xuan Zang 玄奘

Xuancheng 宣城
Xuande 宣德
xuanfeng (zhe) ye 旋風 (摺) 葉
xuanfeng zhuang 旋風裝
Xuanzong 玄宗
Xuetang cang San Dai qi 學堂藏三代器

Yan Lu Gong Duobao Ta bei 顏魯公多寶塔碑
Yan Zhenqing 顏真卿
yang 陽
Yang Shen 楊慎
yangfou 陽浮
Yanghu County 陽湖縣
yangwen 陽文
Yanjing 燕京
yanmei 煙煤
yantai (inkstone) 硯台
Yantai (place) 煙台
Yanyou 延祐
Yao Jinxiu 姚金緒
yaqian 牙簽
ye 葉
Ye Menglong 葉夢龍
ye shanzha 野山楂
Yelikewen (jiao) 也里可溫 (教)
yi (ewer) 匜
Yi li 儀禮
Yi Shan (bei, keshi) 嶧山 (碑, 刻石)
Yi zi shijing 一字石經
Yifeng tang mulu 藝風堂目錄
Yijin Zhai (yin) 詒晉齊 (印)
yin 印
yin shui, si yuan 飲水思源
yingzhen 應真
yinni 印泥
yinse 印色
yinwen zhengzi 陰文正字
yinyang 陰陽
yinzhu 銀硃
Yizhou 義州
Yonghui 永徽
Yongle 永樂
Yongxing (seal) 永瑆
Yongxing (Yu Shinan) 永興
you (wine jar) 卣
You Han Tai Shan duwei Kong jun zhi ming 有漢泰山都尉孔君之銘
You Si 遊似
youni 油泥
youyan mo 油煙墨
Yu (emperor) 禹
yu (character) 于
Yu bei 禹碑
Yu Boshi Fuzi Miaotang bei 虞伯施夫子廟堂碑
Yu Shinan 虞世南
Yu Yongxing Fuzi Miaotang bei 虞永興夫子廟堂碑
Yuan (dynasty, dollar) 元
yuan (*ge*, blade) 援
Yuandi 元帝
yuansi bai 圓絲帛
Yuanyou 元祐
yue 約
Yuelu Shan 嶽麓山
Yuelu Shuyuan 嶽麓書院
Yufo An 玉佛庵
Yungang (shiku) 雲岡 (石窟)
Yunju Si 雲居寺
Yurinkan 有鄰館

zaomu 棗目
zhanbao 氈包
zhang 丈
Zhang Qian (Former Han) 張騫
Zhang Qian (Later Han) 張遷
Zhang Qian (bei, biao) 張遷 (碑, 表)
Zhang Shuwei 張叔未
Zhang Tingqi 張廷齊
Zhang Xuan 張宣
Zhang Yanji 張延濟
Zhang Yanyuan 張顏遠
Zhang Zhidong 張之洞
Zhao Kuan bei 趙寬碑
Zhao Mengfu 趙孟頫
Zhao Song 趙宋
Zhaoling shima 朝陵石馬
Zhe 淛
zheben (folded edition) 摺本
zheben (pleated edition) 褶本
zhebian 折邊

zhen (genuine, script) 真
zheng (script, front) 正
zheng (top of *zhong*-bell) 鉦
Zheng Chenggong 鄭成功
Zheng Wenbao 鄭文寶
zhengbiao(ben) 整裱 (本)
zhengmian 正面
Zhenguan 真觀
zhengzhuang (ben) 整裝 (本)
Zhenzong 真宗
zhi (goblet) 卮
zhi (wrapper) 帙
zhi (paper) 紙
zhi (tankard) 觶
zhifu (keshi) 之(芝)罘(刻石)
zhiyuan 直院
zhong (wine vessel) 鍾
zhong (bell) 鐘
Zhong fu fu dun 仲凫父敦
Zhong Kui 鍾馗
Zhongnan Shan 終南山
Zhongnanzhen 終南鎮
Zhongyuan 中原
Zhou (surname, dynasty) 周
Zhou Kangyuan 周康元
Zhou Shuren 周樹人
Zhou Xiding 周希丁
Zhou yi 周易
zhu (bamboo) 竹
zhu (red) 朱
zhu (vermilion) 硃
zhu (scroll roller) 軸
zhuan 篆
zhuan'e 篆額
zhuanghuang 裝潢
Zhucheng County 諸城縣
zhusha 硃沙
zi (courtesy name) 字
zonglü 椶櫚
zongsao 椶掃
zongshua 椶刷
Zou Shan ji 鄒山記
zouzhen 走針
zun 尊

Notes

1 / HISTORY AND FUNCTIONS OF RUBBINGS

1. Rong Geng, *Shang Zhou yiqi tongkao*, 1:176; Xu Shen, *Shuowen jiezi*, 6a.

2. For *li* and *bafen*, see Nakata, *Chūgoku no bijitsu*, 17; Nakata, *A History of the Art of China*, 113. Brashier, "Evoking the Ancestor," 26, calls Cai "the most famous of the Eastern Han stele writers."

3. Fan Ye, *Hou Han shu*, 90 *xia*: 8b–9a; Weng Fanggang, *Liang Han jinshi ji*, 1:32b–34a. Only fragments of the original remain. For a description and red rubbing of a fragment of the *Zhou yi*, see Shaanxi Provincial Museum, *Xi'an Beilin shufa yishu*, 26–27. For the use of diacritics to mark terms for rubbings and related copying methods, see the initial comments on appendix 2, this volume.

4. Fang Yizhi, *Tongya*, 31:11b; Sun Yuxiu, *Zhongguo diaoban yuanliu kao*, 1; Gerhard Pommeranz-Liedtke, *Die Weisheit der Kunst*, 5.

5. Cheng Dachang, *Yanfan lu*, 7:6a. "Embellish," "adorn" are other meanings of *la*, wax.

6. Qu Wanli and Chang Bide, *Guoshu banbenxue yaolüe*, 16. Su Yinghui, "Tushuguan cang tapian de bianmu gongzuo" (hereafter, "Tapian de bianmu"), 25, concurs that *mo*[b]*xie* does not mean *mo*[a]*ta*[c], common for "rubbing" in Fang's time.

7. Li Shuhua, "Yinzhang yu mota de qiyuan ji qi duiyu diaoban yinshua faming de yingxiang" (hereafter, "Yinzhang yu mota"), 114; Carter, *The Invention of Printing*, 1st ed., 13; Carter, *The Invention of Printing*, 2nd ed., 13, 20.

8. Tsien, *Written on Bamboo and Silk*, 2nd ed., 93; Tsien, *Zhongguo gudai shu shi*, 80. Tsien, *Paper and Printing*, 8, traces rubbings "back to the 6th century or earlier in China"; see also 144.

9. Wei Zheng, *Sui shu*, 32:35a, 36b; Qu Wanli and Chang Bide, *Guoshu banbenxue yaolüe*, 17.

10. Carter, *The Invention of Printing*, 1st ed., 197; Carter, *The Invention of Printing*, 2nd ed., 23.

11. Wang Chi-chen, *Reproductions of Chinese Rubbings*, 2. Wang gives alternative romanizations of *ta* and *tuo*, but with no characters. He uses *ta*[a] on the cover.

12. Early sources vary: On *ta*[b], see *Tang liudian*, 8:3a, 9, 11a, passim; Liu Xu et al., *Jiu Tang shu*, 43, 36a, passim; Ouyang Xiu, *Xin Tang shu*, 47:5b, 49:13b, passim. On *ta*[c], see *Tang liudian*, 8:17b; Sang Shichang, *Lanting kao*, *CSJC*, part 1, 3:17b, passim; Tu Long, *Kaopan yushi*, *CSJC*, part 1, 3:26a–b. Sima Zhen, *Shiji suoyin*, 3:2b, uses *dade . . . beiwen*, "strike-obtain a tablet inscription." Li Shuhua, "The Early Development of Seals and Rubbings" (hereafter, "Seals and Rubbings"), 80, gives "rubbing makers" for *tashu shou*; Tsien, *Written on Bamboo and Silk*, 2nd ed., 94, renders *tashu shou* as "technicians in charge of squeezing inscriptions." Nakata, *Chūgoku shoronshū*, 265–66, gives *tashu ren* and *tashu shou* (*ta*[b]) as ink "copyists," as cited by Harrist, "Copies, All the Way Down," 183. Several reasons favor "rubbing makers." First, historical and modern Chinese sources, including the Beijing Library, favor that interpretation, with some sources referring to paper, ink, and striking/hammering, as do Chinese dictionaries (*Cihai*, *Kangxi zidian*) and Japanese dictionaries (*Daijiten*, *Kenkyusha's New Japanese-English Dictionary*). Second, it is unlikely that the Chinese would have trusted "copyists" to reproduce valued texts, especially calligraphic texts. After all, along with

efficiency, accuracy was a spur for the invention of the technique. Rubbing still is the preferred method of accurately and rapidly reproducing stone texts. Third, Hucker, *A Dictionary of Official Titles in Imperial China*, 475, uses "rubbing maker."

13. Tsien, *Written on Bamboo and Silk*, 1st ed., 93; Tsien, *Zhongguo gudai shu shi*, 80. Tsien initially differentiated "true paper" (*zhi*) from earlier "quasi-paper" (*jiazhi*). See Tsien, *Zhongguo gudai shu shi*, 127 n. 6; Tsien, *Written on Bamboo and Silk*, 2nd ed., 133, and 145 n. 2, where he calls both *zhi* "paper."

14. Tsien, *Written on Bamboo and Silk*, 2nd ed., 150; Tsien, *Zhongguo gudai shu shi*, 131. The availability of paper is also noted by Li Shuhua, "Seals and Rubbings," 77; see also Li Shuhua, "Yinzhang yu mota," 115.

15. Wang Guowei, "Shuowen suowei guwen shuo," 7:6a.

16. Li Shuhua, "Seals and Rubbings," 77; Li Shuhua, "Yinzhang yu mota," 115.

17. For a comprehensive account of the progresses, see Kern, *The Stele Inscriptions of Ch'in Shih-huang*, 106–15. See also Brashier, "Evoking the Ancestor," 48 n. 9, 64–66. For locations of the stones, see the map on pp. 4–5, this volume; see also *Zhongguo lishi dituji*, vol. 2 (Qin, Han), maps 7, 10, 12.

18. The reference to cutting the Yi Shan stone is in Fan Ye, *Hou Han shu*, 90: 3429 (*Lu guo*) and 3430 n. 6.

19. Kern, *Stele Inscriptions of Ch'in Shih-huang*, 13–14.

20. *Beijing Tushuguan cang Zhongguo lidai shike taben huibian* (hereafter, *Beijing tushuguan cang taben*), 1:8. Many traditional sources list the Yi Shan stone, such as Tu Long, *Kaopan yushi*, *CSJC*, part 1:3.

21. Feng Yan, *Feng shi wenjian ji*, 8:2b, cites the *Zou shan ji*, which I could not identify, and whose existence Tsuen-hsuin Tsien has questioned. The title appears in "Zou Shan," *Zhongguo gujin diming dacidian*, 1070.

22. Sima Guang, *Zizhi tongjian*, 125:21a; Shaanxi Provincial Museum, *Xi'an Beilin shufa yishu*, 20.

23. Feng Yan, *Feng shi wenjian ji*, 8:2b.

24. One can point to a similar negative reaction by the townspeople of Cushing, Maine. In an article about Andrew Wyeth that appeared in the *Milwaukee Journal*, 1 July 1974, the artist was quoted as having said that he might leave Maine permanently "because of the popularity—or notoriety—of 'Christina's house' . . . that is attracting 30,000 visitors a year. . . . The natives of this isolated village are unhappy about the hordes of visitors who flood the area every summer."

25. See Shaanxi Provincial Museum, *Shaanxi Sheng Bowuguan*, plates 152–53, and explanations, 219.

26. Li Shuhua, "Yinzhang yu mota," 115; Rong Geng, "Qin shihuang keshi kao," 131.

27. Du Fu, "Li chao bafen xiaozhuan ge," 7:14 (Arabic, 1281); Li Shuhua, "Yinzhang yu mota," 115–16; Rong Geng, "Qin shihuang keshi kao," 130–31; Ye Changchi, *Yu shi*, 1:1.

28. Li Shuhua, "Yinzhang yu mota," 119.

29. Ibid., 115.

30. Wei Zheng, *Sui shu*, 32, passim in the registry of classics (*jingji zhi*), beginning on 1 (Arabic, 468).

31. Li Shuhua, "Seals and Rubbings," 79; Qu Wanli and Chang Bide, *Guoshu banbenxue yaolüe*, 16; Su Yinghui, "Tapian de bianmu," 25; Tsien, *Written on Bamboo and Silk*, 2nd ed., 93–94; Tsien, *Zhongguo gudai shu shi*, 80.

32. Qu Wanli and Chang Bide, *Guoshu banbenxue yaolüe*, 16.

33. Wei Zheng, *Sui shu*, 32:36 (Arabic, 485).

34. Qu Wanli and Chang Bide, *Guoshu banbenxue yaolüe*, 17.

35. Li Shuhua, "Seals and Rubbings," 79.

36. Tsien, *Written on Bamboo and Silk*, 2nd ed., 93–94; Tsien, *Zhongguo gudai shu shi*, 50.

37. Su Yinghui, "Tapian de bianmu," 25.

38. Luo Zhenyu, "Mogaoku shishi milu," 33.

39. Musées Nationaux, *Manuscrits et Peintures de Touen-houang*, 22, describes it as "the oldest known rubbing" and notes that "the Chinese call it the 'Emperor of rubbings.'" Pelliot, *Les débuts de l'imprimerie en Chine*, reads as follows: "4508. Incomplete rubbing . . . of a rhymed composition composed and handwritten in the VIIth century by . . . Tai-tsong of the Tang. Stone missing since the Sung. . . . Tai-tsong died at the beginning of 649, and in 654, someone noted at the end of our rubbing that he had examined it that very year. Very valuable. *Preserve.*" See also Luo Zhenyu, "Mogaoku shishi milu," 1. For the site, see "*Qianfo Dong*" and "*Dunhuang shishi*," *Zhongguo gujin diming dacidian*, 53 and 898, and the provincial atlas *Zhongguo renmin gongheguo fensheng dituji*, 101.

40. Luo Zhenyu, "Mogaoku shishi milu," 31.

41. Li Shuhua, "Yinzhang yu mota," 116, gives the year as 684; Li Shuhua, "Seals and Rubbings," 81, gives the year as 654, as do other sources. Harrist, "Record of the Eulogy on Mt. Tai," 72, gives 648 as the year of the stele's erection.

42. Weng Kaiyun, "'Huadu si bei yanjiu," 14. For Zhongnan Shan, see *Zhongguo lishi dituji*, 6:19, about 34'08" north/108'20" east. See Zhongnan in *Zhongguo gujin diming dacidian*, 103, and modern Zhongnanzhen in *Zhongguo renmin gongheguo fensheng dituji*, 94.

43. Weng Kaiyun, "'Huadu Si bei yanjiu," 14. Weng seems to be on poor ground in citing the *Chunyu ji*. Dr. Ming Sun Poon of the Asian Section at the Library of Congress and Ms. Yue Shu of the Freer-Sackler Library confirmed that there is no *Chunyu ji*, only *Chunyu zashu*. *Chunyu* is one of Xie Jin's alternative names (*bieming*).

44. See Stein, *Serindia*, 2:918 (text), 4:169 (plates). See also Giles, *Descriptive Catalogue of Chinese Manuscripts from Tunhuang in the British Museum*, 194, no. 6182: "*T'ang ou yang hsün hua tu ssu yung ch'an shih t'a ming* [Tang ouyang xun huadu si yong chan shi taming]. Eulogistic inscription relating to the Dhyana master Yung of the Hua-tu monastery, from the calligraphy of Ou-yang Hsün (557–645 C.E.). 5 leaves of a booklet of ink-rubbings, 12 x 8.5 cm. Two more leaves are in the Paris collection [of Pelliot]." There is a wealth of material on Dunhuang in Chinese, Japanese, and Western languages. For a scholarly study, see Su Yinghui, *Dunhuang xue gaiyao*; for a popular book, see Vincent, *The Sacred Oasis*; and for an absorbing historical novel that describes the turbulent times in the eleventh century when the Tangut Xixia ravaged the northwest, occasioning the walling of the Buddhist manuscripts, rubbings, and other treasures, see Yasushi Inoue, *Tunhuang*.

45. See Pelliot, *Les débuts de l'imprimerie en Chine*: "4510. Fragment of a rubbing of the celebrated inscription of Houa-tou- Ssu . . . , handwritten by Nyeou Yang Siun [Ouyang Xun] in the 1st half of the VIIth century. This rubbing was made in the Tang. Three or four [five] other leaves of the same rubbing were found in the manuscripts of Sir Aurel Stein at the British Museum. . . . *Preserve.*" See Luo Zhenyu, "Mogaoku shishi milu," 32.

46. Pelliot, *Les débuts de l'imprimerie en Chine*. Luo Zhenyu, "Mogaoku shishi milu," 32. Conservative scholars question a Tang date, as did Li Shuhua, oral communication, 14 July 1960.

47. Returning from Taiwan in 1960, the author studied the finds at the Bibliothèque Nationale and the British Museum. Limited time, money, and equipment allowed only macro observations. The Dunhuang papers mainly were composed of the woody fibers of the paper mulberry tree (*Broussonetia Papyrifera*) and other plants, along with rags, but none from rags only. Giles, *Six Centuries at Dunhuang*, 13, states that "the paper of even the earliest rolls is of wonderfully good quality"; see

also Giles, *Descriptive Catalogue of the Chinese Manuscripts in the British Museum*, xi, where the author notes that "even the earliest fifth-century papers . . . are of remarkably good quality."

48. Zhou Jiazhou, *Zhuanghuang zhi*, *CSJC*, 1563:7.

49. K. B. Gardner, former keeper, British Museum, oral communication, 28 January 1970.

50. Stein, *Serindia*, 2:918.

51. Carter, *The Invention of Printing*, 1st ed., 40; Carter, *The Invention of Printing*, 2nd ed., 55.

52. Luo Zhenyu, "Mogaoku shishi milu," 32. See also Pelliot, *Les débuts de l'imprimerie en Chine*, where the "original rubbing" (4503) is said to have been "made in the Tang. The stones have been missing since the Northern Sung."

53. Su Yinghui, "Tapian de bianmu," 25.

54. Wang Chang, *Jinshi cuibian*, 50 (Tang, 10):1a (Arabic, 867) lists the stone as *Fang Xuanling bei*, as does Zhu Feng, *Yongzhou jinshi ji*, 1a. Sun Xingyan and Xing Zhu, *Huanyu fangbei lu*, 3:42, list it as *Liang Wenzhao Gong Fang Xuanling bei*.

55. Wang Chang, *Jinshi cuibian*, 41 (Tang, 1):16a (Arabic, 730) lists it as *Kongzi miaotang zhi bei*. Sun Xingyuan and Xing Zhu, *Huanyu fangbei lu*, 3:1a, give it as *Kongzi miaotang bei*; Su Yinghui, "Tapian de bianmu," 25, gives it as *Yu Boshi Fuzi miaotang bei*; and Luo Zhenyu, "Mogaoku shishi milu," 33, gives it as *Yu Yongxing Fuzi miaotang bei*. *Boshi* was Yu's personal name; *Yongxing*, his enfeoffment title.

56. Luo Zhenyu, "Mogaoku shishi milu," 33. *Jingchuang*, literally "scripture streamers," are multisided stone pillars, commonly octagonal, inscribed with the Buddha's name or *dharani* incantations. Colored cloth streamers often decorate the pillars, thus their name.

57. Ibid.

58. Ibid. Dong Juewei, "Zeyang tabei," part 1, 41, refers to "layered ink" (*chongmo*) as similar to *wujinta*, "black-gold rubbing."

59. *Tang liudian*, 8: 17b.

60. Ibid., 9:11a.

61. Ibid., 26:3a.

62. Liu Xu et al., *Jiu Tang shu*, 43: 36a, 40a; Ouyang Xiu, *Xin Tang shu*, 47:5b, 8b, and 49 *shang*:13b.

63. Sima Zhen, *Shiji suoyin*, 8:1b; Dou Ji, "Shushu fu," 6.

64. Qu Wanli and Chang Bide, *Guoshu banbenxue yaolüe* 17; Su Yinghui, "Tapian de bianmu," 25.

65. Ennin, "Nittō guhō junrei gyōki," 3:115; Ennin, *Ennin's Diary*, 254–55; see also Reischauer, *Ennin's Travels in Tang China*, 202, for a free account.

66. Luo Zhenyu, "Mogaoku shishi milu," 33. See also Qu Wanli and Chang Bide, *Guoshu banbenxue yaolüe*, 17, and Su Yinghui, "Tapian de bianmu," 25.

67. Li Shuhua, "Yinzhang yu mota," 117; Li Shuhua, "Seals and Rubbings," 80.

68. Li Shuhua, "Yinzhang yu mota," 117. This substitution was most active with stone-cut calligraphy, which for convenience was wood-cut in positive intaglio (*yinwen zhengzhi*) for rubbing. See also Tsien, *Written on Bamboo and Silk*, 2nd ed., 95; Tsien, *Zhongguo gudai shu shi*, 81.

69. Three terms are helpful in referring to materials susceptible to rubbing. *Substance* connotes the material of an object, such as bronze or stone; *object* refers to an artifact, such as a vessel or stele; and *subject* speaks of intellectual or aesthetic content, such as an inscription or design.

70. Brashier, "Evoking the Ancestor," 50, refers to the indestructible nature of "metal and stone" in preserving memory and immortality. He describes (54) the decline of bronzes in the Han and the growing importance of steles and iron as commemorative materials.

71. Chinese scholars declare that Longmen and Yungang, in the realm of art, and Dunhuang and the Beilin, in that of books, manuscripts, and inscriptions, are China's *baoku*, "treasure houses."

72. *Yunju Si Shijing Shan jianjie*, 3. The main corpus of engravings was cut over a period of five centuries, beginning with the monk Jingwan (d. 639 C.E.). See the comprehensive study by Ledderose, "Thunder Sound Cave," 255, which notes that Jingwan's motivation was concern about *mofa* and preserving the sacred texts. See also Tsien, *Written on Bamboo and Silk*, 2nd ed., 85, 87–88; Tsien, *Zhongguo gudai shu shi*, 73; Tsien, *Paper and Printing*, 28–29, 141.

73. Li Shuhua, "Yinzhang yu mota" 114; Li Shuhua, "Seals and Rubbings," 74. Tsiang, "Monumentalization of Buddhist Texts in the Northern Qi Dynasty," 254, notes that the engraving of sutras predates the mid-sixth-century formulation of the *mofa* doctrine.

74. Qu Wanli and Chang Bide, *Guoshu banbenxue yaolüe*, 17. Su Yinghui, "Tapian de bianmu," 25, also refers to this situation.

75. Li Shuhua, "Seals and Rubbings," 75, lists early engravings of the *Daode jing*; see also Li Shuhua, "Yinzhang yu mota," 114.

76. Wei Zheng, *Sui shu*, 32:35a.

77. Feng, *Feng shi wenjian ji*, 8:2b.

78. Ibid. Dou Ji, "Shushu fu"; Du Fu, "Li Chao bafen xiaozhuan ge," 7:14 (Arabic, 1281); Ye Changchi, *Yu shi*, 1:1; Li Shuhua, "Yinzhang yu mota," 115–16; Li Shuhua, "Seals and Rubbings," 77–78.

79. Tsien, *Written on Bamboo and Silk*, 1st ed., 89; Tsien, *Written on Bamboo and Silk*, 2nd ed., 95; Tsien, *Zhongguo gudai shu shi*, 81.

80. Ledderose, *Mi Fu and the Classical Tradition of Chinese Calligraphy*, 14. After a sixteen-year pilgrimage to Magadha, a central Indian kingdom and Buddhist center, Xuan Zang returned to China in 645 with a great number of Buddhist manuscripts. Taizong (r. 626–649) bestowed on him the honorific *San Zang*, alluding to the three groups of Buddhist writings: *jing*, *lü*, and *lun* (classics, law, and discourses).

81. Carter, *The Invention of Printing*, 1st ed., 14–15; Carter, *The Invention of Printing*, 2nd ed., 21–22.

82. Carter, *The Invention of Printing*, 1st ed., 13; Carter, *The Invention of Printing*, 2nd ed., 20.

83. Chen Yuanlong, *Gezhi jingyuan*, 39:6a–11b; Carter, *The Invention of Printing*, 1st ed., 15, 19; Carter, *The Invention of Printing*, 2nd ed., 22, 25.

84. Ching, Harrist, and Liu, "The Embodied Image."

85. Ouyang Xiu, *Jigu lu*, 4:9a–b. I use the translation in Carter, *The Invention of Printing*, 2nd ed., 24, which differs slightly from that found in Carter, *The Invention of Printing*, 1st ed., 198. Cao Zhao, *Gegu yaolun*, 3:1a–b, describes the collection as being of ten books (*juan*). Bai Qianshen, "The Artistic and Intellectual Dimensions of Chinese Calligraphy Rubbings," 84, states that the calligraphies were "to be engraved on wooden blocks."

86. Carter, *The Invention of Printing*, 2nd ed., 24–25 n. 13; this translation differs slightly from the one in Carter, *The Invention of Printing*, 1st ed., 198–99 n. 9. Chengxin Tang, "Hall of the Pure Heart," was where Li Bian, the founder of the Southern Tang (937–975) and a lover of paintings, kept his favorite paper, which took the name of the hall. The paper was fine, thin, strong, and "as smooth as the skin of a young maid" (*Free China Weekly*, 17 August 1980). See also "Li Bian" and "Nan Tang," in the *Cihai* dictionary.

87. Carter, *The Invention of Printing*, 1st ed., 15; Carter, *The Invention of Printing*, 2nd ed., 22.

88. Carter, *The Invention of Printing*, 1st ed., 15; Carter, *The Invention of Printing*, 2nd ed., 22. Liao Yingzhong, a renowned Southern Song artisan, recut and rubbed the *Chunhua Ge tie*. His work was hand-copied (*lin*) by Dong Qichang, a Ming calligrapher, with a photolithographic edition in 1931. See Liao Yingzhong, *Chunhua Ge mige fatie*.

89. Nakata, "Ni Ō no teki," *Chūgoku no bujitsu*, 2:123; Nakata, "The Masterpieces of Wang Xizhi and Wang Xianzhi," *A History of the Art of China*, 2:118.

90. Bai Qianshen, "The Artistic and Intellectual Dimensions of Chinese Calligraphy Rubbings," 84–85.

91. Ibid., 84.

92. Tsien, *Written on Bamboo and Silk*, 2nd ed., 69; Tsien, *Zhongguo gudai shu shi*, 59.

93. Bai Qianshen, "The Artistic and Intellectual Dimensions of Chinese Calligraphy Rubbings," 85–86. The generic meaning of *jin* is "metal," but in the context of "metal-and-stone studies," *jinshi xue*, the term *jin* essentially connotes the pre-Han ritual bronzes and their inscriptions, and *shi* connotes Qin, Han, and post-Han stone inscriptions. In modern times, the term for "bronze" is *qingtong*.

94. Su Yinghui, "Tapian de bianmu," 26. See also Tao Hongjing, *Daojian lu*; Yu Li, *Ding lu*.

95. Tsien, *Written on Bamboo and Silk*, 2nd ed., 95; Tsien, *Zhongguo gudai shu shi*, 81.

96. Su Yinghui, "Tapian de bianmu," 25.

97. Ibid. See also Wang Guowei, "Shuowen suowei guwen shuo," 7:6a.

98. Zhai Qinian, *Zhou shi*, *CSJC*, *juan shang*:10.

99. Su Yinghui, "Tapian de bianmu" 25. Brashier, "Evoking the Ancestor," 51, notes that *jinshi* was a pre-Han term, widely used in the Han for "indestructible" and only much later for "epigraphy."

100. Rong Geng, *Shang Zhou yiqi tongkao*, 1:176. Other books in this category include an early-twelfth-century work by Wang Fu, *Xuanhe bogu tulu*; a mid-twelfth-century work by Xue Shanggong, *Lidai zhongding yiqi kuanshi fatie*; and a Song-era work by Wang Qiu, *Xiaotang jigu lu*.

101. Bai Qianshen, "The Artistic and Intellectual Dimensions of Chinese Calligraphy Rubbings," 86.

102. The author spent a vividly remembered 1949 backpacking Easter holiday at Baiyun Dong. Said to date from the Song, the Daoist temple floated serenely on a cliff 400 meters above the Yellow Sea. Qing references, with maps, include You Shuxiao and Li Yuanzheng, *Jimo Xian zhi*, 1:5b and 12:4b, and Lin Puzan, *Jimo Xian zhi*, 12:3 (text), 12:4 (illustrations). For a modern reference to the temple, still active, and to the Jin Shan sect, see Yin Zhihong, *Qingdao zhinan*, 47, 176. *Moyai* were being cut at Baiyun Dong in 1949, as they were at Buddhist Jiao Shan, Zhenjiang, in 1993. As for the *ya* character in *Xinhua zidian*, an alternative pronunciation is *moya*; and as for the *yai* character in *Cihai*, the traditional pronunciation is *moyai*. One sees both spellings, with *moya* used by Tsien, passim, and *moyai* used by Nakata, *A History of the Art of China*, 113, and by Harrist, "Record of the Eulogy on Mt. Tai," 68, passim. My Taiwan informants used *moyai*.

103. Among Western collectors of calligraphs, including rubbings, Robert Hatfield Ellsworth and John B. Elliot are prominent. See Bai Qianshen, "The Artistic and Intellectual Dimensions of Chinese Calligraphy Rubbings," and Ching, Harrist, and Liu, "The Embodied Image."

104. Rong Geng, *Shang Zhou yiqi tongkao*, 1:176.

105. For a list of materials susceptible to rubbing, see Su Yinghui, "Tapian de bianmu," 26–27.

106. Provincial, county, and local museums and libraries hold rubbings relating to their jurisdictions. Temples, many now serving as museums, such as the Dai Temple (Dai Miao) in Taian, also have collections.

2 / ORCHID ROOT AND RHINOCEROS-TAIL HAIR

1. Sang Shen, "Quanxing ta zhi chuangcheng yu liubian," 52.

2. Carter, *The Invention of Printing*, 1st ed., 16; Carter, *The Invention of Printing*, 2nd ed., 23; Tsien, *Written on Bamboo and Silk*, 1st ed., 87; Tsien, *Zhongguo gudai shu shi*, 79.

3. Luo Zhenyu, "Mogaoku shishi milu,"33.

4. Three Qing accounts are basic. Wu Shifen, *Jinshi huimu fenbian*, 1a–b, describes materials and techniques, emphasizing the rubbing of steles. The fullest and most cited account, with emphasis on rubbing bronzes, is Chen Jieqi, *Chuangu bielu*. Ye Changchi, *Yu shi*, informs more broadly and deeply about historical stone inscriptions, including terms, types, and forms; famous calligraphers; types of rubbings and rubbing "editions"; and provincial variations in papers and inks (see also Ye Changchi, *Yakuchū goseki*, annotated Japanese translation, including an index and many illustrations). Four recent titles are instructive. Jiang Xuanyi, "Mota shu," details materials and methods for rubbing a wide range of objects. Rong Geng, *Shang Zhou yiqi tongkao*, addresses mainly the ancient bronzes; he appreciably amplifies Chen Jieqi's cryptic earlier text. Jun Yu, "Tan taben," emphasizes techniques of copying fine shell-and-bone inscriptions. Dong Juewei, "Zeyang tabei," details materials and methods for rubbing steles and cliff-cut inscriptions. See also Starr, "Old Stones and Black Tigers in Frederick County"; McCarthy, "Secrets Carved in Stone."

5. Tsien, *Paper and Printing*, comprehensively treats paper in China—history and diffusion, materials and manufacture, roles and uses. See also Tsien, *Written on Bamboo and Silk*, 1st ed.; Tsien, *Written on Bamboo and Silk*, 2nd ed.; and Tsien, *Zhongguo shuji zhimo ji yinshua shi lunwenji*. Su Yijian (Song), *Wenfang sipu*, informs about paper and medieval papermaking materials and methods. See also the account of papermaking in Du Halde, *Description Géographique, Historique, Chronologique, Politique, et Physique de l'Empire de la Chine*, 2:288f, and in Du Halde, *The General History of China*, 2:418f. Song Yingxing, *Tiangong kaiwu*, 217–25, describes Ming papermaking materials and methods; see also Song Yingxing, *T'ien-kung K'ai-wu: Chinese Technology in the Seventeenth Century*. Both Tsien, *Paper and Printing*, 68–73, and Li Ch'iao-p'ing, *The Chemical Arts of Old China*, draw on Song. Chen Jieqi, *Chuangu bielu*, focuses on contemporary rubbing papers, and Jiang Xuanyi, "Mota shu," describes modern papers and their provincial variants. For a general history of Chinese papermaking materials, see Tsien, "Raw Materials for Old Papermaking in China"; Tsien, *Paper and Printing*, 52–64; Tsien, *Zhongguo shuji zhimo ji yinshua shi lunwenji*, 57–66; Tsien, *Written on Bamboo and Silk*, 1st ed., 148–51; and Tsien, *Written on Bamboo and Silk*, 2nd ed., 161–65. For modern papermaking in China and other Asian countries, see Hunter, *A Papermaking Pilgrimage to Japan, Korea and China*, and Hunter, *Papermaking: The History and Technique of an Ancient Craft*. Van Gulik, *Chinese Pictorial Art As Viewed by the Connoisseur*, appendix V, includes samples of common Chinese and Japanese papers.

6. Le Compte, *Memoirs and Observations*, 191. *Papermaking in China* (ca. 1930–1940), an early color film, shows peasants making paper by hand; another color film, *Aspects of Taiwan's Handmade Paper Industry* (1972) illustrates materials, equipment, and methods.

7. Du Halde, *Description Géographique, Historique, Chronologique, Politique, et Physique de l'Empire de la Chine*, 2:288–89.

8. Chen Jieqi, *Chuangu bielu*, 1b.

9. Wang Chi-chen, *Reproductions of Chinese Rubbings Taken from Inscriptions Cut in Stone, Wood, and Also from Bronzes, Monuments and Other Bas-reliefs*, 3–4 (hereafter, *Reproductions*).

10. The *Chunhua Ge tie* is cited endlessly in Chinese sources, which invariably mention Chengxin Tang paper and Li Tinggui ink for rubbing the model. See Cao Zhao, *Gegu yaolun*, 3:1a–b. Chengxin Tang paper, from the "Hall of the Pure Heart," is said to be named from the building where Lie Zu (Li Bian), king of the Southern Tang (937–975), kept this favored paper. Literati prized Chengxin Tang paper for its fineness, smoothness, and strength.

11. See Wu Shifen, *Jinshi huimu fenbian*, 1a; Chen Jieqi, *Chuangu bielu*, 4a. Both authors also mention the need for heavier paper in rubbing large-characters inscriptions.

12. Wu Shifen, *Jinshi huimu fenbian*, 1a. He notes that fine Shaanxi *maotou* paper also is excellent.

13. Su Yinghui, "Tushuguan cang tapian de bianmu gongzuo," 25. Li Zongtong stated that traditional Chinese scholars did not make their own rubbings and cited correspondence between Chen Jieqi and Pan Zuyin in which Pan refers to a girl with small feet in the Chen household who made rubbings. Aside from sexual implications (women with small feet and a tottering gait were favored in old China from the time of Yang Guifei, the Tang courtesan, but foot binding was subsequently spurned), girls were preferred for their carefulness (Li Zongtong, oral communication, 4 April 1960). When the author reported that Sueji Umehara made his own rubbings, Su Yinghui noted that such was unusual with Chinese scholars.

14. Chen Jieqi, *Chuangu bielu*, 1b. Jiang obviously refers to this passage. He amplifies, noting that Zhang Shuwei used Song flyleaves to make rubbings of bronzes and other antiquities, that the current (1939) *luowen* paper was doubled and had to be separated before use, and that a yellow cast gave the paper a pleasing air of antiquity. See Jiang Xuanyi, "Mota shu," part 1, 71.

15. Rong Geng, *Shang Zhou yiqi tongkao*, 1:177. The availability of "thin *mianlian* paper" has varied through time and space in China. Although the paper had existed "formerly," Chen Jieqi could not find it in Wei Xian, his Shandong hometown, in the latter half of the nineteenth century. Rong Geng had access to it in Beijing in the second quarter of the twentieth century but noted that it was not readily available in other provinces. In 1955, Jun Yu, "Tan taben," 73, recommended Liuji *mianlian* paper for fine shell-and-bone inscriptions.

16. Jiang Xuanyi, "Mota shu," part 1, 71. The character for *jing* in Jing County is given as *shi*. Jiang does not locate Xin'an, and it is difficult to know which of the many places by that name he cites.

17. Jiang Xuanyi, "Mota shu," part 2, 51. Jiang expands on a similar account written thirty years earlier by Ye Changchi, *Yu shi*, 10:315–16.

18. Jiang Xuanyi, "Mota shu," part 2, 51, repeats time-honored information on northern and southern papers. The Ming writers Zhang Yingwen, Tu Long, and Wen Zhenheng, among others, make the same observations. Zhang Yingwen, *Qing mi zang*, 195–97, adds that southern papers are strong and thin and very good for rubbing, able to withstand stress and capture fine detail. See also Tu Long, *Kaopan yushi*, 1:3–4, 2:36, and Wen Zhenheng, *Zhangwu zhi*, 5:182, 7:221.

19. Jiang Xuanyi, "Mota shu," part 2, 51.

20. Appendix 3 is a list of papers that appear frequently in the Chinese rubbings literature.

21. In the 1980s and 1990s, the author purchased these papers, including Xuan (both single and double weight), *mianlian*, and *lianqi*, in specialty shops, such as Beijing's legendary Rongbao Zhai. The papers came in large sizes (135 by 67 centimeters), good for rubbing steles, and bore the names of their places of manufacture, such as Anhui *tezhong jingpi mianlian* paper, Fujian *maobian*, and Yunnan *si chi Yunnan* Xuan.

22. Jiang Xuanyi, "Mota shu," part 1, 71.

23. Ibid.

24. Some writers specify these working papers, while others do not, suggesting that they attach less importance to them. Chen Jieqi, *Chuangu bielu*, 1b–2a, gives no names but refers to two papers. Rong Geng, *Shang Zhou yiqi tongkao*, 1:177, who draws heavily on Chen, also gives no names, but mentions only one paper. Jiang Xuanyi, "Mota shu," part 1, 71, 74, gives the names and uses of the two different papers, while Jun Yu, "Tan taben," 73, referring particularly to rubbing shell-and-bone inscriptions, speaks only of *xishui* paper. Stanley, "The Method of Making Ink Rubbings," 83, states merely that "coarser paper is placed over this as a protective layer during the process of applying the thin [rubbing] paper to . . . the incisions."

25. Jiang Xuanyi, "Mota shu," part 1, 71.

26. Ibid.

27. Wang Chi-chen, *Reproductions*, 3.

28. Chen Jieqi, *Chuangu bielu*, 1b.

29. Wang Chi-chen, *Reproductions*, 3.

30. Chen Jieqi, *Chuangu bielu*, 1b.

31. Jiang Xuanyi, "Mota shu," part 1, 71.

32. Linnaean nomenclature for *baiji* varies. In addition to standard botanical dictionaries, a classical Chinese reference is Li Shizhen, *Bencao gangmu*, 12 *xia* (description) and *tu* (*shang*) for illustrations. Xiao Peigen, ed., *Zhongguo bencao tulu*, 1:237, no. 448, is a contemporary listing. Yang Qianzhi, *Changyong zhongyao shouce*, 50, gives common, botanical, and pharmaceutical names. *Baiji* is a traditional element of the native pharmacopoeia as well as a mucilaginous component in making vermilion.

33. Chen Jieqi, *Chuangu bielu*, 1b, refers to rubbing bronzes.

34. Rong Geng, *Shang Zhou yiqi tongkao*, 1:177.

35. Jiang Xuanyi, "Mota shu," part 1, 71; Jun Yu, "Tan taben," 73–74.

36. Stanley, "The Method of Making Ink Rubbings," 83.

37. Jun Yu, "Tan taben," 74, suggests steeping ten or so flakes in a teacup of boiling water. One can experiment, varying the strength with the situation. The stickier the solution feels, the stronger it is.

38. Zhang Xuan, oral communication, 3 November 1960.

39. Chen Jieqi, *Chuangu bielu*, 1b, 4a.

40. Stanley, "The Method of Making Ink Rubbings," 83.

41. Ma Ji, Beilin, Xi'an, oral communication, 16 April 1993. Ma proudly reported that in a national competition at the Beilin in the mid-1970s, Xi'an artisans won the palm for the best rubbings.

42. Wang Chi-chen, *Reproductions*, 3.

43. Jiang Xuanyi, "Mota shu," part 1, 71.

44. Dong Juewei, "Zeyang tabei," part 1, 42.

45. Jiang Xuanyi, "Mota shu," part 1, 71.

46. Ibid., 74.

47. Chen Jieqi, *Chuangu bielu*, 1a.

48. Jiang Xuanyi, "Mota shu," part 1, 74.

49. Chen Jieqi, *Chuangu bielu*, 1a. While in the Nepal Terai in 1970, the author hoped to obtain some rhinoceros-tail hair. Confrontation with a rhinoceros while riding on a palpably trembling elephant through the 20–foot "elephant grass" gave him pause to consider some other means of obtaining it.

50. Rong Geng, *Shang Zhou yiqi tongkao*, 1:177. For *zonglü*, see Makino Tomitarō, *Nihon shokubutsu zukan*, 1154; Ohwi Jisaburo, *Flora of Japan*, 254; Steward, *Manual of Vascular Plants of the Yangtze Valley*, 498.

51. Jiang Xuanyi, "Mota shu," part 1, 71.

52. Stanley, "The Method of Making Ink Rubbings," 84.

53. Jun Yu, "Tan taben," 73.

54. Rong, *Shang Zhou yiqi tongkao*, 1:177. Because of its greater stiffness, Chinese hair is preferable to the author's, which, where it still remains, is too fine. He was forced to bargain for cuttings from a Chinese barber shop.

55. Chen Jieqi, *Chuangu bielu*, 1a.

56. Wang Chi-chen, *Reproductions*, 4.

57. Jiang Xuanyi, "Mota shu," part 1, 74.

58. Chen Jieqi, *Chuangu bielu*, 1a.

59. Su Yinghui, "Tushuguan cang tapian de bianmu gongzuo," 25.

60. Rong Geng, *Shang Zhou yiqi tongkao*, 1:177; Wang Chi-chen, *Reproductions*, 4.

61. Jun Yu, "Tan taben," 74.

62. Jiang Xuanyi, "Mota shu," part 1, 70.

63. Wu Shifen, *Jinshi huimu fenbian*, 1a. Jiang Xuanyi, "Mota shu," part 1, 70, repeats this information. Dong Zewei, "Zeyang tabei," recommends lighter pine or pear for the head.

64. Van Gulik, *Chinese Pictorial Art As Viewed by the Connoisseur*, 87.

65. Ricci, *China in the Sixteenth Century*, 21.

66. Jiang Xuanyi, "Mota shu," part 1, 70.

67. Dong Juewei, "Zeyang tabei," part 2, 46.

68. Wu Shifen, *Jinshi huimu fenbian*, 1a; Wang Chi-chen, *Reproductions*, 3. Similar brief descriptions occur in Jiang Xuanyi, "Mota shu," part 1, 70, and Jun Yu, "Tan taben," 74.

69. Stanley, "The Method of Making Ink Rubbings," 84.

70. Cao Zhao, *Gegu yaolun*, 3:31. The name of Li Tinggui, the celebrated Southern Tang (923–936) ink maker (*mogong*), appears endlessly in studies of Chinese ink, as it still does on commercial ink sticks. Li's inks reputedly were as hard and strong as jade. Chao Guanzhi, *Mo jing*, 1495:2, 10, 13, 23, cites Li and his methods and preferences. For illustrations and descriptions of Li's inks, see Li Xiaomei, *Mo pu*, 4–6.

71. Interpretations of *hei laohu* and *mo laohu* come from scholars and collectors on Taiwan in 1960, and from specialists at the Xi'an Beilin, the Palace Museum, and the Nanjing City Museum in April and May 1993. Wang Chi-chen, *Reproductions*, 4, uses "ink tigers."

72. Jun Yu, "Tan taben," 74.

73. Jiang Xuanyi, "Mota shu," part 1, 70, gives general instruction. Colleagues in Taiwan provided further information, including that on powdered and oil-based inks.

74. Wang Chi-chen, *Reproductions*, 4, states that "it is possible that sized ink [as mentioned by Carter] is used in making cheap rubbings, but good ones are always made with regular Chinese ink of the best quality." Having limited gambling instincts, the author decided against carrying a visibly fragile bottle of Hua Shan ink in his luggage, settling for a label (fig. 2.7).

75. A photograph in *The Free China Journal*, 27 January 1997, shows "two history majors from National Cheng Kung University" as they "press carbon powder onto a monument at Taipei's Confucius Temple to make stone rubbings. . . . Commissioned by the National Central Library, the . . . students are traveling all over Taiwan to make rubbings for the library's collection." The uneven inking is readily apparent.

76. Li Ch'iao-p'ing, *The Chemical Arts of Old China*, 137–40, lists the names and proportions of basic and optional ingredients in *yinni* (*yinse*), the similar red seal ink. Wang Chi-chen, *Reproductions*, 4, notes that "some Japanese traveling archaeologists . . . use a preparation made by soaking silk waste with a mixture of rape seed oil and ink."

77. Wang Chi-chen, *Reproductions*, shows rubbings in colors.

78. Red ochre was associated with skeletal remains in the Upper Cave at Zhoukoudian, the Upper Paleolithic site; see Chang Kwang-chih, *The Archaeology of Ancient China*, 485.

79. Ibid., 122; Tsien, *Written on Bamboo and Silk*, 1st ed., 84, 165; Tsien, *Written on Bamboo and Silk*, 2nd ed., 183; Tsien, *Paper and Printing*, 237–39; and Tsien, *Zhongguo shuji zhimo ji yinshua shi lunwenji*, 112.

80. Li Ch'iao-p'ing, *The Chemical Arts of Old China*, 33–34; Song Yingxing, *Tiangong kaiwu*, 275–76;

Song Yingxing, *T'ien-kung K'ai-wu: Chinese Technology in the Seventeenth Century*, 279–85. Names for vermilion include *zhu* and *yinzhu*, and for cinnabar, *zhusha*. The common name for both is *chensha*, "Chen sand," from one source, Chenzhou, Hunan; see *Dizhi kuangwuxue dacidian*, 341, 878.

81. Song Yingxing, *T'ien-kung K'ai-wu: Chinese Technology in the Seventeenth Century*, 285; for the original passage, see Song Yingxing, *Tiangong kaiwu*, 276.

82. Jiang Xuanyi, "Mota shu," part 2, 50–51; Ye Changchi, *Yu shi*, 10: 316. For *tuzhu*, the less common term for vermilion, see Chen Zunren, *Zhongguo yaoxue dacidian*, 1:48, where it is given as an older name for *daizhe shi*, red ochre.

83. Van Gulik, *Chinese Pictorial Art As Viewed by the Connoisseur*, 88. Zhao Liguang, director of the Duplication Department at the Beilin, confirmed that egg white more commonly was used to make red rubbings (*zhu ta*[a]) than black ones (oral communication, 19 April 1993).

84. Jiang Xuanyi, "Mota shu," part 2, 51.

85. Jiang Xuanyi, "Mota shu," part 1, 70; Jun Yu, "Tan taben," 74; Rong Geng, *Shang Zhou yiqi tongkao*, 1:177–78; Wu Shifen, *Jinshi huimu fenbian*, 1b.

86. Chen Jieqi, *Chuangu bielu*, 2a.

87. Rong Geng, *Shang Zhou yiqi tongkao*, 1:178–79.

88. Jiang Xuanyi, "Mota shu," part 1, 70.

89. Ibid., 70, 75.

90. Ibid., 75.

91. Dong Juewei, "Zeyang tabei," part 1, 42–43, provides a lengthy, highly detailed description of a dabber.

92. Chen Jieqi, *Chuangu bielu*, 3. See also Jun Yu, "Tan taben," 75.

93. Jun Yu, "Tan taben," 74.

94. Wu Shifen, *Jinshi huimu fenbian*, 1a–b.

95. Lu Shihua, "Shuhua shuo," *Shuhua shuoling*, 1:9a.

96. Wu Shifen, *Jinshi huimu fenbian*, 1a–b. See also Su Yinghui, "Tushuguan cang tapian de bianmu gongzuo," 26–27.

97. Wu Shifen, *Jinshi huimu fenbian*, 1a. In a supplement to the report on Chengziyai, Dong Zuobin wistfully describes a situation in nearby Longshanzhen: "Stone tablets were very numerous at the [Tang temple] site of [Taiping Si], but . . . those who built the [modern] school used [the tablets] to make the wall foundations, causing students of antiquity to sigh endlessly"; see Li Chi et al., *Ch'êng-tzŭ-yai*, 102; see also Li Chi, *Ch'êng-tzŭ-yai: The Black Pottery Culture Site at Lung-shan-chên in Li-ch'êng-hsien, Shantung Province*, 173. Such cases are common.

98. Wu Shifen, *Jinshi huimu fenbian*, 1a.

99. Jiang Xuanyi, "Mota shu," part 2, 50.

100. Ibid. Having searched for "old stones" in both China and his native Frederick County, Maryland, the writer exactly shares the feelings of Wu and Jiang. Bai Qianshen, "The Artistic and Intellectual Dimensions of Chinese Calligraphy Rubbings," 83, states that "touching a rubbing is like touching the ancient object itself, such as a stele."

101. Jiang Xuanyi, "Mota shu," part 2, 50. The author has compiled a comprehensive list of equipment for searching out "old stones."

102. Ibid. As an avocational extension of his interest in "old stones," the author in retirement has documented early stone inscriptions, excluding tombstones, in his native county in Maryland; see Starr, "Old Stones and Black Tigers in Frederick County," and McCarthy, "Secrets Carved in Stone."

3 / THE GENTLE ART

1. For distinctions among substance, object, and subject, see chap. 1, n. 69.

2. Chen Jieqi, *Chuangu bielu*, 7b.

3. Ibid.

4. Ibid.

5. Jiang Xuanyi, "Mota shu," part 2, 43.

6. Ibid.

7. Wu Shifen, *Jinshi huimu fenbian*, 1a; Chen Jieqi, *Chuangu bielu*, 4a; Jiang Xuanyi, "Mota shu," part 1, 72.

8. Jiang Xuanyi, "Mota shu," part 2, 46–47. Similar situations occurred in 1960 on Quemoy Island (Jinmen Dao), where late-Ming stones lay fallen, their inscriptions in whole or part buried, and their massive weight, tons, a sobering challenge to rubbers. The memory is the clearer for the author because Mainland forces, through the night, were lobbing shells over his bed from across the narrow strait.

9. Ibid., 47. The indiscriminate secondary use of old steles is common.

10. Chen Jieqi, *Chuangu bielu*, 4a.

11. Wu Shifen, *Jinshi huimu fenbian*, 1a.

12. Ibid. The most frequently used traditional measures for length are *fen* (0.33 centimeters), *cun* (3.3 centimeters, an inch), *chi* (0.3 meters, a foot), *zhang* (3.3 meters), and *li* (0.5000 kilometers, one-third of an English mile). Common weights are *qian* (5 grams), *liang* (50 grams, an ounce), and *jin* (0.5000 kilograms, a catty). Weights and measures have varied greatly over time and space in China. For modern metric and English equivalents, see *Jianming hanying cidian*, 816; *Xinhua zidian*, 603–6.

13. Chen Jieqi, *Chuangu bielu*, 5b–6a.

14. Jun Yu, "Tan taben,", 74.

15. Jiang Xuanyi, "Mota shu," part 1, 76.

16. Ibid. See Hsü Chin-hsiung, *The Menzies Collections of Shang Dynasty Oracle Bones*, 8–10, 13, and plates 265–81.

17. Jiang Xuanyi, "Mota shu," part 1, 72.

18. Jiang Xuanyi, "Mota shu," part 2, 48.

19. Chen Jieqi, *Chuangu bielu*, 4a; Jiang Xuanyi, "Mota shu," part 1, 72; Jiang Xuanyi, "Mota shu," part 2, 51; Dong Juewei, "Zeyang tabei," part 2, 46.

20. Bi Yuan and Ruan Yuan, *Shanzuo jinshi zhi*, 7:1b–2a.

21. See Jiang Xuanyi, "Mota shu," part 2, 46; Chavannes, *La sculpture sur pierre en Chine au temps des deux Han*; Fairbank, "The Offering Shrines of 'Wu Liang Tz'u'"; Wu Hung, *The Wu Liang Shrine*, xxii. Liu, Nylan, and Barbieri-Low, *Recarving China's Past*, esp. 131–32, 171, 176, depicts the complex levels of the reliefs; see also Bernstein, "An Uncertain History," 23–25.

22. Jiang Xuanyi, "Mota shu," part 1, 72; Dong Juewei, "Zeyang tabei," part 2, 46.

23. Jun Yu, "Tan taben," 73.

24. Chen Jieqi, *Chuangu bielu*, 9a.

25. Ibid.

26. Ibid., 9a–b.

27. Ibid., 9a; Jiang Xuanyi, "Mota shu," part 2, 43–44.

28. Jiang Xuanyi, "Mota shu," part 2, 43; Chen Jieqi, *Chuangu bielu*, following 10b, recommends a bamboo knife.

29. Chen Jieqi, *Chuangu bielu*, 9b.

30. Jiang Xuanyi, "Mota shu," part 2, 44.

31. Chen Jieqi, *Chuangu bielu*, following 10a–b. Judging from Chen's account, the paste made from hill-haw apples is effective because of its mildly acidic nature. The agent, malic acid, is present in many fruits, especially apples, hence its name. John Gettens, former conservator at the Freer Gallery, and Thomas Chase, his successor at the Sackler, reported using certain fruits, including plums, as mild acidic agents for softening copper corrosion (Thomas Chase, oral communication, 28 March 1974).

32. Chen Jieqi, *Chuangu bielu*, 7a–8a.

33. Ibid., 8; Jiang Xuanyi, "Mota shu," part 2, 44.

34. Jiang Xuanyi, "Mota shu," part 2, 43–44.

35. Chen Jieqi, *Chuangu bielu*, 10a.

36. Ibid., 7b.

37. Ibid., 7b–8a.

38. Ibid., 10a–b.

39. Ibid., 19b.

40. Ibid., 10a.

41. Ibid., 10b.

42. Ibid.

43. Ibid., 7a–8a.

44. Ibid., 5a; Jiang Xuanyi, "Mota shu," part 1, 75–76; Jiang Xuanyi, "Mota shu," part 2, 43. The *Cihai* dictionary describes *Baila* (*beila*), "white wax," as either beeswax, more likely here, or the secretion of the white-wax insect (*Flata limbata, Fab.*) or the water-wax insect (*Ericerus pela*); see also *Dongwuxue dacidian*, 327. Whatever its type, the wax should not have an oil base.

45. Chen Jieqi, *Chuangu bielu*, 1b, 4a; Jiang Xuanyi, "Mota shu," part 2, 47.

46. Chen Jieqi, *Chuangu bielu*, 5b; Jiang Xuanyi, "Mota shu," part 1, 74–75.

47. Jiang Xuanyi, "Mota shu," part 1, 74–75.

48. Chen Jieqi, *Chuangu bielu*, 5b. Again, many will sigh at such use of rare old Chinese books.

49. Ibid., 3b.

50. Jiang Xuanyi, "Mota shu," part 1, 75.

51. Jun Yu, "Tan taben," 73. This method apparently is standard, for workers at the Institute of History and Philology, in Taiwan, also used it in 1960.

52. Ibid. Jun Yu suggests using *youni*, a term that the author could not identify. The character and purpose of the foundation are clear, and it should not be oily.

53. Bi Yuan and Ruan Yuan, *Shanzuo jinshi zhi*, 1:1b–2a.

54. Ibid., 2:4b–5a; Ma Heng, "Ge ji zhi yanjiu," 745–46.

55. Ding Fubao, *Gu qian dacidian, xia bian*, 237a. There are illustrations of round coins in Wang Yuquan, *Early Chinese Coinage*, plates 51–55, and in Cribb and Williams, "Who Made the First Coins?"

56. Bi Yuan and Ruan Yuan, *Shanzuo jinshi zhi*, 4:13b (knife), 4:14a (spade); Ding Fubao, *Gu qian dacidian, xia bian*, 16a, 54a. Wang Yuquan, *Early Chinese Coinage*, illustrates spade and knife coins (plates 7–27, 28–50) coins, as do Cribb and Williams, "Who Made the First Coins?"

57. See Long Dayuan, *Gu yu tupu*, 12:9a–10a (*bi* discs), 55:11a–12a (*huan* discs).

58. Chen Jieqi, *Chuangu bielu*, 1b, 4a.

59. Jiang Xuanyi, "Mota shu," part 1, 71.

60. Ibid.

61. Ibid., 71; Jiang Xuanyi, "Mota shu," part 2, 45–47, 49.

62. Wu Shifen, *Jinshi huimu fenbian*, 1a.

63. Ibid.

64. Jun Yu, "Tan taben," 73.

65. Jiang Xuanyi, "Mota shu," part 1, 75.

66. Chen Jieqi, *Chuangu bielu*, 5b; Jiang Xuanyi, "Mota shu," part 1, 71–72.

67. Wu Shifen, *Jinshi huimu fenbian*, 1a. Dong Juewei, "Zeyang tabei," part 1, 43, recommends only 2 centimeters all around, insufficient for colophons and seals.

68. Chen Jieqi, *Chuangu bielu*, 6a. Illustrations of these vessels are in Rong Geng, *Shang Zhou yiqi tongkao*, 2:239–41 (*jia* wine cups, plates 452–63), 2:234–38 (*jue* wine cups, plates 443–51), 2:220–344 (*jue* wine goblets, plates 415–42), 2:291–97 (*gu* beakers, plates 557–58), 2:351–62 (*guang* jars, plates 674–85), 2:297–307 (*zhi* goblets, plates 569–89), 2:259–91, 2:363–73 (*zun* wine goblets, plates 493–556, 686–703), and 2:316–50 (*you* wine jars, plates 607–73).

69. Chen Jieqi, *Chuangu bielu*, 6a. The meaning of Chen's *zhong* (?) character is unclear, for its position in his list, between eight vessels above and three weapons below, makes it difficult to know in which category, if either, the object falls. It probably is a bell, one of the most difficult objects to rub.

70. Ibid., 3a; Jiang Xuanyi, "Mota shu," part 1, 72, 74.

71. Chen Jieqi, *Chuangu bielu*, 3a; Jiang Xuanyi,"Mota shu," part 1, 72.

72. Wu Shifen, *Jinshi huimu fenbian*, 1b; Jiang Xuanyi, "Mota shu," part 1, 72. Dong Juewei, "Zeyang tabei," part 1, 43, recommends a 1–centimeter overlap.

73. Dong Juewei, "Zeyang tabei," part 1, 43.

74. There are many studies of the early bronzes and their inscriptions, including the *Mao Gong ding* cauldron and the *San shi pan* basin, among the most difficult to rub. Particularly useful is Tang Funian, *Xi Zhou qingtong qi mingwen fendaishi zhengqi yingji*. Tang describes and illustrates vessels by class, with chronological listings of references. The list includes the *Mao Gong ding* (text, 22; picture, no. 83) and the *San shi pan* (text, 107; picture, no. 417). See also Rong Geng, *Shang Zhou yiqi tongkao*, 2:432–49 (plates 821–51, illustrating *pan* basins).

75. Rong Geng, *Shang Zhou yiqi tongkao*, 1:114, fig. 107. Ruan Yuan, *Jigu zhai zhongding yiqi kuanshi*, 8:3a–8b, gives the text of the *San shi pan* in its original characters and modern equivalents. Stanley, "The Method of Making Ink Rubbings," 84, vaguely states that "to take an impression from a concave surface the paper is cut at the sides in strips which are applied to the surface and fixed in position by the [adhesive] seaweed [agar] solution."

76. Liu Tizhi, *Xiaojiaojing Ge jinwen taben*, 9:85a–88b, reproduces an excellent rubbing of the *San shi pan* inscription and a commentary on the vessel. The notes repeat the common view about the rarity of the length of the inscriptions on the *San shi pan*, the *Mao Gong ding*, and the two *Qi Hou lei*.

77. Jun Yu, "Tan taben," 74–75. See also Rong Geng, *Shang Zhou yiqi tongkao*, 2:220–34 (plates 415–42, illustrating *jue* goblets).

78. Illustrations of rubbings of inscriptions and designs under and flanking the handles of *jue* goblets appear in many bronze studies. See Rong Geng, *Song Zhai jijin tulu*, 11a–13a, plates 17–21; Liu Tizhi, *Xiaojiaojing Ge jinwen taben*, 6:1a–77b; Umehara, ed., *Kankarō kikinzu, maki naka*, 14a–37b.

79. For illustrations of a *zhong* bell, see fig. 3.7, this volume; Rong Geng, *Shang Zhou yiqi tongkao*, 2:495–511 (plates 942–75). For illustrations of rubbings, see Liu Tizhi, *Xiaojiaojing Ge jinwen taben*, *juan* 1, passim.

80. Chen Jieqi, *Chuangu bielu*, 5b.

81. Ibid. For three-quarter representations of bells and their bosses, see Liu Tizhi, *Xiaojiaojing Ge jinwen taben*, 1:26a–b, 1:30a–b. Liu's illustrations are photolithographic reproductions, making identification difficult, but they suggest that the originals are composite rubbings rather than rubbings of or prints from woodcuts.

82. Chen Jieqi, *Chuangu bielu*, 5b–6a.

83. Chen Jieqi, *Fu Zhai cang jing*, shows the results of both methods. Liu Tizhi, *Xiaojiaojing Ge jinwen taben, juan* 15–17, illustrates a greater number and range of examples; plate 2.19 illustrates laying the paper over the bail of a Zhou *ding* tripod lid.

84. Rong Geng, *Shang Zhou yiqi tongkao*, 1:177; Jiang Xuanyi, "Mota shu," part 1, 71.

85. Ibid.; ibid.; Jun Yu, "Tan taben," 73–75; Dong Juewei, "Zeyang tabei," part 2, 46.

86. Jun Yu, "Tan taben," 74.

87. Jiang Xuanyi, "Mota shu," part 1, 71.

88. Ibid., 75. For *jingta* and *wujin ta* rubbings, see chap. 7, this volume.

89. It is intriguing to speculate whether this method of hanging wallpaper moved west with wallpaper, and whether the method of application originated in laying rubbing paper.

90. Chen Jieqi, *Chuangu bielu*, 1b.

91. Arthur Stanley, "The Method of Making Ink Rubbings, 84; Wang Chi-chen, *Reproductions of Chinese Rubbings Taken from Inscriptions Cut in Stone, Wood and Also from Bronzes, Monuments and Other Bas-reliefs*, 3 (hereafter, *Reproductions*).

92. Wu Shifen, *Jinshi huimu fenbian*, 1a; Jiang Xuanyi, "Mota shu," part 1, 72; Chen Jieqi, *Chuangu bielu*, 1a; Rong Geng, *Shang Zhou yiqi tongkao*, 1:177. Dong Juewei, "Zeyang tabei," part 1, 43, describes a similar method, but wetting only every third sheet, allowing moisture to diffuse to intervening dry sheets.

93. Conversation with Orient Lee (Lee Tung-fang), Milwaukee, 11 March 1977.

94. Rong Geng, *Shang Zhou yiqi tongkao*, 1:177.

95. Jun Yu, "Tan taben," 74.

96. The Metropolitan Museum invited Zhang to make rubbings of objects in its collection; see Reif, "Ink Rubbings, Ancient Art, Revived at Museum Here."

97. Dong Juewei, "Zeyang tabei," part 2, 46, recommends wetting the stele with *baiji*.

98. Liu Yuanjian, head artist at the Institute of History and Philology, Academia Sinica, Taiwan, oral communication, 7 April 1960.

99. Chen Jieqi, *Chuangu bielu*, 1b, 3a.

100. Jiang Xuanyi, "Mota shu," part 1, 73, refers to rewetting edges that lift. Wang Chi-chen, *Reproductions*, 3, suggests using a soft brush to remoisten the paper. Contemporary artisans also sometimes use a mister. James Plummer, formerly of the University of Michigan, observed an artisan spraying water from his mouth onto the rubbing paper, as laundry workers do to moisten shirts in ironing.

101. Wu Shifen, *Jinshi huimu fenbian*, 1a; Chen Jieqi, *Chuangu bielu*, 1b; Jiang Xuanyi, "Mota shu," part 1, 73.

102. Jiang Xuanyi, "Mota shu," part 1, 73.

103. Ibid., 72. Dong Juewei, "Zeyang tabei," part 2, 46, advises brushing *baiji* solution on the stone to hold the paper down. Chinese workers often use a smear of cooked rice, rather than commercial rice paste, which often contains deleterious chemicals. Wheat paste, or paste made from ordinary flour, also works, especially on soft, friable surfaces, such as plaster. Going contemporary, one can use duct tape, Garrison Keillor's favorite product.

104. Jiang Xuanyi, "Mota shu," part 1, 73.

105. Wu Shifen, *Jinshi huimu fenbian*, 1a; Jiang Xuanyi, "Mota shu," part 1, 72; Wang Chi-chen, *Reproductions*, 3.

106. Wu Shifen, *Jinshi huimu fenbian*, 1a.

107. Jiang Xuanyi, "Mota shu," part 1, 72; Dong Juewei, "Zeyang tabei," part 2, 46.

108. Dong Juewei, "Zeyang tabei," part 2, 46.

109. Ibid.

110. Ibid.

111. Wu Shifen, *Jinshi huimu fenbian*, 1a.

112. Jiang Xuanyi, "Mota shu," part 1, 72.

113. Ibid.

114. Ibid.

115. See Rong Geng, *Shang Zhou yiqi tongkao*, 2:11–70 (plates 1–119, illustrating round-bellied *ding* cauldrons), 2:414–19 (plates 784–95, illustrating *lei* jars), and 2:374–413 (plates 704–83, illustrating *hu* jars).

116. Chen Jieqi, *Chuangu bielu*, 3a.

117. Rong, *Shang Zhou yiqi tongkao*, 1:179, and 2:45 (plate 69), where Rong illustrates the *Mao Gong ding*. Dong Zuobin, *Mao Gong ding*, includes the text and analysis of its date. Dong also illustrates the famous tripod and its long inscription as well as a two-sheet rubbing of the latter; a colophon by Tan Danyong describes the vessel's history since its unearthing in 1850, and another by Su Yinghui reviews its dating. For a reference to a description of the vessel, see n. 74, above. For a popular account and picture, see *Free China Journal*, 25 February 1992, 5. Rubbings of the cauldron are highly prized. In the second quarter of the nineteenth century, rubbings of the vessel and its inscription are said to have sold for fifty ounces (*liang*) of silver (Li Lincan, oral communication, 14 March 1962). The tripod now is in the National Palace Museum, Taibei. For rubbings, see Sang Shen, "Qingtong qi quanxing ta jishu fazhan de fenqi yanjou," 36.

118. Chen Jieqi, *Chuangu bielu*, 3b. Liu Tizhi, *Xiaojiaojing Ge jinwen taben*, 9:85a, cites the *San shi pan* along with the *Mao Gong ding* and the two *Qi Hou lei.*

119. Chen Jieqi, *Chuangu bielu*, 3b. It seems likely that Chen used the term *mo*^{c}*ke* in the sense of *mo*^{c}*ta*, "tracing from a rubbing." See Wang Zhuangwei, *Shufa zongtan*, 119; Wang Zhuangwei, *Shufa yanjiu*, 31.

120. Jiang Xuanyi, "Mota shu," part 1, 74.

121. Ibid.

122. Jun Yu, "Tan taben," 73.

4 / GENTLER STILL

1. Jiang Xuanyi, "Mota shu," part 1, 74; Stanley, "The Method of Making Ink Rubbings," 84.

2. Rong Geng, *Shang Zhou yiqi tongkao*, 1:177.

3. Ibid. Jun Yu, "Tan taben," 73, calls this "absorb-water paper" (*xishui zhi*), as does Jiang Xuanyi, "Mota shu," part 1, 74, who recommends it if the paper is too wet for inking. Artisans at the Institute of History and Philology and the Historical Museum in Taiwan used liner sheets on bronzes, stones, and oracle bones.

4. Jiang Xuanyi, "Mota shu," part 1, 74, and part 2, 45.

5. Jiang Xuanyi, "Mota shu," part 1, 74.

6. Dong Juewei, "Zeyang tabei," part 2, 46.

7. Ibid.

8. Jiang Xuanyi, "Mota shu,", part 1, 72–73.

9. Ibid., 74, 76.

10. Wang Chi-chen, *Reproductions of Chinese Rubbings*, 4.

11. Jiang Xuanyi, "Mota shu," part 2, 46, 49. Orient Lee (Lee Dongfang) referred to the dry dabber, oral communication, 6 August 1977.

12. Jiang Xuanyi, "Mota shu," part 1, 76; Jun Yu, "Tan taben," 74–75.

13. Jun Yu, "Tan taben," 73.

14. Jiang Xuanyi, "Mota shu," part 1, 72–73.

15. Ibid. See also Chen Jieqi, *Chuangu bielu*, 1a, and Jun Yu, "Tan taben," 73. Stanley, "The Method of Making Ink Rubbings," 84, speaks of "vertical taps," adding that "this takes a considerable time and requires care to prevent tearing of the paper."

16. Jiang Xuanyi, "Mota shu," part 1, 74.

17. Chen Jieqi, *Chuangu bielu*, 2b.

18. Rong Geng, *Shang Zhou yiqi tongkao*, 1:179.

19. Jiang Xuanyi, "Mota shu," part 1, 73.

20. Chen Jieqi, *Chuangu bielu*, 1a.

21. Wang Chi-chen, *Reproductions of Chinese Rubbings*, 3–4.

22. Jiang Xuanyi, "Mota shu," part 2, 46, 48.

23. Chen Jieqi, *Chuangu bielu*, 1a. Stanley, "The Method of Making Ink Rubbings," 84, and Jun Yu, "Tan taben," 73, also emphasize a vertical stroke.

24. Jun Yu, "Tan taben," 73.

25. Jiang Xuanyi, "Mota shu," part 1, 73.

26. Chen Jieqi, *Chuangu bielu*, 1a. Ye Changchi, *Yu shi*, 9:298, also mentions this.

27. Ye Changchi, *Yu shi*, 9:298.

28. Ibid., 9:299. The pressure to sell rubbings at the Beilin and other museums threatens the integrity of the more famous inscriptions. Cutting copies eases the situation.

29. Chen Jieqi, *Chuangu bielu*, 8a, comments in the context of what he calls "evil practices" by careless rubbers.

30. Dong Juewei, "Zeyang tabei," part 2, 46.

31. Jiang Xuanyi, "Mota shu," part 1, 73.

32. Ibid.

33. Ibid.

34. Chen Jieqi, *Chuangu bielu*, 2a–b. Jiang Xuanyi, "Mota shu," part 1, 73, offers similar advice.

35. Jiang Xuanyi, "Mota shu," part 1, 74.

36. Chen Jieqi, *Chuangu bielu*, 2a–b. See below for the aesthetic effects of differential inking.

37. Rong Geng, *Shang Zhou yiqi tongkao*, 1:177; Jun Yu, "Tan taben," 73.

38. Jiang Xuanyi, "Mota shu," part 1, 73.

39. Wang Yuqing, National Historical Museum, Taibei, oral communication, 8 June 1960.

40. Chen Jieqi, *Chuangu bielu*, 2a.

41. Ibid.

42. Jiang Xuanyi, "Mota shu," part 1, 73–75.

43. Stanley, "The Method of Making Ink Rubbings," 84.

44. Jiang Xuanyi, "Mota shu," part 1, 73.

45. Jun Yu, "Tan taben," 73. Dong Juewei, "Zeyang tabei," part 2, 47, gives a similar description of dabber movement.

46. Chen Jieqi, *Chuangu bielu*, 2b.

47. Jiang Xuanyi, "Mota shu," part 1, 73; Jun Yu, "Tan taben, 73–74.

48. Dong Juewei, "Zeyang tabei," part 2, 47.

49. Jiang Xuanyi, "Mota shu," part 1, 73; Jun Yu, "Tan taben," 73–74.

50. Chen Jieqi, *Chuangu bielu*, 2b. Dong Juewei, "Zeyang tabei," part 2, 47, also emphasizes striving for an even tone.

51. Jiang Xuanyi, "Mota shu," part 1, 74.

52. Ibid., 73–73; Jun Yu, "Tan taben," 74; Dong Juewei, "Zeyang tabei," part 2, 47.

53. See Jun Yu, "Tan taben," 74; Chen Jieqi, *Chuangu bielu*, 2a; Dong Juewei, "Zeyang tabei," part 1, 41.

54. Jiang Xuanyi, "Mota shu," part 1, 75; Jun Yu, "Tan taben," 73.

55. Jiang Xuanyi, "Mota shu," part 1, 73. Having too much or too moist ink on the dabber also results in blotches.

56. Chen Jieqi, *Chuangu bielu*, 2b.

57. Jiang Xuanyi, "Mota shu," part 1, 73. See also *xiang*[b]*ta*[a], Appendix 2, this volume. Dong Juewei, "Zeyang tabei," part 2, 47, describes hand movement as well.

58. Jiang Xuanyi, "Mota shu," part 1, 74.

59. Chen Jieqi, *Chuangu bielu*, 3a.

60. Jiang Xuanyi. "Mota shu," part 1, 75.

61. Dong Juewei, "Zeyang tabei," part 2, 47.

62. Chen Jieqi, *Chuangu bielu*, 3b.

63. Jiang Xuanyi, "Mota shu," part 1, 76; Jun Yu, "Tan taben," 75–76.

64. Rong Geng, *Shang Zhou yiqi tongkao*, 1:179.

65. Jun Yu, "Tan taben," 74.

66. The term "black-gold rubbing" connotes a dark, burnished appearance; van Gulik, *Chinese Pictorial Art As Viewed by the Connoisseur*, 87 n. 1, describes *wujin* as a mixture of nine parts copper and one part gold, with a dark, purplish luster as the sheen of good-quality ink. Dong Juewei, "Zeyang tabei," part 1, 41, cites the use of "layered ink" in the Tang and the Song; Jiang Xuanyi, "Mota shu," part 1, 75, assigns its use to smaller objects.

67. Wen Zhenheng, *Zhangwu zhi*, 182.

68. Jiang Xuanyi, "Mota shu," part 1, 75. Dong Juewei, "Zeyang tabei," part 1, 41, recommends fine, pure white Xuan paper and jet-black oil-soot ink.

69. Van Gulik, *Chinese Pictorial Art As Viewed by the Connoisseur*, 87.

70. Ibid. Chen Zhongyu of the Institute of Archaeology, Academia Sinica, Taiwan, spoke of brushing the dried ink with a palm-fiber brush (oral communication, 4 April 1960). Liu Yujian, head of the Art Department, Institute of History and Philology, Taiwan, stated that the quality of the ink was as important as the polishing (oral communication, 7 April 1960). Luo Jimei, a Taibei collector, recommended egg white instead of *baiji* in sizing the paper, and brushing or polishing the finished rubbing with a smooth object (oral communication, 6 March 1960). Others gave similar explanations. I have experimented with all of the suggested methods and have had the most success with polishing the finished rubbing with a hard, smooth object. My lackluster success, pun intended, speaks more of my modest skills than of the inadequacy of the techniques.

71. Commercial inks designed especially for making rubbings contain adhesive ingredients and those that produce a gloss; see chap. 2, this volume.

72. Ma Ji, Beilin, Xi'an, oral communication, 16 April 1993.

73. Ibid. For *cata*[a] and *chui*[d]*ta*[a], Ma Ji of the Beilin cited Nakata, *Chūgoku shoronshū*, 251–66, which discusses terms relating to copying,.

74. Dong Juewei, "Zeyang tabei," part 1, 42 and part 2, 47–48.

75. Chen Jieqi, *Chuangu bielu*, 2a–b.

76. Ibid., 2b; Jiang Xuanyi, "Mota shu," part 1, 75.

77. Jiang Xuanyi, "Mota shu," part 1, 75.

78. Ibid. See also Chen Jieqi, *Chuangu bielu*, 2b. Dong Juewei, "Zeyang tabei," part 1, 41, cites the existence of *chanyi ta* in the Tang and the Song.

79. Jiang Xuanyi, "Mota shu," part 1, 75.

80. Jiang Xuanyi, "Mota shu," part 2, 49.

81. Jiang Xuanyi, "Mota shu," part 1, 75.

82. Ibid. See also Dong Juewei, "Zeyang tabei," part 1, 41; Chen Jieqi, *Chuangu bielu*, 2b.

83. Jun Yu,"Tan taben," 74.

84. Jiang Xuanyi, "Mota shu," part 2, 49.

85. Dong Juewei, "Zeyang tabei," part 1, 41, refers to "black rubbings" (*mo*[a]*ta*[a]) or "charcoal rubbings" (*meita*) made with powdered charcoal mixed with glue. He does not specify whether the technique is wet or dry but says that the medium is fugitive.

86. For allied reasons, officials at the Calligraphy Museum (Shodō Hakubutsukan) in Tokyo in 1960 provided me not only with clean cotton gloves but also with a fresh cotton dust cap before allowing me to study their rare documents. In response to my puzzled look, they explained, with exquisite tact, that small particles of hair or skin fall on the paper and produce oil stains that, in storage, expand and spread to adjoining sheets.

87. In visiting museums, Sueji Umehara carried a small rubbing kit with oil *sumi*. He laid on the ink when the rubbing paper was only 60 to 70 percent dry without the ink bleeding. The inking done, he washed the host piece with soap and water.

88. Jiang Xuanyi, "Mota shu," part 2, 45–50.

89. Jiang Xuanyi, "Mota shu," part 2, 47, gives *Xilengyinshe* but elsewhere in the same text (52) gives *Xiyinlengshe*. It may be a village in the Hangzhou area.

90. There were three "editions" of the limestone "Zhaoling stone horses" (*Zhaoling shima*), "six piebalds" (*liubo*), or, simply, "warhorses" (*junma*). Taizong cut the original set of six tablets on the death of Wende, his empress, and placed them near her tomb in Liquan Xian, northwest of Xi'an. Four are in the Shaanxi Provincial Museum in Xi'an; the other two, Saluzi, "Whirlwind Victory," and Telepiao, "Teghin," are in the University Museum, Philadelphia, "stolen" in 1914 (see Yang Guanlin, *Zhongguo mingsheng cidian*, 1021). A full-size reproduction was cut in 1089, along with a miniature set, and placed in the memorial temple to Tai Zong in Liquan. Ferguson, "The Six Horses at the Tomb of the Emperor T'ai Tsung of the T'ang Dynasty," gives the history of the cuttings. Shaanxi Provincial Museum, *Shaanxi Sheng Bowuguan*, describes the six horses as low relief and illustrates three of them (plates 116–18).

91. Jiang Xuanyi, "Mota shu," part 2, 49, gives a spare description.

92. Ibid., 50.

93. Chen Jieqi, *Chuangu bielu*, 2a, 3a; Jiang Xuanyi, "Mota shu," part 2, 50; Rong Geng, *Shang Zhou yiqi tongkao*, 1:179; Jun Yu, "Tan taben," 73.

94. Chen Jieqi, *Chuangu bielu*, 3a.

95. Ibid.

5 / VARIATIONS ON THE THEME

1. Rong Geng, *Shang Zhou yiqi tongkao*, 1:179–80. Bao Changxi, *Jinshi xie*, 1:33a–34a, pictures a woodcut of the Han *Zhenguan xi* basin and describes its uncertain history. The owner was unknown, as was the date of the rubbing, which was in the collection of Bao's fellow Jiaxing native Ma Fuyan (fl. 1798), the "venerable Qifeng." See also Xu Kang, *Qianchenmeng yinglu*, 234. Sang Shen, "Qingtong qi quanxing ta jishu fazhan de fenqi yanjou," expands on these masters and assigns them to three periods: initial (Ma Qifeng, Da Shou, Li Jinhong), developmental (Chen Jieqi), and flowering (Zhou Xiding, Ma Ziyun).

2. See fig. 5.1 for an outline longevity character filled with small rubbings, done by the author. For an outline grass-style *shou* character by a Song calligrapher containing thirty different long-life characters from early bronze, stone, and tile inscriptions, see Su Yinghui, "Jinshi tongshou," 14 (the original rubbing, in auspicious red on the cover of the issue in which this article appears, is in Su's personal collection).

3. Rong Geng, *Shang Zhou yiqi tongkao*, 1:180.

4. Ibid.

5. Chen Jieqi, *Chuangu bielu*, 3b–4a.

6. Rong Geng, *Shang Zhou yiqi tongkao*, 1:181.

7. Su Yinghui, letters of 8 March and 6 June, 1959.

8. Zhang Xuan visited me at the Field Museum in November 1960, shortly after my return from Taiwan. He was on his way home to Hong Kong, whence the Metropolitan Museum had invited him to rub selected pieces in its collections. Zhang came from a scholarly family, with maternal connections to Chen Jieqi. He was knowledgeable in etymological studies and ancient scripts, and he was a skilled calligrapher and seal carver. He also was highly adept in making rubbings, including composite rubbings, and he very kindly gave me a simplified demonstration using a Qing-dynasty (1858) iron gong, greatly augmenting my understanding of the technique. For his work at the Metropolitan, see Reif, "Ink Rubbings, Ancient Art, Revived at Museum Here."

9. Rong Geng, *Shang Zhou yiqi tongkao*, 1:181.

10. Zheng Shanshan et al., "Zhimo liuxiang—chuanta jifa, quanxing ta; chuanji shou de rongyao," 38–51.

11. Zhang Xuan, oral communication, 3 November 1960.

12. See Sang Shen, "Quanxing ta zhi chuangcheng yu liubian"; see also Zheng Shanshan et al., "Zhimo liuxiang—chuanta jifa, quanxing ta; chuanji shou de rongyao." One can find other brief accounts online through CNKI (China National Knowledge Infrastructure), published by Tsinghua University Academic Journals Electronic Publishing House, Beijing.

13. Letter from William B. Jones, 26 November 1959. I thank Sona Johnston, curator of painting and sculpture before 1900, for her courtesy in permitting me to review the files.

14. See Beedell, *Brasses and Brass Rubbing*, for an account of and bibliography on the brasses and brass rubbing.

15. Cheng Dachang, *Yanfan lu*, 7:6a.

16. This observation differs with van Gulik, *Chinese Pictorial Art As Viewed by the Connoisseur*, 88, 89, who recommends the method for rough and irregular surfaces and opines that "technically the 'dry method' is more difficult than the wet one," a point on which one also could take serious issue. Hard, carnauba-base ink cakes capture fine line more clearly, with softer, candilla-base cakes smudging easily.

17. "Squeeze," definitions 7a–b, *Oxford English Dictionary*, 2nd ed. (compact disc), 1992.

18. Wang Chi-chen, *Reproductions of Chinese Rubbings*, 2–3, also speaks of molding with papier-mâché and concludes that the term "rubbing" is "more or less accepted." Others who use "rubbing" or "ink rubbing" include Bai Qianshen, T. F. Carter, Lionel Giles, Robert E. Harrist Jr., Li Shuhua, Gilbert Mattos, and Nakata (in Jeffrey Hunter's translation). Carter, *The Invention of Printing*, 2nd ed., 23 n. 8, mentions both "ink squeeze" and *estampage*, which latter is also used by Pelliot, *Les débuts de l'imprimerie en Chine.* Tsien prefers "ink squeeze." R. Thomas Berner, "The Ancient Chinese Process of Reprography" (unpublished manuscript), uses "reprography."

19. One hears two pronunciations of *ta*[a], the most common form for rubbing, with dictionaries differing. *Cihai* gives *tuo*, the traditional pronunciation. *Jianming hanying cidian* and *Xinhua zidian* give *ta*[a] as "to make rubbings," with the alternative pronunciation, *tuo*, having a different meaning. See "rub," definition 1e, and "rubbing," definition 4, in *Oxford English Dictionary*, 2nd ed. (compact disc).

6 / WHEN THE WORK IS DONE

1. A few rubbings reflect both intaglio and relief. From the Tang on, there was a practice of cutting an inscription in stone and insetting metal to create a relief effect. If the insets fell out, leaving the original intaglio inscription, a rubbing then shows both black and white characters. Carter also notes that the broken stone blocks of the *Chunhua Ge Model Book* "were mended with silver wire, the impression of which could often be detected in the rubbing"; see Carter, *The Invention of Printing*, 1st ed., 15, 22.

2. Jiang Xuanyi, "Mota shu," part 1, 74.

3. Chen Jieqi, *Chuangu bielu*, 3a; Jiang Xuanyi, "Mota shu," part 1, 74; Dong Juewei, "Zeyang tabei," part 2, 47.

4. Chen Jieqi, Chuangu bielu, 3a.

5. Jiang Xuanyi, "Mota shu," part 1, 75.

6. Dong Juewei, "Zeyang tabei," part 2, 47.

7. Jiang Xuanyi, "Mota shu," part 1, 74. Weng Fanggang, *Liang Han jinshi zhi*, 6:30a, cites Niu Yunzhen, *Jinshi tu*, who locates the Kong Zhou Stele "on the east side of the Tongwen Gate, facing south, at the Confucian Temple in Qufu [Shandong]." Niu shows rubbings of miniature steles, including the Kong Zhou Stele, and portions of their original texts, pasted in stitch-bound volumes.

8. Jiang Xuanyi, "Mota shu," part 1, 74.

9. Jiang Xuanyi, "Mota shu," part, 46. Northern Song scholars noted the reliefs, dated to 151 C.E. The Qianlong scholar Huang Yi first visited the site in 1786 and in the course of his studies made notes and rubbings; see Wu Hung, *The Wu Liang Shrine*, xvii, 3–10. Rong Geng published Huang's rubbings, and Jiang Gusun, a Taiwan antiquarian who as a boy had Wang Guowei as his tutor, owned a manuscript set of Huang's notes; see Ma Ziyun, "Tan Wu Liang Ci huaxiang de Song ta yu Huang Yi taben," 171.

10. Jiang Xuanyi, "Mota shu," part 2, 46.

11. The Institute of History and Philology in Taiwan used such a classification.

12. Jiang Xuanyi, "Mota shu," part 2, 53.

13. Ibid.

14. Jiang Xuanyi, "Mota shu," part 1, 74, and part 2, 50.

15. Jiang Xuanyi, "Mota shu," part 1, 74.

16. The catalogue is in the Field Museum.

17. *Guoli zhongyang tushuguan zhongwen tushu bianmu guize*, 129–39, details rules for cataloging rubbings.

18. See Shaanxi Provincial Museum, *Xi'an Beilin shufa yishu*; see also *Beijing Tushuguan cang Zhongguo lidai shike taben huibian*.

19. Jiang Xuanyi, "Mota shu," part 2, 53.

20. Ibid., 48–49; see also chap. 4, this volume.

21. Ye Changchi, *Yu shi*, 10:317. Van Gulik, *Chinese Pictorial Art As Viewed by the Connoisseur*, 73–78, details backing.

22. Ye Changchi, *Yu shi*, 10:316. Zhang Yanyuan was a Tang connoisseur of and author on calligraphy and painting; see *Zhongguo renming dacidian*, 943. Van Gulik, *Chinese Pictorial Art As Viewed by the Connoisseur*, provides a comprehensive description of mounting paintings; see chaps. 1–4. The present account emphasizes rubbings.

23. Van Gulik, *Chinese Pictorial Art As Viewed by the Connoisseur*, 278, cites Jiangnan as the Ming and Qing center. Su Yinghui named the modern cities (oral communication, 30 March 1960).

24. For the evolution from scroll to album, see van Gulik, *Chinese Pictorial Art As Viewed by the Connoisseur*, 218–21.

25. Ibid. Aside from several minor points of question, van Gulik (86–89) provides an excellent brief account of rubbings lore but devotes only a few lines to their mounting (94). He refers to the difficulties of handling the rubbing paper and its tendency to expand but does not mention the adverse effects of stretching the wet paper and "fattening" the characters. Pomeranz-Liedtke, *Die Weisheit der Kunst: Chinesische Steinbreibungen*, also broadly treats stone rubbings.

26. Jiang Xuanyi, "Mota shu," part a, 50–51, 53; van Gulik, *Chinese Pictorial Art As Viewed by the Connoisseur*, 150, 229, also refers to vermifugal additions.

27. Zhou Jiazhou, *Zhuanghuang zhi*, 44:9b–10a.

28. Ye Changchi, *Yu shi*, 10:316. See also Jiang Xuanyi, "Mota shu," part 2, 52; van Gulik, *Chinese Pictorial Art As Viewed by the Connoisseur*, 94–95, 97.

29. Van Gulik, *Chinese Pictorial Art As Viewed by the Connoisseur*, 97.

30. Jiang Xuanyi, "Mota shu," part 2, 52.

31. It is intriguing to note how closely the borders of mounted paintings and rubbings resemble those in the coffin complex of the Marchioness of Dai, the ageless lady in the Former Han tomb at Mawangdui, Changsha. The similar proportions, general format, and dominance of horizontal elements over vertical are striking. See Kenneth Starr, "An 'Old Rubbing' of the Latter Han *Chang Ch'ien pei*," 292 n. For an illustration of the coffin complex, see *Changsha Mawangdui yihao Han mu*, 2, plate 8.

32. Van Gulik, *Chinese Pictorial Art As Viewed by the Connoisseur*, 218. In chaps. 2 and 3 he gives a comprehensive description of mounting, especially paintings. The focus here is on rubbings.

33. Ye Changchi, *Yu shi*, 10:316–17.

34. Jiang Xuanyi, "Mota shu," part 2, 52.

35. Ye Changchi, *Yu shi*, 10:317.

36. Zhou Jiazhou, *Zhuanghuang zhi*, 44:10a–b.

37. Zhou Erxue, *Shangyan suxin lu*, 45: 6b.

38. Ye Changchi, *Yu shi*, 10:318.

39. Van Gulik, *Chinese Pictorial Art As Viewed by the Connoisseur*, 215–23, tracks the history of title labels in China. The emphasis here is on rubbings.

40. Zhou Jiazhou, *Zhuanghuang zhi*, 44: 7b; Zhang Yanchang, *Jinsu jian shuo*, 127.

41. Zhou Erxue, *Shangyan suxin lu*, 45: 6b; Zhang Yanchang, *Jinsu jian shuo*, 127; van Gulik, *Chinese Pictorial Art As Viewed by the Connoisseur*, 301 n.

42. Jiang Xuanyi, "Mota shu," part 2, 53.

43. Zhou Erhxue, *Shangyan suxin lu*, 45: 6b. Zhou frowns on carved labels.

44. Van Gulik, *Chinese Pictorial Art As Viewed by the Connoisseur*, 215–25, summarizes the evolution of wrappers, traditional since the Han.

45. Zhou Erxue, *Shangyan suxin lu*, 45: 9a.

46. For *xia* boxes, see Tu Long, *Kaopan yushi*, part 2:35, and Zhou Erxue, *Shangyan suxin lu*, 45: 8b–9a.

47. Jiang Xuanyi, "Mota shu," part 2, 52.

48. Ibid.

7 / THE RICE AND THE CHAFF

1. Shaughnessy, afterword to Tsuen-hsuin Tsien, *Written on Bamboo and Silk*, 2nd ed., 209.

2. Dong Zuobin was one of many who have drawn on historical records to supplement archeology. See Li Chi et al., *Ch'êng-tzŭ-yai*, 93; Li Chi, *Ch'êng-tzŭ-yai: The Black Pottery Culture Site at Lung-shan-chên in Li-ch'êng-hsien, Shantung Province*, 154. See also Shaughnessy, afterword to Tsuen-hsuin Tsien, *Written on Bamboo and Silk*, 2nd edition.

3. Yan Gengwang, ed., *Shike shiliao congshu*.

4. Chang Kwang-chih. *The Archaeology of Ancient China*, 113–14, 274–75; Cheung Kwong-yue, "Recent Archaeological Evidence Reflecting the Origin of Chinese Characters"; Shaughnessy, afterword to Tsuen-hsuin Tsien, *Written on Bamboo and Silk*, 2nd ed., 223.

5. For a biography of Xu and an account of his work, see Erickson, *Words Without Meaning, Meaning Without Words*.

6. Mattos, *The Stone Drums of Ch'in*, 24. Ledderose, "Thunder Sound Cave," 251, notes the utility of Qing rubbings of the engravings at Stone Sutra Mountain.

7. Ye Changchi, *Yu shi*, is a basic source on stone inscriptions, rubbings, and related aspects. Subjects include the history of inscribed stones; provincial stone inscriptions; terminology relating to *bei*, including differences between *bei* and *tie*; types and subjects of stone inscriptions; and rubbings, including mounting and identifying their provincial origins from their paper and ink. Later writers draw on the *Yu shi*, including Weng Kaiyun, "Beitie mantan," 70–73, in describing the origins and development of *bei* and *tie*. David, *Chinese Connoisseurship*, 36 n. 3, differentiates the two; Ledderose, *Mi Fu and the Classical Tradition of Chinese Calligraphy*, 10–12, describes their characteristics, as does Dong Juewei, "Zeyang tabei," part 1, 41.

8. Ye Changchi, *Yu shi*, 3:73; Weng Kaiyun, "Beitie mantan," 71; Dong Juewei, "Zeyang tabei," part 1, 41. For the form and function of *jie*, see Brashier, "Evoking the Ancestor," 72–73, 80.

9. Xu Shen, *Shuowen jiezi*, 9 *xia*:4b; Ye Changchi, *Yu shi*, 3:73; Weng Kaiyun, "Beitie mantan," 71.

10. Brashier, "Evoking the Ancestor," 47–48.

11. Ibid., 72–84, discusses *jie* grave markers and differentiates six stele shapes.

12. Letter from Liu Hui, Dai Miao, Taian, 5 August 2001.

13. Ye Changchi, *Yu shi*, 3:73; Weng Kaiyun, "Beitie mantan," 70–71. Brashier, "Evoking the Ancestor," 80–84, recites traditional explanations but posits that steles mutated from earlier tem-

porary preburial wooden *chong* markers; he concludes "that the *bei* by the time of the *Shuowen jiezi* in 100 C.E. was defined as an upright stone without any reference to its function" (47–48). See also Xu Shen, *Shuowen jiezi*, 9 *xia*:4b.

14. Ye Changchi, *Yu shi*, 3: 73. For *bei* stylistic changes, see Nakata, "Shin koku seki to Kan hi," 116–17; Nakata, "Qin Stone Inscriptions and Han Steles," 112.

15. Ye Changchi, *Yu shi*, 4:112; Weng Kaiyun, "Beitie mantan," 71. Nakata, "Rikuchō no sekikoku," 125; Nakata, "Stone Inscriptions of the Six Dynasties," 120. For economic reasons, see Brashier, "Evoking the Ancestor," 111–13, and Harrist, "Record of the Eulogy on Mt. Tai," 70.

16. Weng Kaiyun, "Beitie mantan," 71. For the development of *tie*, see Ledderose, "Rubbings in Art History"; for a fuller account, with differences between *bei* and *tie*, see Ledderose, *Mi Fu and the Classical Tradition of Chinese Calligraphy*, 10–12.

17. Weng Kaiyun, "Beitie mantan," 71–72, states that while some hold that cutting *tie* in stone began as early as the Southern Tang (937–975), he concurs with Weng Fanggang that it did not begin until the Northern Song, with the *Chunhua Ge fatie* (992) the first example.

18. Ibid.

19. Ibid., 72.

20. Ye Changchi, *Yu shi*, 3:85; Weng Kaiyun, "Beitie mantan," 70.

21. Ye Changchi, *Yu shi*, 3:85; Wang Zhuangwei, *Shufa zongtan*, 101–2; Weng Kaiyun, "Beitie mantan," 70. Ledderose, *Mi Fu and the Classical Tradition of Chinese Calligraphy*, 12, differentiates two eighteenth-century schools of thought, the "*Tie* School" (*Tie Xue*) and the "*Bei* School" (*Bei Xue*). Bai Qianshen, "The Artistic and Intellectual Dimensions of Chinese Calligraphy Rubbings," 86–88, calls these the "Model Book School," which focused on Wang Xizhi and the classical calligraphic tradition, and the "Stele School," which looked to early metal and stone inscriptions.

22. David, *Chinese Connoisseurship*, 36 n. 3.

23. Ibid.

24. Weng Kaiyun, "Beitie mantan," 70.

25. Ye Changchi, *Yu shi*, 3:85; Zhou Jiazhou, Zhuanghuang zhi, 44:9b–10a; Weng Kaiyun, "Beitie mantan," 70.

26. Wang Zhuangwei, *Shufa zongtan*, 103. See Ye Changchi, *Yu shi*, juan 3–5, for Ye Changchi's list of *shike*.

27. Li Shuhua, who participated in the survey; oral communication, 8 May 1960.

28. Cheng Jilin, Dai Miao, Taian, oral communication, 2 May 1993. Harrist, "Record of the Eulogy on Mt. Tai," 78, reported that Li Peng, former premier of the People's Republic, set a self-legitimizing stone cut of his own calligraphy on the summit of Mt. Tai, near Tang and Qing inscriptions.

29. Shaughnessy, afterword to Tsuen-hsuin Tsien, *Written on Bamboo and Silk*, 2nd ed., 223.

30. The provinces take their regular names (Shandong, "east of the mountains," and Shanxi, "west of the mountains") and their literary names (Shanzuo, "left of the mountains," and Shanyou, "right of the mountains") from their relationships with the dividing Tai Hang (mountains). The regular names relate to compass directions; the literary, as seen looking south from Beijing, as in Bi Yuan and Ruan Yuan, *Shanzuo jinshi zhi*.

31. Cost considerations required elimination of many references and illustrations, spanning the humanities through the sciences and technology, and connoisseurship as well; figures 7.16–7.26 provide a sampling of the disciplinal range. For additional examples, see Walravens, ed., *Catalogue of Chinese Rubbings from Field Museum*, and the rubbings catalogue of the East Asian Library at the University of California, Berkeley. See also note 33.

32. Shaughnessy, afterword to Tsuen-hsuin Tsien, *Written on Bamboo and Silk*, 2nd ed., 224. The

preface to Brashier, "Evoking the Ancestor," is definite: "Even in China and Japan, Han stelae are studied for their calligraphy. . . . To my knowledge there exists no extended exploration of their textual content."

33. Notable exceptions in the United States are the Field Museum, strong in stone rubbings, and the East Asian Library at Berkeley, strong in *fatie* and bronze inscriptions. The Field Museum has a printed catalogue of a large part of its collection, and a team from the United States and China is preparing a bilingual Web site with a database of information and photographs. The East Asian Library has its collection online and is preparing a printed catalogue, due out in 2007. See Walravens, ed., *Catalogue of Chinese Rubbings from Field Museum*, bibliography; see also Keng Huilin et al., *Rubbings of Chinese Inscriptions: Notes on Rubbings in the Collection in the East Asian Library at the University of California, Berkeley.* Princeton University Art Museum has a large rubbings collection.

34. Jiang Xuanyi, "Mota shu," part 2, 51.

35. In a letter of 8 March 1959, Su Yinghui stated that Zhou was not in Taiwan and that he did not know if Zhou still was alive. Zhou died in 1961. Su added that one could not buy composite rubbings in Taiwan at that time.

36. Rong Geng, *Shang Zhou yiqi tongkao*, 1:176.

37. See Hummel, *Eminent Chinese of the Ch'ing Period*, 521; see also *Zhongguo renming dacidian*, 1063.

38. Rong Geng, *Shang Zhou yiqi tongkao*, 1:176.

39. Su Yinghui, "Tushuguan cang tapian de bianmu gongzuo," 25. Jiang Xuanyi, "Mota shu," part 2, 51, notes that when he was writing, in the late 1930s, the most skilled rubbers were from Shandong.

40. Jiang Xuanyi, "Mota shu," part 2, 51.

41. See Taiwan Cultural Commission, *Taiwan wenxian*, special issue devoted to the Lu Wang inscription. Other historic Quemoy steles include *Huang Ming Shijing Zheng shi fenzhiming* (epitaph of Zheng [Chengggong] of Shijing [Fujian] in the imperial Ming). Zheng was a defender of the Ming in its final days.

42. Jiang Xuanyi, "Mota shu," part 1, 69, recalls urging his younger sisters to make rubbings of the family jades and potsherds.

43. Conversation with Qu and Jiang, Taiwan, 20 May 1960.

44. Ibid.

45. Su Yinghui (oral communication, 23 April 1960) pointed out that a seal of Rong Geng in blue on a rubbing in the National Central Library in Taiwan indicated that one of Rong's parents had died in the past twenty-four months. Li Zongtong (24 June 1960) noted that some people also used yellow. Such coloring is a further means of documenting the ownership, authenticity, and date of a rubbing.

46. Mattos, *The Stone Drums of Ch'in*, exhaustively examines their location, purpose, and language and script, and it elucidates texts and compares them with other Zhou texts.

47. Ma Heng, "Shigu wei Qin keshi kao," 13b–14b, summarizes traditional and current (1923) opinions on dating the cuttings, including the views of Guo Moruo, *Shigu wen yanjiu*, 1:8b–10a, and of Zhang Guangyuan, "Shigu wen de renshi." See also Wu Bolun, "Zhongguo shufa yanbian lishi zuoyao," 2 (the English brochure, 7–8, transposes the Guo and Ma assignments).

48. Mattos, *The Stone Drums of Ch'in*, 369.

49. *Beijing Tushuguan cang Zhongguo lidai shike taben huibian*, 1.

50. Ma Heng, "Shigu wei Qin keshi kao," 1b. Mattos, *The Stone Drums of Ch'in*, 52, describes the attrition as recorded by Ouyang Xiu (1007–1072) and states (23) that "at present [1988], only around 272 graphs remain."

51. Ma Heng, "Shigu wei Qin keshi, kao," 1a–b.

52. For general references to the Stone Drums and rubbings of them, see Mattos, *The Stone Drums of Ch'in*; Tsien, *Written on Bamboo and Silk*, 1st ed., 65–66; Tsien, *Written on Bamboo and Silk*, 2nd ed., 70–72. Tsien, *Zhongguo gudai shu shi*, 60–61; and Tsuen-hsuin Tsien's biographical sketch of An Guo in Goodrich and Chao, *Dictionary of Ming Biography*, 9–12. Older Chinese studies include Guo Moruo, *Shigu wen yanjiu*; Ma Heng, "Shigu wei Qin keshi kao"; and Na Zhiliang, *Shigu tongkao*. Tang Lan, "Shigu niandai kao," includes photographs of all ten stones and rubbings of all but number eight, whose inscription is gone. Mattos, *The Stone Drums of Ch'in*, 55–56, describes these rare Song rubbings, now in Japan.

53. Letter of 9 July 1993 from Li Yingji of the Palace Museum, following the author's visit in April of that year.

54. Wu Shifen, *Jinshi huimu fenbian*, 1a.

55. Compilers of catalogues have recorded these imitative recuts. Wu Shifen, *Jinshi huimu fenbian*, lists those at Shaoxing and Changsha.

56. Ma Ji, Beilin, Xi'an, oral communication, 16 April 1993.

57. Oral communication from Zhuang Yan, former director, Palace Museum, Taibei, 6 March 1962.

58. One hears two terms for rubbings, *hei laohu*, "black tigers," and *mo*[a] *laohu*, "ink tigers." *Hei* and *mo*[a] have both different and overlapping meanings. The basic meaning of *hei* is "black," whereas the primary meaning of *mo*[a] is "ink," with "black" and "dark" as secondary meanings. Usage varies. The Song writer Zhai Qinian, *Zhou shi, juan shang*, 10, used *mo*[a] in *mo*[a] *qikuan*, "to ink (or blacken) inscriptions on bronze vessels." Wang Chi-chen, *Reproductions of Chinese Rubbings Taken from Inscriptions Cut in Stone, Wood and Also from Bronzes, Monuments and Other Bas-reliefs*, 4, uses the term in its primary sense of "ink," as in "ink tigers." Colleagues at the Beilin, the Palace Museum, and the Nanjing City Museum gave differing interpretations. All concurred on *hei* meaning "black" and on the derived negative connotations, including blackhearted, unscrupulous dealers. The majority held that *hei laohu* was the common term for "rubbings." One Beilin authority stated that the term *mo*[a] *laohu*, "ink tigers," was not common for rubbings but that some people used it interchangeably with *hei laohu*. A specialist at the Palace Museum was emphatic that *mo*[a] *laohu* referred to calligraphy, to brush-written characters and not to rubbings, which were *hei laohu*.

Bibliography

ABBREVIATIONS

BIHP	*Guoli Zhongyang yanjiuyuan lishi yuyan yanjiusuo jikan.* (Bulletin of the Institute of History and Philology, Academia Sinica). Nanjing and Taibei, 1928–.
CSJC	*Congshu jicheng* (Collection of collectanea). Shanghai and Taibei: Commercial Press, 1936–91.
MSCS (1936)	*Meishu congshu* (Collectanea on fine arts). Shanghai: Shenzhou guoguangshe, 1936.
MSCS (1975)	*Meishu congshu* (Collectanea on fine arts). Taibei: Yiwen Press, 1975.
PXZCS	*Pangxi zhai congshu* (Collectanea in the Studio of Abundant Happiness). Wu Xian: Pan Zuyin, Tongzhi–Guangxu-reign periods (1862–1908).
SBCK	*Sibu congkan* (Collected works in four divisions). Shanghai: Commercial Press, 1929.
ZDCS	*Zhaodai congshu* (Collectanea on literary writings). Location unknown: Shikai Tang, 1876.

Aspects of Taiwan's Handmade Paper Industry. Appleton, Wis.: Institute of Paper Chemistry, 1972 (color film).

Bai Qianshen. "The Artistic and Intellectual Dimensions of Chinese Calligraphy Rubbings: Some Examples from the Collection of Robert Hatfield Ellsworth." *Orientations* 3 (March 1999), 82–88.

———. *Fu Shan's World: The Transformation of Chinese Calligraphy in the Seventeenth Century.* Cambridge, Mass.: Harvard University Asia Center, 2003.

Bao Changxi. *Jinshi xie* (Bits and pieces on metal and stone), 8 vols. Jiaxing, 1877.

Beedell, Suzanne. *Brasses and Brass Rubbing.* Edinburgh: John Bartholomew, 1973.

Beijing Tushuguan cang Zhongguo lidai shike taben huibian (Chinese stone rubbings from successive dynasties in the Beijing Library), 101 vols. Zhengzhou: Zhongguo guji chubanshe, 1989–91.

Bernstein, Mark F. "An Uncertain History." *Princeton Alumni Weekly,* 23 March 2005, 22–25 (interview with Cary Y. Liu on the Wu Liang reliefs).

Bi Yuan and Ruan Yuan. *Shanzuo jinshi zhi* (Record of Shandong metal and stone), 12 vols. 1797.

Brashier, Kenneth Edward. "Evoking the Ancestor: The Stele Hymn of the Eastern Han Dynasty (25–220 C.E.)." Ph.D. diss., University of Cambridge, 1997.

Cao Pi (Wei Wendi). *Dian lun* (Codes of conduct). *Wenjintang congshu*, vol. 8.

Cao Zhao. *Gegu yaolun* (The essential criteria of antiquities), 13 *juan*. Xindu [Sichuan] Huang shi jiao keben, 1598(?). In Percival David, trans., *Chinese Connoisseurship: The Ke Ku Yao Lun: The Essential Criteria of Antiquities.* New York: Praeger, 1971 (includes a photocopy of the 1388 three-*juan* edition).

Carter, Thomas Francis. *The Invention of Printing in China and Its Spread Westward*, 1st ed. New York: Columbia University Press, 1925; rev. ed. by L. C. Goodrich, New York: Ronald Press, 1955.

———. *The Invention of Printing in China and Its Spread Westward*, 2nd ed. New York: Ronald Press, 1955.

Chang Kwang-chih. *The Archaeology of Ancient China*, 3rd ed. New Haven, Conn.: Yale University Press, 1977.

Changsha Mawangdui yihao Han mu (Han tomb no. 1 at Mawangdui, Changsha). 2 vols. Beijing: Wenwu chubanshe, 1973.

Chao Guanzhi. *Mo jing* (Classic on ink). *CSJC*, series 1, vol. 1495.

Chavannes, Edouard. *La sculpture sur pierre en Chine au temps des deux Han.* Paris: Ernest Leroux, 1893.

———. "Les inscriptions des Ts'in." *Journal Asiatique* 9:2 (1893), 484–86.

Chen Baochen. See Sun Zhuang.

Chen Jieqi. *Chuangu bielu* (Separate record on perpetuating antiquity). PXZCS, vol. 28; for a Japanese version of the section on making rubbings, see "Kodōki no takuhō" (The method of rubbing ancient bronzes), *Shōen* 1:7 (1939), 16–18, and *Shōen* 1:10 (1939), 28–30.

———. *Fu zhai cang jing* (Mirrors in the Studio of the Sacrificial *Fu*-vessel). Photolithographic ed. Location and publisher unknown, 1925.

Chen Naiqian. *Baiyi lu jinshi congshu* (Collectanea on metal and stone in the Hundred-and-one Cottage). Location and publisher unknown, 1921.

Chen Yuanlong. *Gezhi jingyuan.* (Encyclopedia of scientific and technical origins). 24 vols., 1735.

Chen Zunren. *Zhongguo yaoxue dacidian* (Dictionary of Chinese medicine). 3 vols. Shanghai: Shijie shuju, 1935.

Cheng Dachang. *Yanfan lu* (Extension of the string of pearls on the Spring and Autumn Annals). *Xuejin taoyuan* (1805), vols. 116–18.

Cheung Kwong-yue. "Recent Archaeological Evidence Reflecting the Origin of Chinese Characters." In David N. Keightley, ed., *The Origins of Chinese Civilization.* Berkeley: University of California Press, 1983, 323–91.

Ching, Dora C. Y., Robert E. Harrist Jr., and Cary C. Liu. "The Embodied Image: Chinese Calligraphy from the John B. Elliot Collection." *Orientations* 3 (March 1999), 97–105.

Cihai (Sea of Words), 2 vols. Shanghai: Zhonghua shuju, 1938.

Ciyuan (Spring of Words), rev. ed., 1 vol. Taibei: Commercial Press, 1970.

Cribb, Joe, and Jonathan Williams. "Who Made the First Coins?" *British Museum* 27 (1997), 18–20.

Daijiten (The great dictionary [Japanese]), American ed. Cambridge, Mass.: Harvard University Press, 1942.

David, Percival. *Chinese Connoisseurship: The Ke Ku Yao Lun: The Essential Criteria of Antiquities.* New York: Praeger, 1971.

Ding Fubao. *Gu qian dacidian* (Dictionary of ancient coins), 12 vols. Shanghai: Yixue shuju, 1938.

Dizhi kuangwuxue dacidian. (Dictionary of geology and mineralogy). Location unknown: Commercial Press, 1944.

Dong Juewei. "Zeyang tabei" (How to rub steles), part 1. *Shufa* 1 (1986), 41–43.

———. "Zeyang tabei" (How to rub steles), part 2. *Shufa* 2 (1986), 46–48.

Dong Zuobin. "*Mao Gong ding*" (The *Mao Gong ding* cauldron). Taibei: *Continent Magazine*, 1952.

Dongwuxue dacidian. (Dictionary of zoology). Shanghai: Commercial Press, 1933.

Dou Ji. "Shushu fu" (Prose poem on explaining calligraphy). *MSCS* 16 (1975), 1–52.

Du Fu. "Li Chao bafen xiaozhuan ge" (Poem on the *bafen* "small-seal" calligraphy of Li Chao). Peng

Dingqu et al., *Quan Tang shi* (Complete book of Tang poetry), vol. 2, *juan* 7:14. Taibei: Fuxing shuju, 1974 (reprint of the 1706 ed.).

Du Halde, Jean Baptiste. *Description Géographique, Historique, Chronologique, Politique, et Physique de l'Empire de la Chine*, 4 vols. The Hague: Henri Scheurleer, 1736.

———. *The General History of China*, 3rd ed. Trans. Richard Brookes. 4 vols. London: J. Watts, 1736–41.

Du Yaquan. *Dongwuxue dacidian* (Dictionary of zoology). Shanghai: Commercial Press, 1933.

Encyclopaedia Britannica 2003. Compact disc. Chicago: Britannica, 2003.

Ennin (Jikaku Daishi). *Dai Nihon Bukkyō Zensho* (Collected works of Japanese Buddhism). Tokyo: Suzuki gakujitsu zaidan, 1970.

———. *Ennin's Diary: The Record of a Pilgrimage to China in Search of the Law.* Trans. Edwin O. Reischauer. New York: Ronald Press, 1955.

———. "Nittō guhō junrei gyōki" (Travels of Ennin in Tang China in search of the Law). Entry 563 in *Dai Nihon Bukkyō Zensho* (Collected works of Japanese Buddhism). Tokyo: Suzuki gakujitsu zaidan, 1970.

Erickson, Britta. *Words Without Meaning, Meaning Without Words: The Art of Xu Bing.* Washington, D.C., and Seattle. Wash.: Arthur M. Sackler Gallery, Smithsonian Institution, and University of Washington Press, 2001.

Fairbank, Wilma. "The Offering Shrines of 'Wu Liang Tz'u.'" *Harvard Journal of Asiatic Studies* 6:1 (1941), 1–36.

Fan Ye. *Hou Han shu* (History of the Later Han). Shanghai: Tongwen shuju, 1884 (photolithographic reproduction of the palace edition of 1739).

———. *Hou Han shu* (History of the Later Han). Beijing: Zhonghua shuju, 1965.

Fang Yizhi. *Tongya* (Understanding elegance). Tongshan: Tao shi, 1666.

Feng Yan. *Feng shi wenjian ji* (Record of what Mr. Feng has seen and heard). *Qifu congshu*, vol. 36, 1879.

Ferguson, John C. "The Six Horses at the Tomb of the Emperor T'ai Tsung of the T'ang Dynasty." *Eastern Art* 3 (1931), 61–71.

———. "Wang Ch'uan." *Ostasiatische Zeitschrift*, 1914–15, 51–60.

Free China Journal. Government Information Office, Republic of China. Taibei: 1964– .

Giles, Lionel. *Descriptive Catalogue of the Chinese Manuscripts from Tunhuang in the British Museum.* London: Trustees of the British Museum, 1957.

———. *Six Centuries at Dunhuang: A Short Account of the Chinese Manuscripts in the British Museum.* London: The China Society, 1944.

Goodrich, L. Carrington, and F. Y. Chao. *Dictionary of Ming Biography, 1368–1644.* 2 vols. New York: Columbia University Press, 1976.

Gu Yanwu. *Jinshi wenzi ji* (Record of metal and stone inscriptions), 2 vols. Location and publisher unknown, ca. 1695.

Gu Yewang (519–581). *Yupian lingjuan* (Jade tablet miscellany). *CSJC, chubian.* Shanghai: Commercial Press, 1935.

Guo Moruo. *Shigu wen yanjiu* (Research on the Stone Drum inscriptions), 2 vols. Changsha: Commercial Press, 1940.

———. "Shigu wen yanjiu." *Moruo wenji, juan* 16. Beijing: Renmin chubanshe, 1962.

Guoli zhongyang tushuguan zhongwen tushu bianmu guize (Rules for cataloging Chinese-language books in the National Central Library). Taibei: National Central Library, 1959.

Guoyeu Tsyrdean. (Dictionary of the national language), 4 vols. Taibei: Commercial Press, 1953.

Harley, J. B., and David Woodward, eds. *The History of Cartography*, vol. 2, book 2: *Cartography in the Traditional East and Southeast Asian Societies.* Chicago: University of Chicago Press, 1994.

Harrist, Robert E. Jr. "Copies, All the Way Down: Replication in Chinese Calligraphy." *East Asian Library Journal* 10:1 (2002), 176–96.

———. "Record of the Eulogy on Mt. Tai and Imperial Autographic Monuments of the Tang Dynasty." *Oriental Art* 46:2 (2000), 68–79.

Hosking, R. F., and G. M. Meridith-Owens, eds. *A Handbook of Asian Scripts.* London: Trustees of the British Museum, 1966.

Hsü Chin-hsiung. *Oracle Bones from the White and Other Collections.* Toronto: The Royal Ontario Museum, 1979.

———. *The Menzies Collections of Shang Dynasty Oracle Bones.* Toronto: The Royal Ontario Museum (preface dated 1970).

Hucker, Charles O. *A Dictionary of Official Titles in Imperial China.* Stanford, Calif.: Stanford University Press, 1958.

Hummel, Arthur W., ed. *Eminent Chinese of the Ch'ing Period (1644–1912).* Washington: Library of Congress, 1943.

Hunter, Dard. *A Papermaking Pilgrimage to Japan, Korea and China.* New York: Pynson Printers, 1936.

———. *Papermaking: The History and Technique of an Ancient Craft*, 2nd ed. New York: Knopf, 1947.

Imms, A. D. *A General Textbook of Entomology.* 9th rev. ed. London: Methuen, 1957.

Inoue Yasushi. *Tunhuang*, 1st paperback ed. New York: Kodansha, 1983.

Jia Rukai, ed. *Dai Miao* (The Dai Miao [temple-museum, Taian]), 2nd printing. Location unknown: Wenwu chubanshe, 1992.

Jiang Xuanyi. "Mota shu" (The rubbing technique), part 1. *Shuowen yuekan* 1:10–11 (1939), 69–76.

———. "Mota shu," (The rubbing technique), part 2. *Shuowen yuekan* 1:12 (1939), 43–54.

Jianming hanying cidian (The Concise Chinese English Dictionary). Beijing: Commercial Press, 1982.

Jun Yu. "Tan taben" (Discussing rubbings). *Kaogu tongxun* 5 (1955), 72–75.

Kangxi zidian (The Kangxi dictionary). Hong Kong: Zhonghua shuju, 1958 (reprinted 1973).

Keightley, David N., ed. *The Origins of Chinese Civilization.* Berkeley: University of California Press, 1983.

Keng Huilin et al. *Rubbings of Chinese Inscriptions: Notes on Rubbings in the Collection in the East Asian Library at the University of California, Berkeley.* Berkeley: East Asian Library, University of California, 1992.

Kenkyusha's New Japanese-English Dictionary, American ed. Cambridge, Mass.: Harvard University Press, 1942.

Kern, Martin. *The Stele Inscriptions of Ch'in Shih-huang: Text and Ritual in Early Chinese Imperial Representation.* New Haven, Conn.: American Oriental Society, 2000.

Le Compte, Louis Daniel. *Memoirs and Observations.* London: Tooke, 1697.

Ledderose, Lothar. *Mi Fu and the Classical Tradition of Chinese Calligraphy.* Princeton, N.J.: Princeton University Press, 1979.

———. "Rubbings in Art History." In Hartmut Walravens. ed., with research by Hoshien Tchen and M. Kenneth Starr. *Catalogue of Chinese Rubbings from Field Museum.* Chicago: Field Museum of Natural History, 1981, xxvii–xxxvi.

———. "Thunder Sound Cave." In Wu Hung, ed., *In Between Han and Tang: Visual and Material Culture in a Transformative Period.* Beijing: Wenwu chubanshe, 2003, 235–60.

Li Chi et al. *Ch'êng-tzŭ-yai* (A report on excavations at Chengziyai, Licheng Xian, Shandong). Nanjing: Academia Sinica, 1934.

———. *Ch'êng-tzŭ-yai: The Black Pottery Culture Site at Lung-shan-chên in Li-ch'êng-hsien, Shantung Province.* Trans. Kenneth Starr. New Haven, Conn.: Yale University Press, 1956.

Li Ch'iao-p'ing. *The Chemical Arts of Old China.* Easton, Pa.: Journal of Chemical Education, 1948.

Li Fang. *Taiping yulan* (The Taiping [976–983] encyclopedia). *SBCK.* Shanghai: Commercial Press, 1935.

Li Shizhen, ed. *Bencao gangmu* (Catalogue of plants). Facsimile of Guangxu ed. (1885). Beijing: Renmin weisheng chubanshe, 1957.

Li Shuhua. "The Early Development of Seals and Rubbings." *Tsing Hua Journal of Chinese Studies* 1:3 (1958), 61–87.

———. "Yinzhang yu mota de qiyuan ji qi duiyu diaoban yinshua faming de yingxiang" (The early development of seals and rubbings, and their influence on the invention of woodblock printing). Taipei: *BIHP* 28, part 1 (1956), 107–21.

Li Xiaomei. *Mo pu* (*Mo yuan*) (Treatise on ink). Supplemented by Pan Yingzhi, *Mo ping* (Notes on ink). Beiping: Palace Museum (copy of a Ming Wanli ed., 1930).

Liao Yingzhong. *Chunhua Ge mige fatie* (Calligrapic model book from the Chunhua Pavilion), hand copied (*lin*) by Dong Qichang (Ming), photolithographic ed. Beiping: Guwu chenlie suo, 1931.

Lin Puzan. *Jimo Xian zhi* (Gazetteer of Jimo Xian, Shandong), 12 *juan.* 1783.

Liu, Cary Y., Michael Nylan, and Anthony J. Barbieri-Low. *Recarving China's Past: Art, Archaeology, and Architecture of the "Wu Family Shrines."* Princeton, N.J., and New Haven, Conn.: Princeton University Art Museum and Yale University Press, 2005.

Liu Tizhi. *Xiaojiaojing Ge jinwen taben* (Rubbings of metal inscriptions in the Small Pavilion for Collating the Classics), 18 vols. Location and publisher unknown, 1935.

Liu Xu et al. *Jiu Tang shu* (Old history of the Tang dynasty). Shanghai: Tongwen shuju, 1884.

Long Dayuan. *Gu yu tupu* (Illustrated catalogue of ancient jades). Kangshancao tang cangben, 1779.

Lu Shihua. *Shuhua shuoling* (Observations on calligraphy and painting). *Yuyuan congshu* 16. Location and publisher unknown, 1893.

Lu You. *Mo shi* (History of ink). *CSJC,* series 1, vol. 1495.

Lü Dalin. *Kaogu tu* (Illustrations of antiquities). Location unknown: Yizheng tang, 1752.

Luo Ergang. *Taiping Tianguo jinshi lu* (Record of metal and stone from the Taiping Rebellion). Shanghai, 1948.

Luo Zhenyu. "Mogaoku shishi milu" (The secret contents of the walled chamber at Mogaoku). *Kaoguxue lingjian, Dongfang wenku* 71 (1923), 1–41.

Ma Heng. "Ge ji zhi yanjiu" (Research on *ge* and *ji* halberds). *Yanjing xuebao* 5 (June 1929), 745–53.

———. "Shigu wei Qin keshi kao" (Research on the Stone Drums being cut in Qin). *Guoxue jikan* (Sinological Quarterly of the National University of Peking) 1 (1923), 17–23 (reissued as a separate photolithographic ed., 1931).

Ma Xulun. *Shuowen jiezi liu shu shuzheng* (Clarifying the six scripts in the *Shuowen jiezi).* Beijing: Kexue chubanshe, 1957.

Ma Ziyun. "Tan Wu Liang Ci huaxiang de Song ta yu Huang Yi taben" (Discussing Song rubbings of the Wu Liang pictorials and those made by Huang Yi in Qing). *Bulletin of the National Palace Museum* (Beijing) 2 (1960), 170–77.

Makino Tomitarō. *Nihon shokubutsu zukan* (Illustrated encyclopedia of Japanese plants), 11th ed. Tokyo: Hokuryūkan, 1935.

Mao Fengzhi. *Guanzhong jinshi wenzi cunyin kao* (Research on extant Shaanxi metal and stone inscriptions). Shaoxing, 1901.

Mathews, Robert Henry. *Chinese-English Dictionary*, rev. American ed. Cambridge, Mass.: Harvard University Press, 1943.

Mattos, Gilbert L. *The Stone Drums of Ch'in*. Nettetal: Steyler Verlag, 1988.

McCarthy, Mary. "Secrets Carved in Stone." *Frederick* (Maryland), Aug. 2000, 60–61.

Metcalf, Z. P. *General Catalogue of the Homoptera*, fasc. 4, part 13. Raleigh: North Carolina State College, 1957.

Moule, Arthur Christopher. *Christians in China Before the Year 1500*. New York: Macmillan, 1930.

Musées Nationaux. *Manuscrits et Peintures de Touen-houang: Mission Pelliot, 1906–1909*. Paris: Imprimerie Frazier-Soye, 1947.

Na Zhiliang. *Shigu tongkao* (Comprehensive study of the Stone Drums). Taibei: Zhonghua congshu weiyuanhui, 1958.

Nakata, Yūjirō, ed. *Chūgoku no bujitsu* (History of the art of China, vol. 2: Calligraphy). Kyoto: Tankōsha, 1982.

———. *Chūgoku shoronshū* (Discussion of Chinese calligraphy). Tokyo: Nigensha, 1970.

———. *A History of the Art of China*, vol. 2: *Chinese Calligraphy*. Trans. Jeffrey Hunter. New York, Tokyo, and Kyoto: Weatherhill/Tankōsha, 1983.

———. "Qin Stone Inscriptions and Han Steles." In Yūjirō Nakata, ed., *A History of the Art of China*, vol. 2: *Chinese Calligraphy*. Trans. Jeffrey Hunter. New York, Tokyo, and Kyoto: Weatherhill/Tankōsha, 1983.

———. "Rikuchō no sekikoku." In Yūjirō Nakata, ed., *Chūgoku no bujitsu* (History of the art of China, vol. 2: Calligraphy). Kyoto: Tankōsha, 1982.

———. "Shin koku seki to Kan hi." In Yūjirō Nakata, ed., *Chūgoku no bujitsu* (History of the art of China, vol. 2: Calligraphy). Kyoto: Tankōsha, 1982.

———. "Stone Inscriptions of the Six Dynasties." In Yūjirō Nakata, ed., *A History of the Art of China*, vol. 2: *Chinese Calligraphy*. Trans. Jeffrey Hunter. New York, Tokyo, and Kyoto: Weatherhill/Tankōsha, 1983.

Niu Yunzhen. *Jinshi tu* (Illustrations of metal and stone), 1745 (rubbings of miniature copies of steles and selected portions of the original texts, pasted in stitch-bound volumes).

Ohwi, Jisaburo. *Flora of Japan*. Washington, D.C.: Smithsonian Institution, 1965.

Ouyang Xiu. *Jigu lu* (Record of collections of antiquities), 10 *juan*, 1653.

———. *Xin Tang shu* (New history of the Tang dynasty). Tongwen shuju, 1884.

Pan Zuyin, *PXZCS*. Wu Xian: Tongzhi–Guangxi periods (1862–1908).

Papermaking in China. Dalton, Mass.: Beloit Corporation, Jones Division, n.d. (color film).

Pelliot, Paul. *Les débuts de l'imprimerie en Chine*. Paris: Imprimerie Nationale, 1953.

Peng Dingqiu et al. *Quan Tang shi* (The complete Tang poems). Taibei: Fuxing shuju, 1974 (reprint of the 1706 ed.).

Pommeranz-Liedtke, Gerhard. *Die Weisheit der Kunst: Chinesische Steinbreibungen* (The wisdom of art: Chinese stone rubbings). Leipzig: Insel Verlag, 1963.

Qian Dian. *Shiliu changle tang guqi kuanshi kao* (Research on inscriptions on ancient objects in the Hall of Sixteen Eternal Happinesses). Beiping: Kaiming shuju, 1933 (copy of 1796 ed.).

Qu Wanli and Chang Bide. *Guoshu banbenxue yaolüe* (A review of book printing in China). *Xiandai guomin jiben zhishi congshu*, series 1, no. 16, 1962.

Reif, Rita. "Ink Rubbings, Ancient Art, Revived at Museum Here." *New York Times*, 20 July 1960.

Reischauer, Edwin O. *Ennin's Travels in T'ang China*. New York: Ronald Press, 1955.

Ricci, Matteo. *China in the Sixteenth Century: The Journals of Matteo Ricci, 1583–1610.* Trans. Louis J. Gallagher. New York: Random House, 1953.

Rong Geng. "Qin shihuang keshi kao" (Research on the stone cuts of Qin Shihuang). *Yanjing xuebao* (Yenjing Journal of Chinese Studies) 17 (June 1935), 125–82.

———. *Shang Zhou yiqi tongkao.* (Comprehensive study of Shang and Zhou ritual objects), 2 vols. Beiping: Harvard-Yenching Institute, 1941.

———. *Song zhai jijin tulu* (Illustrations of auspicious metals in the Praising Studio). Taibei: Tailian guofeng chubanshe, 1978.

———. *Song zhai jijin xulu* (Supplemental catalogue of auspicious metals [bronzes] in the Praising Studio). *Kaoguxueshe zhuanji* (Special issue of the Archeological Society) 14. Beiping: Wenkuei tang, 1938.

Ruan Yuan. *Jigu zhai zhongding yiqi kuanshi* (Inscriptions on ritual objects in the Accumulated Antiquities Studio). Wuchang: Hubei chongwen shuju, 1879.

———. *Liang zhe jinshi zhi* (Record of metal and stone in eastern and western Zhejiang). Hangzhou: Zhejiang shuju, 1890.

———. *Zhongding kuanshi* (Inscriptions on ritual objects). Hanyang: Ye Zhishen, 1848.

Rudolph, Richard C., with Wen You. *Han Tomb Art of West China.* Berkeley: University of California Press, 1951.

Sang Shen. "Qingtong qi quanxing ta jishu fazhan de fenqi yanjou" (Research on periods in the development of the composite technique). *Dongfang bowu* 3 (2004), 32–39.

———. "Quanxing ta zhi chuangcheng yu liubian" (Transmission and changes in composite rubbing). *Zijin cheng* 5 (2006), 52–55.

Sang Shichang. *Lanting kao* (Study of the Lanting), 12 *juan. CSJC,* chubian, vol. 1598.

Shaanxi Provincial Museum. *Shaanxi Sheng Bowuguan* (Shaanxi Provincial Museum). *Zhongguo bowuguan congshu* (Collectanea on Chinese museums), no. 1. Beijing: Wenwu chubanshe, 1983.

———. *Xi'an Beilin shufa yishu* (Calligraphic art in the Xi'an Beilin). Xi'an: Shaanxi renmin yishu chubanshe, 1983.

Shaughnessy, Edward L. Afterword to Tsuen-hsuin Tsien, *Written on Bamboo and Silk: The Beginnings of Chinese Books and Inscriptions*, 2nd ed. Chicago: University of Chicago Press, 2004.

Shen Jisun. *Mo fa jiyao* (Essentials of ink making). *CSJC,* series 1, vol. 1496. Changsha: Commercial Press, 1939.

Shoen (Garden of calligraphy). Tokyo: Sanshōdo, 1937–44.

Shufa (Calligraphy). Shanghai: Shanghai shuhua chubanshe, c. 1978– .

Shuowen yuekan (Shuowen monthly). Shanghai, Chongqing: Shuowenshe, 1939–47.

Sima Guang. *Zizhi tongjian* (Comprehensive mirror for aiding government, a history of China from late Zhou to Five Dynasties). Hubei: Chongwen shuju, 1871.

Sima Qian. *Shiji* (Records of the grand historian). Shanghai: Tongwen shuju, 1884.

Sima Zhen. *Shiji suoyin* (Commentary on records of the grand historian). Location and date unknown: Jigu ge keben.

Song Yingxing. *Tiangong kaiwu* (Exploitation of works of nature). Guoxue jiben congshu. Shanghai: Commercial Press, 1937.

———. *T'ien-kung K'ai-wu: Chinese Technology in the Seventeenth Century*, trans. Sun E-tun Zen and Shiou-chuan Sun. University Park, Pa.: Pennsylvania State University Press, 1966.

Stanley, Arthur. "The Method of Making Ink Rubbings." *Journal of the North-China Branch of the Royal Asiatic Society* 48 (1917), 83–84.

Starr, Kenneth. "An 'Old Rubbing' of the Latter Han *Chang Ch'ien pei.*" In David T. Roy and Tsuen-hsuin Tsien, eds., *Ancient China: Studies in Early Civilization.* Hong Kong: Chinese University of Hong Kong Press, 1978, 283–313.

———. "Inception of the Rubbing Technique: A Review." In *Qingzhu Li Ji xiansheng qishi sui lunwenji* (Symposium in honor of Dr. Li Chi on his seventieth birthday), part 1. Taibei: Qinghua xuebaoshe, 1965, 281–301.

———. "Old Stones and Black Tigers in Frederick County." *Maryland Surveyor* 24:3 (1997), 1, 3–8.

Stein, Mark Aurel. *Serindia: Detailed Report of Explorations in Central Asia and Westernmost China.* 5 vols. Oxford: Clarendon Press, 1921.

Steward, Albert H. *Manual of Vascular Plants of the Yangtze Valley.* Corvallis: Oregon State College, 1958.

Su Yijian. *Wenfang sipu* (Treatise on the four articles in a scholar's studio). *CSJC,* series 1, vol. 1493. Changsha: Commercial Press, 1939.

Su Yinghui. *Dunhuang xue gaiyao* (Introduction to Dunhuang studies). Taibei: Zhonghua congshu bianshen weiyuanhui, 1964.

———. "Jinshi tongshou" (Combined longevity characters on bronze and stone). Taibei: *Continent Magazine,* 1954.

———. "Tushuguan cang tapian de bianmu gongzuo" (Cataloging work on rubbings in the National Central Library). *Zhuyi yu guoce* 42 (1955), 24–30.

Sun Xingyan and Xing Zhu. *Huanyu fangbei lu* (Comprehensive record of searching for steles). Jiangsu shuju, 1883.

Sun Yuxiu (pseud. Liuan). *Zhongguo diaoban yuanliu kao* (Study of the origins of printing in China), 5th printing. Shanghai: Commercial Press, 1926.

Sun Zhuang, ed. *Ch'eng ch'iu guan jijin tu* (Illustrations of auspicious bronzes in the Clear Autumn Studio). Minhou (Fujian): Chen Baochen, 1930.

Taian Shi Bowuguan (Taian City Museum). *Dai Miao.* Location unknown: Wenwu chubanshe, 1992.

Taiwan Cultural Commission (Taiwan Wenxian Weiyuanhui). *Taiwan wenxian* 11:1 (1960), entire issue (*Ming jianguo Lu Wang teji* [Special issue of *Taiwan wenxian* (Taiwan culture) on the last Ming prince]).

Tang Funian. *Xi Zhou qingtong qi mingwen fendaishi zhengqi yingji.* Beijing: Zhonghua shuju, 1993.

Tang Lan. "Shi gu niandai kao" (Research on the date of the Stone Drums). *Gugong bowuyuan yuankan* (Bulletin of the Palace Museum) 1 (1958), 4–34.

Tang Xuan Zong, ed. *Tang liudian* (Codes and regulations of the six boards of the Tang Dynasty). 8 vols. Japanese ed., 1836.

Tao Hongjing. *Daojian lu* (Record of swords). *MSCS* 17 (1975), 333–46.

Tsiang, Katherine R. "Monumentalization of Buddist Texts in the Northern Qi Dynasty: The Engraving of *Sūtras* in Stone at the Xiangtangshan Caves and Other Sites in the Sixth Century." *Artibus Asiae* 56:3/4 (1966), 233–61.

Tsien, Tsuen-hsuin. *Paper and Printing.* In Joseph Needham, ed., *Science and Civilisation in China,* vol. 5, part 1. Cambridge: Cambridge University Press, 1985.

———. "Raw Materials for Old Papermaking in China." *Journal of the American Oriental Society,* 93:4 (1973), 510–19.

———. *Written on Bamboo and Silk: The Beginnings of Chinese Books and Inscriptions,* 1st ed. Chicago: University of Chicago Press, 1962.

———. *Written on Bamboo and Silk: The Beginnings of Chinese Books and Inscriptions,* 2nd ed. Chicago: University of Chicago Press, 2004.

———. *Zhongguo gudai shu shi* (History of Chinese books in ancient times). Hong Kong: Chinese University of Hong Kong Press, 1975.

———. *Zhongguo shuji zhimo ji yinshua shi lunwenji* (Studies on the history of the Chinese book, paper, ink, and printing). Hong Kong: Chinese University of Hong Kong Press, 1992.

Tu Long. *Kaopan yushi* (Odds and ends in the retirement cottage by the mountain torrent). *CSJC*, series 1, vol. 1559. Shanghai: Commercial Press, 1937.

Umehara, Sueji, ed. *Kankarō kikinzu* (Illustrations of auspicious metals in the Kankarō [Guanjia Lou, studio]). Kyoto: Kobayashi chōbun, 1947.

Van Gulik, R. H. *Chinese Pictorial Art As Viewed by the Connoisseur.* Rome: Istituto Italiano per Medio ed Estremo Oriente, 1958.

Vincent, Irene V. *The Sacred Oasis.* Chicago: University of Chicago Press, 1953.

Walravens, Hartmut, ed., with research by Hoshien Tchen and M. Kenneth Starr. *Catalogue of Chinese Rubbings from Field Museum.* Chicago: Field Museum of Natural History, 1981.

Wang Chang. *Jinshi cuibian* (Catalogue of metal and stone). 4 vols. Taibei: Guofeng chubanshe, 1964 (photolithographic copy of 1805 ed.).

Wang Chi-chen. "Notes on Chinese Ink," part 1. *Metropolitan Museum Studies* 3 (1930), 114–33.

———. *Reproductions of Chinese Rubbings Taken from Inscriptions Cut in Stone, Wood, and Also from Bronzes, Monuments and Other Bas-reliefs.* New York: Huxley House, 1938.

Wang Fu. *Xuanhe bogu tulu* (Illustrated catalogue of antiquities in the Song imperial collection). Location unknown: Yizheng tang, 1752.

Wang Guowei. "Shuowen suowei guwen shuo" (Commentary on the so-named *guwen* script in the *Shuowen jiezi*). In *Haining Wang Jing'an xiansheng yishu* (Collected writings of Wang Guowei), *Guantang jilin*, 7:5b–7a. Changsha: Commercial Press, 1940.

———. "Wei shi jing kao" (A study of the Wei Stone Classics). *Haining Wang Jing'an xiansheng yishu*, vol. 8. Shanghai: Commercial Press, 1936.

Wang Houzhi. *Wang Fu Zhai zhongding kuanshi* (Inscriptions on ritual vessels in the Wang Fu Studio). In Chen Naiqian, *Baiyi lu jinshi congshu* (Collectanea on metal and stone in the Hundred-and-one Cottage), vol. 3. Location and publisher unknown, 1921.

Wang Qiu. *Xiaotang jigu lu* (Record of accumulated antiquities in the Whistling Studio). In Chen Naiqian, *Baiyi lu jinshi congshu* (Collectanea on metal and stone in the Hundred-and-one Cottage), vols. 1–2. Location and publisher unknown, 1921.

Wang Yuquan. *Early Chinese Coinage.* New York: American Numismatic Society, 1951.

Wang Zhuangwei. *Shufa zongtan* (General discussion of calligraphy). Taibei: Zhonghua congshu bianshen weiyuanwei, 1965.

———. *Shufa yanjiu* (Research on calligraphy). Taibei: Commercial Press, 1967.

Wei Zheng. *Sui shu* (History of the Sui dynasty). Taibei: Yiwen Press, 1974 (reprint of the 1739 Wuyingdian ed.).

Wen You. *Sichuan Han dai huaxiang xuanji* (Selected Sichuan Han-dynasty pictorials). Shanghai: Qunlian chubanshe, 1955.

Wen Zhenheng. *Zhangwu zhi* (Record of superfluous things). *MSCS* 15 (1975), 115–258.

Weng Fenggang. *Baosu shi jinshi shuhua biannian lu* (Register of metal and stone, and calligraphy and painting in the Precious Simplicity Studio). In *Fojiao mingren nianpu* (Register of Buddhist notables). Beijing: Beijing tushuguan chubanshe, ca. 1930, 537–772.

———. *Liang Han jinshi zhi* (Record of metal and stone from the two Han dynasties). Beiping, 1789.

Weng Kaiyun. "Beitie mantan" (Chatting about steles and calligraphic models). *Shupu* 37 (1980), 70–75.

———. "'Huadu si bei yanjiu" (Research on the Huadu Temple stele). *Shupu* 66 (1985), 14–49.

West China Union University. *Zhufei jiu cang ming zhi mulu* (Catalogue of the Zhufei collection of notable Chinese papers). *Guidebook Series,* no. 10. Chengdu: West China Union University Museum, 1947.

Wu Bolun. "Zhongguo shufa yanbian lishi zuoyao" (Introduction to the history of changes in Chinese calligraphy). In Shaanxi Provincial Museum, *Xi'an Beilin shufa yishu* (Calligraphic art in the Xi'an Beilin). Xi'an: Shaanxi renmin yishu chubanshe, 1983.

Wu Hung, ed. *In Between Han and Tang: Visual and Material Culture in a Transformative Period.* Beijing: Wenwu chubanshe, 2003.

———. *The Wu Liang Shrine: The Ideology of Chinese Pictorial Art.* Stanford, Calif.: Stanford University Press, 1989.

Wu Rongguang. *Yunqing Guan jinshi lu* (Record of metal and stone in the Hall of the Clear-Skinned Bamboo). Guangzhou, 1842.

Wu Shifen. *Jinshi huimu fenbian* (Classified register of metal and stone). Wenlu tang kanben ed. Location and date unknown. "Takuhi no hō," a simplified Japanese version of the section on making rubbings, is in *Shoen* 1:3 (1939), 43.

Xiandai guomin jiben zhishi congshu (Citizens' Library of Fundamental Knowledge). Shanghai and Taibei, date and publisher unknown.

Xiao Peigen, ed. *Zhongguo bencao tulu* (Illustrated flora of China), 2 vols. Taibei: Commercial Press, 1988.

Xinhua zidian (New China dictionary). Beijing: Commercial Press, 1971.

Xu Kang. *Qianchenmeng yinglu*(Record of reflections from the past). *MSCS* 1 (1975), 141–250.

Xu Shen. *Shuowen jiezi* (Explanation of words and elucidation of characters). Location unknown: Tenghuaxie keben, 1807.

Xue Shanggong. *Lidai zhongding yiqi kuanshi fatie* (Model book of inscriptions on historical ritual objects). Guichi: Liu shi, 1907.

Yan Gengwang, ed. *Shike shiliao congshu* (Collectanea of stone-cut historical materials). *Jiayi* series. Taibei: Yiwen Press, 1968.

Yang Guanlin et al. *Zhongguo mingsheng cidian* (Dictionary of scenic places in China). Shanghai: Shanghai cishu chubanshe, 1981.

Yang Qianzhi. *Changyong zhongyao shouce* (Handbook of common Chinese herbs and formulas), 2nd ed. Rosemead, Calif.: Institute of Chinese Medicine, 1996.

Ye Changchi. *Yakuchū goseki.* Trans. and annotation Fujiwara Sossui. Tokyo: Shōshin shobō, 1975 (reissue of Ye Changhi, *Shina kinseki shodan* [Discussing Chinese metal and stone], trans. Fujiwara Sossui, 1929).

———. *Yu shi* (Discussing stones), 2 vols. In *Guoxue jiben congshu,* series 1, no. 40. Taibei: Commercial Press, 1956.

Yee, Cordell D. Y. "Reinterpreting Traditional Chinese Geographical Maps." In J. B. Harley and David Woodward, eds., *The History of Cartography,* vol. 2, book 2: *Cartography in the Traditional East and Southeast Asian Societies.* Chicago: University of Chicago Press, 1994.

Yin Zhihong. *Qingdao zhinan* (Qingdao guidebook). Qingdao: Zhongguo shicheng xiehui Qingdao fenhui, 1947.

You Shuxiao and Li Yuanzheng. *Jimo Xian zhi* (Gazetteer of Jimo Xian, Shandong). 12 *juan* plus introductory *juan,* 1764.

Yu Li. *Ding lu* (Record of *ding* cauldrons). *MSCS* 17 (1975), 273–82.

Yunju Si Shijing Shan jianjie (Introduction to Cloud-Dwelling Temple, Stone Sutra Mountain). Location and publisher unknown, 1990(?)

Zhai Qinian. *Zhou shi* (History of the *zhou* script). *CSJC,* vol. 1513.

Zhang Guangyuan. "Shigu wen de renshi" (The Stone Drums Speak). *Zhonghua wenhua fuxing yuekan* (Chinese Cultural Renaissance Monthly) 5:7 (1972), 5–9.

Zhang Haipeng. *Xuejin taoyuan* (Studying the crossing places and tracing the sources). Yu Shan [Jiangsu]: Zhang shi Zhaokuang ge kanben, 1805.

Zhang Tingji. *Qingyi ge suo cang gu qiwu wen* (Inscriptions on ancient objects in the Studio of Refined Manners). Shanghai: Commercial Press, 1925.

Zhang Yanchang. *Jinsu jian shuo* (Talking about Jinsu paper). *MSCS* 8 (1975), 127–56.

Zhang Yanyuan. *Lidai ming hua ji* (Compilation of famous paintings through the dynasties). Beijing: Renmin chubanshe, 1963 (reprint of the ninth-century original).

Zhang Yingwen. *Qing mi zang* (Storehouse of the clear and the hidden). *MSCS* 4 (1975), 182–252.

Zheng Chao. *Tongzhi* (Comprehensive annals). *Guoxue jiben congshu,* vol. 4, part 1. Taibei: Xinxing shuju, 1959.

Zheng Shanshan et al. "Zhimo liuxiang—chuanta jifa, quanxing ta; chuanji shou de rongyao" (Retaining the fragrance of paper and ink: the rubbing technique and composite rubbing, transmitting the glory of the hand). *Zijin cheng* 5 (2006), 38–51.

Zhiwuxue dacidian (Dictionary of botany). Shanghai: Commercial Press, 1918.

Zhongguo gujin diming dacidian. (Dictionary of ancient and modern Chinese place names), 2nd ed. Taibei: Commercial Press, 1966.

Zhongguo lishi dituji (Historical atlas of China), 8 vols. Shanghai: Ditu chubanshe, vols. 1–7 (1982), vol. 8 (1987).

Zhongguo renming dacidian. (Cyclopedia of Chinese Biographical Names), 4th ed. Taibei: Commercial Press, 1966.

Zhongguo renmin gongheguo fenshing dituji (Atlas of the People's Republic of China), 2nd printing. Beijing: Ditu chubanshe, 1983.

Zhonghua renmin gongheguo fensheng dituji (Provincial atlas of the People's Republic of China), 3rd printing. Beijing: Ditu chubanshe, 1976.

Zhongwen dacidian (Encyclopedia of the Chinese language), 12 vols. Taibei: Zhonghua xueshuyuan, 1973.

Zhou Erxue. *Shangyan suxin lu* (Record of prolonged gratification of the simple heart). *ZDCS,* 45.

Zhou Jiazhou. *Zhuanghuang zhi* (Record of mounting). *CSJC,* chubian, vol. 1563. Shanghai: Commercial Press, 1939.

Zhu Feng. *Yongzhou jinshi ji* (Record of metal and stone in Shaanxi and Gansu). *Xiyin'gan congshu,* vols. 28–29.

Index

www.ingramcontent.com/pod-product-compliance
Lightning Source LLC
LaVergne TN
LVHW082157080826
844660LV00046B/1264

9780295988115